Digital Bouncers

European Monographs Series Set

VOLUME 118

Editor

Prof. Andrea Biondi is Professor of European Law and Director of the Centre of European Law at King's College London

Introduction & Contents/Subjects

As the process of European integration assumes an increasingly complex character, the EU legal system continues to undergo sweeping changes. The European Monographs series offers a voice to thoughtful, knowledgeable, cutting edge legal commentary on the now unlimited field of European law. Its emphasis on focal and topical issues makes the series an invaluable tool for scholars, practitioners, and policymakers specializing or simply interested in EU law.

Objective

The aim is to publish innovative work appealing to academics and practitioners alike. The result is an original and ongoing library of detailed analyses, theories, commentaries, practical guides, and proposals, each of which furthers the cause of meaningful European integration. Cumulatively, the series may be regarded as a 'work in progress' engaged in building a sharply defined representation of law in Europe.

Readership

Academics and practitioners dealing with EU law.

The titles published in this series are listed at the end of this volume.

Digital Bouncers

A European Roadmap to Navigate Access Rights and Moderation Issues on Social Media Platforms

Berdien B.E. van der Donk

Wolters Kluwer

Published by:
Kluwer Law International B.V.
PO Box 316
2400 AH Alphen aan den Rijn
The Netherlands
E-mail: lrs-sales@wolterskluwer.com
Website: www.wolterskluwer.com/en/solutions/kluwerlawinternational

Sold and distributed by:
Wolters Kluwer Legal & Regulatory U.S.
920 Links Avenue
Landisville, PA 17538
United States of America
E-mail: customer.service@wolterskluwer.com

ISBN 978-94-035-2858-8

e-Book: ISBN 978-94-035-2868-7
web-PDF: ISBN 978-94-035-2878-6

Table of Contents

List of Abbreviations

AG	Advocate General
BGB	Bürgerliches Gesetzbuch
BGH	Bundesgerichtshof
BverfG	Bundesverfassungsgericht
BW	Burgerlijk Wetboek
CDSM	Copyright in the Digital Single Market Directive Directive (EU) 2019/790
Charter	Charter of Fundamental Rights of the European Union
CJEU	Court of Justice of the European Union
Cod. Civ.	Codice Civile
Cod. Cons.	Codice Consumo
DE	Germany
DK	Denmark
DMA	Digital Markets Act Regulation (EU) 2022/1925
DSA	Digital Services Act Regulation (EU) 2022/2065
EC/Commission	European Commission
eCD	eCommerce Directive Directive 2000/31/EC
ECHR	European Convention on Human Rights
ECtHR	European Court of Human Rights
EDPB	European Data Protection Board
EP	European Parliament
EU	European Union
GDPR	General Data Protection Regulation Regulation (EU) 2016/679

HR	Hoge Raad der Nederlanden
IHRL	International Human Rights Law
ISP(s)	Internet Service Provider(s)
IT	Italy
NetzDG	Netzwerkdurchsetzungsgesetz
NL	The Netherlands
RIVM	Rijksinstituut voor Volksgezondheid en Milieu
TEU	Treaty on European Union
TFEU	Treaty on the Functioning of the European Union
UCPD	Unfair Commercial Practices Directive Directive 2005/29/EC
UCTD	Unfair Contract Terms Directive Directive 93/13/EEC
UK	United Kingdom
US	United States of America
VLOPs	Very Large Online Platforms

List of Figures

List of Tables

Preface

This book addresses the complex issue of questionable content removals and account suspensions on social media platforms in the European Union. The unique nature of the internet's infrastructure and the differing normative views on the role of social media platforms make resolving access restriction and moderation issues a challenging task. The greatly varying outcomes in recent years in case law in the Member States show that a universal approach to address these issues is currently lacking. The Digital Services Act, which came into effect in 2024, offers new opportunities for redress. However, a unified approach is essential to ensure that all European users have equal opportunities for redress. This book provides a European roadmap to navigate online access rights and moderation issues on social media platforms as a solution to the existing legal ambiguity.

The roadmap's elements are deduced from a technology-neutral comparative case law study of four Member States (Denmark, Germany, Italy, and the Netherlands), in which access and moderation restrictions to physical property have been compared to restrictions on social media platforms. The six substantive chapters provide four independent layers for a roadmap: the foundational layer, the access layer, the content layer, and the enforcement layer. The design of each of these layers is subsequently amended to reflect the legal landscape applicable to social media platforms' terms of service.

The first layer – called the foundational layer – outlines the legal basis for social media platforms to impose restrictions. Following the case law of the Member States, national courts have almost exclusively relied on the right to property to resolve access and moderation decisions, both concerning physical property and virtual spaces. On the basis of this observation in combination with a doctrinal study, the right to property forms the starting point to address access and content restrictions on social media platforms. The second layer – the access layer – covers the three ways a platform operator can exercise the exclusive rights protected by the right to property to shape the access possibilities to its platform. This layer also outlines the limitations to the platform's right to exclude users. These limitations form the legal basis for users to force the platform to contract them. After accessing the platform through either open, conditional, or forced access, the legal issues shift from accessing the platform to decisions that the platform takes in relation to the users' content. The third layer – the content layer – covers two paths: the doctrine of the general right of use on open access-platforms and the validity and enforceability of user terms on conditional access-platforms. The fourth and final layer – the enforcement layer – covers users' and platforms' remedies for breaches of the terms of service. It covers users' legal redress against a content moderation decision, the procedural obligations in the Digital Services Act that platform operators have to uphold when enforcing contractual sanctions for a user's breach of contract, and the consequences for infringements of those procedural obligations.

This book's biggest contribution to the legal field lies in the unifying power of the roadmap. Streamlining the application of the various fields of law allows decision-makers to reach (more) uniform outcomes, which will ultimately benefit European platform users. 'Decision-makers' should be understood broadly. The roadmap guides all parties involved in content moderation decisions on platforms, including judges in the Member States, social media platforms, and out-of-court dispute resolution bodies. In addition to the development of the roadmap, the research has led to several concrete findings along the way. First, from the comparative study on the national case law, it follows that courts in the Member States rely on property law to adjudicate issues resulting from access and moderation restrictions on both physical property and social media platforms. Second, *ex ante* access problems cannot be resolved by applying the same rationale, arguments, and laws as applicable to *ex post* content moderation issues. The distinct problems arising from *ex ante* restrictions have not previously been highlighted in the literature. Lastly, the research clearly demonstrates that, currently, the primary way to safeguard fundamental rights on social media platforms is through contract law.

Disclaimer

This book is based on the author's dissertation submitted for fulfilment of the requirements for the degree of PhD in Law at the Faculty of Law at the University of Copenhagen, which was successfully defended in public on 25 August 2023.

The information and views set out in this book reflect those of the author and do not necessarily reflect the official opinion of the European Institutions. In particular, the matters addressed in this book dealing with the work of the European Union solely reflect the personal views of the author.

Introductory Part

CHAPTER 1
Terms of Service as a Source of Power

1.1 SOCIAL MEDIA PLATFORMS' PRIVATE GOVERNANCE POWER

How many times have you *actually* read a full set of user terms in your life? If you did, you are amongst a very exclusive group of people. In 2016, a study by Obar and Oeldorf-Hirsch showed that people accepted user terms despite the terms dictating to give up their first-born child and to share all their data with the NSA.[1] In 2019, Benoliel and Becher confirmed empirically that user terms are unreadable for basically anyone.[2] Despite this, people all around the globe accept various *user terms, terms and conditions, community guidelines*, and *terms of service* every day. Without reading hardly anything – the average time spent reading user terms is less than one minute[3] – people may accept contracts that include clauses that are not beneficial to them. The internet has increased and accelerated this development. When buying a house or signing a work agreement, people tend to (thoroughly) read the contracts. However, with online user terms, the same people click 'I agree' on a computer screen without paying much attention.

Although users may agree to such terms, a platform operator cannot legally provide access to any content that is prohibited by law. This is exemplified by the absence of legitimate platforms for the sale of illegal drugs despite the potential economic benefits such a platform could bring. Since it is in the best interest of society

1. Jonathan A Obar and Anne Oeldorf-Hirsch, 'The Biggest Lie on the Internet: Ignoring the Privacy Policies and Terms of Service Policies of Social Networking Services' (Social Science Research Network 2018) SSRN Scholarly Paper ID 2757465 https://papers.ssrn.com/abstract=2757465 (accessed 21 September 2021).
2. Uri Benoliel and Shmuel I Becher, 'The Duty to Read the Unreadable' (2019) 60 Boston College Law Review; Obar and Oeldorf-Hirsch (n. 1).
3. Thomas J Maronick, 'Do Consumers Read Terms of Service Agreements When Installing Software? – A Two-Study Empirical Analysis' (2014) 4 International Journal of Business and Social Research 137.

to curb illegal activities, it is unlikely that many would object to the removal of such content. Rather, social media platforms are increasingly urged to swiftly remove any content that includes terrorism, child sexual abuse material, and listings of defective, counterfeit products in order to keep the internet a safe and pleasant place.[4] However, the user terms of large-scale social media platforms go beyond restricting access solely to illegal content as defined by the law. Whereas platforms cannot make the illegal legal, they can remove posts that are *lawful, but awful.*[5] In addition, social media platform user terms limit access to content that may be perfectly legal in some jurisdictions but is deemed undesirable by the specific platform. This exercise of *private governance power* through the terms and conditions of the service negatively impacts users' freedom of expression[6] and grants the platform operators a (quasi-) normative power over their users.[7] This normative power effectively transforms social media platform operators into *digital bouncers*.

The issue is that a user cannot simply choose to disregard the user terms on a social media platform. The technical interface often requires users to create an account to access the content, and in doing so, they must accept the user terms. These user terms also dictate the process to (permanently) restrict a user's access to the account in

4. Most recently with the Regulation (EU) 2022/2065 (Digital Services Act), but also prior through initiatives such as Commission Recommendation (EU) 2018/334 of 1 March 2018 on measures to effectively tackle illegal content online 2018 [OJ L 63]; The EU Code of conduct on countering illegal hate speech online 2016; European Commission, Memorandum of Understanding on the sale of counterfeit goods 2011 [Ref Ares (2016) 3934515]; Proposal for a Regulation of the European Parliament and of the Council on preventing the dissemination of terrorist content online A contribution from the European Commission to the Leaders' meeting in Salzburg on 19-20 September 2018 [COM (2018) 640 final].
5. As coined by Daphne Keller in 'Lawful but Awful? Control over Legal Speech by Platforms, Governments, and Internet Users' (*The University of Chicago Law Review Online*, 28 June 2022) https://lawreviewblog.uchicago.edu/2022/06/28/keller-control-over-speech/ (accessed 3 August 2022).
6. David Kaye, *Speech Police: The Global Struggle to Govern the Internet* (Columbia Global Reports 2019) https://www.jstor.org/stable/j.ctv1fx4h8v (accessed 15 January 2023); Luca Belli and Jamila Venturini, 'Private Ordering and the Rise of Terms of Service as Cyber-Regulation' [2016] Internet Policy Review https://policyreview.info/articles/analysis/private-ordering-and-rise-terms-service-cyber-regulation (accessed 22 March 2021); Jamila Venturini and others, 'Terms of Service and Human Rights: An Analysis of Online Platform Contracts'; Marco Bassini, 'Fundamental Rights and Private Enforcement in the Digital Age' (2019) 25 European Law Journal 182; Matteo Monti, 'Privatizzazione della censura e Internet platforms: la libertà d'espressione e i nuovi censori dell'agorà digitale' (2019) 1 Rivista italiana di informatica e diritto 35; Michael Karanicolas, 'Too Long; Didn't Read: Finding Meaning in Platforms' Terms of Service Agreements' (2021) 52 University of Toledo Law Review 1. Matthias C Kettemann, *The Normative Order of the Internet: A Theory of Rule and Regulation Online* (Oxford University Press 2020).

   The use of the term 'private governance' is not limited to this situation, but exists in general where private actors regulate activity, *see* on this: Ole Hansen, Vibe Ulfbeck and Clement Salung Petersen, 'Private Governance and the Potential of Private Law' (2020) 28 European Review of Private Law https://kluwerlawonline.com/api/Product/CitationPDFURL?file=Journals\ERPL\ERPL2020017.pdf (accessed 23 January 2023) DOI: https://doi.org/10.54648/erpl2020017.
7. Luca Belli, 'Structural Power as a Critical Element of Social Media Platforms' Private Sovereignty' in Edoardo Celeste, Amélie Heldt and Clara Iglesias Keller (eds), *Constitutionalising Social Media* (Bloomsbury Publishing Plc 2022) 82 http://ebookcentral.proquest.com/lib/kbdk/detail.action?docID=7027117 (accessed 28 January 2023); Kettemann (n. 6).

case of a (recurrent) breach of the rules.[8] As a result, social media platforms effectively hold the power to determine what content is permissible to share. Simultaneously, the *networking effect* of social media platforms – the service of a platform becomes more attractive as more people join – makes it hard for individual users to move to another platform.[9]

Despite the negative effects on users' freedom of expression, it is not easy to restrict social media platforms' private governance power. There is a widely accepted belief that since platforms are private companies, they have the authority to restrict their services as they see fit.[10] There is also an underlying feeling that *some* platforms should not moderate *too much* speech. However, it is unclear exactly when user terms cross the border between the freedom of contract and an excessive restriction of speech. The scope of the terms should be dictated by the parties involved – a process that falls within the scope of their freedom of contract. European consumer law protects consumers when contracting with powerful undertakings, but the rules do not fit seamlessly into the digital challenges posed by the technical power giants. The various stakeholders (platform operator, user, the user community, advertisers) complicate matters further, as the relationships between either one of them are governed by different fields of law. This creates legal uncertainty and puts the user in a vulnerable and dependent situation.

If users cannot bypass normative restrictions or find a suitable alternative service, what recourse do they have when their social media account is blocked, or their content is removed? Are there any legal mechanisms available to users seeking to restore deleted content or to regain access to a suspended or terminated account? Can users seek compensation for unjustified content removal? This book addresses the legal remedies available to users challenging the private governance power of social media platforms, with a focus on the European Union.

In this introductory chapter, the necessary background information is presented. The chapter starts with an overview of the content infrastructure of social media platforms and narrows the research focus to two legal relationships: the private governance power of social media platforms over their users and the regulation of

---

8. *See* for a demonstration of this possibility an earlier case-study: Berdien van der Donk, 'Ex-Ante and Ex-Post Access Restrictions in Online Marketplace's Terms of Service' (2022) 6 European Review of Private Law, DOI: https://doi.org/10.54648/erpl2022044.
9. Spencer Waller, 'Antitrust and Social Networking' (2011) 90 North Carolina Law Review. The 'social lock-in' that is created by these networking effects has been discussed in light of competition law and the necessary interoperability of social media platforms' services, *see*, for example, Inge Graef, 'Mandating Portability and Interoperability in Online Social Networks: Regulatory and Competition Law Issues in the European Union' (2015) 39 Telecommunications Policy 502. The Digital Markets Act has a brand-new provision on mandatory interoperability for gatekeepers (Art. 6), though this obligation does not extend to the inclusion of content normatively banned by another platform and will therefore unfortunately not address nor solve this issue.
10. *See* for an in-depth analysis on online platforms' ability to freely draft user terms a previous study on the scope of the freedom of contract of private parties: Berdien van der Donk, 'The Freedom to Conduct a Business as a Counterargument to Limit Platform Users' Freedom of Expression' (Springer International Publishing) https://doi.org/10.1007/16495_2021_33 (accessed 20 April 2022).

social media platforms by states. Next, the foundational disagreements on the qualifications of social media platforms in national case law and legal literature are addressed. Rather than taking a fragmented approach, the research presented in this book takes a unified approach, drawing on multiple fields of law to develop a European roadmap on online access rights and content moderation. The chapter concludes with a presentation of the research questions, the structure, and the methodology of the research, as well as further explanations of the rationale behind the research's scope.

1.1.1 The Infrastructure of Content-Issues on Social Media Platforms

To ensure a clear and concise understanding of the applicable legal fields related to legal problems concerning social media platforms, this chapter dissects the infrastructure of these issues. Depending on the actors involved, the legal field and related problems may vary. When looking at the relationship between a state and social media platform users, problems relate to the regulation of illegal speech ('is misinformation illegal?' or 'should doxing be illegal?'). These questions of illegality do not differ from states' traditional speech regulations. If something is illegal in the physical world, it is also illegal online. Platforms cannot deviate from national laws on illegality. Moreover, the state has an obligation to protect its nationals from harm. The relationship between the state and the platform, therefore, mainly concerns the effective banning of illegal content, focusing on the regulation of the operator's infrastructure. When social media platforms exert their private governance power to restrict lawful speech, they intervene in the traditional legal interaction between the state and the speaker. The contractual relationship between the platform and the users, therefore, gives rise to questions on the limits of the freedom of contract ('can platforms limit the freedom of expression?' or 'can platforms delete a user without giving a warning?').

Balkin visualised this difference between traditional speech regulation and social media platforms' speech regulation in a speech triangle.[11] Balkin included three groups of main actors: states and regulators, privately owned internet-infrastructure companies, and the speaker. However, Balkin's triangle is insufficient in capturing the full scope of content-related issues on social media platforms. Although it aptly addresses the challenge of regulating speech in the digital sphere, it neglects to account for a fourth stakeholder impacted by such intervention: the online community of users.[12] When a social media platform deletes content on the basis of its terms of service, then not only the individual user who had posted the deleted content is affected; the entire

11. Jack M Balkin, 'Free Speech Is a Triangle', *Columbia Law Review* https://columbialawreview.org/content/free-speech-is-a-triangle/ (accessed 1 June 2022).
12. *See* in this line: Niva Elkin-Koren, Maayan Perel (Filmar) and Giovanni De Gregorio, 'Social Media as Contractual Networks: A Bottom up Check on Content Moderation' (Social Science Research Network 2021) SSRN Scholarly Paper ID 3797554 https://papers.ssrn.com/abstract=3797554 (accessed 29 March 2021). The authors argue that the terms of service do not solely create a contractual relationship between the platform and one individual user, but rather as a contractual network between the platform, the user sharing content, and all other users in the community. *See* similar: Roberta Cosio, 'Facebook e Social. Natura del contratto tra utente e social' [2020] Ricerche giuridiche JournalArticle_3077, 143.

user community will no longer have access to it. This limits the community's right to impart information. Moreover, content published by an individual can affect other users in the online community, leading to issues of direct liability, and the platform operator can, under certain circumstances, be held liable for such content. To account for all these interrelated relationships, Balkin's speech triangle should best be extended into a *content square.*[13]

Figure 1.1 The Content Square Based on Balkin's Speech Triangle

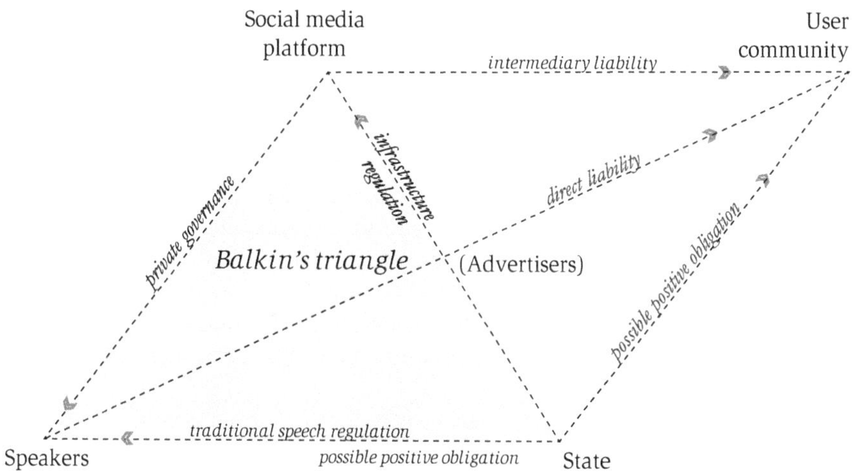

In the content square, Balkin's third group of 'end users' has been split into two groups: the user that posts the content (referred to by Balkin as 'the speaker') and a new group that represents the online community of users on social media platforms (*see* Figure 1.1). Between this fourth group and the other three groups, independent legal relationships exist. In addition to the interactions between Balkin's three groups (traditional speech regulation, infrastructure regulation,[14] and private governance), this updated visualisation also includes the discussions on direct and indirect liability for illegal content on the platform, and it pinpoints the discussion on the existence of a positive state obligation to safeguard speech on social media platforms. Arguably, one could add the group of 'advertisers' as a fifth group located in the centre of the square. Advertisers interact with all other four groups: first, they have a contractual relationship with the social media platform to supply advertisements; second and third, these advertisements are distributed to the speaker and the user community, and fourth, advertisers' behaviour is regulated by the state. Since advertisers' business

13. Despite calling it square, the interaction has been visualised here as a parallelogram to be able to integrate Balkin's triangle in its triangle-shape.
14. Balkin refers to these two categories as 'Old-School Speech Regulation' and 'New-School-Speech Regulation'. I have chosen for more descriptive terminology but refer to the same interaction between the parties.

models do not form a part of the research outlined in this book, their role is not further elaborated on in this context.

The study only addresses two of the lines indicated by the content square above: the private governance line between the social media platform and the speaker, and the infrastructure regulation between the State and the social media platform. Consequently, several topics related to social media platforms and content moderation are not addressed in this book. First, the study does not contribute to the discussion on whether specific types of content are, could, or should be illegal and removed (the traditional speech regulation-line between state and speaker). Platform governance and platform regulation studies have focused substantially on the question of who should remove illegal content and who is liable at exactly what point in time.[15] In this book, the point of reference to differentiate between illegal or legal content will be (national) positive law, in line with the definition in Regulation (EU) 2022/2065 ('Digital Services Act' or 'DSA').[16] Second, this book does not contribute to the (developments in the) discussion on direct and indirect liability for content on social media platforms (the lines between the user community and, respectively, the speaker and the social media platform), nor does it address the (potential) positive obligation of a state towards either the speaker or the user community.[17] However, at times, the latter discussion crosses paths with the discussion on the private governance power of social media platforms. The arguments related to the discussion on positive state obligations are therefore included where relevant but do not form an independent topic of study.

1.1.2 A Foundational Disagreement on the Qualification of Platforms

Having defined the two legal relationships that will be addressed, we can start the journey to unravel the legal redress options for users. One of the ways to oppose a social media platform's normative decision to restrict access is through *must-carry*

15. Discussions on the justification, and/or desirability of the classifications of content are necessary. Research into these factors is carried out mostly in relation to mis-and disinformation, harmful content, and rules in repressive regimes. This research will not dive into this discussion specifically, but the developments and findings of these discussions have nonetheless been followed and are referred to when coinciding with the restriction of legal content.
16. Regulation (EU) 2022/2065 of the European Parliament and of the Council of 19 October 2022 on a Single Market For Digital Services and amending Directive 2000/31/EC (Digital Services Act). The discussions on the Digital Services Act reflect the state of play in March 2023, and have not been adapted to the situation after the Regulation came into force.

    Recital (12): 'In order to achieve the objective of ensuring a safe, predictable and trustworthy online environment, for the purpose of this Regulation the concept of 'illegal content' should broadly reflect the existing rules in the offline environment. In particular, the concept of 'illegal content' should be defined broadly to cover information relating to illegal content, products, services and activities. In particular, that concept should be understood to refer to information, irrespective of its form, that under the applicable law is either itself illegal, such as illegal hate speech or terrorist content and unlawful discriminatory content, or that the applicable rules render illegal in view of the fact that it relates to illegal activities. (...)'
17. *See* for a recent study into the (non-)existence of positive obligations based on the case law of the ECtHR: Matthias Smed Larsen, 'A Right to Post? Structural Human Rights Law and Social Media' (2022) 6 Retskraft.

claims: demanding a court to reinstate content that has been removed based on a social media platform's normative decision. The discussion on these must-carry claims for social media platforms has been on the rise during the last few years. In the United States, all must-carry claims to date[18] have been unsuccessful due to platform's protection under section 230.[19] In the European Union, however, the discussion on must-carry claims is far from settled. The (European) legal literature has solely addressed individual Member States or compared the practice in an individual Member State and the practice in the United States, sometimes even concluding on a 'European approach' based on one Member State.[20] However, the studies on the national Member States and recent case law in Germany, Italy, and the Netherlands show that the 'European approach' simply does not exist. Courts in the Member States have reached diverging conclusions, leading to broad differences in implications for users and platforms in different Member States. For example, in Italy, social media platforms have been forced to pay non-material damages for wrongful content removals as high as EUR 14,000 for a personal social media account and EUR 3,000 for removed content.[21] Contrarily, in the Netherlands, a claim for reputational damage was rejected even in the case of *wrongful removal*.[22] Similarly, the influence of fundamental rights through open norms in private law is the focus point in German case law, demonstrating a far more complex discussion than the Dutch case law demonstrates. The subtle differences in the perception of social media platforms in the Member States have a significant impact on the outcome of cases that challenge content moderation decisions.[23] The perception defines, for example, whether the relationship between a social

18. This book has been based on a PhD dissertation that was submitted in March 2023.
19. Daphne Keller, 'Why D.C. Pundits' Must-Carry Claims Are Relevant to Global Censorship' http://cyberlaw.stanford.edu/blog/2018/09/why-dc-pundits-must-carry-claims-are-relevant-global-censorship (accessed 3 August 2022); Daphne Keller, 'Who Do You Sue? State and Platform Hybrid Power Over Online Speech' Stanford University https://www.hoover.org/sites/default/files/research/docs/who-do-you-sue-state-and-platform-hybrid-power-over-online-speech_0.pdf.
20. For a comparison between Germany and the US, *see* Amélie Heldt, *Intensive Third-Party Effect* (1st edn, Mohr Siebeck 2023); Matthias C Kettemann and Anna Sophia Tiedeke, 'Back up: Can Users Sue Platforms to Reinstate Deleted Content?' (2020) 9 Internet Policy Review https://policyreview.info/articles/analysis/back-can-users-sue-platforms-reinstate-deleted-content (accessed 3 August 2022); For a comparison between Italy and the US, *see* Marco Bassini, 'Libertà di espressione e social network, tra nuovi "spazi pubblici" e "poteri privati". Spunti di comparazione' 33; Luca Rinaldi, 'Le Piattaforme Tra Diritto Pubblico e Diritto Privato: Libertà d'espressione, Discorso Politico e Social Network in Alcuni Casi Recenti Tra Italia e Stati Uniti' 211; For a comparison between the Netherlands and the US, *see* Michael Klos, 'Wrongful Moderation Regulation of Internet Intermediary Service Provider Liability and Freedom of Expression' (2022).
21. *Tribunale di Bologna sez II (De Gaetano)* [2021] RG 5206/2020; *Corte appello L'Aquila (Correggiari)* [2021] N 1659/2021.
22. *Rechtbank Amsterdam (BLCKBX/Google)* (2021) ECLI:NL:RBAMS:2021:4308, §4.17. A wrongful removal refers to a removal that is not in line with the user terms of a social media platform. The exact definition of a wrongful removal will be explained further below.
23. Compare for example the Dutch cases *Rechtbank Noord-Holland (Van Haga/LinkedIn)* (2021) ECLI:NL:RBNHO:2021:8539; *BLCKBX/Google* (n. 22); *Bundesgerichtshof (Inhaltesperrung)* (2021) III ZR 192/20, ECLI:DE:BGH:2021:290721UIIIZR192.20.0; *Bundesgerichtshof (Kontosperrung)* (2021) III ZR 179/20, ECLI:DE:BGH:2021:290721UIIIZR179.20.0. The Dutch users have – apart from social media platforms who do not substantiate their user terms – no right to claim

media platform and its users is viewed as a purely contractual matter (Italy), a relationship with elements of a public forum (Denmark), private property (the Netherlands), or a private service with potential public/social interest (Germany).

The disagreement over the qualification of social media platforms extends beyond the national case law in the Member States. Not only have the national courts in the Member States applied divergent qualifications, but the academic literature also portrays social media platforms in varying ways. Platforms have been addressed as part of various regulatory doctrines related to competition law, such as public utilities,[24] essential facilities,[25] and essential facilities and public utilities combined.[26] Their role has been compared to general public spaces,[27] public spheres,[28] a public forum,[29] multiple coexisting and competing public spheres,[30] as private businesses taking over (at least partially) the role of the state,[31] systems 'synchronizing offline and

reinstatement or regain access to a platform, whereas German users could indirectly claim access to a platform that is open to the general public and claim reinstatement if content is removed from such a platform without an objective reason.

24. Christoph Busch, 'Reguliering Digitaler Plattformen als Infrastrukturen der Daseinsvorsorge' 36; Vicente Bagnoli, 'Digital Platforms as Public Utilities' (2020) 51 IIC – International Review of Intellectual Property and Competition Law 903; Friso Bostoen, 'Are Online Platforms the New Utilities – And Should They Be Regulated as Such? Inspiration from over 100 Years of Telecommunications Regulation' https://fsr.eui.eu/bostoen-f-are-online-platforms-the-new-utilities-and-should-they-be-regulated-as-such-inspiration-from-over-100-years-of-telecommunications-regulation/ (accessed 14 September 2021); K Sabeel Rahman, 'The New Utilities: Private Power, Social Infrastructure, and the Revival of the Public Utility Concept' (2017) 39 Cardozo Law Review 1621; Jean-Christophe Plantin and others, 'Infrastructure Studies Meet Platform Studies in the Age of Google and Facebook' (2018) 20 New Media & Society 293; Tarleton Gillespie and Mike Ananny, 'Exceptional Platforms' (*The Internet, Policy & Politics Conferences*, 2016) http://blogs.oii.ox.ac.uk/ipp-conference/2016/programme-2016/track-b-governance/platform-studies/tarleton-gillespie-mike-ananny.html.
25. Inge Graef, 'Rethinking the Essential Facilities Doctrine for the EU Digital Economy' https://papers.ssrn.com/sol3/papers.cfm?abstract_id=3371457.
26. Adam Thierer, 'The Perils of Classifying Social Media Platforms as Public Utilities' [2012] SSRN Electronic Journal.
27. Edoardo Celeste, Amélie Heldt and Clara Iglesias Keller, *Constitutionalising Social Media* (Bloomsbury Publishing Plc 2022) http://ebookcentral.proquest.com/lib/kbdk/detail.action?docID=7027117 (accessed 28 January 2023); Jacquelyn Burkell and others, 'Facebook: Public Space, or Private Space?' (2014) 17 Information, Communication & Society 974; Pamela L Morris and Susan H Sarapin, 'You Can't Block Me: When Social Media Spaces Are Public Forums' (2020) 54 First Amendment Studies 52; Margaret McCartney, 'Online Is Not a Private Space' (2011) 343 BMJ d7109.
28. Mike S Schäfer, 'Digital Public Sphere', *The International Encyclopedia of Political Communication* (American Cancer Society 2016) https://onlinelibrary.wiley.com/doi/abs/10.1002/9781118541555.wbiepc087 (accessed 14 September 2021); Manuel Castells, 'The New Public Sphere: Global Civil Society, Communication Networks, and Global Governance' (2008) 616 Annals of The American Academy of Political and Social Science, 78.
29. Amélie Pia Heldt, 'Merging the "Social" and the "Public": How Social Media Platforms Could Be a New Public Forum' (Social Science Research Network 2019) SSRN Scholarly Paper 3460067 https://papers.ssrn.com/abstract=3460067 (accessed 22 April 2022); Micah Telegen, 'You Can't Say That!: Public Forum Doctrine and Viewpoint Discrimination in the Social Media Era' (2018) 52 University of Michigan Journal of Law Reform 235, DOI: https://doi.org/10.36646/mjlr.52.1.you.
30. Axel Bruns and Tim Highfield, 'Is Habermas on Twitter?: Social Media and the Public Sphere', *The Routledge Companion to Social Media and Politics* (Routledge 2015).
31. Susan Benesch, 'But Facebook's Not a Country: How to Interpret Human Rights Law for Social Media Companies' (*Yale Journal on Regulation*) https://www.yalejreg.com/bulletin/but-facebo

online spaces',[32] and digital mediums.[33] More towards the idea of property law, social media platforms have been referred to as proprietary or privately governed spaces[34] and something in between a public and a private space.[35] A final conclusion is yet to be reached[36] *if* reaching a consensus is at all possible. More problematically, this discussion on the qualification of social media platforms has taken away the focus on reaching a functioning framework for the opposition of normative decisions by social media platforms. Arguably, a social media platform has elements of multiple of the above-mentioned qualifications, which would render an *outcome*-based approach to resolve access restriction issues more suitable than an *origin*-approach. Not the qualification of the nature of social media platforms should be the deciding factor for the applicable legal framework, but the restricting outcome for platform users should be the focus point.

Instead of seeking a shared solution or approach, legal scholars in fields such as constitutional law, contract law, consumer protection law, and competition law have focused on debating the most effective way for their respective fields to address access restriction issues. This is understandable as each field is complex, and scholars may not possess comprehensive knowledge of other related fields to build bridges for problem-solving. This research demonstrates the involvement and relevance of all the aforementioned legal fields to different aspects of access restriction problems, illustrating how each field contains a puzzle piece to solve the bigger issue.

1.1.3 Striving Towards a Uniform Approach to Access Restrictions

The main goal of this research is to develop a roadmap that structures *how* to address issues concerning social media platforms' access and moderation restrictions rather than solving one explicit problem. The outcome of this book is a roadmap that can be

oks-not-a-country-how-to-interpret-human-rights-law-for-social-media-companies/ (accessed 13 September 2021); Natali Helberger, Jo Pierson and Thomas Poell, 'Governing Online Platforms: From Contested to Cooperative Responsibility' (2018) 34 The Information Society 1, DOI: https://doi.org/10.1080/01972243.2017.1391913.

32. Human Rights Council (Advisory Committee), 'New and Emerging Digital Technologies and Human Rights. Study of the Human Rights Council Advisory Committee' (2021) A/HRC/AC/25/CRP.2.
33. John McMullan, 'A New Understanding of "New Media": Online Platforms as Digital Mediums' (2020) 26 Convergence 287, DOI: https://doi.org/10.1177/1354856517738159.
34. Przemyslaw Jacek Palka, 'Terms of Service Are Not Contracts – Beyond Contract Law in the Regulation of Online Platforms' in Stefan Grundmann (ed.), *European Contract Law in the Digital Age*, vol. 3 (Intersentia 2018) https://www.cambridge.org/core/books/european-contract-law-in-the-digital-age/terms-of-service-are-not-contracts-beyond-contract-law-in-the-regulation-of-online-platforms/06837F552C19D1F4BB8F2A1D63445AFF (accessed 15 November 2022).
35. José van Dijck, 'Governing Digital Societies: Private Platforms, Public Values' (2020) 36 Computer Law & Security Review 105377; Hilde Sakariassen, 'A Digital Public Sphere: Just in Theory or a Perceived Reality for Users of Social Network Sites?' (2020) 36 MedieKultur: Journal of media and communication research 126; Keller, 'Who Do You Sue? State and Platform Hybrid Power Over Online Speech' (n. 19); Mike Ananny, 'From Noxious to Public? Tracing Ethical Dynamics of Social Media Platform Conversions' (2015) 1 Social Media + Society 20563051 15578140, DOI: https://doi.org/10.1177/2056305115578140.
36. Andrea Buratti, 'Framing the Facebook Oversight Board: Rough Justice in the Wild Web?', 25 July 2022.

used within the European Union to address and/or resolve *any* access and moderation problem on social media platforms. This means that this study deviates, to a large extent, from the traditional format and design of legal research, focusing on increasing expert knowledge on one specific topic. Pandya refers to these singular topic experts as *divers* and describes their research process as follows:

> Divers go narrow and deep with their research. They pick a broad spot in the ocean, jump in, and gradually narrow down to explore what that thread of the ocean has to offer. In the original spot they pick, there is a decent amount of other people, and most can communicate with each other about what they see. As they dive deeper and more narrowly into the thread that interests them, there are fewer people. Communication between divers gradually becomes more difficult since what the divers see becomes more detailed. When divers are several threads away from each other, they have no idea what the other is saying; they can't communicate. We could define 'experts' as divers.[37]

However, when dealing with complex problems where multiple fields of law are involved – such as the private governance power of social media platforms – a diving study simply does not suffice to create the necessary overview and linkage to contribute to a workable solution. Single-topic experts, by themselves, cannot overcome the foundational problems that result from the application of various legal orders in a complex, globalised system. To curb this, Pandya refers to the need for a second category of researchers. A second category of experts embodies interdisciplinary research and paves the way for the various single-topic experts to communicate with one another. He refers to this group as *surfers*:

> Now, surfers start in the same spot as divers: a broad spot in the ocean. However, surfers then take the opposite route. Instead of diving in and gradually narrowing down to explore a particular thread, surfers decide to explore the ocean horizontally. They realise that the ocean is large, unimaginably large, so they don't want to limit themselves to a particular thread of the ocean. They would rather spend their time seeing what a large area of the ocean has to hold. The surfer is interested in discovering connections between what different parts of the ocean hold. They have binoculars and scuba gear on them. As they travel, they use their binoculars for horizontally scanning which areas are most connected to where they currently are. They go to those areas next to continue connecting the dots. They also use their binoculars for vertically scanning downwards to see what threads of the ocean are most relevant to the connections they've made. The problem is binoculars can't see that far down. This is where the scuba gear comes in handy. When relevant threads are found, the surfer pauses their journey, throws on the scuba gear and does some diving. However, they don't go as deep as the diver. They go as far as they need to, gaining relevant information, resurfacing, and then continuing to surf.

To streamline the outcome of access problems in the European Union, a surfer-study to sort and align the different types of access restriction is highly needed. The right framework allows one to see potential solutions to problems and enables a

37. Tejas Pandya, 'In Academia, We Need Two Types of Researchers: Divers and Surfers' (*University Affairs*) https://www.universityaffairs.ca/career-advice/career-advice-article/in-academia-we-need-two-types-of-researchers-divers-and-surfers/ (accessed 6 February 2023).

transparent discussion on the future of content moderation and access restrictions. This book is the result of such a surfer-study. Consequently, the book does not focus on one field of law but touches upon and combines European law, constitutional and fundamental rights law, competition law, equality law, property law, and contract law. Moreover, all of these fields are reflected on and assessed through both a European and a national lens. That approach has advantages. The outcome of this project forms a roadmap that can be used by all the above-mentioned fields of law. It guides the reader to the field of law necessary to find the solution and connects the edges to the other relevant fields of law, allowing scholars from different fields to intercommunicate, and, most importantly, it demonstrates which problems are to be addressed by which fields of law. The main contribution of this book lies in the identification and mapping of the multiple legal frameworks that govern access and moderation restrictions on social media platforms. This mapping provides a meta-level overview that aims to establish a uniform and comprehensive approach to addressing these issues. The resulting European roadmap serves as a guide for navigating online access rights and content moderation, streamlining the academic discourse, and highlighting areas for further research. By clarifying the complex legal landscape, this roadmap offers a starting point for constructive discussions on how to address access and content moderation challenges in the European Union.

A surfer-study also has disadvantages. The study to form the roadmap has stumbled upon various problems that have not been fully addressed or resolved in the academic literature. Since the aim of this study is to create a source of interoperability, the focus has not been to address these individual problems in the detail necessary to resolve them in full. With the scuba gear, the various problems are explored and mapped to the extent that future divers can pick them up. To ease this process, several ready-to-go 'diving research projects' are included in the final chapter. Working together in this way, hopefully, most pending legal issues outlined in this book can be solved within the next decade. Even though it is not the aim to provide concluding answers to how these discussions must be solved – for many problems touched upon in this book, solutions and answers are presented.

The roadmap thus serves as a blueprint, pinpointing various unresolved discussions related to access and moderation restrictions on social media platforms. The aim to develop a European roadmap is founded on the observation that there is a lack of consensus on which law should be applied to resolve disputes between social media platforms and their users. Rather than answering whether specific claims of access restrictions would be successful, the roadmap guides judges, lawyers, legal scholars, internet users, and social media platforms through the overlapping legal orders and points in the direction of exactly which European or national laws must be applied to resolve the exact access restriction on a social media platform. It marks gaps in the existing legislation, offering the European and national legislators a stable foundation to build future legislation on. The roadmap paves the way for structured discussions on the role social media platforms play in the creation of norms on the internet and allows for an answer to the question of whether internet users in different European Member States have (equal) redress mechanisms to (re)claim access to a social media platform.

Lastly, while the roadmap outlines a uniform approach for access and content restrictions in the European Union, it is important to note that the roadmap does not necessarily lead to *equal outcomes* in all Member States. The research highlights the interplay between European and national rules governing the user term-based relationship between a user and a platform operator. Some access restrictions can only be resolved by applying Member States' national laws. Consequently, if these national laws vary, the outcome of the dispute will vary too. In resolving matters of content on the internet, it is crucial to consider these national variations. The choice to allow flexibility for such national variations in the roadmap secures a future-proof solution that accommodates (cultural) deviations in Member States. Moreover, this study purposely does not follow the idea of *exceptionalism* of platforms but rather discusses the issues on social media platforms from within the current legal framework.[38]

1.2 THE MAIN RESEARCH QUESTION

The main objective of this book is to pave a uniform path to address access and moderation issues on social media platforms in the European Union. This objective is reflected in the main research question:

> How can the positive law applicable to access and moderation decisions by social media platforms be consolidated in a roadmap that can guide decision-makers in the European Union?

The roadmap is intended to guide decision-makers in the European Union when deciding on issues related to access and content restrictions. The term 'decision-makers' is to be understood broadly. It includes, *inter alia*, decision-making by the judiciary in the Member States, social media platforms deciding on the scope and application of their content moderation systems, and any out-of-court dispute resolution bodies. With the Digital Services Act being applicable as of early 2024, a streamlined, unified approach is direly needed to ensure equal outcomes for users across the Union. This roadmap fulfils that role and paves the way for a uniform basis.

Drawing up a roadmap to address access restrictions relies on two inextricably linked factors. First, the identification of the roadmap's elements and, second, these elements' application to access and moderation issues on social media platforms. The book's structure follows that distinction and is therefore divided into two parts. The two parts will be individually explained in detail after a first limitation of the scope of the research and a justification of the theory that has served as the objectives' foundation.

1.3 LIMITATIONS OF THE SCOPE OF RESEARCH

There are limitations to the scope of the conducted research. Access and moderation decisions, in the scope of this study, concern restrictions on either accessing a platform

38. *See infra*, §1.4: 'The Underlying Theory: A Technology-Neutral Approach'.

(access restriction) or on the scope of the communication of platform users (content). Furthermore, this research only includes redress mechanisms on *social media platforms.* This term can be understood in various ways. Here, the terminology refers to a private undertaking that offers to (temporarily) host information created by users of the service and which information is made available to third parties. To those users, the access to server space is represented by an 'online environment' where users intercommunicate. Excluded from the scope are, therefore, messaging services (e.g., WhatsApp, Signal), market places and other services whose core business focuses on selling (physical products) (e.g., amazon.com, Steam, Etsy, eBay), search engines (e.g., Google, DuckDuckGo), and private cloud storing services. It is possible that one service includes multiple of the aforementioned services. If that is the case (e.g., Facebook, which offers a communication platform, a messaging service, and an online marketplace), then only the redress mechanisms applicable to the *private users' communication platform* form a part of the scope of this research.

A second limitation forms the exclusive focus on the European Union. Social media platforms have users worldwide. Their problems exist worldwide. The choice to solely include the European Union and European law to address the problems that arise from these global players, therefore, might seem out of place and requires some justification. The problem addressed in this study is jurisdiction-specific. Depending on national legislation, a *voluntary* decision to remove content might simultaneously be a *mandatory* removal in another jurisdiction.[39] As such, one cannot simply compare different jurisdictions that apply to social media platforms since the underlying contract law that governs the relationship between platform and user is not harmonised. Therefore, rather than, for example, comparing the limitations imposed by social media platforms on the European freedom of expression and the United States' freedom of speech, such as recent works have done,[40] it focuses on the internal comparisons of the European Union's Member States. Designing a flexible, overarching framework for those has proven complicated enough.

Furthermore, attempting to find a worldwide consensus on matters as fundamental as the freedom of expression is a daunting task, especially given the different legal systems and cultural values across the globe. As such, to make progress in this field of research, the choice was made to start on a smaller scale by focusing on (parts of) the European Union. If a uniform roadmap can be created within the Union, it can potentially serve as a model for other parts of the world. However, it must be stretched that the aim and European basis of this study by no means strives to add another topic

39. *See, e.g.*, the introduction in: van der Donk, 'The Freedom to Conduct a Business as a Counterargument to Limit Platform Users' Freedom of Expression' (n. 10). The problem of French Alain Cocq whose account was suspended from Facebook, because the latter equalled suicide and euthanasia, would not exist equally in other jurisdictions, either because euthanasia is legal, or the public perceives euthanasia as suicide. The same goes for the hate speech-example referring to the tradition of Black Pete in the Netherlands. Without the existing tradition in the Netherlands, a social media platform blocking access to content depicting the tradition would not constitute (as big) a problem.
40. Klos (n. 20); Amélie Heldt, 'Intensivere Drittwirkung: Die Mittelbare Drittwirkung Der Meinungsfreiheit in Öffentlichkeiten Der Digitalen Gesellschaft – Eine Verfassungsrechtliche, Rechtsvergleichende Und Interdisziplinäre Analyse' (2022).

to the scope of the *Brussels-effect*.[41] The development of a roadmap could serve as an inspirational outline for other jurisdictions, but the building blocks should be filled with local norms to create an inclusive online environment for communication. This book demonstrates the ability to adapt for flexibility within a uniform approach and provides space for deviations in national legislation on illegal or unwanted content. Just as the different views of Member States fit into the roadmap, other jurisdictions can adapt its blueprint to create a locally applicable one.

1.4 THE UNDERLYING THEORY: A TECHNOLOGY-NEUTRAL APPROACH

The search for a roadmap departs in legal theory, focusing on the separation of the presumed legal issue and the (technological) change. The main research question involves technological development: the emergence of social media platforms and the *platformisation* of society in general. The problem of access restrictions on social media platforms is explicitly not addressed from the perspective of *platform law*. The problem of access restrictions is taken out of the context of platforms to assess whether the problem similarly exists outside the realm of platforms. A broader context is more suitable and will prevent side-tracked solutions to solely technological problems that are also experienced outside of the technological field. Simultaneously, it will prevent any proposals that lead to a patchwork of legislation.

The underlying conception of the research is that platforms should not be treated as exceptional cases. Historically, technological developments are not exclusive to our time, and while some sector-specific regulation is needed and even welcomed, it should be reserved for those developments that are unable to be covered by existing rules and principles. Therefore, the issue of access restrictions on social media platforms is addressed from a technology-neutral perspective, comparing it to access restrictions in physical places rather than starting with the platform's unique features. That does not mean that these latter characteristics of platforms are left out of this research's design. The platform's specific role and characteristics are examined within the existing framework that applies to their brick-and-mortar equivalents in the physical world.

The choice to frame the research as technology-neutral as possible - only referring to the role of platforms where it reflects a socio-technical change - has been based on legal theory regarding technology regulation as developed by Easterbrook, Bennett Moses, Dizon, and Cockfield & Pridmore. It departs from Easterbrook's call to study cyberspace through the lens of well-established, overarching legal fields rather than as an isolated topic, drifting away from the depth of the assessment.[42] It is further

41. Anu Bradford, *The Brussels Effect: How the European Union Rules the World* (Oxford University Press 2020).
42. Frank H Easterbrook, 'Cyberspace and the Law of the Horse' The University of Chicago Legal Forum 11. The main point Easterbrook makes in his article is that a specialised topic, such as horses, are best to be studied through the application of general rules. Rather than studying conflicts related to horses, such as the regulation of horse races, the selling of horses, horses

inspired and based on the reinforcement model and the theory of Bennet Moses' on how to address problems relating to emerging technology,[43] Cockfield and Pridmore's synthetic theory of law and technology,[44] and the third phase of Dizon's reinforcement model.[45] Their individual contributions to the theory of technology-neutrality are discussed in more detail below.

Placing the problem in a broader context opens up a discussion that aims to address the underlying issue rather than just the symptoms of technological change. This *search for newness*, as described by Bennett Moses, assesses whether the problem is part of a larger societal change. If the technological change is not significantly new, it can be solved by working within existing legal frameworks, as Easterbrook suggests. This approach prevents creating unnecessary laws for specific platforms.

If the problem exists beyond the scope of platforms, the current legal framework may already provide solutions, rendering new legislation unnecessary. This aligns with the third stage of Dizon's reinforcement model, which involves incorporating seemingly technology-induced problems into existing structures.[46] The reinforcement model consists of three stages: an initial utopian view of technological development, a dystopian phase, and finally, the reinforcement phase. Dizon argues that these stages are, and have been, present in the entire field of science and technology for over fifty years. When observing social media platforms, one can clearly see the contours of the reinforcement model's first two stages and a starting third stage. The rise of online platforms triggered the utopian phase. Users were (globally) interconnected and could exchange experiences. Access to information surged, and new (economical) opportunities arose. Then, the scandals rolled in. Platforms were caught harvesting and hoarding personal data, were using manipulating algorithms to bind consumers to their platforms, were involved in voting fraud, and have, over time, turned into dominant players that export their norms on a worldwide scale. These scandals led to the dystopian phase with calls for specific legislative packages and negative public

kicking people, or horses winning prizes at horse shows, the different aspects should be studied through the legal field governing these overarching problems. Injury caused by horse kicks can be resolved by tort law, the sale of horses by property law, and so forth. A quarter century after Easterbrook published his article on Cyberspace and the Law of the Horse, his metaphor still seems to perfectly apply to emerging fields of regulation such as platform regulation.

43. Lyria Bennett Moses, 'How to Think about Law, Regulation and Technology: Problems with "Technology" as a Regulatory Target' (2013) 5 Law, Innovation and Technology 1. In line with Easterbrook, Bennett Moses states that creating a 'law of the horse' will lead to duplicative and compartmentalised rules. Bennett Moses transferred and applied Easterbrook's thoughts to the field of technology regulation. A problem caused by a specific subject, whether horse, technology, or platform, could potentially be sufficiently governed by existing, more general regulatory regimes. Bennett Moses' interpretation of Easterbrook's proposal resulted in two questions that determine whether the object of study should be viewed through the specified lens of 'technology regulation': *Does addressing issues related to technology through the lens of technology regulation allow one to say something about the regulation of technology in a general way?* and *Does the technology-aspect add a unique dimension to the existing problem that does not apply when considering the problem in a more general way?*

44. Arthur Cockfield and Jason Pridmore, 'A Synthetic Theory of Law and Technology' (2007) 8.

45. Michael Anthony C Dizon, 'From Regulating Technologies to Governing Society: Towards a Plural, Social and Interactive Conception of Law' SSRN Scholarly Paper ID 2123105 https://papers.ssrn.com/abstract=2123105 (accessed 6 April 2021).

46. *Ibid.*

opinion. In line with the model, that means the next phase in addressing platform problems would be the reinforcement phase. The reinforcement phase is based on the idea that technology, or in this case, social media platforms, does not offer anything substantially new, and thus, these new technologies will, over time, be absorbed and addressed by the existing structures. If this is not possible, it implies that platformisation offers something unprecedented, justifying specific legislation.

Dizon's reinforcement model and the theory of Bennet Moses' on how to address problems relating to emerging technology seamlessly fit Cockfield and Pridmore's *synthetic theory of law and technology*. They argue that problems of a technological nature are best addressed through a two-step test: first, to define (doctrinally) whether technological change threatens traditional interests the law seeks to protect, and second, to decide what should be done about it by placing the issue in a broader context. Following these steps will answer whether specific legislation is recommended or whether the experienced problem can be addressed within the existing legislative framework. The study's design draws upon these approaches. Part one examines whether access and moderation decisions on social media platforms differ significantly from those in the physical world. Once this is established, part two focuses on finding solutions to the problem.

1.5 PART I: THE IDENTIFICATION OF THE ROADMAP'S ELEMENTS

In Part I, the central focus point lies with the identification of the relevant elements for the European roadmap. In line with the technology-neutral theory's aim to dissect technological change from its context, the search for the elements will be based on a comparison with the existing legal framework on physical access restrictions. It concretely consists of a two-fold comparative study of the case law of four Member States of the European Union.

1.5.1 Sub-questions and Methodology of Part One

In this first part, the following two sub-questions will be answered:

(i) Have access restrictions on social media platforms been resolved differently from those regarding physical places, and to what extent do the Member States differ in their approach?

(ii) Based on the findings of the comparative study, which elements can be used as the building blocks of the roadmap?

1.5.1.1 Comparative Legal Research Methodology

The roadmap's various elements will be identified through a two-fold comparative analysis. A comparative legal research methodology is the most appropriate approach for defining the applicable law to user terms in the European Union. European (private) law cannot develop independently of the legal systems in the Member States, and conversely, the legal systems of the Member States are influenced by European law.[47] In this line, Lenaerts points to Article 3(3) TFEU, stating that '[the Union] shall respect its rich cultural and linguistic diversity, and shall ensure that Europe's cultural heritage is safeguarded and enhanced'. Referring to Article 340 TFEU, he underpins the importance of comparative analyses to fill any legal lacunae in European law.[48] Comparative analysis plays a crucial role in regulating and harmonising the various legal systems in the European Union. To reach a uniform system to adjudicate access and content moderation issues on social media platforms, achieving both objectives seems desirable. First, social media platforms operate online in a borderless space. Uniformity in the rules applied within the European Union ensures legal certainty for platforms and guarantees that all Union citizens have access to the same safeguards and legal remedies. Second, comparative research can reveal the rules of different Member States that can serve as a source of inspiration for setting new rules or filling legal gaps.

The research follows the comparative methodological framework developed by Oderkerk.[49] After deciding that the comparative method is suitable to achieve the research goals, Oderkerk distinguishes various choices underlying a comparative study and offers guidance to reach a justified decision for these choices. Consequently, the goal and relevance of the study are explained, followed by an explanation of the legal systems and objects to be studied, and the sources that were included in the research project.

1.5.1.2 The Goal and Relevance of the Comparative Study

The comparative research has, first, a non-normative goal[50] and serves to explore and describe how the Member States' legal frameworks function when dealing with access and moderation restrictions on respectively social media platforms and physical property. The results from the comparative study are used to decide on the elements of the roadmap. The comparative study exposes the (potentially diverging) solutions in the Member States and demonstrates the viability of a roadmap based on a theory of technology neutrality.

The first part of the comparative study is based on two hypotheses. These hypotheses have an internal (within one Member State) and an external (between

47. Schwartze, 'Comparative Law' in Karl Riesenhuber and Fritz Thyssen-Stiftung (eds), *European legal methodology* (Intersentia 2017), p. 63.
48. Lenaerts, Koen, 'The Court of Justice and the Comparative Law Method' (2016) https://www.europeanlawinstitute.eu/fileadmin/user_upload/p_eli/General_Assembly/2016/K._Lenaerts_ELI_AC_2016.pdf (accessed 27 September 2021).
49. Marieke Oderkerk, 'The Need for a Methodological Framework for Comparative Legal Research: Sense and Nonsense of "Methodological Pluralism" in Comparative Law' (2015) 79 Rabels Zeitschrift für ausländisches und internationales Privatrecht/The Rabel Journal of Comparative and International Private Law 589, DOI: https://doi.org/10.2139/ssrn.2422265.
50. *Ibid.*, 600-601. Oderkerk distinguishes non-normative from normative comparative legal research. The first one serving to describe and explore, whereas normative research has an inherent evaluative and/or regulatory aim.

Member States) component, and therefore, the comparative analysis follows an identical dichotomy. First, it is presumed that a discrepancy exists within the individual Member States regarding the way they address access restrictions imposed by social media platforms as opposed to non-platform actors. This internal discrepancy is suspected to be caused by the Member States' difficulty in weighing the overlapping legal orders as a consequence of the unclear role that social media platforms fulfil in society. If the role of social media platforms is unclear, courts struggle to define the obligations of these platforms in relation to the content they are obliged to host. The latter would, in turn, lead to difficulty in balancing contract law with users' fundamental rights protection. The assessment of a potential internal discrepancy in the different Member States is based on the technology-neutral approach following from platform regulation theory as outlined above. Second, it is presumed that the individual Member States resolve conflicts with social media platforms' user terms differently from their fellow Member States, creating an external European discrepancy. This second discrepancy could be caused by a disagreement on the qualification of social media platforms. Therefore, after the initial comparative analysis of a potential *internal* discrepancy that will demonstrate how the individual Member States view social media platforms (as opposed to non-platforms), a second comparative analysis will test whether an *external* discrepancy exists between the selected Member States.

For the internal part, the legal framework applied by national courts to access restrictions to physical places (e.g., restaurants, bars, football stadiums) is compared to that of online places (social media platforms, chat boxes). The findings resulting from the internal comparative analysis will allow for several conclusions. First, from this assessment, it can be deducted *whether*, and if yes, *how*, the individual Member States resolve user term disputes when dealing with social media platforms as opposed to non-platform actors. It will show whether Member States apply different legal standards when dealing with social media platforms' user terms as opposed to the user terms applied by non-platform actors.

However, one Member State displaying a uniform approach between social media platforms and non-platform actors does not provide a solid base for a roadmap. Rather, it demonstrates how the national law in said Member State functions. Therefore, following the internal comparison, an external comparison of the practice in the four Member States is conducted to reveal any existing discrepancies in the national practices. The external part of the comparison is meant to shed light on current European trends by comparing the findings of the internal comparative analysis at a European level and to find out whether the elements for a roadmap can be derived from the case law in the Member States.

After the identification of the different types of access restrictions, the legal orders applicable to the individual access restriction categories are mapped. This leads to the final roadmap on the overlapping legal orders applicable to access restrictions.

1.5.1.3 *Selection of Member States for the Comparative Analysis*

A selection of Member States has been made for this study.[51] Therefore, the research will not provide a conclusive overview of how *all* Member States address access and moderation issues. Since the main goal of the comparative study is to explore and describe discrepancies in Member States' adjudication of access and moderation issues, both physical and online, legal systems should be included in which one expects to find objects that relate to the topic of the study.[52] Moreover, the selected systems must function as a source of solutions for the evaluative aim of the second part of the research. This is only possible if the selected systems share essential common features.[53] Based on these selection criteria, the study has focused on four Member States: Germany, Italy, the Netherlands, and Denmark.[54]

The German legal system has been included first because it is the first Member State in which the Supreme Court has directly addressed the norm-setting behaviour of social media platforms in user terms.[55] Second, it has a long-standing tradition of the horizontal application of fundamental rights in private agreements, which gives an interesting perspective on how to address the problem.[56] Furthermore, the German Civil Code covers an explicit provision on the exclusion of access to private property (§1004 BGB), which offers a useful point of departure for the comparison of physical access restrictions since the *doctrine of house rights* was developed thereon.

The Italian legal system has been selected due to the particularities in its case law on access rights, such as the existence of a possibility to claim non-material damages for wrongful moderation and the opportunity to claim access on the basis of an individual pressing social need. Moreover, the Italian system grants ex officio power to the Italian Competition Authority to enforce unfair clauses in user terms. The case law of these decisions - which are publicly available - provides valuable insight and ground for comparison to the other systems. Lastly, similar to the German civil code, the Italian civil code is explicit in the possibility of excluding others from private property and allows for a good comparison to the German system on access restrictions to physical property.

---

51. *Ibid.*, 603.
52. *Ibid.*, 605.
53. As such, a comparison between the US-system and the European Member States proves unsuitable for this study since the US' First amendment in combination with the specifics 47 U.S.C. §230 do not prove 'transplantable' building blocks for a roadmap on access and content restrictions in the European Member States' systems. *See ibid.*, 605.
54. Since the study does not have the aim to *harmonise* the European systems, but to allow for a roadmap that can accommodate different systems, a selection of Member States has been made. If the aim would have been to harmonise the European system, all 27 Member States would have to be studied, which would have to be carried out by a group of researchers. *See* reflections on the harmonisation of European approaches: Oderkerk (n. 49) 606. Since this project is the result of a study by a single person in a limited timeframe, a harmonisation study would simply not be feasible.
55. *Bundesgerichtshof (Kontosperrung)* (n. 23); *Bundesgerichtshof (Inhaltesperrung)* (n. 23).
56. Matthias C Kettemann and Torben Klausa, 'Regulating Online Speech: Ze German Way' (*Lawfare*, 20 September 2021) https://www.lawfareblog.com/regulating-online-speech-ze-german-way (accessed 27 September 2021).

The Netherlands has been selected because of the developments in its case law. During the COVID-19 pandemic, numerous cases were filed by individual users against social media platforms, challenging the normativity of access and content moderation decisions on 'misinformation'. In this stream of cases, Dutch courts have made several references to physical property and their access restrictions, posing a viable source of inspiration for the aims of comparison in this study. Furthermore, inspired by the German doctrine of *house rights*, the Dutch courts have applied a similar, but unsuccessful, doctrine to Dutch access restrictions in physical property.

Lastly, Denmark has been selected to test the elements following from the three rather similar legal systems of Germany, Italy, and the Netherlands and to add a perspective from another legal family. Denmark forms a part of the Scandinavian legal family and distinguishes itself from the other Member States selected in this study as it does not have a codified civil law. The Danish system is similar – and at points identical – to the other Scandinavian legal systems, and the inspiration drawn from the Danish system, therefore, forms a gateway to the other Scandinavian systems. Furthermore, the Scandinavian countries are remarked as 'non-litigators', meaning that their nationals file lawsuits significantly less often than other European countries.[57] Contrarily, multiple quasi-judicial bodies and dispute resolution bodies exist. When looking at redress mechanisms for users against access and moderation decisions, this is an interesting factor to include in the comparison, as it would increase the applicability of the roadmap even in countries where the threshold of litigation is high. Lastly, the Danish system offers an interesting overlap with the Italian system. The Danish system regulates individuals' access to certain types of private property, such as access to privately owned forests.

1.5.1.4 The Objects to Be Compared

To usefully compare objects in a comparative study, they must share a common element – a *tertium comparationis*.[58] As the comparative study is descriptive and exploratory in nature, the *tertium comparationis* should focus on the function of rules in the selected legal systems.[59] Following a *problem-solving method*,[60] objects which function to address/solve the problem are included in the comparative evaluation of the four legal systems. As the goal of the comparative study is, first, to identify *internal*

57. Uwe Kischel, 'Variety of the Civil Law Context' in Uwe Kischel and Andrew Hammel (eds), *Comparative Law* (Oxford University Press 2019) 109 https://doi.org/10.1093/oso/978019879 1355.003.0007 (accessed 9 February 2023).
58. Oderkerk (n. 49) 610.
59. *Ibid*. Oderkerk states that 'If the aim of the comparison is descriptive but the topic of the research is the regulation of a certain societal phenomenon, the tertium comparationis will not be form but function because the researcher will describe the (different or similar) regulation of a similar societal phenomenon in several legal systems. The researcher will thus describe those rules that deal with this situation. In this way, the tertium comparationis is not determined by the aim of the research: the researcher selects objects that have an identical function not because the aim of the project requires this but because the topic logically calls for objects that fulfill a similar function.'
60. Oderkerk (n. 49) 612-613.

discrepancies in the selected legal systems, the objects sought after are the rules that function to resolve access and moderation conflicts between an undertaking and a private person, both when dealing with physical undertakings and social media platforms. The rules will be grouped by functions. Second, the identified groups of functions will be compared *externally* between the different Member States to see if overlapping elements can be found.

1.5.1.5 The Sources of the Comparative Study

The selection of sources for the comparative study depends on a combination of the study's objectives and focus areas.[61] The aim of this study is to explore and describe the differences in the Member States to resolve access and content moderation issues, respectively, in the physical and online world. As the object of study, the rules that are used to resolve these issues have been chosen. Consequently, the most logical choice for legal sources to find the rules in the selected legal systems is the national case law. Despite the lacking binding nature of case law in some of the included legal systems, the case law proves valuable insight into the (potential discrepancy in the) way access and moderation restrictions are addressed. Problems of (questionable) content removals and suspensions of accounts on social media platforms exist and are (increasingly) addressed in national courts. Courts have to apply and interpret the existing rules in their national legal system to reach a verdict, also in cases related to social media platforms, for which the national laws potentially do not per se pose a direct answer. The case law has been identified through multiple sources in the respective jurisdictions.[62]

61. *Ibid.*, 615.
62. *Germany*: The two most important sources (the Federal Constitutional Court and the Federal Court of Justice) have been sourced as follows: for the cases from the Federal Constitutional Court (*Bundesverfassungsgericht – BVerfG)*, the register of cases on bundesverfassungsgericht.de has been used, and similarly, the cases from the Federal Court of Justice (*Bundesgerichtshof – BGH)* have been identified through the database on juris.bundesgerichtshof.de. These two databases contain cases from respectively 1998 and 2000 onwards. Additionally, the online database of beck-online has been applied to find additional cases. Case law covering access restrictions based on legal grounds outside private law have been excluded from this study. On administrative law, *see, e.g.*, the discussion on access to an e-mail service in *Bundesverfassungsgericht* (2006) 2 BvR 1458/03, ECLI:DE:BVerfG:2006:rk 20060703.2bvr145803; on competition law and the access to dominant services: *Bundesverfassungsgericht* (2003) 1 BvR 1712/01, ECLI:DE:BVerfG:2003:rs20031007.1bvr171201; and *Bundesgerichtshof* (2002) KVR 15/01.
    Italy: For specific cases on the unfairness of clauses in terms and conditions used in consumer contracts, all cases issued by the Italian Consumer Authority (ICA) were assessed. In 2012, ICA was granted competency to enforce unfair contract terms (*clausole vessatorie*) either ex officio or after a complaint (Article 37-bis of the Consumer Code). The ICA publishes all decisions on unfair terms on its website. As of 2012 – the start of the investigative competency of the ICA – there have been issued 65 decisions on unfair contract terms, of which six were directly relevant for this study. The cases are accessible at Italian Consumer Authority, Tutela del Consumatore – Clausole Vessatorie – 'Provvedimenti ed estratti', available at: https://www.agcm.it/competenze/tutela-del-consumatore/clausole-vessatorie/provvedimenti-ed-estratti (accessed 6 May 2022). Additionally, general civil and administrative cases have been located through the database of dejure.it. Excluded from the study are the cases on refusals of access to (football) stadiums on the basis of a *DASPO, Divieto di accedere alle manifestazioni sportive* (prohibition to access

1.6 PART II: CREATING A ROADMAP FIT FOR SOCIAL MEDIA PLATFORMS

In the second part, the roadmap will be customised to address specific issues on social media platforms. The elements identified in part one will be adjusted to fit the specific issues concerning access restrictions and content moderation on social media platforms. As quickly touched upon above, the answer to the main research question exists of two interdependent challenges: without the study of the practice in the Member States' case law, it is hard to identify the (interaction between the) different legal orders while simultaneously, without the assessment of the legal orders, the practice in the Member States cannot be interpreted sufficiently clear to form a roadmap for future adjudication. The comparative study of the case law in the Member States will show that an identical approach to resolving access restrictions does not exist, though it is possible to deduct four overlapping layers with identical and/or similar elements.[63] For the roadmap to function effectively, these different elements must be adjusted to the specific circumstances of social media platforms.

Each of the four distinct layers that emerge from the comparative study (foundation, access, content, and enforcement) presents its own set of interpretational

sporting events), which is a criminal measure that can be imposed on a person to prevent violence in relation to sports events - mainly football matches. For the prohibition to access sporting events to be imposed on a person, a criminal conviction is not required. The prohibition is seen as a preventive measure, *see* Corte Costituzionale, Sentenza 512/2002, 20 November 2002, ECLI:IT:COST:2002:512. These decisions are excluded from this study due to the origin of the exclusion of access. Rather than the normative choice (through house rules or general terms and conditions) of the stadium to deny access, the refusal is based on national (criminal) law.

Netherlands: The cases have been sourced through the Dutch judiciary's official website (rechtspraak.nl), to which all court cases after 2002 are published (online, for free). For court cases prior to 2002, the online service *Navigator* (navigator.nl) has been used to search through Dutch legal literature. The literature subsequently pointed in the direction of relevant cases, which full texts were also included in Navigator. Furthermore, most cases on social media platforms in relation to COVID-19 were frequently referenced in the Dutch national news. Only cases including references to user terms (*algemene voorwaarden*) and the right to property have been included in this study. Case law covering access restrictions based on other legal grounds have been excluded from this study Despite being interesting and a potential source for future research. *See, e.g.*, the criminal case *Rechtbank Amsterdam* (2021) ECLI:NL:RBAMS:2021:5796, where a social media prohibition was imposed after the suspect issued threats over WhatsApp and Instagram.

Denmark: The Danish cases have been sourced through the newly established online case law database (*Domsdatabasen*, https://domsdatabasen.dk), and Karnovs case law database (https://pro.karnovgroup.dk). Additionally, inquiries have been made to the Danish Institute for Human Rights (https://www.humanrights.dk), the independent legal thinktank Justitia (http://justitia-int.org), and the IT-political association.

63. The decisions on the outline and methodology for the second part were taken after the first part had been finished. This allowed for an adjustment of the research questions to seamlessly fit the conclusions in the Member States. This had one main practical reason: depending on whether the outcome of the comparative study showed overlapping elements, a roadmap could or could not be build. As the conclusions of the comparative study showed that there were overlapping elements, the second part focuses on these elements in detail. If the opposite result had been reached, the second part would have been an evaluative study to see how the systems of the Member States could have been brought closer together for a uniform approach on access and moderation restrictions.

challenges. First, the foundational layer concerns the legal basis for access restrictions. As the comparative study will show, the right to property forms the basis for *physical* restrictions in all four legal systems (whether directly or indirectly). However, whether also social media platforms can invoke this basis, and if yes, what the scope and application of the right to property is when dealing with social media platforms, is unclear. Second, the possibility to claim access to private property varies in the different national legal systems. It is unclear whether these possibilities could be transposed to social media platforms, mainly because of the differences in the qualification of social media platforms by the national courts (dominant player, public forum, essential service). Third, in the content layer, the interpretation of the elements differs between physical property and social media platforms due to specific legislation that affects social media platforms. Similarly, the consequences of a breach of the contractual terms are different when dealing with social media platforms as opposed to physical properties because the DSA's procedural obligations have a direct effect on the users' options for (legal) redress against an access or moderation decision by a social media platform. These procedural obligations must be considered to create a roadmap that efficiently addresses access and moderation issues on social media platforms.

1.6.1 Sub-questions and Methodology of Part Two

The second part of this book provides answers to the following sub-questions:

(i) Which fundamental rights form the foundational basis for access restrictions on social media platforms, and what is their scope of application?
(ii) Which types of access restrictions are imposed by social media platforms, and what possibilities do users have to oppose them?
(iii) When and how can users oppose platforms' moderation decisions?

1.6.1.1 Doctrinal Legal Research Methodology

The interpretation of legal rules is central to the doctrinal legal research methodology, making it an ideal approach for interpreting the elements of the roadmap identified in the comparative study of the book's first part.[64] The second part departs from the assumption that legal rules are made up of a combination of positive law, legal principles, and the interpretation of legal rules by courts. Preparatory works and (legal) academic literature can serve as a pointer towards a correct interpretation of the former

64. Mark Van Hoecke, *Methodologies of Legal Research: Which Kind of Method for What Kind of Discipline?* (Bloomsbury Publishing Plc 2013) 3 http://ebookcentral.proquest.com/lib/kbdk/detail.action?docID=1772966 (accessed 8 February 2023). Jan M Smits, 'What Is Legal Doctrine? On the Aims and Methods of Legal-Dogmatic Research' (1 September 2015) 5 https://papers.ssrn.com/abstract=2644088 (accessed 9 February 2023). Smits describes legal doctrine as 'research that aims to give a systematic exposition of the principles, rules and concepts governing a particular legal field or institution and analyses the relationship between these principles, rules and concepts with a view to solving unclarities and gaps in the existing law'.

but are not, in itself, included as legal sources. With this in mind, the elements of the roadmap are interpreted and adjusted to fit social media platforms.

To define the scope of 'positive law', inspiration has been drawn from the theory on plural legal orders outlined by Vanessa Mak.[65] Globalisation has led to an increase in private lawmaking 'beyond the state', which has consequences for contract and consumer law. Mak highlights specifically 'the balancing of interests between parties in the light of (social) justice, consumer protection, or fundamental rights', as well as the increase of rules that do not derive from the state regulator, such as the role of the European Union, transnational rules, and private regulation by industry. The balancing of that plurality of legal norms lies at the core of the second part's interpretational problems. Opposed to a monist approach, the legal pluralist approach does not limit itself to sources of national state law but 'includes all relevant sources of norms in its analysis – including non-state law – and therefore can perhaps do more justice to the real interests of consumers in the global marketplace'.[66] However, the division between a monistic and a pluralistic approach is not a simple dichotomy but exists in a continuum of several factors (*see* Figure 1.2). Depending on the sources of norms included in the definition of 'law' and the belief in an inherent hierarchy, varieties within legal pluralism can be identified.[67]

Figure 1.2 The Continuum of Legal Monism and Pluralism

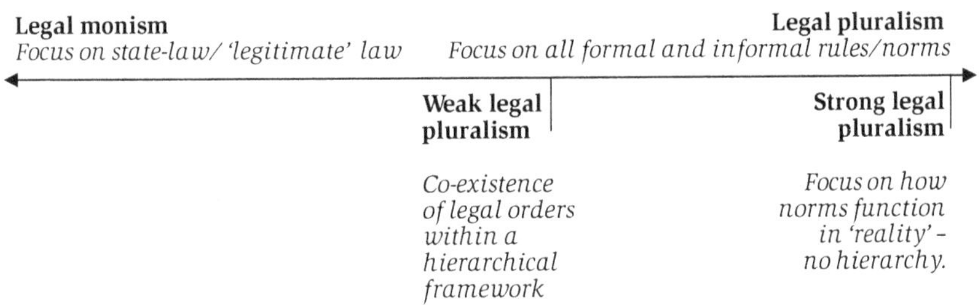

The first, weak legal pluralism (also called state-law or juridical legal pluralism), concerns the co-existence of legal orders within a hierarchy.[68] Opposed to the approach of legal monism, the weak legal pluralist approach does not solely include state law as a source of law but also other norms following from supranational or intranational sources or private lawmaking. Despite including all these legal orders, weak legal pluralists acknowledge a legal hierarchy. Strong (or 'deep') legal pluralists also include

65. Vanessa Mak, *Legal Pluralism in European Contract Law* (First edition, Oxford University Press 2020).
66. *Ibid.*
67. Mak, *Legal Pluralism in European Contract Law* (n. 65) 28-34. Keebet von Benda-Beckmann and Bertram Turner, 'Legal Pluralism, Social Theory, and the State' (2018) 50 The Journal of Legal Pluralism and Unofficial Law 255.
68. It has also been argued that the weak version of legal pluralism simply represents legal centralism, Baudouin Dupret, 'Legal Pluralism, Plurality of Laws, and Legal Practices'.

all those sources of law, but its application differs from its weak counterpart by an absence of a hierarchy of those norms.

In the scope of this study, 'law' is understood broadly, following the approach of legal pluralists. However, the assessment of the interaction of the different legal orders follows a hierarchy. Norms – which form incentives for an individual to act or not act – can have numerous sources outside the legal sphere, such as norms that are the consequence of platforms' technical interface[69] or norms imposed through the terms of service of social media platforms.[70] Despite the norm-setting consequences of terms of service or the technical interface on platforms, the idea is rejected that all norms have the same value as state- or supernational lawmaking when resolving access and moderation issues (on social media platforms). The content of terms (and arguably even the technical interface) can be challenged in national courts.[71] The fact that users often use the platform's own internal dispute resolution mechanisms because taking a dispute to a national court proves challenging, more expensive, and time-consuming and does not alter the hierarchical nature of these norms.[72] After the platform has taken a decision on an internal complaint, that complaint can nonetheless be brought before a national court. Contrarily, after a decision by a national court, a platform cannot take another decision concerning the same content through an internal complaints process.

Since this focus is to map the *legal* redress options of social media platform users, the *effect* of non-legal norms can play a role in the assessment of legal norms (e.g., very strict terms in an exclusive technical interface can lead to a limitation of the freedom of contract),[73] but they are not included as *sources* of legal redress. The 'positive law' in this study is therefore understood within the approach of weak legal pluralism with a focus on the legal mechanisms deriving from state and international/multinational lawmaking, without disregarding the effect that non-legal norms can have on the outcome and interpretation of the former.

For the first three layers, the aim is to describe how the existing plural orders apply, identify legal gaps, and interpret how the law would apply in the context of access and content moderation problems on social media platforms. The main legal problem in the foundational layer relates to the interpretation and applicability of the exclusive rights of the right to property by social media platforms, and the influence of the freedom to conduct a business. For the access layer, the interpretation concerns the rules of competition law, (in)direct horizontal effect of fundamental rights, the protection of the rights and freedoms of others, and the rules on social and public interest rights following from the national legal systems. For the content layer, the

69. Lawrence Lessig and Lawrence Lessig, *Code* (Version 20, Basic Books 2006).
70. Kettemann (n. 6).
71. Both can lead to unfair outcomes for consumers, which can be opposed by the Member States' national transpositions of either the Unfair Commercial Practices Directive or the Unfair Contract Terms Directive.
72. Opposing the view set out by Mak, *Legal Pluralism in European Contract Law* (n. 65) 31. Mak refers to this lack of access to national adjudication as a reason to opt for a strong legal pluralist approach.
73. The dilemma in this example will return in various parts of the book, such as on the access rights to 'essential' platforms (§5.5.5) or to answer whether the platform's scope of freedom of contract allows full restrictions of fundamental rights (§6.4.3.3).

general principles of contract law and the increasing European consumer protection laws that are an extension thereof give rise to numerous interpretational problems when applied to normative content moderation decisions. The fourth layer faces its own interpretational problem, as the enforcement of terms of services is highly influenced by the DSA's new obligations on social media platforms. Most importantly, Article 14 DSA imposes increased obligations of transparency and due diligence on these players when enforcing their terms of service. However, the interpretation and application of these obligations is unclear. As case law and literature on the interpretation of these obligations are (still) scarce, the interpretation of the legal texts will be based on a textual interpretation of the legal texts and the preparatory works.

1.7 THE OUTLINE OF THE BOOK

This book contains an introduction chapter, six substantive chapters (chapters two to seven), and two concluding chapters. The first part of this book is covered in Chapters 2 and 3, which cover the comparative study and the results. In Chapter 2, each jurisdiction's section includes an explorative part on physical access restrictions and online access restrictions. Chapter 2 concludes with an external comparative study, which addresses the internal discrepancies in the four legal systems. Chapter 3 utilises the findings from the comparative study in Chapter 2 to identify the access restriction elements that could serve as building blocks for a European roadmap.

The second part builds on the European roadmap established in Part I, focusing on its application to social media platforms. Chapters 4 to 7 correspond to the four layers identified in Chapter 3. Chapter 4 covers the foundational layer, tracing access and moderation restrictions to their origin in the right to property. Chapter 5 addresses the access layer and examines the various ways in which users can be denied and/or claim access to a platform. Chapter 6 discusses the conditions for conditional access and the permissible scope of terms applied by social media platforms. Finally, Chapter 7 addresses the enforcement of terms of service on social media platforms.

The answering of the sub-questions corresponds to the chapters of this book, meaning that sub-question (i) will be answered in Chapter 2, sub-question (ii) in Chapter 3, sub-question (iii) in Chapter 4 and sub-question (iv) in Chapter 5. Lastly, deviating from the others, the answer to sub-question (v) is divided between Chapters 6 and 7. The main research question is answered in Chapter 8. Finally, Chapter 9 covers an overview of the additional findings, reflections and recommendations, and concrete opportunities for further research.

Part I The Identification of the Roadmap's Elements

CHAPTER 2

Access Restrictions in a European Comparative Perspective

2.1 THE OUTLINE OF THE TWO-FOLD COMPARATIVE STUDY

The comparative study outlined in this chapter serves to explore and describe how the Member States' legal frameworks function when dealing with access and moderation restrictions on respectively social media platforms and physical property. The comparative study is two-fold and consists of an internal and an external comparison (*see* Figure 2.1).[74]

Figure 2.1 Visual Representation of the Two-Fold Comparative Study

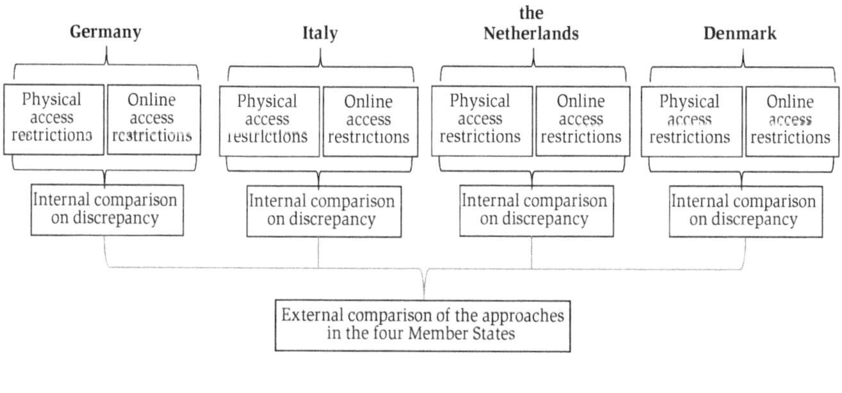

74. *See* §1.5.1 above for a full disclosure of the methodology, underlying hypotheses, the scope and limitations, and the objects and sources of the comparative study.

The internal comparison allows us to conclude whether there are overlapping legal elements in the adjudication of access and content restrictions to physical properties and social media platforms. Subsequently, the overlapping elements in the individual Member States are compared with the other three Member States' outcomes further below in §2.3. Combining these two steps – the internal and external comparison – forms the foundation for the identification of the roadmap's elements, which are outlined in Chapter 3.

2.2 THE *INTERNAL* COMPARATIVE STUDY

The internal comparison focuses on the potential differences between the way a Member State resolves access and moderation issues in relation to physical proprietors and their customers and compares that approach to the one applied to social media platforms and their users. It tests whether a technology-neutral approach poses a viable framework for a roadmap to deal with access restrictions on social media platforms. The internal comparative analysis consists of three parts:

(i) an assessment of the applicable law and an analysis of the case law on physical actors' access restrictions.
(ii) an assessment of the applicable law and an analysis of the case law analysis of social media platforms' access restrictions.
(iii) a comparison of the conclusions on (i) and (ii).

Each of these three points is outlined per selected Member State, starting with Germany, followed by Italy, the Netherlands, and Denmark.[75]

2.2.1 Germany

2.2.1.1 Physical Access Restrictions

The case law on access restrictions for physical places shows that German courts deal with physical access restrictions predominantly through a system of *Hausrecht* ('house right'). Several other categories referring to access restrictions (invalid user terms, equal treatment, termination) have been included in the system of house rights. Additionally, discriminating access and moderation decisions are illegal, as well as between two private parties.[76] This includes discrimination on the grounds of race or ethnic origin, sex, religion, disability, age, or sexual orientation.

The cases studied in relation to house rights cover not only the access to publicly accessible places (supermarkets, airports, public squares) but also the access to generally more restricted places where people, for example, have to buy an entrance ticket or make a reservation (hotel rooms, stadiums, thermal spas). The doctrine of house rights emerged in 1966 in *Bundesgerichtshof*'s *Hausverbot* and has since been

75. The comparative study contains data until March 2023.
76. General Act on Equal Treatment, section 19.

developed in more detail. House rights follow from the proprietor's right to property, which is codified in §903 of the German Civil Code (*BGB*). According to §903, the owner of the property may, 'unless the law or the rights of third parties conflict therewith, dispose of the property as he pleases and exclude others from any interference with the property'. The right consists of both a positive and a negative aspect. The positive side allows the property owner to decide freely what to do with the property and how to make use of it. The negative aspect provides the owner with a right to exclude others from interfering with his property. It is this negative aspect that is referred to as the *Hausrecht*. If a third party that interferes with the property owner's house right does not comply with the exclusion of access (e.g., a person does not leave the premises after being asked to do so), book 3, paragraph 3, title 4 of the BGB ('claims arising from ownership' – §§985-1007) prescribes redress mechanisms. These include a claim for restitution of the property (§985) and a claim for removal and injunction (§1004).

Therefore, in principle, a property owner is free to deny access to the property and to set conditions limiting third parties' access to the property based on §§903 and 1004 BGB. However, these access refusals are not unlimited (§1004(2) BGB). In later case law, the scope of use of the house right has been limited in the following ways.

First, if a private property is 'open to the general public', the users have a 'general right of use' (*generellen Nutzungsbefugnis*). The act of offering a service to the general public is conceived as an implicit waiver of the proprietor's right to exclude, and thus, the proprietor cannot later invoke this right to deny access.[77] The assessment of whether a property is open to the public is based on various grounds. For example, the property is open if the service is offered or access to the property is granted to anyone ('open to general traffic'[78]) and impacts the person's participation in social life. Moreover, a property is also open to the general public if the place constitutes a public forum.[79] These places are 'characterised by the fact that it can be used to pursue a variety of different activities and concerns the development of a varied and open communications network'.[80] These 'open private places' do not include property where an individual assessment is carried out, thereby excluding, for example, the airport zone after the security check, wellness hotels, and thermal baths.[81] Private squares and shopping malls fall within the scope of open private places.[82] A football stadium is open to the general public, even though a ticket is required because the proprietor 'in principle grants anyone – against payment – access to the stadium'.[83]

77. *Bundesgerichtshof (Therme)* (2020) V ZR 275/18, ECLI:DE:BGH:2020:290520UVZR275.18.0; *Bundesgerichtshof (Hausrecht des Hotelbetreibers)* (2012) V ZR 115/11.
78. *Bundesverfassungsgericht (Fraport)* (2011) 1 BvR 699/06, §66.
79. *Ibid.*, §70.
80. *Ibid.*
81. *Ibid.*; *Bundesgerichtshof (Hausrecht des Hotelbetreibers)* (n. 77); *Bundesgerichtshof (Therme)* (n. 77).
82. *Bundesgerichtshof (Stadionverbot I)* (2009) V ZR 253/08; *Bundesverfassungsgericht (Bierdosen-Flashmob)* (2015) 1 BvQ 25/15, ECLI:DE:BVerfG:2015:qk20150718.1bvq002515; *Bundesverfassungsgericht (Fraport)* (n. 78).
83. *Bundesgerichtshof (Stadionverbot I)* (n. 82).

Second, this general right of access can, in turn, be limited by either valid user terms and/or by an objective reason. The proprietor may make accessing the property subject to general terms and conditions. However, these terms must fulfil the general requirements in the BGB and thus must be sufficiently clear and unambiguous.[84] For the assessment of the validity of the terms, the general provisions of §§307 ff BGB apply. In *Einzelhandelsmarkt*, the shop owner only indicated at the entrance that customers were 'kindly asked' to hand in their bags at the information desk and that otherwise, bags might be searched if deemed necessary.[85] The *Bundesgerichtshof* concluded that the proprietor had not unequivocally declared an intention to only allow customers who consent to a bag check, and thus, all customers had acquired a general right to access the store *with a bag*. A polite question does not fulfil the criteria of clarity and unambiguity.

Third, even without valid terms and conditions, access can be denied if the proprietor has an objective reason to do so. This objective reason must reflect all the circumstances involved, which means it must strike a fair balance between the interests of all parties.[86] Following German case law,[87] for powerful proprietors, striking a fair balance between the interests of all parties involved means that the objective reason must also strike a fair balance between and take into consideration constitutional norms. Under German law, constitutional norms are not automatically applicable to a relationship between private parties, but they can be included in the interpretation of open norms through 'third-party effect' (*Drittwirkung*).[88] In this way,

84. *Ibid.*, II. under 1: 'Das schließt es aber nicht aus, daß er von seinem Hausrecht gegenüber solchen Kunden Gebrauch macht, die hierzu, insbesondere durch Störungen des Betriebsablaufs, Anlaß geben, oder daß er die generelle Erlaubnis zum Betreten seiner Geschäftsräume von bestimmten Bedingungen abhängig machen und denjenigen, der diese Bedingungen nicht erfüllen will, vom Zutritt ausschließen kann.' However, any access restrictions in the terms and conditions may not disproportionally infringe the personal rights of a customer. The Court found that the inspection of bags without a concrete suspicion of theft was disproportional. Therefore, the owner of a shop that is open to the general public cannot deny a customer, which was not suspected of any unlawful behaviour, access to the store based on the mere fact that she did not want her bag searched.
85. The *Bundesgerichtshof* valued the formulation of the request and the fact that the seller had not taken measures to *prevent* people from entering with their bags highly for reaching the conclusion of a non-binding term: 'Der "höflichen Bitte" um Abgabe der Taschen kommt ein hinreichend deutlicher Regelungscharakter im Sinne einer verbindlichen Hausordnung nicht zu. Einer Bitte nicht Folge zu leisten, steht im Belieben des Kunden. Damit stimmt überein, daß die Bekl. im Eingangsbereich des Marktes keine Maßnahmen zur Durchsetzung dieser Bitte getroffen hat.'
86. *Bundesgerichtshof (Stadionverbot I)* (n. 82); *Bundesgerichtshof (Hausrecht des Hotelbetreibers)* (n. 77).
87. *See* for an overview of the general development and specifically the principle of equality: Peter Rott, 'Powerful Private Players in the Digital Economy: Between Private Law Freedoms and the Constitutional Principle of Equality' (2020) 18 Baltic Yearbook of International Law Online 32, DOI: https://doi.org/10.1163/22115897_01801_004.
88. Since the aim of the comparative study is to identify building blocks for the European roadmap that overlap between Member States, the scope of this comparative study does not allow for an extensive study into the full details of German third-party effect, but the existence and possibility to invoke constitutional norms in private relationships is an important element to include in the external comparative analysis.

they serve as an objective principle.[89] Based on this third-party effect of constitutional rights, fundamental rights such as equal treatment and freedom of expression can have an effect on access restrictions.[90] Following the decision in *Stadionverbot II*, the principle of equal treatment is applicable to access restrictions on publicly offered services if the refusal has a significant effect of the refusal on a person's social life.[91] The proprietor is subject to a 'special legal responsibility' if the restriction would objectively impact the social life of the refused person, meaning that the proprietor needs to adhere to procedural requirements.[92] In effect, that means that a person can claim forced access to the property in case refusal would mean a significant reduction or practical impossibility of a person to participate in his/her social life.[93]

Based on the case law of the German doctrine of house rights, four layers can be identified (*see* Figure 2.2). The first layer covers the proprietor's right to property and the therewith intertwined right to refuse access (§§903 and 1004 BGB). These form the legal basis for the existence of both the house right and the house ban. The second layer covers the potential users' general right of use/access. Such a general right exists when the property is open to the general public. The third layer comes into consideration in case the proprietor, in user terms, applies general restrictions to enter the property. These restrictions limit the general access right the users can claim under layer two. Fundamental rights *could* come into play to review the content of the terms of service.[94] If no restrictions to the general access right exist, then the third layer can be omitted – in that case, the users have an *unlimited* general right of access/use. The fourth and

89. *Bundesverfassungsgericht (Bierdosen-Flashmob)* (2015) 1 BvQ 25/15, ECLI:DE:BVerfG:2015:qk20150718.1bvq002515, §6.

90. *Bundesverfassungsgericht (Stadionverbot II)* (2018) 1 BVR 3080/09, ECLI:DE:BVerfG:2018:rs20180411.1bvr308009; *Bundesgerichtshof (Therme)* (n. 77). However, invoking the requirement of equal treatment presupposes an imbalance in the social power balance between the two parties, *see Bundesgerichtshof (Private banking)* (2013) XI ZR 22/12. *See* on the third-party effect of the freedom of expression Heldt, 'Intensivere Drittwirkung: Die Mittelbare Drittwirkung Der Meinungsfreiheit in Öffentlichkeiten Der Digitalen Gesellschaft – Eine Verfassungsrechtliche, Rechtsvergleichende Und Interdisziplinäre Analyse' (n. 40).

91. *Bundesverfassungsgericht (Stadionverbot II)* (n. 90); *see also* a confirmation in *Bundesgerichtshof (Therme)* (n. 77).

92. *Bundesverfassungsgericht (Stadionverbot II)* (n. 90); Rott (n. 87). The legal obligation follows from the social dimension of the property right in Art. 14(2) of the German Basic Law, *see also* Stefan Muckel, 'Mittelbare Drittwirkung Des Allgemeinen Gleichheitssatzes' [2018] Juristische Arbeitsblätter 553.

93. *See Bundesgerichtshof (Therme)* (n. 77). Between the lines, one can deduct that the basis of the argumentation and conclusion on what constitutes 'impact on social life' refers to the existence of relevant alternatives. The *Bundesgerichtshof* underlines for example the existence of other, similar thermal baths that the refused person could have visited (§3). The subjective experience of the refused person is explicitly refused as an argument – in *Therme*, the refused person used the thermal bath for social gatherings and had built up friendly relationships with the other guests. The latter argument was dismissed as irrelevant for determining whether the service contributed to the person's social life.

94. *See Bundesverfassungsgericht (BVerfG zur Inhaltskontrolle von Bürgschaften einkommens- und vermögensloser Familienangehöriger)* [1993] 1 BvR 56789, concluding that civil courts, especially when interpreting open clauses such as §242 BGB, must take the fundamental right of private autonomy in Article 2(1) Basic Law in consideration. According to the Court, 'this follows from their duty to review the content of contracts that place an unusually heavy burden on one of the two contracting parties and are the result of structurally unequal bargaining power'.

last layer addresses whether other refusals of access can be justified even outside or without the applicability of valid terms. In those circumstances, despite the existence of a general right of access, a proprietor can use its house right to deny access to its property if an objective reason exists.

Figure 2.2 The Different Layers of the German Hausrecht

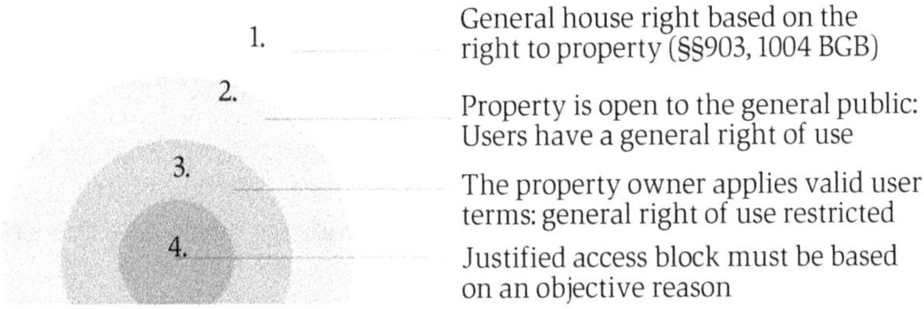

2.2.1.2 Online Access Restrictions[95]

For social media platforms with more than two million users, the (criticised[96]) German Network Enforcement Act stipulates procedural obligations (procedures for handling complaints, obligation to create public reports) for dealing with illegal content (*rechtswidrige Inhalte*).[97] German law does not offer social media platform-specific regulation on access and content restrictions outside the scope of illegal content. Disputes related to access and content restrictions that go beyond the scope of illegality are, therefore, dealt with within the regular legal framework.

Online platforms that are available without mandatory sign-up (e.g., an open chat box) follow an approach similar to the house right doctrine observed in physical places. For this type of online platform, a *virtual* house right exists.[98] A chat forum owner's virtual house right cannot be used to deny access to a free-of-charge publicly

95. The case law analysis for access restrictions on (social media) platforms only covers disputes involving privately owned platforms. Cases covering disputes between the blocking of access to 'public social media pages' have been omitted, such as the case on the restriction of access to the 'comment-section' of an internet platform governed by the national public communication channel: *Verwaltungsgericht München (Sperrung der Kommentarfunktion auf einer Diskussionsplattform)* (2017) M 26 K 16.5928.
96. Critics mainly refer to the laws' incentive for over-removal and the inspiration the law serves for restrictive regimes, *see* Justitia, 'The Digital Berlin Wall: How Germany (Accidentally) Created a Prototype for Global Online Censorship – Act Two' (2020) https://justitia-int.org/wp-content/uploads/2020/09/Analyse_Cross-fertilizing-Online-Censorship-The-Global-Impact-of-Germanys-Network-Enforcement-Act-Part-two_Final-1.pdf (accessed 17 February 2023); Heidi Tworek and Paddy Leerssen, 'An Analysis of Germany's NetzDG Law' https://www.ivir.nl/publicaties/download/NetzDG_Tworek_Leerssen_April_2019.pdf.
97. Netzwerkdurchsetzungsgesetz vom 1. September 2017 (BGBl. I S. 3352), das zuletzt durch Artikel 3 des Gesetzes vom 21. Juli 2022 (BGBl. I S. 1182) geändert worden ist.
98. *Landsgericht Offenburg (Virtuelles Hausrecht II)* (2018) ECLI:DE:LGOFFEN:2018:0926. 2O310.18.00 2 O 310/18, §34.

accessible chat forum without an objectively justified reason. The users of such a forum have a 'general right of use' equal to the general right of use for physical places. However, the existence of these types of platforms has decreased over the last years, and thus, so has the importance of the virtual house right. Platforms that are not open access, such as the majority of the social media platforms offered online, can delete content or refuse access to the platform. It is settled in German case law that a social media platform is allowed to impose such sanctions.[99] For content restrictions, these sanctions must be based on either the law or the terms of service.[100]

The analysis of the cases on social media platforms shows that the assessment of the justification and legitimacy of content restrictions follows a three-step test. First, the platform must uphold its own rules for removal.[101] If the restriction is evidently wrong (e.g., content was removed that is not illegal or against the terms), the user has a 'right to claim the reinstatement of content'.[102] Second, the terms' validity is assessed. According to the case law, terms on social media platforms generally pass the test of transparency in §307 of the Civil Code. The mere fact that social media platforms make use of 'layered user terms' (linking from one set of user terms to another) does not, per default, make the user terms untransparent. User terms can be unilaterally amended by the platform as long as the platform user – at some point – clicks 'I agree' and is made aware that clicking said button means that the user terms are updated. The fact that the platform only grants the user the opportunity to agree to the new terms or leave the platform does not change this.[103] Third and lastly, it is examined whether the

---

99. *Ibid.* The *LG Offenburg* concluded that a virtual house right exists, though it cannot be invoked to overrule the agreement between the parties and therefore does not apply to social media platforms that require sign-up, as the user terms accepted at the time of signing up will overrule the virtual house right.

100. *Landsgericht Köln (Hate speech)* (2018) ECLI:DE:LGK:2018:0727.24O187.18.00 24 O 18718, §42 (translation by the author). Illegal content can *always* be deleted, even without a basis in the user terms. In §42, the *Landsgericht Köln* concludes that *'even without the requirements of the Network Enforcement Act and without a provision in its user terms, including the Community Standards, the [platform] would be entitled to delete comments with criminal content and to prevent the sharing of further similar offences by appropriate means because – which does not require any further justification – no one has to assist criminal acts to be committed'.* (translation by the author).

101. *Bundesgerichtshof (Inhaltesperrung)* (n. 23), §40: 'There is a contract of use between the parties, in the context of which the platform makes its products and services available and to enable the user to contact other users and to exchange information with other users, in particular to send messages and share data such as texts, photos and videos. It follows from the user terms that content posted by the user on the platform's network may not be deleted without reason.'

102. *Landgericht Frankfurt am Main (Restore claim)* (2018) 2-03 O 182/18; ECLI:DE:LGFFM:2018:0514.2.03O182.18.0A. Later confirmed in *Bundesgerichtshof (Kontosperrung)* (n. 23).

103. *See Bundesgerichtshof (Inhaltesperrung)* (n. 23) §§46-51; *Oberlandesgericht Dresden (Unfair platform terms)* (2018) 4 W 577/18 §13; *Oberlandesgericht Schleswig* [2020] 9 U 125/19 §39; *Oberlandesgericht Dresden (Amended user terms)* (n. 103). Interestingly, that means that a platform can unilaterally change the user terms and subsequently demand that the user either accepts the new terms or leaves the platform's service all together. Opposingly, if the platform would not have this opportunity, the platform would not be able to make its service reflect to updated societal norms and/or laws (for example a stricter interpretation of hate speech or a law increasing the scope of illegal content). Furthermore, the use of legal terms such as 'hate speech' in a way that deviates from the law is not per se untransparent. *See also* Gerald

terms unreasonably disadvantage the platform user. (Clauses in) the user terms are unfair if the party that has drafted the terms (the platform) abusively and at the expense of the contractual partner (the user) favours its own interests and does not adequately compensate the user for that balancing difference.[104] To find out whether the platform has favoured its own interests at the expense of the users' interests, a comprehensive assessment and weighing of the mutual interests, the goal, the nature of the agreement, and to what extent the agreement deviates from the law is required.[105] A social media platform is allowed to restrict content in its user terms that would otherwise be legal.

Opposed to the constitutional rights imposing a duty on the state, in German civil disputes between private parties, the aim is not to minimise the interference with constitutional freedoms but rather to reconcile the freedom of one party with the freedom of the other.[106] Thus, all the (legal) interests of the involved parties (including the platform's own) must be balanced.[107]

If the user terms pass the three-step test, the decision to remove content is, in principle, valid. However, recently, the *Bundesgerichtshof* has put more emphasis on procedural safeguards for users when dealing with social media platforms restricting content. In *Inhaltesperrung*, the court concluded that specific restrictions in the user terms that deviate from the law (e.g., the removal of legal content) are only fair if the following criteria are met. First, there must be an objective reason to delete the content. In line with prior case law, this means that the decision of whether content infringes the

---

Spindler, 'Löschung und Sperrung von Inhalten aufgrund von Teilnahmebedingungen sozialer Netzwerke – Eine Untersuchung der zivil- und verfassungsrechtlichen Grundlagen' (2019) 35 Computer und Recht 238.

104. *Bundesgerichtshof (Inhaltesperrung)* (n. 23), §66.

105. *Ibid.* The *Bundesgerichtshof* also concludes in §70 that a private undertaking such as a social media platform is not directly bound by fundamental rights as a State would be and thus fundamental rights do not need to be directly included in this assessment, though they can be used as a balancing mechanism. A social media platform does not overtake the communication function of the State as is the case for private telecommunication service providers. It cannot be compared to a state monopoly, nor a privatised equivalent. The *Bundesgerichtshof* highlights that large-scale social media platform (in the case Facebook) offer a significant communication possibility on the internet, but they do not guarantee access to the internet as such.

106. Referred to as 'practical concordance' or *Praktische Konkordanz* in German.

107. The *Bundesgerichtshof*'s decision follows the previous decisions in *Oberlandesgericht Dresden (Unfair platform terms)* (n. 103); *Landsgericht Heidelberg (Hate speech II)* (2018) 1 O 71/18; *Landgericht Frankfurt am Main (Access blocks)* (2018) 2-03 O 310/18. The *Oberlandesgericht* concluded that the freedom of expression cannot, without any further balancing, be invoked to oppose the deletion of content that would otherwise be protected by the freedom of expression. Similarly, in *Hate Speech II*, the LG Heidelberg finds that limiting hate speech content in the user terms is not unreasonably disadvantaging the user, despite the effect such a restriction has on the freedom of expression. The users' right to freedom of expression must be weighed against the interest of the platform (Facebook in this case) to create a profitable communication platform. Consequently, the platform can make a decision to create an online environment without 'harmful content', as long as the decision is based on objective criteria, does not restrict one specific type of expression, and is foreseen in the user terms. The same conclusion is reached in *Access Blocks*. In *Hate Speech II*, the *Landsgericht Heidelberg* formulates it clear and precisely: 'An unreasonable disadvantage of the contractual partner of the [platform] within the meaning of §307 BGB is given if the [platform] abusively tries to enforce his own interests at the expense of his contractual partner by a unilateral drafting of the contract without sufficiently taking into account the interests from the [user] and without granting him an adequate compensation.'

user terms may not be left to the subjective interpretation of the platform.[108] Undefined and unobjective user terms do not reflect a fair balance, do not withstand the content review of §307, and are therefore invalid. Second, the platform has the duty of effort to find and clearly communicate the facts that have led to the removal of content. The decision to delete content must be based on objective, verifiable facts, may not arbitrarily exclude content, and must be understandable. To fulfil these requirements, the decision to remove content must be communicated to the user immediately, must contain the reason for deletion and must give the user the opportunity to complain. The latter includes an effective possibility to have the content reinstated. Due to legitimate interests of the platform (mainly avoiding liability and providing an attractive platform)[109] or pressing needs to prevent crime,[110] content may be removed, and accounts may be suspended with immediate effect and before the user has been heard. If these requirements are not present, the removal of the content is unreasonably disadvantaging for the user.

The case law regarding restrictions of access to the platform follow a similar focus on procedural rules. Equal to content removals, a (temporarily) suspension of access to a user account is bound by rules of procedure.[111] An account may not be blocked on the sole basis of a third-party complaint.[112] Furthermore, the access block must be based on an objective reason and may not be taken arbitrarily.[113] Additionally, a platform may issue an access block if the user has repeatedly committed an identical offence (e.g., posting hate speech content) and has thus both violated the rights of other users and permanently disrupted the course of the discussion on the platform. In addition to the 'right to claim the reinstatement of content' outlined above, users have a 'right to unblock' in case of evidently wrongful access suspensions or terminations.[114]

However, a general 'right to access a social media platform' does not exist.[115] The right to unblock only applies to previous users of the platform's service and does not

108. *Oberlandesgericht München (Content block)* (2018) 18 W 858/18; ECLI:DE:OLGMUEN:2018:0717.18W858.18.0A; *Oberlandesgericht Dresden (Unfair platform terms)* (n. 103). In *Content Block*, the *Oberlandesgericht München* concluded that user terms that allow the platform to decide which content breaches the 'community norms', unreasonably disadvantages the platform's user (§307 (1) BGB). Subsequently, in *Unfair Platform Terms*, the *Oberlandesgericht Dresden* followed the *Content Block* decision and states that: '*the Terms of Use no longer link the removal of contributions and the other sanctions regulated therein – as the platform's provision still did [in Content Block] – to a unilateral right of determination by the platform, but to a breach of Facebook's terms of use, community standards and other conditions and guidelines and thus to criteria that can in principle be objectified*'.

109. *Bundesgerichtshof (Inhaltesperrung)* (n. 23), §104.

110. *Landsgericht München (Reinstatement request)* (2022) 42 O 4307/19. The account was suspended with immediate effect because it was used to share Child Exploitative Imagery.

111. *Landgericht Frankfurt am Main (Access blocks)* (n. 107); *Landgericht Frankfurt am Main (Restore claim)* (n. 102); *Bundesgerichtshof (Kontosperrung)* (n. 23); *Bundesgerichtshof (Inhaltesperrung)* (n. 23).

112. *Landgericht Frankfurt am Main (Access blocks)* (n. 107).

113. *Ibid.*; *Verwaltungsgericht München (Sperrung der Kommentarfunktion auf einer Diskussionsplattform)* (n. 95).

114. *Landgericht Frankfurt am Main (Access blocks)* (n. 107).

115. Despite the platform's strong position on the market of social media platforms, the platform cannot be subjected to an obligation to contract as that would undermine the platforms own legal interests. The platform is free to select its contractual partners within the framework of the

grant a legal foundation to claim access. That does not mean that a platform can simply refuse persons from accessing the service. The *Bundesgerichtshof* applies the legal argumentation from the 'physical' house right to the digital sphere of platforms and finds that social media platforms 'offer [a service] to an unlimited number of people without regard to the person and which, for a considerable part of those affected, determine to a considerable extent their participation in social life'.[116] Moreover, the court applies the requirements of equal treatment in Article 3 of the Basic Law to interpret the unfairness of the contractual clauses under §307.[117] As is the case for physical access restrictions, constitutional norms are not automatically applicable to the relationship between private parties. The third-party effect of constitutional rights depends on several factors, such as the dominant position of the operator, the orientation of the platform, the degree of user dependence on the platform, and the affected interests of the platform operators and other third parties.[118] If a social media platform has millions of users in Germany, the service is of dominant importance for users' communication (in at least a certain group of the population), and accessing the service does not have any specific, person-related limitations, then the requirements of Article 3 Basic Law apply directly.[119] That means that a social media platform cannot simply deny the first entry to the platform. The positive right under the right to property, which would allow the platform to freely choose its contractual partners, is outweighed by the persons' interests in accessing the service.

general prohibition of discrimination, *see Bundesgerichtshof (Inhaltesperrung)* (n. 23) §14. The *Bundesgerichtshof* confirms that the platform's scope plays a role in the determination of which specific (groups of) persons can be denied access.

116. *Ibid.*, §§78-79. The Court finds a considerable impact on the participation in social life due to the difficulty to switch platform and the necessity to 'meet' one's friends on the same platform. Therefore, alternatives are scarce – the output of content shared on a social media platform cannot be compared to content shared generally somewhere on the internet.

117. Previously, in *Bundesverfassungsgericht (der III Weg)* (2019) 1 BvQ 42/19, ECLI:DE:BVerfG:2019:qk20190522.1bvq004219, the *Bundesverfassungsgericht* concluded that, under specific circumstances, social media platforms may be bound by requirements pertaining to the laws on equal treatment, therewith applying the prior decision of the *Bundesverfassungsgericht* in *Stadionverbot II* to the realm of platforms.

118. *Bundesverfassungsgericht (der III. Weg)* (n. 117), §15, and later confirmed in *Bundesgerichtshof (Inhaltesperrung)* (n. 27) and *Bundesgerichtshof (Kontosperrung)* (n. 23).

119. Starting with *Der III. Weg*, the court concludes that Meta (Facebook at that time) had a decision-making power over the communication of its users similar to the power of the proprietor of the stadium in *Stadionverbot II*. In *Inhaltesperrung* and *Kontosperrung*, the *Bundesgerichtshof* built further upon the decision in *Der III. Weg*. It concludes that a platform is 'open to the general public' if it does not have any general restrictions on the type of content that can be shared, and it offers its service to an unlimited number of people without regard to the person. The latter argumentation corresponds directly to the limitation of the scope of house rights for proprietors of physical spaces. The *Bundesgerichtshof* continues and states that if such an open platform has a significant impact on the social life of its users, it must adhere to the requirements of the laws on equal treatment. The impact on a user's social life depends on whether the operator of the platform has a dominant position, to what extent users would be able to switch from one platform to another ('lock-in' effect), the orientation of the platform, and the affected interests of the platform operators and other third parties. Thus, applying the criteria developed in *Stadionverbot II* for the third-party effect of constitutional rights directly to social media platforms.

2.2.1.3 *Existence of an Internal Discrepancy*

Comparing the practice in the German case law between physical places and online places, several overlapping elements can be observed. First, the case law on physical access restrictions and online access restrictions equally shows the existence of a general right of use for open access-properties/platforms. If a person is able to access a property or use a social media platform's service without access restrictions, the proprietor cannot refuse the person's access. If the proprietor decides to impose rules on the use of the property or the platform, it is, in principle, free to do so. The imposed restrictions – whether effective physically or online – must have a basis in the law or in valid terms of service. The validity of the terms is assessed by the provisions in §§307 ff of the German Civil Code.

However, the legal basis for refusing access differs between physical and online access restrictions. While this seems a discrepancy at first, the legal application is, in fact, nearly identical. Access restrictions to physical property are dealt with through the doctrine of house rights, which is based on the proprietor's right to property. Disputes on access restrictions to social media platforms are dealt with from the perspective of agreements. This difference results from the fact that 'property' is interpreted strictly in the German Civil Code and only covers physical objects (§90 BGB). The opinions differ greatly as to whether software and hardware can be included in that sphere and, thus, whether access to social media platforms can fall within the scope of house rights.[120] This discrepancy does not extend into the scope of application. Whereas the legal foundation differs, the scope of the restrictive powers that can be used to either protect (property) or define (agreement) the object is defined and interpreted in an equal way. Despite the differences in the underlying legal basis to resolve disputes related to access

120. Compare: Gabriella Piras, *Virtuelles Hausrecht?*, vol. 7 (1st edn, Mohr Siebeck 2016); Götz Schulze, 'Das private Hausrecht. Schutzrecht für die Gebrauchsnutzung von Räumen' (2015) 70 JuristenZeitung 414; Lennart Elsaß, Jan-Hendrik Labusga and Rolf Tichy, 'Internet und E-Commerce. Löschungen und Sperrungen von Beiträgen und Nutzerprofilen durch die Betreiber sozialer Netzwerke' (2017) 33 Computer und Recht 234; Thorsten Feldmann and Joerg Heidrich, 'Rechtsfragen Des Ausschlusses von Usern Aus Internetforen' (2006) 22 Computer und Recht https://www.degruyter.com/document/doi/10.9785/ovs-cr-2006-406/html (accessed 2 February 2022); Philipp Maume, 'Bestehen Und Grenzen Des Virtuellen Hausrechts' [2007] Multimedia und Recht Zeitschrift für Informations-, Telekommunikations- und Medienrecht 620. Piras argues that software can never be qualified as 'physical' property, and that a qualification of the server as physical property would lead to an impossible situation. *If* the server would be qualified as property, then any change to a file stored on the server would lead to an infringement of §1004 BGB. Arguably, even accessing a website would require changes in the server's data which could be prohibited as an infringement of §1004. However, Piras takes the server as a physical object as a starting point and concludes on the basis thereof that an online space (e.g., a social media platform) cannot be property as it solely consists of data *inside* actual property: the server. A server is not a 'space' but an 'object' that cannot be entered. Opposingly, it has been argued that an online space poses a virtual representation of a physical space and thus, consequently, a virtual house right should exist in line with a regular house right for physical spaces. That would create a 'general virtual house right' (Schulze). Less drastic is the argument that a virtual house right could be based on the hardware infrastructure of the platform, and that thus the criteria of 'physical property' are fulfilled (Elsaß et al). The same has been argued for software alone (Maume), and for the interplay between software and hardware (Kohl).

restrictions, overlap can be observed when looking more closely at the application of the two. Both the application of the house right and the assessment of the fairness of the agreement depend on unspecific, open norms. Their definition, interpretation and exact scope depend on the circumstances of the case. In German (case)law, the interpretation of such open norms in private law has led to the rise of the third-party effect of constitutional rights (*Drittwirkung*).

Figure 2.3 Overlap in the Scope of Restrictive Powers

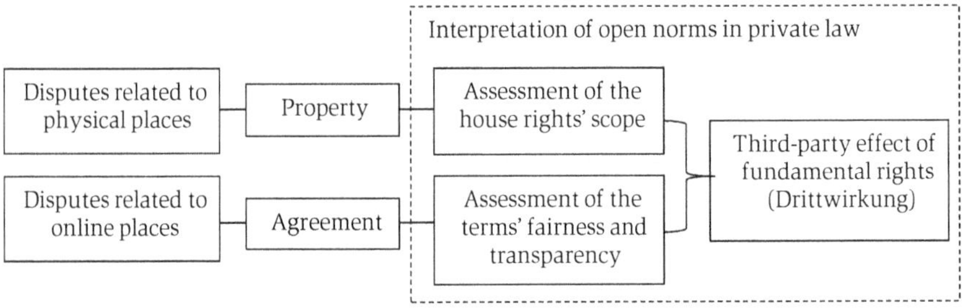

Third-party effect means that a constitutional right of either one of the parties can have an effect on the private relationship with another party – in this case, to interpret the open norms related to the scope of the house right or the assessment of an agreement's fairness (*see* Figure 2.3). The criteria for third-party effect overlap for physical access restrictions and online access and content restrictions. This overlap consists of two elements: whether the place is 'open to the general public' and whether the refusal of access has a significant impact on the social life of the refused. If the interpretation of the open norms for either of the types of access restrictions is identical, then what is the practical consequence of the difference pointed out above on the differentiation on a legal basis (property/agreement)?[121] The determination of the scope of these two open norms – the proprietor's scope to invoke its house right and the fairness of a user term – are seemingly assessed identically. If an online or physical place is not open to the general public, the provider/proprietor can refuse access – either through terms of service or by invoking a house right and providing an objective reason. If the place is open to the general public – whose requirements for assessment are also identical for physical places and social media platforms – and the provider has significant decision-making power over the communicative space of its users, the provider is subjected to a special legal responsibility, meaning that it must weigh the interests of all the parties involved. The overlap in the application of this third-party effect demonstrates that the discrepancy found in regard to the legal basis dissolves when viewed from a meta-level.

121. Frederik Vinding Kruse argues for a 'general right to property' as opposed to differentiating between material right to property and rights of resource ('*tingsretten*' and '*fordringsretten*').

The internal comparison of the German case law on physical access and moderation restrictions to private property and online access and moderation restrictions to social media platforms demonstrates that the (initially observed) discrepancy in resolving these disputes dissolves when looking at the underlying interpretation and application. As demonstrated by the identical requirements applied to fill in the open norms in both circumstances, the differences do not extend beyond the choice of wording, which wording, in turn, stems merely from a stringent reading of the word 'property' in the BGB, rather than on any significant normative or legal arguments.

2.2.2 Italy

2.2.2.1 Physical Access Restrictions

The legal framework to resolve issues on access rights and restrictions can be found in their entirety in Italian law, as the protection of property follows from the Italian Constitution, and both the positive and the negative right to property have been codified in the Italian Civil Code. However, the law does leave room for judicial interpretation, and open norms pose a problem for actual effective dispute resolutions. Public and private property are protected by Article 42 of the Italian Constitution. A proprietor's general right to property is codified in Article 832 of the Italian Civil Code. The latter safeguards the full and exclusive enjoyment of the property within the obligations of the law and constitutes a positive right to decide how to use the property freely. Additionally, Article 841 grants a proprietor a right to exclude others from using the property. The latter, referred to as the *ius excludendi*, corresponds to the negative aspect of the right to property. Neither the positive right to use the property nor the proprietor's right of exclusion is absolute. The second paragraph of Article 42 of the Italian Constitution provides limitations to the right to property foreseen by law 'in order to ensure its social function and to make it accessible to all'. The limitations to the right to property can be divided into two separate categories, depending on whether the limitation stems from the public and social interest to access the property or from an obligation to contract.[122]

The first category, public and social use rights, regulates both a person's *individual* need to access private property[123] and safeguards access to the *function* of

122. Additionally, under Italian law, the right to property can also be limited on the basis of *diritti reali su cosa altrui* (rights on another person's property), such as the *diritto di superficie* (Article 952 Italian Civil Code), *diritto di enfiteusi* (Article 957), *diritto di usufrutto* (Articles 978, 981), *diritto di uso* (Article 1021), *diritto di abitazione* (Article 1022), and the *diritto di servitù* (Articles 1027, 1031). As these do not apply directly to access restrictions, further discussion has been omitted.

123. Examples of such individual needs are a third-party's access to private property for hunting, which cannot be denied even against the will of the owners, however, consent is needed to enter private property for fishing (Article 842) or photography purposes. Compare *Cassazione Civile (Volpi)* (1962) 86 N 2329 793/794 and *Corte Costituzionale nr 57/1976 (Fotografia)* ECLI:IT:

the property.[124] The function exemption applies to property that, due to its function, has become part of the public domain.[125] Private property falls within the public domain when, first, the proprietor has allowed the property to be used by an indeterminate number of persons, and second, this use serves a general public interest.[126] Whether or not the proprietor had the intention to open the property for general use is irrelevant; the owner's conduct denoting the intention that an indeterminate number of persons can use the property for a public need automatically renders it public.[127] The property must be accessible to the service of the community, without reservations or limitations, voluntary, unlimited and free of charge.[128]

The second limitation to the *ius excludendi* consists of two obligations to contract. The first concerns Article 2597 of the Civil Code, which obliges regulated monopolies to contract.[129] Failure to comply with this obligation gives the counterpart who was denied service a direct claim of access based on Article 2932. The content of the contract under which the monopolist must offer the service remains free (subject to the general rules on terms and conditions). If a contract is refused by a monopoly, it must disclose its reasons for doing so, observing objective criteria such as urgency of

---

COST:1976:57. In that same line, the proprietor must allow a third-party to retrieve lost objects or animals (Article 843), but for an escaped swarm of bees, access can only be claimed within two days (Article 924).

124. This would be the case when a private property functions as a public domain, or accessing it is necessary to reach a public domain, such as access to the sea. Crossing and thus accessing these private beach properties is often necessary to reach the shore, which is public property. Therefore, despite large parts of the beach being private property, persons wanting to access the see can legally cross these private properties - even without consent of the proprietor. Blocking (the only) access to the sea, for example with a fence, is a criminal offence since the sea is marked as state property, *see also Cassazione penale sez III n2205 (Accesso al mare)*.

125. The access to such private properties in the public domain is referred to as *dicatio ad patriam*, which is a legal principle following from Roman law. Everything placed in the public domain can be subject to public use rights, even when owned by a private person, *see* more on this Salvatore Settis, 'The Cultural Heritage of the Church in Contemporary Culture' in Francesco Buranelli, Jean-François Rauzier and Katholische Kirche (eds), *Ventennale della Pontificia Commissione per i Beni culturali della Chiesa: Twenty Years of the Pontificial Commission for the Cultural Patrimony of the Church* (Libreria editrice Vaticana 2011). The principle is codified in Art. 825 of the Italian Civil Code, prescribing that private property can be subjected to the regime of public property if necessary for the achievement of purposes of public interest.

126. *Cassazione Civile sez II (Uti cives)* [2001] n 6924; *Cassazione Civile sez II (Uso pubblico)* [2021] n 28869; *Consiglio di Stato n 3316/2007 (Dicatio ad patriam)*; *Consiglio di Stato n 311/2021 (Servitù pubblica)* (2021) ECLI:IT:CDS:2014:2542.

127. *Consiglio di Stato n. 311/2021 (Servitù pubblica)* (n. 126), §7.7, and the case law cited.

128. *Consiglio di Stato n. 3316/2007 (Dicatio ad patriam)* (n. 126); *Cassazione Civile sez II (Uti cives)* (n. 126); *Cassazione Civile sez I (Dicatio ad patriam)* [2012] n. 4207.

129. Article 2597. (Obligation to contract in the case of a monopoly). Whoever exercises an undertaking under a legal monopoly has the obligation to contract with anyone requesting the services of the undertaking, observing equality of treatment. (translation by the author).

Original text: (Obbligo di contrattare nel caso di monopolio). Chi esercita un'impresa in condizione di monopolio legale ha l'obbligo di contrattare con chiunque richieda le prestazioni che formano oggetto dell'impresa, osservando la parita' di trattamento. The article's scope concerns solely monopolies that are imposed and regulated by Italian law, such as public transport companies, telephone services, energy companies, and other state regulated monopolies such as tobacco shops. In addition, some of the services are separately regulated in the Civil Code, such as public transportation in Article 1679.

the request or increased necessity.[130] The second concerns the rules following the Royal Decree 635/1940.[131] Article 187 dictates that those who offer a service to the public 'may not, without a legitimate reason, refuse the services of their establishment to anyone who requests them and pays for them', apart from the situations that exist under Articles 689 and 691 of the Criminal Code (respectively selling alcohol to minors and selling alcohol to persons clearly intoxicated).[132] Based on the latter law, one cannot refuse access to a publicly accessible bar nor refuse to provide the services offered to anyone requesting them. To what extent this law from 1940 means that public places can freely limit the scope of their service is unclear.[133] The scope of the 'legitimate reason to refuse service' is unsettled due to lacking legislation and case law on the matter. When transposing the obligations from Council Directive 2004/113/EC (Gender Goods and Services Directive), the Italian legislator has chosen to stick closely to the minimum protection outlined in the Directive. As such, discrimination when accessing goods and services only includes gender,[134] race and ethnic origin.[135] The region of Tuscany tried to prohibit commercial operators from refusing service, in particular, for reasons attributable to sexual orientation or gender identity. The legislation was deemed unconstitutional.[136]

In 2006, the Constitutional Court referred to Article 187 specifically as a 'general obligation to contract',[137] but this obligation only applies to places without formal

130. Francesco Galgano, *Trattato Di Diritto Civile. Volume II* (III, Wolters Kluwer 2020) 196.
131. Regio Decreto 6 maggio 1940, n. 635. Approvazione del regolamento per l'esecuzione del testo unico 18 giugno 1931-IX, n. 773, delle leggi di pubblica sicurezza. (040U0635) 1940.
132. Regio Decreto 6 maggio 1940, n. 635. Approvazione del regolamento per l'esecuzione del testo unico 18 giugno 1931-IX, n. 773, delle leggi di pubblica sicurezza. (040U0635). Art. 187's full original text: 'Salvo quanto dispongono gli articoli 689 e 691 del codice penale, gli esercenti non possono, senza un legittimo motivo, rifiutare le prestazioni del proprio esercizio a chiunque le domandi e ne corrisponda il prezzo'.
133. *See, e.g.*, the discussion of the law's application to restaurants offering 'no-kids'-spaces and the lacking case law on 'legitimate reasons': Roberta Stella, 'È legale vietare l'accesso alle famiglie con bambini nei ristoranti?' (*Studio Cataldi*, 27 July 2017) https://www.studiocataldi.it/articoli/26965-e-legale-vietare-l-accesso-alle-famiglie-con-bambini-nei-ristoranti.asp (accessed 31 May 2022).
134. Decreto Legislativo 6 novembre 2007, n. 196. Attuazione della direttiva 2004/113/CE che attua il principio della parità di trattamento tra uomini e donne per quanto riguarda l'accesso a beni e servizi e la loro fornitura.
135. Decreto Legislativo 9/7/2003 n° 215.-Attuazione della direttiva 2000/43/CE per la parità di trattamento tra le persone indipendemente dalla razza e dall'origine etnica. GURI n° 186 del 12/8/2003.
136. The legislation was deemed unconstitutional, as the violation was 'connected to the imposition of an administrative penalty, which affects the negotiating autonomy of private individuals and, therefore, on a matter reserved, pursuant to Art. 117, para. 2, letter l) of the Constitution, to the exclusive legislative competence of the State' according to the *Corte Costituzionale nr 253/2006 (Gender equality)*.
137. Stella (n. 133); 'Ristoranti vietati ai bambini, l'ingresso «childfree» è legale?' (*LCA Studio Legale*, 25 October 2022) https://www.lcalex.it/ristoranti-vietati-ai-bambini-lingresso-childfree-e-legale/ (accessed 20 February 2023). 'Le disposizioni censurate, le quali prevedono il divieto per gli operatori commerciali appartenenti a determinate categorie di rifiutare la loro prestazione, o di erogarla a condizioni deteriori rispetto a quelle ordinarie senza un legittimo motivo e, in particolare, fra l'altro, per motivi riconducibili all'orientamento sessuale o all'identità di genere, disciplinano, in sostanza, un obbligo legale a contrarre – obbligo già previsto, in via generale, dal legislatore statale all'art. 187 r.d. 6 maggio 1940 n. 635 – alla cui violazione è

access restrictions.[138] The latter obligation to contract on the basis of Article 187 RD 635/1940 resembles the obligation to offer access to open property as observed in the German case law on the *generellen Nutzungsbefugnis* (§2.2.1.1). As such, this obligation would, despite fitting under the obligation to contract in the Italian system, rather be treated as an individual's right to access a publicly accessible place and/or service.

Figure 2.4 Physical Access Restrictions under Italian Law

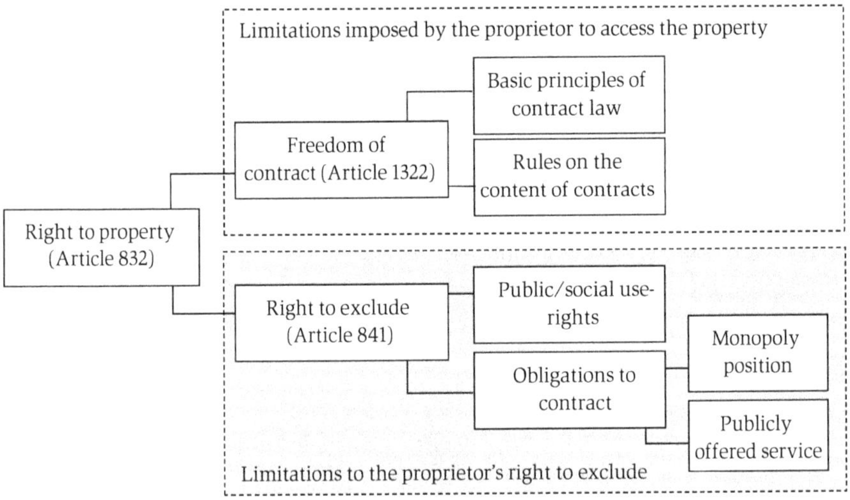

If a proprietor wants to offer access to its property, it is free to do so. The contractual freedom of the parties is recognised explicitly in the Italian Civil Code (Article 1322), though the scope of the freedom is limited by the basic principles of contract law and the rules on the content of contracts (*see* Figure 2.4). First, the user must be able to

connessa la comminatoria di una sanzione amministrativa, e introducono una normativa incidente sull'autonomia negoziale dei privati e, quindi, su di una materia riservata in via esclusiva, dall'art. 117 comma 2 lett. l), cost., allo Stato.'

138. Attilio Pecora, 'L'art. 187 del Regolamento T.U.L.P.S. (R.D. 6.5.1940. N. 635): Problemi Interpretativi' 4. The obligation to contract applies to services that are offered to a general public and which are accessible without fulfilling any prior criteria, such as for example restaurants, bars, hotels, coffee shops, and gaming halls. In R.D. 635/1940, these types of services are referred to as *esercizi pubblici* (public establishments), which constitute a separate category from *spettacoli e trattenimenti pubblici* (public shows and entertainment). The latter covers for example horse races, sports events, vehicle speed races, and dancing halls/discotheques. Arguably, all places to which an entry ticket must be bought and/or which do not cover an essential service (lodging, food) are excluded from the scope of *esercizi pubblici*.

Access restrictions on the basis of gender and/or sexual orientation *could* constitute a legitimate reason. Interestingly, that would mean that a bar in light of Art. 187 could limit its services to 'gay-only', 'hetero-only', or 'female-only'. If not, the law imposed by the Region of Tuscany would not impair the private autonomy, as the freedom to refuse access on the basis of gender or sexual orientation would have already been prohibited by Art. 187.

voluntarily express to be bound by a set of terms and conditions, even though, in practice, this *voluntary* action is often a formality: the user can either accept the terms or not receive the goods or services.[139] Furthermore, Article 1322 of the Italian Civil Code codifies the parties' freedom of contract and adds that 'the parties may freely determine the content of the contract within the limits imposed by law'. Such limitations to the freedom of contract can be found in various legislation, such as the rules on invalid clauses in unilateral contracts (Article 1341 of the Civil Code).

2.2.2.2 Online Access Restrictions

Unlike the clear and codified legal framework for physical access restrictions, there are no specific laws to address similar issues on social media platforms. Case law is useful to paint a picture of the outcome of these platform-specific cases under Italian law and clarifies the legal framework applicable to disputes regarding wrongful moderation decisions and the scope of the freedom to draft the terms of service.

From the case law, it follows that platforms have a legal obligation to remove illegal content from their service, which means that they can delete such content even when not explicitly mentioned in their terms of service.[140] Equally, the platform has a legal obligation to terminate or suspend an account breaching legal provisions.[141] All other sanctions imposed on users must be included in their terms of service. If a sanction is not based on the law or the terms, there is no justified ground for removal. The enforcement and interpretation of social media platforms' terms have proven difficult. Wrongful decisions to remove content or suspend access to a platform occur due to the misinterpretation of Italian law or by imposing a sanction that is not a part of the user terms. The first situation, the misinterpretation of the law, can be observed in the decision of the *Corte d'Appello di L'Aquila (Correggiari)*. The social media platform's terms stipulated that content in violation of (national) law would be removed. Consequently, the platform removed posts containing images of Mussolini, a flag of the Salò Republic, and a few other similar posts, claiming it breached the Italian laws against fascism. The *Corte d'Appello* concluded that the posts were, in fact, not in violation of Italian law and since the user terms did not explicitly prohibit the content, the removal was wrongful.[142] User terms must be interpreted according to the jurisdiction in which the service is offered, or their wording should explicitly refer to certain types of content. The counterargument that such regulation would render it

139. Galgano (n. 130) 190. Specifically, for the Italian discussion on the use of personal data on social media platform as the users' counter-performance to gain access to the service and the issue of whether such a forced accept to give up personal data can be seen as 'voluntarily given' in light of data protection laws *see* the case of *Consiglio di Stato n 02631/2021 (Payment with personal data)* (2021) ECLI:IT:CDS:2021:2631SENT, concluding that such practice constitutes an aggressive commercial practice, which imposes strict criteria on providing transparency on how and for which (commercial) purposes the personal data will be processed.
140. *Tribunale di Roma (Forza Nuova)* [2020] RG 648942019, §3.1.1. and §4. *Tribunale di Roma (Casapound IV)* [2022] n 17909/2022.
141. *Provvedimento n 29817 – CV194 – Google Drive* (Italian Competition Authority).
142. *Ibid.*, §§9.4.-9.5.

impossible to offer a worldwide service was explicitly dismissed by the Italian Competition Authority.[143]

A second wrongful removal follows from social media platforms that do not live up to their own terms of service, which forms a simple breach of contract for which the user can request damages and other contractual remedies. When imposing a sanction foreseen in the user terms, the platform must follow its own outlined procedure for removal. In *Tribunale di Bologna (De Gaetano)*, the user terms of Facebook at the time of the proceedings only prescribed termination or suspension of a user account when the platform would have a legitimate reason to do so, plus the platform must inform the user of the (grounds for the) decision to suspend or terminate the account. Facebook had permanently deleted *De Gaetano*'s account without informing the user of the decision or the underlying reasons.[144] The court found that Facebook's user terms did not foresee the possibility for *ad nutum* termination of a user account and concluded in favour of the claiming user that the removal was unjustified. In Italy, users who had their content wrongfully removed and/or access to their account blocked have successfully claimed non-material damages in several cases. In the case before the *Tribunale di Bologna*, the user was awarded EUR 14,000 for the wrongful removal of two Facebook pages featuring (historical) military items and his personal Facebook account. The Court specifically stated that the economic value of the pages – estimated at around EUR 100 – was irrelevant to the determination of the damages since a user cannot monetise the pages in the same way as Facebook monetises them by selling advertisement space. The court based the value of the accounts on the impact the removal has had on the social life of the user, included in Article 21 of the Italian Constitution (freedom of expression). In the case before the *Corte d'Appello di L'Aquila*, the user was awarded EUR 3,000 for the wrongful removal of his posts. Equal to this practice on content decisions, users of social media platforms who have had their pre-existing account wrongfully suspended or terminated can request (immaterial) damages.[145]

Decisions to remove content or suspend access to the platform are justified if they follow the platform's own user terms. However, the freedom to decide on the scope of the user terms is not absolute. Social media platforms may suspend user profiles for numerous breaches of the user terms,[146] but they may not create, in effect, unlimited discretionary powers to suspend or exclude users.[147] Clauses that prescribe the

143. *Provvedimento n 26596 – CV154 – WhatsApp* (Italian Competition Authority), §61: 'No correlation exists between the opportunity/need to provide a "single and uniform service, widespread and available throughout the world" and the need to regulate it everywhere in the same way. The provision of a service that is technically usable by consumers all over the world does not seem in any way incompatible with the adaptation of the Terms of Use to the different legal contexts of the countries where the Professional's service is offered, least of all if this practice results in limitations for the users.' (translation by the author).

144. *Tribunale di Bologna sez. II (De Gaetano)* (n. 21).

145. *Ibid.*; *Corte appello L'Aquila (Correggiari)* (n. 21).

146. *Tribunale di Varese (n 2572/2021), §4.5* referring to Article 1460 of the Italian Civil Code. The social media platform may suspend its own obligations (providing access to the platform) if the user breaches the conditions in the user terms – even if the breached provision was an accessory obligation rather than a primary one.

147. *Provvedimento n 26596 – CV154 – WhatsApp* (n. 143), §74, §83.

termination of a user account without giving a reason and without notice are unfair[148] because, first, without a provision of the reason(s) for termination or suspension, the users' right to defend themselves would be impaired,[149] and second, users would not be able to export their data or acquired products captured in the offered service to a third-party, meaning a loss of data that can have a significant impact on the consumer.[150] Consequently, if the termination by the platform has the effect that users lose virtual goods and/or virtual money that has intrinsic economic value, the platform will have to reimburse the costs made by the user. Excluding such refund payments in the user terms negatively distorts the balance between the platform and the consumer.[151]

Furthermore, there must be a breach of the user terms in order to justify termination of a user account. The mere fact that the account was used to link to external sources and that the information on those external sources would breach the user terms was inadequate. Neither the aims/goals pursued by the party behind the social media account nor the (potentially criminal) behaviour of any members outside the platform may be taken into consideration – the behaviour *on the platform* must breach the user terms.[152] Access restrictions on social media platforms must be proportional, even if the sanction is set out in the user terms, meaning that minor breaches of the user terms, such as posting – in good faith – two short clips including copyright-protected material,[153] should not lead to suspension or termination of a user account.

The case law points predominantly in the direction of general Italian contract law to resolve access and moderation conflicts, but one can observe different views on the role of social media platforms in the Italian case law on online access restrictions. On the position of social media platforms, the courts disagree. In the 2019 *Casapound* case, the *Tribunale di Roma* reached the conclusion that the relationship between Facebook and its users is not merely 'two random private parties', and consequently, Facebook must adhere to constitutional principles until a violation of the user terms on the side of the user has been proven.[154] Also, the *Tribunale di Varese* reaches the conclusion that a social media platform's user terms could potentially infringe on a user's constitutional right to freedom of expression.[155] That opinion has been reversed. In

148. *Provvedimento n 29976 – CV224 – TikTok* (Italian Competition Authority); *Provvedimento n 29817 – CV194 – Google Drive* (n. 141); *Provvedimento n. 26596 – CV154 – Whatsapp* (n. 143).
149. *Provvedimento n 29817 – CV194 – Google Drive* (n. 143), §34.
150. *Provvedimento n 29818 – CV195 – Dropbox* (Italian Competition Authority); *Provvedimento n 26729 – CV157 – App Pokemon GO* (Italian Competition Authority), §44.
151. *Provvedimento n. 26729 – CV157 – App Pokemon GO* (n. 150), §44: 'In particular, what determines a significant imbalance in the rights and obligations of consumers under the contract is the failure to provide any form of reimbursement for those who have purchased Exchange Items, virtual money or virtual goods that have been lost or not used as a result of the unilateral cancellation, suspension or termination of the user's account by the merchant.'
152. *Tribunale di Roma (Casapound)* (n. 140), p. 8.
153. *Tribunale di Pordenone (Preliminary reinstatement request)* [2018] n 2139/2018. The user had posted two short video clips including copyright-protected material. The user terms explicitly prohibited this. After making the user aware of the infringing material, the user immediately removed the content and apologised to the copyright holder. The court concluded (preliminary) that suspension of the user account was not proportionate.
154. *Tribunale di Roma (Casapound)* [2019] RG 59264/2019 p. 4.
155. *Tribunale di Varese (n. 2572/2021)* (n. 146).

December 2022, the *Tribunale di Roma*, in another case concerning far-right party *Casapound*, takes a more balanced stance, concluding that social media platforms carry out an activity of social importance but that the platform is first and foremost a private party, whose contractual conditions the user has accepted to agree to.[156] This opposing view that the body of user terms defines the service offered by a social media platform rather than its societal impact can also be observed in other cases.[157] The *Tribunale di Milano* concludes that the service offered by YouTube is solely what is defined in their user terms. Outside of the possibilities stipulated in the contract, users cannot claim access to the service to express their freedom of expression.[158] The *Corte d'Appello di L'Aquila* follows this view and adds thereto that 'the use of the platform by the users has as its object the use of a service that is certainly not essential' (speaking of Facebook).[159] A social media platform has not accepted to host *all* content - rather, it has accepted to host content that, first, does not breach the law and, second, does not breach its user terms.[160]

2.2.2.3 Existence of an Internal Discrepancy

The Italian case law does not necessarily demonstrate a discrepancy in resolving cases on physical access restrictions as opposed to online access restrictions. However, the focus on resolving either case differs. The system of physical access restrictions is based on the right to property and the exclusive rights of the proprietor to choose to conditionally grant access to the property or to exclude access. Against the latter, a person can oppose that decision and claim access on the basis of either a public/social use right or based on an obligation to contract. In online access restriction cases, it is noticeable that the courts treat these issues as purely contractual problems, focusing on the validity of the contract in light of the basic principles of contract law (can a user 'pay' with personal data or not?[161]) and on the content of the user terms (are the user

156. *Tribunale di Roma (Casapound IV)* (n. 140).
157. *Tribunale di Roma (Casapound)* (n. 154), p. 4. Here referred to as 'body of user terms' as the social media platform discussed (Facebook) uses numerous sets of intertwined user terms that all have to be taken into consideration.
158. *Tribunale di Milano (ByoBlu II)*, p. 4: '(...) outside and apart from the contract, it is unimaginable that Google is obliged to guarantee the complainants the exercise of their freedom under Article 21 of the Constitution or their right to inform their subscribers and publicly express their opinions through Google's social media.'
159. *Corte appello L'Aquila (Correggiari)* (n. 21), §8.5.
160. In *Corte appello L'Aquila (Correggiari)* (n. 21), §9, the court described the service offered by Facebook as a 'civil coexistence' based on the platform's user terms. Within that coexistence, a user is not fully free to post anything it wishes. Rather, 'the balance between the possibility for the user to express himself and share content deemed important and the harm that certain modes of expression or certain content may cause to the safety and well-being of others or to the integrity of the community itself, which is to say that those modes of expression are accepted insofar as they do not end up becoming an attack on the safety and well-being of other users and/or the integrity of the values of the community itself.' A breach of the principles underpinning this civil coexistence 'may well therefore be assessed as a breach of contract that, if it exists, entitles the other party [the platform] to suspend its own performance, removing or blocking the contents that violate these contractual provisions.'
161. *Consiglio di Stato n. 02631/2021 (Payment with personal data)* (n. 139).

terms on social media platforms unfair?[162]). However, since contract law within the Italian legal framework falls within the positive side of the right to property, there is no inherent discrepancy. The courts merely apply the rules of the positive aspect of the right to property. This observation implies that the service offered by social media platforms does not fall within any of the limitations of the negative aspect of the right to property. If either of the latter were the case, the courts should have taken into consideration the limitations to the negative right to property. However, when dealing with online issues, the courts depart from the freedom of contract (Article 1322), thereby dismissing the existence of a limitation to the platforms' *ius excludendi*. That means that a social media platform is: (i) not a monopoly service, (ii) not a publicly offered service, (iii) no individual need to access the property exists, and (iv) the service does not fall in the public domain.

More explicitly, several courts have argued for this normative stance. The *Tribunale di Milano* and the *Corte d'Appello di L'Aquila* both treated social media platforms' services as non-essential, fully contractually defined services.[163] Compare these views to, for example, the earlier decision of the *Tribunale di Roma* in *Casapound*, where the Roman court reached the conclusion that social media platforms cannot be compared to regular contractual relationships and consequently have the obligation to adhere to constitutional principles. The absence of a discrepancy lies exactly in this normative choice. Either normative choice (essential service or contractually defined service) fits within the system applied to physical access restrictions, whether the conclusion is that social media platforms' services are solely defined by their contracts or, opposingly, that the function of their services falls within the public domain. If platforms do not fulfil a public/social function and neither one of the obligations to contract applies, the platform has an unlimited right to exclude. Thus, the user terms are decisive for what can be posted and who should or should not have access to the service.

However, in light of the latter, it is important to note that the discussion on the qualification of platforms is not final. In numerous cases on (defamatory) content on social media platforms, Italian courts have reached the conclusion that social media platforms are 'able to reach an indeterminate or quantitively appreciable number of persons'.[164] That corresponds to the first requirement for the existence of public/social use rights, the second one being whether the use of the property serves a general public interest. Thus, a normative choice that a social media platform's service fulfils some kind of general public interest (e.g., the Roman court) could impose a limitation on the platform's right to exclude access. This inconsistency in the qualification of social media platforms in Italy must be resolved to guarantee a foreseeable and uniform approach to access restrictions. Thereafter, the system for physical access restrictions

162. *Provvedimento n. 29976 – CV224 – TikTok* (n. 148); *Provvedimento n. 29818 – CV195 – Dropbox* (n. 150); *Provvedimento n 29819 – CV196 – iCloud Apple* (Italian Competition Authority); *Provvedimento n. 29817 – CV194 – Google Drive* (n. 141); *Provvedimento n. 26596 – CV154 – Whatsapp* (n. 143); *Provvedimento n. 26729 – CV157 – App Pokemon GO* (n. 150).
163. *Tribunale di Milano (ByoBlu II)* (n. 158); *Corte appello L'Aquila (Correggiari)* (n. 21).
164. Tribunale di Pavia, sez. III, 14/03/2019, n. 468, Tribunale di Firenze, sez. II, 13/07/2021, n. 1916, Tribunale di Cassino, 09/07/2021, and n. 506 Tribunale di Vicenza, 03/05/2021, n. 426.

can sufficiently resolve any future problems – whether from the perspective of contractual law or the public/social function of the platforms' services.

2.2.3 The Netherlands

2.2.3.1 Physical Access Restrictions

The right to property is codified in the Dutch Civil Code (*burgerlijk wetboek* or *BW*) in Article 5:1. Like the German §903 BGB, Article 5:1 BW consists of a positive and a negative right, respectively allowing or refusing the free use of the property. In relation to access refusals in (football) stadiums, this right to exclude has been referred to as a 'house right', but an elaborate doctrine of house rights as observed in the German case law does not exist.[165]

The right to exclude under Article 5:1 is not absolute. The second half of Article 5:1 allows a proprietor to exclude access to and use of the property, solely when 'provided that this use does not violate the rights of others and the restrictions based on statutory provisions and rules of unwritten law'. A proprietor can only refuse access to property it owns, and an access restriction cannot exceed the property's limits.[166] Outside the premises, restrictions can only be imposed when explicitly agreed upon, thus requiring a contractual agreement.[167] If a decision to restrict access is solely intended to harm the refused, the decision is void (Article 3:13 BW). The proprietor must have an interest in the refusal of access, but the margin to define that interest is big. Moreover, an access restriction can be imposed for unwanted behaviour, as well as for illegal behaviour of the refused,[168] and if the ground for the access restriction is illegal activity, the refusal may be based on a presumption, rather than a conviction.

165. The first reference to a Dutch house right was made in *Hoge Raad (NOS/KNVB)* (1987) ECLI:NL:PHR:1987:AD0055. A more explicit confirmation can be observed in *Rechtbank Gelderland (Stadionverbod Vitesse)* (2015) ECLI:NL:RBGEL:2015:452. In the case on the lawfulness of the stadium ban, the court confirms the existence of the house right and elaborates that '[the stadium owner] can derive from the right to property the power to deny third parties' access to the premises or to impose restrictions on the permission to access. It must be assumed that [the football club] can invoke this house right in principle as an independent ground for a stadium ban.'

166. *Rechtbank Maastricht (Stadionverbod)* (2009) ECLI:NL:RBMAA:2006:AY7409.

167. *Gerechtshof Den Haag (User Terms KNVB)* (2006) ECLI:NL:GHSGR:2006:AY6000, §14; §33: In the dispute before the Appeals Court of The Hague, the question was raised whether a private undertaking, without the mandate and or delegated task from the government, can impose on a natural person a restraint of their liberty (not physically being allowed near and in a stadium). The court clarifies that these are not 'liberty restraints', but merely contractual consequences (suspension of the obligations under the contract and/or (temporary) refusal to enter into an agreement with the supporter to attend a football match). A private undertaking does not need a delegated task from the government '*to agree with an opposing party that certain sanctions may be imposed, or certain powers granted, if that opposing party acts contrary to what has been agreed*'.

168. *Gerechtshof Amsterdam (Toegangsverbod winkelcentrum)* (2017) ECLI:NL:GHAMS:2017:1285, §3.7.

The criminal law principle of the presumption of innocence does not apply in a contractual relationship between private parties, nor when invoking the right to exclude access to private property.[169] If the property serves a *public* or *social* function, access restrictions must be accompanied by a reasonable ground. Such a reasonable ground could be a breach of the house rules or aggressive behaviour.[170] Properties with public and/or social functions include nursing homes,[171] football stadiums,[172] and houses of worship,[173] but the exact definition is unclear. The decision to refuse access to property with a public or social function must include, at a minimum, the facts and circumstances that have led to the refusal.[174] The latter does not apply to places that have been accessed illegally (e.g., when squatting private property), regardless of whether the property had been publicly accessible.[175] Moreover, an absolute requirement of proportionality does not seem to exist according to the Dutch case law on physical access restrictions. The proprietor can refuse access to the property (in the case of a shopping mall) even without an attempt to solve the issues in a less intrusive manner.[176] Lastly, discrimination on the grounds of religion, belief, political opinion, race, sex, nationality, heterosexual or homosexual orientation or marital status when offering access to goods or services and for the conclusion, performance, or termination of contracts is forbidden.[177] Only in case the nature of the (intended) contract is private, an exemption might apply.[178]

In addition to the right to exclusion, Article 5:1 BW also grants the proprietor the right to provide conditional access to the property (the positive right). A breach of the conditions is a valid ground for a refusal of access (and termination of the contract).[179] The assessment of the imposed conditions and a potential breach follows the laws on agreements. In principle, a proprietor can agree with an opposing party that certain sanctions may be imposed, if the opposing party acts contrary to what has been agreed.[180] For unilaterally imposed contracts to be valid, the terms must have been

169. *Rechtbank Maastricht (Stadionverbod)* (n. 166), §3.2.
170. *Gerechtshof Arnhem-Leeuwarden (Nursing home)* (2013) ECLI:NL:GHARL:2013:6873.
171. *Ibid.*
172. *Stadionverbod Vitesse* (n. 165).
173. *Rechtbank 's-Hertogenbosch (Refusal of entry to a mosque)* (2009) ECLI:NL:RBSHE:2009:BH4029.
174. *Stadionverbod Vitesse* (n. 165), §4.2.
175. *Rechtbank Oost-Brabant (Squatters)* (2018) ECLI:NL:RBOBR:2018:3237.
176. *Gerechtshof Amsterdam (Toegangsverbod winkelcentrum)* (2017) ECLI:NL:GHAMS:2017:1285, §3.8.
177. *Algemene wet gelijke behandeling*, https://wetten.overheid.nl/BWBR0006502/2020-01-01, Arts 1 and 7.
178. This does explicitly not cover offering a service or access to a public place to the general public, *see* the explanation by the Dutch Ministry of Internal Affairs: Ministerie van Binnenlandse Zaken en Koninkrijksrelaties, 'Algemene Wet Gelijke Behandeling – Discriminatie op de woningmarkt – Home | Volkshuisvesting Nederland' (15 March 2022) https://www.volkshuisvestingnederland.nl/onderwerpen/discriminatie-op-de-woningmarkt/algemene-wet-gelijke-behandeling (accessed 15 March 2023).
179. *Rechtbank Overijssel (Camping Olst)* (2020) ECLI:NL:RBOVE:2020:1955, §5.12.
180. *Gerechtshof Den Haag (User Terms KNVB)* (2006) ECLI:NL:GHSGR:2006:AY6000, §33.

communicated to the users before invoking them as a basis for an access restriction.[181] When communicated in due time, these house rules will become a part of the contractual relationship between the parties.[182] A sole reference to the existence of terms and conditions, without including the terms and conditions themselves, can be sufficient to fulfil the requirement of communication.[183]

When the conclusion of the contract is proven to be valid, its content is assessed according to the rules on unfair contract terms (as set out in Part 3, book 6 of the Dutch Civil Code) and by open norms in private law such as the reasonableness and fairness in Article 6:248 BW. In case of doubt, contract terms will be interpreted according to the *Haviltex* standard.[184] Through Article 3:12 BW, fundamental rights may be used to define the scope of the generally recognised legal principles and the fundamental concepts of law in the Netherlands and can, therefore, play an indirect role in the interpretation and application of contractual terms through the open norm of reasonableness and fairness. Despite the proprietor's obligation in Article 5:1 BW not to violate the rights of others and the inclusion of fundamental rights as legal principles, parties that have been refused access to private property cannot directly invoke their fundamental or constitutional rights horizontally. Constitutional rights do not provide a base for a general right of access to private property'.[185] Only when an access restriction fully hinders constitutional freedom can the freedom be included in the assessment of the fairness of an access restriction.[186] The threshold for the latter is high, as demonstrated by, for example, in *Toegangsverbod zorginstelling*, where a nursing home issued an entry ban against the brother of one of the patients. The brother had broken various house rules and was therefore denied future access to the nursing home where his sibling resided. Due to the access ban, he claimed that his right to family life protected in Article 8 ECHR was impaired. However, as the nursing home offered him to see his sister in the common areas or to arrange for him to visit his sister outside the nursing home's facilities, the court dismissed the argument. Although the

181. *Gerechtshof Amsterdam (Leeuwenhose)* (2006) ECLI:NL:GHAMS:2006:AZ3550, §2.10; *Stadionverbod* (n. 6). If the invoked house rule is not known prior to the decision, it breaches the principle of reasonableness and fairness.
182. *Rechtbank Utrecht* (2006) ECLI:NL:RBUTR:2006:AX6427, §§5.4-5.7.
183. *Stadionverbod* (n. 6).
184. *Hoge Raad (Haviltex)* (1981) ECLI:NL:HR:1981:AG4158, §2: 'The question of how the parties intended to regulate their relationship in a written contract and whether that contract leaves room for interpretation cannot be answered on the basis of a purely linguistic interpretation of the provisions of that contract. The answer to that question depends on the intention the parties had when agreeing to those provisions in the given circumstances and on what they could reasonably expect from each other in that regard. The social circles to which the parties belong and the legal knowledge which can be expected from such parties may also be of importance in this respect.'
185. *Rechtbank Groningen (Demonstration on private grounds)* (2012) ECLI:NL:RBGRO:2012:BW7184, with a reference to *Appl. Nos 39343/98, 39651/98, 43147/98 and 46664/99 (Kleyn and others v. The Netherlands)* [2003] ECLI:CE:ECHR:2003:0506JUD003934398 (ECtHR).
186. On the balancing of an access refusal and the right to family life, *see Rechtbank Den Haag (Toegangsverbod zorginstelling)* (2019) ECLI:NL:RBDHA:2019:9411. For the freedom of expression, *see Rechtbank Groningen (Demonstration on private grounds)* (2012) ECLI:NL:RBGRO:2012:BW7184; and earlier *Hoge Raad (Plakverbod II)* (1989) ECLI:NL:HR:1989:ZC8243.

access ban restricted the free visit of his sister on the grounds of the privately owned nursing home, his right to family life had not been *fully* impaired due to the offered alternatives. On the freedom of expression, a similar conclusion was reached. Only a completely arbitrary or general ban on manifestations imposed by a proprietor could violate third parties' fundamental right 'if such a ban on access results in the absence of any effective exercise of freedom of expression within a given municipality'.[187]

2.2.3.2 Online Access Restrictions

The Dutch legislation does not offer specific legislation on access and moderation restrictions on social media platforms. Issues concerning those restrictions are dealt with within the existing legal framework, predominantly from the right to property. The choice to resolve online access restrictions through the view of the social media platform's right to property has been explicit. On the assessment of the fairness of online access restrictions, the court refers to the decision of the ECtHR in *Appleby & others v. United Kingdom*,[188] a case on a physical access restriction to a shopping centre.[189] Moreover, other Dutch courts have, on numerous occasions, concluded that the decision to exclude access falls within the platform's right to property.[190] Social media platforms can, therefore, in principle, deny access to their service. A general right of access to a social media platform nor a general right to have legal content hosted does not exist.

Furthermore, platforms can freely decide on the scope of the rules applicable to the service. From the case law on access and moderation restrictions on social media platforms, it follows that private companies are, in principle, free to agree with their users on the rules that are applicable to their service. This applies equally in cases where the social media platform imposes and decides unilaterally on the applicable rules.[191] The conditions drawn up by social media platforms define the possibilities for using the service. The assessment of the validity of the applied terms follows the general provisions in Dutch law on contract validity. However, from a perspective of proportionality, a social media platform must adhere to procedural safeguards when terminating or suspending access to its service on the basis of its user terms. In *Van Haga/LinkedIn*, the court qualifies the agreement between the platform and its users as a *continuous agreement*.[192] The termination of a continuous agreement is bound by

187. *Rechtbank Groningen (Demonstration on private grounds)* (2012) ECLI:NL:RBGRO:2012:BW7184, §4.6.
188. *Appl. No. 44306/98 (Appleby and Others/United Kingdom)* (2003) ECLI:CE:ECHR:2003:0506JUD004430698 (ECtHR).
189. *Rechtbank Amsterdam (FvD/Google)* (2021) ECLI:NL:RBAMS:2021:5117; *BLCKBX/Google* (n. 22).
190. *Rechtbank Amsterdam (Café Weltschmerz/YouTube)* (2020) ECLI:NL:RBAMS:2020:4435; *Rechtbank Amsterdam (Smart Exit/Facebook)* (2020) ECLI:NL:RBAMS:2020:4966; *FvD/Google* (n. 189); *BLCKBX/Google* (n. 22); *Rechtbank Rotterdam (Engel/Facebook)* (2021) ECLI:NL:RBROT:2021:10459.
191. *FvD/Google* (n. 189).
192. Specific requirements regarding the termination of continuous agreements (*duurovereenkomsten*) have been developed in Dutch case law. An unlimited continuous agreement can in

additional safeguards to comply with the requirements of reasonableness and fairness in Article 6:248 BW.[193] Based on the court's interpretation of (the at that time still proposed) articles of the DSA and the Dutch law, these procedures must safeguard the principle of transparency, the principle of justification, and the principle of due care.[194] This means that a decision to block access to a social media platform is void if the user was not informed or if the decision did not highlight the reason for suspension. The court adds thereto that a social media platform's 'obligation to provide reasons in concrete cases increases, the more vaguely defined and/or less known the policy it claims to be applying in its decisions is'.[195] Whether a user should be given a warning and opportunity to resolve the infringement prior to the access restricting decision does not follow from the case law, but the opposite scenario has been confirmed. If a platform has warned the user of illegal or infringing behaviour, the user cannot claim the invalidity of the access restriction on the basis of reasonableness and fairness.[196]

Lastly, users have not been able to successfully invoke their freedom of expression to oppose restrictive terms. As long as the exercise of the user's fundamental or constitutional right is not *fully* impaired, social media platforms are not obliged to host specific statements from users.[197] If another option exists where users can express their opinion, their right to freedom of expression has not been fully impaired. In the eyes of the court, users can turn to newspapers or create a website to disseminate their opinions.[198] The above does not mean that social media platforms can simply impose access restrictions as they see fit. For wrongful access restrictions, a right to reinstatement exists.[199] There is no case law on the possibility of claiming (immaterial) damages in the case of a (wrongful) permanent removal of a user account or content, but injunctions have been imposed on social media platforms prohibiting the permanent removal of account information. These injunctions include penalty payments in case of non-compliance to prevent irreparable harm.[200] For platforms, that concretely implies that (the data underlying) user accounts and content should not be *permanently* removed until the user has exhausted all legal measures.

principle be terminated, even if the agreement does not have a termination clause. The termination must live up to the standards of reasonableness and fairness in Art. 6:248 BW, meaning that the terminating party must either have a compelling reason to terminate the agreement, damages should be paid, or the termination should include a notice period.

193. *Hoge Raad (Duurovereenkomst)* (2018) ECLI:NL:HR:2011:BQ2213.
194. *Van Haga/LinkedIn* (n. 23), §§4.14-4.15.
195. *Van Haga/LinkedIn* (n. 23), §4.22.
196. *Rechtbank Amsterdam (Google AdSense)* (2020) ECLI:NL:RBAMS:2020:7179. Google had warned the plaintiffs numerous times that their conduct breaches the user terms, they were aware of the infringing activity, and were given the chance to resolve the matter, which they chose not to do. The Court thus concludes that the accounts were blocked in accordance with Google's user terms and therefore the plaintiffs' accounts did not need to be reinstated.
197. *Smart Exit/Facebook* (n. 190); *FvD/Google* (n. 189); *Engel v. Facebook* (n. 190); *BLCKBX/Google* (n. 22).
198. *Smart Exit/Facebook* (n. 190), §4.23.
199. *Rechtbank Midden-Nederland (Microsoft OneDrive)* (2020) ECLI:NL:RBMNE:2020:4348; *Rechtbank Midden-Nederland (Microsoft OneDrive II)* (2020) ECLI:NL:RBMNE:2020:5773.
200. *Rechtbank Midden-Nederland (Microsoft OneDrive)* (n. 199).

2.2.3.3 *Existence of an Internal Discrepancy*

For both physical and online access restrictions, Dutch courts depart from the proprietor's right to property. The two systems overlap. The case law on the two types of access restrictions addresses both a positive and a negative right to property (respectively deciding to provide access and/or on what terms and to exclude access). Moreover, when dealing with both types of access restrictions, one can observe a strict interpretation of the horizontal effect of fundamental and constitutional rights on the relationship between private parties. The reasoning underlying this caution is equal for both types of access restrictions. Compare, for example, the physical access restriction in *Toegangsverbod zorginstelling* with the cases on online access restrictions. In the first, an access ban was imposed on the brother of a patient in a private nursing home. Despite the fact that the brother was not allowed to enter the nursing home, meetings with his sister were still facilitated outside the premises. Therefore, the access ban did not impair his fundamental right to family life as the right had not been *fully* impaired. The same reasoning was applied in the online access restriction cases. If users have the possibility to express their opinions elsewhere (online), the right to freedom of expression is not fully impaired, and as such, access restrictions to a social media platform do not constitute an unjust impairment of the users' fundamental rights. The above disproves the hypothesis that a general discrepancy exists between the way Dutch courts resolve disputes on physical access restrictions as opposed to online access restrictions. The proprietor's protection under the right to property obstructs a general right of access for users to either physical or online property. However, in case access to the property would prove to be the *only viable option* to exercise the protection of a fundamental right, access must be allowed. In the light of social media platforms, the Dutch courts find that unlikely. After all, there are plenty more ways to express oneself than through social media platforms alone, both on the internet and beyond.

Apart from the overlapping foundational basis, one important difference can be observed. In cases involving social media platforms, the interpretation of the reasonableness and fairness of contracts, in conjunction with the articles of the Digital Services Act (then not yet in force), have led to an increase in procedural safeguards. These procedural safeguards are further reaching than the safeguards observed in the case law on physical access restrictions. For example, the references to the principles of transparency, justification, and due care for online access restrictions contrast the explicit waiver of the principle of proportionality for physical access restrictions. Whether and to what extent the inclusion of these procedural safeguards when dealing with online access restrictions will have a spill-over effect on physical access restrictions is currently unclear. Such an effect could be expected given the fact that both systems are based on the same legal framework, and both types of restrictions involve private individuals and a powerful private party. That would then, in time, resolve this discrepancy in applying the existing legal framework to both online and physical access restrictions.

2.2.4 Denmark

2.2.4.1 Physical Access Restrictions

Opposed to the previous three Member States, Denmark proves a difficult case. In the other Member States, a proprietor can derive both a positive and a negative right from the right to property. The proprietor can decide freely how to use its property (positive element) or choose to exclude others from using it (negative element). Contract law, in these Member States, is used as a tool to govern the powers that derive from the positive aspect of the right to property. Danish law does not (explicitly) infer from the right to property a positive and negative right. The Danish constitution grants an inviolable right to property in §73,[201] where 'property' is interpreted broadly. The right protects anything from economic rights to physical objects from both private individuals and businesses.[202] However, the protection has a narrow scope. The scope of protection under §73 is limited to expropriation by the State and has a vertical effect only. It does not affect the decision to (exclude) access to a private property between two private parties. Laws governing the *access* to private property do not necessarily qualify as expropriation.[203] These types of laws merely regulate the use of the property and thus fall outside §73's protection.[204]

In Denmark, two specific laws exist on the access to private property. The legislation governing access to private property has been based on arguments of public safety, which was the case for the *Rockerlaw*,[205] and on public/social interest. The

201. Opposingly, §§72, 74 and 78 of the Danish Constitution (respectively the right to peacefully enjoy one's own home, the free entry to business property, and the freedom to conduct a business) do explicitly not concern access restrictions to a property, *see Højesteret (Hells angels Rockerforbud)* (1999) I 248/1998-U.1999.1798H. (original text: 'For så vidt angår spørgsmålet om, hvorvidt der ved meddelelsen af forbudet er sket en krænkelse af sagsøgerens grundlovssikrede rettigheder, bemærkes, at hverken grundlovens §72, §74 eller §78 efter disse bestemmelsers ordlyd eller almindeligt anerkendte forståelse vedrører den omstændighed, at en person forbydes at opholde sig et bestemt sted.')

202. Folketinget, 'Grundlovens paragraf 73', https://www.ft.dk/da/dokumenter/bestil-publikationer/publikationer/mingrundlov/min-grundlov/kapitel-8/paragraf-73 (accessed 10 March 2022), Kommentar stk 1: '*de rettigheder, som er grundlaget for folks økonomiske eksistens*'.

203. *Højesteret (Bandidos Rockerforbud) (2001) I 67/2000-U.2001.1057H*: 'the law [the rocker law] concerns a general regulation of the use of property (...) the regulation solely concerns certain persons' prohibition to access the property. Even if a prohibition is imposed without any time limit, the prohibition must be expected to be lifted after a certain time (...) Prohibiting an owner from residing on the property does not entail any restriction on other powers of ownership, such as sale or letting.' (translation by the author). *See* on this also Frederik Vinding Kruse, *Ejendomsretten*, 3rd edn (1951), p. 257, where he defines the difference as 'a limitation of the right of disposal' versus a 'transfer of ownership'.

204. The discussion on which regulatory measures from the State fall within the scope of 'expropriation' is interesting from a compensational point of view. For the expropriation of property, the State must pay a reasonable compensation, whereas for the sole regulation of the use of property, no such duty exists. That discussion falls, unfortunately, outside the scope of the discussion addressed here.

205. *Rockerlaw*: Lov 1996-10-15 nr. 907 om forbud mod ophold i bestemte ejendomme, changed by LOV nr 672 af 08/06/2017, Lov om ændring af straffeloven, lov om forbud mod ophold i bestemte ejendomme og lov om fuldbyrdelse af straf m.v., accessible at: https://www.retsinformation.dk/eli/lta/2017/672.

latter can be observed in the *naturbeskyttelseslov* Chapter 4, where the Danish legislator has chosen to regulate *public access to nature.*[206] Apart from these specific laws protecting the public enjoyment of nature and the protection of public safety when dealing with criminal organisations, the (limitations to the) power to exclude private parties from accessing private property has not been explicitly regulated elsewhere in Danish law. Case law on the topic is scarce[207] despite the fact that similar problems have occurred in Denmark as compared to the other Member States.[208] The only case law addressing access restrictions to private property concerns cases on equal treatment. In Denmark, the laws on equal treatment[209] apply directly to private parties offering services to the general public.[210] The laws limit the proprietor's freedom to choose to enter into an agreement in certain situations – or rather, limit the freedom to exclude persons on the basis of gender, handicap, and ethnicity.[211] Cases regarding the

206. For example, §23 Naturbeskyttelsesloven regulates the access to private forests over 5 hectares, and as a result, a proprietor cannot refuse public access to the forest's paths between 6 in the morning and sunset when used in the public's interest ('to provide people with access to and enjoyment of nature and to improve opportunities for outdoor recreation'). Similarly, §22 regulates the access to a beach.
207. The scarcity is the result of two factors. First, Denmark (like other Scandinavian countries) is not known as high volume litigation-countries. Second, Denmark was one of the only two Member States in the European Union that did not provide online access to national case law, the other one being Cyprus. *See* for a full overview the register of the European e-justice portal at https://e-justice.europa.eu/13/EN/national_case_law?DENMARK&member=1. In 2022, the Danish database *Domsdatabasen* was launched at domsdatabasen.dk. (Historical) case law is slowly added to the system but accessing case law remains problematic in Denmark.
208. For example, comparable to the Dutch case on a refusal to enter a supermarket/shopping centre, *see*: Fyens.dk: 'Mand blev nægtet adgang til Rema 1000 – gik ud og smadrede sidespejl af bil: – Personalet har bøvlet med ham før', 1 September 2022, https://fyens.dk/artikel/det-blev-han-temmelig-vred-over-mand-n%C3%A6gtet-adgang-til-rema-1000-gik-ud-og-smadrede-sidespejl-af-bil; *see* on (unfair enforcement of) house rules in night clubs: EkstraBladet 'Smidt ud af natklub: I er for gamle', 1 September 2014, https://ekstrabladet.dk/nyheder/samfund/article4994113.ece; on a supermarket that refuses access to children from a specific elementary school: TV2: 'Netto-butik forbyder skoleelever', 14 January 2015, https://nyheder.tv2.dk/2015-01-14-netto-butik-forbyder-skoleelever.
209. Law on ethnic equal treatment (*lov om etnisk* ligebehandling), law on equality between women and men (*lov om ligestilling af kvinder og mænd*) and the law on prohibiting discrimination on grounds of disability (*lov om forbud mod forskelsbehandling på grund af handicap*).
210. For example, denying access to a football stadium on the basis of ethnicity infringed the law on ethnic equal treatment, *see Ligebehandlingsnævn KEN nr 9790 (Foreign surname).* The same goes for the denial of access to a night club (ken nr. 10007) or hairdresser (ken nr. 10261).
211. §3 a. law on equality between men and women, §7 law on prohibiting discrimination on grounds of disability, and §3 stk 3 of the law on ethnic equal treatment. Equality laws prohibit two types of discrimination: direct and indirect. *Direct* discrimination on the basis of one of the protected categories is prohibited under all circumstances. *Indirect* discrimination is prohibited unless the decision is justified by a legitimate aim and the means of achieving that aim are proportionate. The difference between direct and indirect discrimination depends on the formulation of the provision and/or the decision taken. Indirect discrimination occurs 'when an apparently neutral provision, criterion or practice would put [the protected group of persons] at a particular disadvantage compared to other persons, unless that provision, criterion or practice is objectively justified by a legitimate aim and the means of achieving that aim are appropriate and necessary'. *see* Law on equality between women and men §2 stk 3, law on ethnic equal treatment §3 stk 3, and law on prohibiting discrimination on grounds of disability §5 stk. 3, where [protected group of persons] in the respective law refers to either gender, handicap, or ethnic/racial origin.

laws on equal treatment can be brought - free of charge - before the Equal Treatment Board (*Ligebehandlingsnævn*), an administrative body that was enacted on 1 January 2009.[212] If the complaint is successful, the complainant can be awarded compensation.

Drawing the line between a justified decision based on a proprietor's house rules and a violation of equality laws can be a delicate matter. This issue is evident in cases involving 'stiletto-discounts' at Copenhagen nightclubs. Male visitors have lodged complaints about events offering free or discounted entry and drinks to individuals wearing stilettos. The complainants argued that this practice favoured women, constituting a breach of equality laws. The Board agreed with the complainants, concluding that this practice forms a disguised gender discrimination against men. Since stilettos are produced primarily for women, men are less likely to wear them, putting them at a disadvantage compared to women in terms of access to these discounts.[213] The case was upheld by the Copenhagen City Court.[214] The case law from the Equal Treatment Board offers some other examples of legitimate aims, such as reserving access to the first day of a clothing sales event without dressing rooms for women only (protecting women's sexual integrity),[215] limiting service to one gender when due to the competences of the party offering the service (e.g., hairdresser salon or tailored suits),[216] and a general refusal of dogs to enter a restaurant (food hygiene).[217] Discrimination against one sex may be justified on the basis of the promotion of equality between men and women.[218] Opposingly, dedicating one of the twenty-three floors of a hotel for female guests only was found disproportionate. In *Bellasky*,[219] the hotel was found to discriminate on the basis of gender because the restriction did not serve a legitimate aim. According to the Appeals Court: 'prohibiting men from access to certain sections of the hotel cannot be regarded as necessary to safeguard considerations of modesty or privacy or to meet genuinely demonstrated problems of women's safety in relation to violence or sexual harassment'. The case law of the Equal Treatment Board proves furthermore that wrongful moderation decisions also exist in physical access restrictions.[220]

212. The Equal Treatment Board's decisions are based on written complaints only - there is no oral procedure involved. If the case cannot be handled on a written basis, the case will be dismissed and can be brought before a regular court.
213. *Ligebehandlingsnævn KEN nr 10007, 5 September 2012; Ligebehandlingsnævn KEN nr. 10024, 20 February 2013; Ligebehandlingsnævn KEN nr. 10032, 29 May 2013; Ligebehandlingsnævn KEN nr. 9404, 28 August 2013; Ligebehandlingsnævn KEN nr. 9792, 27 August 2014; Ligebehandlingsnævn KEN nr. 10011, 22 April 2015.* In all cases, the complainants were awarded 2.500DKK in compensation.
214. Københavns Byret, January 2014, (*Olgun/Natklub Penthouse*). Concluding, in essence, that stilettos were 'essentially targeting women' and 'the discrimination was not objectively justified by a legitimate aim nor that the means of achieving that aim were appropriate and necessary'.
215. *Ligebehandlingsnævn KEN nr 9998 (Women only sales).*
216. *Ligebehandlingsnævn KEN nr 10261 (Men's hairdresser).*
217. *Ligebehandlingsnævn KEN nr 9852 (Refusal of service dog),* though the restaurant cannot generally prohibit the entry of service dogs, as that would discriminate on the basis of handicap. It will have to make a case-by-case decision.
218. *Ligebehandlingsnævn KEN nr 9687 (Event for men only).*
219. *Østre Landsret B-2983-12* (*Bella Sky*) (2014) U.2014.2286.
220. *Ligebehandlingsnævn KEN nr 9853 (access to a night club).* In case number 9853, the dispute did not regard the house rules of the night club, but rather the decision taken by the bouncer

The interpretation and justification of all other access restrictions that do not touch upon equality laws fall under general Danish contract law. The regulation and governance over private persons' access rights are left to the (general limitations of the) freedom of contract. However, neither the freedom of contract nor its scope is mentioned in the constitution or in Danish legislation, such as the contract act (*aftaleloven*).[221] This makes it difficult to fully define its scope. In principle, a proprietor can choose freely to open up its property to the general public and to allow unlimited access. Similarly, the proprietor can choose to enter into an agreement with another party and, in that way, provide access to its property under certain conditions.[222] The validity of access agreements is stipulated by the general provisions of the contract act. Acceptance of conditions applicable to accessing property can be explicitly or tacitly.[223] The contract act's §36 provides a general ground for invalidity: an agreement can be altered or set aside in whole or in part if unfair or contrary to good faith. §36 provides an opportunity to rebalance unequal agreements, such as agreements between a professional party and a weaker (consumer) party.[224] The wording of §36 allows Danish courts to balance the interests at stake and, where needed, to alter parts of the agreement or declare (parts of) the agreement invalid. If upholding a contractual term is unfair or unreasonable, the balancing of interests can limit a proprietor's right to property[225] or alter/invalidate contractual terms used for conditional access to the property (*see* Figure 2.).[226]

in light of the applicable house rules. The case was left undecided as it required substantial evidence (oral statements of the parties and witnesses), which falls outside the competences of the Equal Treatment Board.

221. The freedom can be traced back to the *Danske Lov* of 1683, mentioning that agreements must be honoured if they 'are not against the law or honour' (*ikke er imod Loven eller Ærbarhed*). From early to mid-20th century, the wish to create a more social, balanced system of contracts led to increased legislation imposing limitations to the freedom, *see* Lennart Lynge Andersen, *Aftalelovens §36-Fra Kontraktfrihed Til Urimelighedskontrol* (Foerste udgave, foerste oplag, Ex Tuto Publishing 2018) 151.

222. *See, e.g.*, *Højesteret 16/2013 (Private car parking)* (2014) U.2014.1719 on the terms and conditions to park a car on privately owned parking spaces.

223. Such as by parking a car on a privately owned car park with signs indicating the application of terms and conditions, *see ibid*

224. *Ibid.*

225. *Højesteret I 241/1985 (Oil tanks)* (1987) U.1987.531. The Danish Supreme Court agrees with the Western Appeal Court that the claimant (an oil company) cannot claim property rights over a set of oil tanks that have been buried under the property of the defendant (a gas station). Considering that the oil tanks do not have individual value once dug up and the fact that the digging process would put a heavy financial burden on the defendant, the Supreme Court dismisses the right to property on the oil tanks and dismisses the contractual obligation to return the oil tanks to the claimant. An identical outcome was reached in Højesteret I 234/1985 (1987) U.1987.526.

226. *Højesteret 16/2013 (Private car parking)* (n. 222).

Figure 2.5 Access Restrictions to Publicly Accessible Private Property under Danish Law

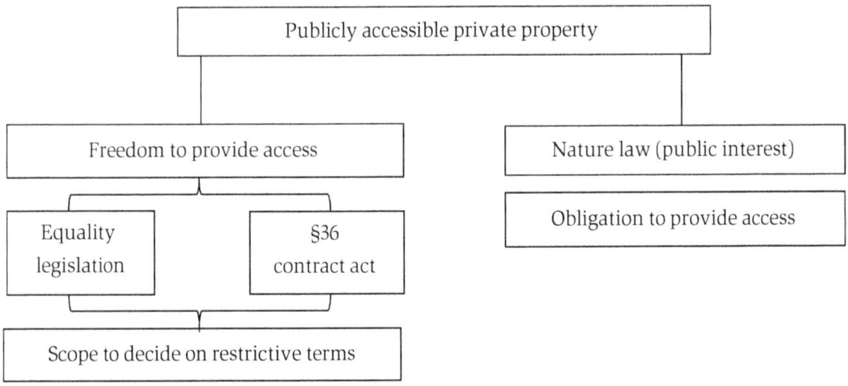

Either one of the contracting parties can suspend its obligations under the contract on the basis of a material breach of contract. Other sanctions can be stipulated in the contract. For a breach of the conditions to use the property, a proprietor can, under specific circumstances, be allowed to impose a contractual penalty payment. Though, arguably, for publicly accessible places, such a penalty can only be imposed when an explicit ground is provided by law.[227]

2.2.4.2 *Online Access Restrictions*

In March 2022, the Danish legislator published a *proposed law on the regulation of social media*, in which it – initially – defined the service offered by social media platforms as communication platforms.[228] From the preparatory works, it follows that social media platforms, through their communication platforms, provide fora for the dissemination of opinions, news and information, and public debate. If the latter is the case, deleting posts that fall within the scope of protection of the freedom of expression

227. *See Højesteret 16/2013 (Private car parking)* (n. 222) U.2014.1719 and the reference to the Danish traffic act (LBK nr 1710 13 August 2021). The Supreme Court concludes that a fine for breach of the terms was allowed, though references the Danish traffic act, which explicitly prescribes that possibility in §122 c.: '*Unless there is a general and clearly marked prohibition on parking on the publicly accessible private area, a parking charge may only be imposed if this is clearly indicated on the spot*'. It is unclear whether a fine or sanction can be imposed on publicly accessible private places without explicitly being provided by law. As the imposition of fines is regulated strictly in the traffic act (§122 c sub 2 and 3 regulate a complaint body and the requirements for signs), it seems unlikely that other publicly available private properties could freely impose fines, as the legislator seemingly has chosen to regulate that area exhaustively.
228. Lovforslag nr. L 146 – Forslag til Lov om regulering af sociale medier, 15 March 2022, https://www.ft.dk/ripdf/samling/20211/lovforslag/l146/20211_l146_som_fremsat.pdf. The proposal has been withdrawn on 2 June 2022.

would constitute a breach of contract because, in that situation, the social media platform no longer offers a communication platform that serves as a public forum. The latter seems a bridge too far, as that would indicate that social media platforms have agreed to host all content that is protected by the freedom of expression, which would render the user terms they impose on their users superfluous. The legislator seems to have changed opinion during the legislative process. In more recent (May 2022) answers to questions raised by Meta/Facebook in regard to the proposed law, the legislator describes the role of social media as purely private, and 'as social media platforms are private companies, they do not, in principle, have any obligation to respect users' freedom of expression. The legal starting point is, therefore, that it is not contrary to freedom of expression for a company to remove posts on its platform'.[229] That points in the direction of an interpretation of the obligations in line with the contract as drawn up between the parties without mitigation for the potential influence the user terms may have on the users' ability to express themselves.

A conclusion on the role of platforms was never reached. The proposed law was withdrawn in June 2022, and apart from this legislative attempt, Danish law does not offer specific legislation addressing access and/or moderation issues on social media platforms, nor are there any cases before a Danish court that deal with these issues. This makes the scope of the obligations of social media platforms unclear. In the absence of mandatory statutory provisions and in accordance with the parties' freedom of contract, the provisions of the agreement between the parties serve as the only blueprint for the parties' mutual obligations. The terms are supplemented by the mandatory provisions on equal treatment. Identical to physical property, equality laws are directly applicable to social media platforms' services.[230] As a result, social media platforms' user terms may not include directly discriminating provisions nor seemingly neutral provisions that indirectly result in discrimination.

Equality laws pose an opportunity to oppose restrictive user terms on social media platforms, though their application is limited. In a case concerning the discriminative nature of user terms of a social media platform (a dating service), the Equal Treatment Board concluded that neither men nor women were affected differently by imposing a minimum and/or maximum age to use the service.[231] Age in itself was disregarded as a ground of discrimination. However, other terms applied by social media platforms would fall within the Danish prohibition and can pose an obstacle to the platform's freedom to decide on the scope of hosted content. For example, the censorship of female nipples on social media platforms would be prohibited, in line

229. Erhvervsministeriet, 'Besvarelse af spørgsmål 9 ad L 146 stillet af udvalget den 6. april 2022', 11 May 2022 https://www.ft.dk/samling/20211/lovforslag/l146/spm/9/svar/1882999/2573412.pdf, p. 5 (answer to question 4).

230. Law on equality between women and men §1 a. Chapter 2 is applicable to 2): 'authorities and organisations and all persons supplying goods and services which are available to the public in both the public and private sectors, including public bodies, and which are offered outside private and family life, and transactions relating thereto. *See also* law on ethnic equal treatment §2 and law on prohibiting discrimination on grounds of disability §2. Neither of the rules prescribed by these three laws cannot be derogated from by agreement if that would be against the protected party's interest.'

231. *Ligebehandlingsnævn KEN nr 9189 (Dating website).*

with the law on equality between women and men, because such a provision directly differentiates between men and women. As the provision itself refers to *female* nipples rather than general nudity,[232] it breaches §2 stk. 2 of the law on equal treatment unless there is an objective reason. In December 2022, the scope of the grounds for discrimination in the law on gender equality has been increased and now includes not only gender but also sexual orientation, gender identity, gender expression, and sex characteristics.[233] That is an (important) increase of opportunities to challenge restrictive terms because even a seemingly neutral provision in the user terms can be challenged if it: (a) results in an access restriction that indirectly affects one protected group in particular, (b) the platform does not have a legitimate aim, and (c) the measure is not necessary to achieve that aim. Sadly, due to the lack of case law regarding access restrictions on social media platforms, it is hard to predict which legitimate aims can be invoked to impose access restrictions and to what extent such measures are proportionate.

There have not been brought other cases (or rather: no other cases are known)[234] before a Danish court or complaints body on access restrictions on social media platforms.[235] Due to this lack of case law, it remains unclear how the obligations of the social media platform and the user will be interpreted under Danish law. That is problematic because the obligations of the contracting parties form a decisive ground in defining whether suspension or termination of a user account is justifiable. The conclusion that a social media platform offers a platform service that, in principle, hosts *all legal content* leads to a different outcome on the justifiability of user account terminations than a narrower interpretation of obligations would. In case a platform offers all content, removing a post that consists of legal content can trigger a claim for compensation on the users' side. Similarly, defining the obligation of the users is necessary to define whether it is proportionate to terminate the user's account for a one-time breach of one of the conditions. Consequently, one can only guess whether social media platforms should adhere to the principles of proportionality and necessity, even when the user terms foresee in termination and suspension clauses, and whether, in case of an unjust removal, suspension or termination, the user would be able to claim compensation for the time the user account was 'down'.

232. *See, e.g.*, the Facebook Community Guidelines (15 September 2022), available at: https://transparency.fb.com/en-gb/policies/community-standards/adult-nudity-sexual-activity/:

> Do not post: (...) Uncovered *female* nipples except in the context of breastfeeding, birth giving and after-birth moments, medical or health context (for example, post-mastectomy, breast cancer awareness or gender confirmation surgery) or an act of protest (emphasis by the author).

233. Ligestillingsloven, §2 stk. 2 (direct discrimination) and §2 stk 3 (indirect discrimination).
234. Due to the historical lack of public access to case law in Denmark and the *Domsdatabase* only recently becoming available with a large backlog of cases, it cannot be ruled out that, despite the efforts and searches, a case has been missed.
235. In addition to online searches, the following Danish institutions have been consulted for advice on retrieving unknown case law: The Danish Institute for Human Rights (https://www.humanrights.dk/), Independent Think-tank Justitia (https://justitia-int.org), and IT-politisk Forening (https://itpol.dk/).

2.2.4.3 *Existence of an Internal Discrepancy*

Due to the lack of case law on access restrictions in Denmark, the conclusion on an internal discrepancy between the handling of access restrictions in physical places as opposed to online places remains unclear, though some remarks can be made. Equality laws are directly applicable to both types of access restrictions and, therefore, play a role in the assessment of both types. Access restrictions to both physical places and online platforms that possibly infringe equality laws can, therefore, be brought before the Danish Equal Treatment Board. The exact scope of application of the prohibition and the implications for social media platforms' freedom of contract is unclear. Furthermore, the above results show that the Danish legislator has only intervened in property rights of physical parties, but a legal possibility to intervene in platforms' right to property exists equally. For physical property, the Danish legislator has restricted both the owner's *own* access to the property (on the basis of public safety) and the access rights between two private parties (based on the public interest). Due to the specificity of the way these limitations were drafted (access to one's own *house*, access to a *forest*), neither one of these restrictions can, in its current form, apply to social media platforms. That does not rule out any future interventions. In the words of Vinding Kruse: 'It is a matter for legislators to give private property rights a free rein wherever they lead to valuable productive work, but to tighten the reins, i.e., to intervene with coercive rules, where production goes astray, leads to confusion and waste of values, and where private property rights, in short-sighted self-interest, prey on the interests of the general public and of future generations.'[236] The use of property by social media platforms tends (way) more towards the latter, highlighted by, for example, social media platforms' bad influence on children and teenagers' concentration and self-esteem, the high consumption of their datacentre's electricity and the influence on the environment, or the exposure to disinformation and its effects on democracy. Arguments to intervene in the property rights of social media platforms are, therefore, plenty. However, whether social media platforms have gone a bridge too far in favouring their own economic interests over the interests of the general public remains a political discussion, which, unfortunately, falls outside of the scope of the legal discussion addressed here.

2.3 THE *EXTERNAL* COMPARATIVE STUDY

The previous paragraphs have outlined the practice of the four Member States, which has allowed for conclusions on the presumed discrepancy in resolving access and moderation restrictions on physical property and social media platforms. The aim of this external part is to compare those internal findings to see if an overlapping approach or overlapping elements can be identified. From the internal comparative study, five

236. Vinding Kruse (n. 203), p. 331.

objects have been identified, which all function to address and/or contribute to solving access and moderation problems on physical and/or online property:[237]

(i) the legal basis to address access restrictions;
(ii) the service offered by social media platforms;
(iii) the existence of rights to claim access to private property;
(iv) the influence of fundamental rights;
(v) the existence and influence of procedural safeguards; and
(vi) the possibility to claim remedies for wrongful access restrictions.

2.3.1 The Legal Basis to Address Access Restrictions

The internal comparison of the case law reveals the legal foundation courts have referred to in order to resolve access problems. At first glance, the results of the internal comparative study show that the four Member States do not uniformly apply the same legal foundation to online and physical access restrictions, as shown in the table below.

Table 2.1 Conclusions on the Legal Basis for Access Restrictions

The Legal Basis	*Physical Access Restrictions*	*Online Access Restrictions*
Germany	House rights/right to property	Freedom of contract
Italy	Right to property	Freedom of contract
The Netherlands	Right to property	Right to property/freedom of contract
Denmark	Freedom of contract	Inconclusive

However, when looking further into the theory of the right to property in the different Member States, a more homogenous framework appears on a meta-level. Germany, Italy, and the Netherlands, despite not using the same terminology, base access restrictions on the positive and negative aspects of the right to property. These refer to, respectively, a proprietor's ability to freely make use of its property and to exclude anyone else from entering and/or using the property. Interestingly, regarding physical access restrictions, both aspects of the right to property have been addressed (indirectly). The Italian legislation is the most thoroughly defined. The positive and negative sides of the right to property can be found in the Italian Civil Code. The positive right and the therefrom emerging freedom of contract are encoded and provide the legal basis to dictate the conditions to access. The negative right, referred to as the *ius excludendi*, allows one to refuse access to private property. The latter is, in turn, restricted in numerous ways, which will be discussed in the following paragraph. The Dutch courts have explicitly referenced the right to property both for physical access restrictions as well as for online restrictions. Despite not referring explicitly to the positive and negative aspects of the right to property, their line of reasoning signals the

237. In line with the theory of selection of the *tertium comparationis* by Oderkerk, *see* §1.5.1.4.

courts' implicit application of these two aspects of the right to property (e.g., social media companies are private property and, as such, can dictate their terms of use). Similarly, in Germany, the doctrine of house rights demonstrates a focus on balancing the negative and positive aspects of the right to property.

Therefore, despite the differences in terminology, the German, Italian, and Dutch systems demonstrate an overlapping legal basis to address access restrictions - both when imposed by a social media platform as a proprietor of physical property. The practice in Denmark does not explicitly follow this distinction. The reason, therefore, is not necessarily the explicit choice of the legislator or national courts not to refer to a positive and negative right to property but is the result of a lack of case law. The results for online access restrictions in the tables above have, therefore, been marked as *inconclusive*. In addition to the lacking case law, the Danish legislative system complicates matters further. Danish law, and Nordic law in general for that matter, has a tradition of broader, less-defined legislation as compared to the other three Member States addressed in this study. It does not have a civil code, nor are principles such as the freedom of contract specifically defined anywhere. That allows for a broad interpretation and adaptation of the system to various legal problems, but it also causes legal uncertainty, as is the case for access restrictions.

Table 2.2 Consolidated Outcome of the Legal Basis for Access Restrictions

The Legal Basis	*Physical Access Restrictions*	*Online Access Restrictions*
Germany	Positive and negative aspects of the right to property	
Italy		
The Netherlands		
Denmark	Freedom of contract	Inconclusive

The choice of the legal basis to apply to online access restrictions exposes a normative stance on the role of social media platforms in society. In the introduction, the lack of consensus on the qualification of social media platforms in the academic literature was pointed out. From the results of the internal comparative study, however, a more uniform interpretation can be deducted, namely that the majority of the national courts apply contract law to define the service offered by these platforms.[238] In Germany, Italy, and the Netherlands, the interpretational choice can be traced back to the right to property of social media platforms. In the assessed Member States, it has been explicitly pointed out that social media platforms' services are predominantly seen as a contractual offer by a private undertaking rather than the creation of a (near-)public space. The German, Italian, and Dutch courts have explicitly rejected the notion that social media platforms are essential and fulfil the role of a public forum. Rather, the terms of use between the platform and the user are the reference point to define the scope of the service.

238. *See* further §3.2.1 on the discussion of the right to property as a base for access restrictions.

2.3.2 The Service Offered by Social Media Platforms

As social media platforms' services are predominantly viewed as a contractual offer to the users, the interpretation of the scope of the service is decisive for the content to be hosted. However, the interpretation of the service offered by social media platforms varies from Member State to Member State. Italian courts have referred to a 'civil co-existential space' in which the platform is obliged to offer a communication platform in which the users can freely communicate.[239] The users are, in turn, obliged to observe the rights of other users. Platforms, however, have not offered to host *all* content. They have offered to host the content that is allowed in the user terms. According to the German *Bundesgerichtshof*, social media platforms offer users a general service to contact and exchange information with other users.[240] A platform's service obligation does not include guaranteed access to the internet, nor do social media platforms have a monopoly or state-like position. Referring to the network effect of platforms and the resulting difficulty with which users can switch, the German court concludes that if a user is excluded from a large-scale social media platform, it does not have an equal alternative to voice an opinion. The stance of the Dutch courts has been the exact opposite: social media platforms form a limited part of the available (online) options to voice an opinion. A refusal of access does, therefore, not interfere with the freedom of expression. In Denmark, online access restrictions have not been addressed by a court, though the preparatory works for the 2022 proposed (and revoked) law on the regulation of social media show that the decision on how to interpret platforms' services is highly normative. In a matter of months, the Danish legislator has shifted from arguing that platforms function as public fora to arguing that the service offered by a platform is solely contractually defined.

2.3.3 Obligations to Contract and Limitations to the Right to Property

In Germany, Italy, and the Netherlands, courts reference predominantly the positive aspect of the right to property (the freedom of contract) when dealing with access and content restrictions on social media platforms. The reference implicitly exposes that the courts handling the cases on online access restrictions did not see any indication that social media platforms' right to property should be limited nor that users would have any right to claim access to a platform. Rather, the power of social media platforms was solely reviewed in light of the positive aspect of the right to property, indicating that

239. *Corte appello L'Aquila (Correggiari)* (n. 21), §9. Within that coexistence, a user is not fully free to post anything it wishes. Rather, 'the balance between the possibility for the user to express himself and share content deemed important and the harm that certain modes of expression or certain content may cause to the safety and well-being of others or to the integrity of the community itself, which is to say that those modes of expression are accepted insofar as they do not end up becoming an attack on the safety and well-being of other users and/or the integrity of the values of the community itself.' A breach of the principles underpinning this civil coexistence 'may well therefore be assessed as a breach of contract that, if it exists, entitles the other party [the platform] to suspend its own performance, removing or blocking the contents that violate these contractual provisions.'

240. *Bundesgerichtshof (Inhaltesperrung)* (n. 23); *Bundesgerichtshof (Kontosperrung)* (n. 23).

these platforms have the unlimited freedom to decide on the use of their property. However, the right to exclude (*ius excludendi*) is not absolute in any of the examined Member States. Limitations to the *ius excludendi* can result in an obligation to contract or an obligation to allow the use of the property. Both of these types - obligation to contract and the obligation to allow use - are forms of *forced access*.

The grounds for forced access in the different systems overlap to a certain extent. First, all Member States allow limitations to the physical right to property in the interest of the public and society. Germany and Italy's systems go even further, imposing an obligation to provide access to all publicly offered services. In those two jurisdictions, the act to offer a service to the general public is conceived as an implicit waiver of the proprietor's *ius excludendi,* and thus, the proprietor cannot later invoke its right to exclude. Second, access can be claimed to certain types of property if those types of property fall in the public domain. Danish users can claim access to a limited number of specific types of property that fall in the public domain, such as forests and beaches. Italy and the Netherlands define the scope of public and social use rights by the nature of the public property and cover forests, beaches, nursing homes, football stadiums, and houses of worship, respectively. In Italy, the rules on forced access can also be based on a person's individual interest in accessing the property. The German system does not offer public and social use rights as a form of limitation, but it does weigh the open nature as a factor that could limit a house right. However, despite Denmark, Italy, and the Netherlands offering a system of public and social rights to limit the right to property's right of exclusion, these systems are not generally applicable to social media platforms. The Danish system is the strictest, only allowing public/social use rights to types of property that have been pre-defined in the law. Applicability of these rules to the realm of social media platforms is impossible without legal intervention. In Italy, the threshold for application is high: social media platforms have to form part of the public domain to fall within the scope, and the threshold for a personal interest for an obligation to contract is high. In the Netherlands, the practice follows from case law, leaving room for the Dutch courts to include social media platforms in the scope. Third and lastly, in all Member States, due to the implementation of European directives 2000/43/EC and 2004/113/EC, equality/anti-discrimination laws are generally applicable to access restrictions to both online and physical places if their services are offered publicly.

2.3.4 The Influence of Fundamental Rights

To resolve access restrictions, Member States apply fundamental rights to a varying degree. In two out of the four jurisdictions (Italy and Denmark), fundamental rights did not play a role in the assessment of physical or online access restrictions. In Italy, fundamental rights were not included in the assessment of access restrictions, neither in the discussion on entering property nor on suspending access. Only one Italian case referenced fundamental rights,[241] but this line of reasoning by the preliminary court in

241. *Tribunale di Roma (Casapound)* (n. 154).

Rome has not been followed by any other courts, has not been mentioned in any of the appeal cases, and was more recently rejected in a similar case.[242] In Denmark, the influence of fundamental rights did not show from the limited cases available. In Germany and the Netherlands, however, fundamental rights have had a significant influence on the assessment of the fairness of access restrictions. Both legal systems resemble each other, but there are some differences in the application of fundamental rights. In both systems, fundamental rights are generally not directly applicable to a relationship between private parties. Fundamental rights have a vertical effect and protect private parties against influence from the State. However, both the German and the Dutch civil codes have open norms, for example, the Dutch 'reasonableness and fairness' and the German 'objective reason'. It is through these open norms that fundamental rights can find their way into the private agreement.[243] When defining whether a refusal of access is based on an objective reason or whether the enforcement of certain house rules is reasonable and fair, fundamental rights can serve as normative principles.

Table 2.3 Conclusions on the Influence of Fundamental Rights on Access Restrictions

Fundamental Rights	*Physical Access Restrictions*	*Online Access Restrictions*
Germany	Through open norms in private law (*Drittwirkung*) if the place is open to the general public or access restriction has a significant impact on social life.	
Italy	Seemingly not applicable to access restriction cases	Only applied in one preliminary request
The Netherlands	Through open norms in private law (*'reasonableness and fairness'*) – strict application, only when right is *fully* impaired	
Denmark	Inconclusive	

Interestingly, the application of these normative principles and their (potential) influence is virtually identical in both jurisdictions for both physical and online access restrictions. In Germany, when addressing online access problems, the courts refer specifically to the previous case law on physical restrictions. In the Netherlands, the outcome of the balancing is uniform in all access cases, both online and physical. As

242. In *Tribunale di Roma (Casapound IV)* (n. 140), the court included an assessment of the freedom of expression, but this assessment was not used to define the justifiability of the moderation decision. Rather, the court's assessment showed that the posted hatespeech content was not protected by the freedom of expression and left the decision on the justifiability depend on the contractual terms applied by the platform.

243. Note that these findings are based on the internal comparative study, but do not represent the full potential of the application of fundamental rights in private parties' relationships. In fact, the Italian legal system offers a similar possibility of application through open norms, but that finding did not show from the case law on access restrictions to physical property or social media platforms. *See* for a full discussion on the functioning of fundamental rights §5.5.3 below.

long as the fundamental freedom is not *fully* impaired, the right to property prevails. Consequently, the practical effect of fundamental rights on access restrictions has proven limited in the Netherlands, and invoking the fundamental right to freedom of expression to oppose an access restriction seems useless. Dutch courts, weighing the users' fundamental right to freedom of expression against the right to property of the platform owners, systematically conclude that users have other possibilities to express their thoughts or opinions - both online (websites, other platforms) and offline (newspapers).

2.3.5 The Existence of Procedural Safeguards

Under the Digital Services Act, social media platforms must observe procedural safeguards for (certain types of) access and content moderation decisions. For three Member States, this European regulation proves to be merely a codification of existing practice. For Denmark, it was not possible to conclude on the existence of procedural safeguards.

For the German legal system, the practical consequence of the above-described *Drittwirkung* of constitutional rights is a shift towards procedural safeguards, both in an online and physical context. The development of the indirect application of fundamental rights allows these rights to be used to fill in the open norm of 'unfairness'. When balancing the different constitutional rights, the *Bundesgerichtshof* concluded that terms applied on a social media platform are unfair if they allow access or moderation restrictions without procedural safeguards. Decisions on access restrictions must be based on an objective reason, must be clearly communicated to allow the refused to appeal the decision, and may not be taken arbitrarily. Those safeguards apply equally to both types of access and moderation restrictions. Similarly, also in the Italian case law on online access restrictions, a shift towards increased procedural safeguards can be observed. Like the Germans, the Italian case law shows that the basis for this shift is the interpretation of the (national implementation of the) Unfair Contract Terms Directive. The Italian Competition Authority - which has ex officio competency to assess user terms' potential unfairness - has consistently held that clauses are unfair when they allow the termination of a user account without giving a reason and without notice. An access or content limitation decision must include the reasons for the decision and a time notice before the measure becomes effective, as well as an obligation to adhere to the principle of proportionality. The Italian argumentation for the unfairness is equal to the German: users must have an opportunity to appeal the decision and to make effective use of their rights.

In the Netherlands, the safeguards do not generally apply to access restrictions to private property, but they have been in place for physical access restrictions to property with a public or social function. For these types of property, the proprietor must give a reasonable ground for the refusal, which could be either a breach of the user terms or public safety. Access decisions must be reasonable and fair, and in order to assess this, the decision must include the facts and circumstances that have led to the refusal. For online access restrictions, procedural safeguards have been introduced by the courts through the open norm of reasonableness and fairness, by reference to the DSA and the fundamental principles underlying the regulation to conclude on a necessity for procedural safeguards for social media platforms' access and moderation decisions.

2.3.6 Remedies for Wrongful Access Restrictions

Wrongful access restrictions were observed in all Member States. When the proprietor has chosen to make use of its property and to agree with a third party on the terms for access, it must subsequently live up to these conditions. Wrongful access restrictions – the access denial is not in line with the conditions – result in a breach of contract. Due to the large number of access decisions taken on a daily basis by social media platforms, wrongful access restrictions are mostly observed in the case law on online access restrictions. A case before the Danish Equality Board is the only occurrence of a wrongful access restriction to a physical place and concerned the grounds to refuse access to a night club. Most likely, wrongful access restrictions occur as frequently in the physical world as in the online world, but the online interface of the latter makes them more accessible and visible and, therefore, makes their assessment easier.[244] In the other Member States, wrongful decisions have occurred in relation to online access restriction. In all instances of wrongful decisions, users have successfully claimed a right to reinstatement – both of their content and their account. In the Netherlands, when a user fears a potential wrongful access restriction, it can request a preliminary injunction to prevent the permanent removal of the data concerning the account or post to safeguard a future reinstatement. Italy has proven to impose the most far-reaching consequences for wrongful moderation decisions by social media platforms. Users have successfully claimed non-material damages for the time their account or post has been unjustly blocked, and in case a user faces the loss of virtual goods bought within the system, the proprietor is obliged to refund those items.

2.4 SUMMARY OF THE RESULTS OF THE COMPARATIVE STUDY

After concluding the internal and external comparative analysis of the Member States' case law, the first sub-question can be answered: *have access restrictions on social media platforms been resolved differently from those regarding physical places, and to what extent do the Member States differ in their approach?* The answer is summarised in three concluding statements, but first, the underlying hypotheses of the comparative study, as outlined in the introduction, are revisited.

244. This is only true for 'regular' access restrictions on social media platforms and does not apply to more opaque moderation measures taken by some platforms. This is, for example, the case with shadow banning, a practice where a users' post is downgraded by the platform's algorithm and virtually deleted. Because the content has never been 'officially' deleted, it is hard to challenge and sustain and argument of wrongful moderation. *See* for an in-depth analysis of these opaque moderation measures: Paddy Leerssen, 'An End to Shadow Banning? Transparency Rights in the Digital Services Act between Content Moderation and Curation' (2023) 48 Computer Law & Security Review 105790, DOI: https://doi.org/10.1016/j.clsr.2023.105790.

In the introduction, two hypotheses were outlined that led to this two-fold comparative study. First, the discrepancy within the individual Member States regarding the way they address access restrictions imposed by social media platforms as opposed to physical property proprietors. It was expected that this internal discrepancy would be caused by the Member States having difficulty weighing the overlapping legal orders. This hypothesis has been (partly) disproven. In the Member States, where case law was available on both types of access restrictions (all, excluding Denmark), these two types of restrictions were resolved in a similar way and on an identical legal basis (the freedom of contract and the right to property). However, the national courts in the Member States nonetheless had difficulties weighing the overlapping legal orders. This caused differences in language and terminology but did not lead to substantial differences in the way access restrictions have been resolved. Second, it was suspected that the individual Member States would resolve conflicts with social media platforms differently from their fellow Member States, creating an external discrepancy. Additionally, it was presumed that this external discrepancy could be caused by a disagreement on the qualification of social media platforms. Contrarily, it follows from the findings of the comparative study that the majority of the examined Member States uniformly qualify social media platforms' services as a contractual obligation rather than as public services.

Following the disproval of both hypotheses, the comparative study's most important findings can be summarised in three concluding statements.

(i) The Member States base both online and physical access restrictions on the right to property

The case law in Germany, Italy, and the Netherlands shows that the legal foundation for the proprietor's competence to impose access restrictions to physical and online places is the right to property. In these Member States, the right to property consists of two elements. The negative element grants the proprietor a right of exclusion (*ius excludendi*). This right can be used to deny access to the property against any third party. It is therewith, on basis, the core foundation of access restrictions in its purest form: it allows a proprietor to fully exclude the use of its property. The positive element allows the proprietor to make use of its property in the way it pleases. That includes opening the property fully (open access) or under certain conditions (conditional access). The latter part of the positive element of the right to property is what is commonly referred to as the freedom of contract. In Denmark, the basis for physical access restrictions referenced solely the freedom of contract. Referring to the freedom of contract as the basis for access restrictions means that the proprietor makes use of its positive right to property to set the conditions for access and exclusion. It seems unlikely that proprietors do not have any right of exclusion in Denmark, but the negative element has not been explicitly codified and has not (yet) led to any disputes.[245] In that sense, the extent to which the legal foundation for access restrictions differs in Denmark as opposed to the other three Member States seems limited.

245. *See* on the matter Vinding Kruse (n. 203), p. 134: 'Det er derfor meget forklarligt, at man tilsidst – som almindeligt i nordisk jura – opgiver at finde nogen enkelt eller enkelte beføjelser som

The conclusion on the basis of access restrictions is important when digging deeper into the permissible conditions for conditional access, which will be addressed in part two. As shown by several examples in the national case law, these conditions are increasingly interpreted by taking into consideration and balancing constitutional principles - at least in some Member States. Concluding that the right to exclude and the right to choose the conditions for conditional access form an intrinsic part of the right to property means that these elements must be balanced against the different interests at stake. That means that a user's right to access the property, an obligation to contract, and disregarding contractual terms form a limitation of the proprietor's right to property.

(ii) The substantial influence of fundamental rights on access restrictions is limited in all Member States

Despite their inclusion through national Member States' open norms, the effects of fundamental rights on substance of normative access and moderation decisions have proven limited. In neither of the assessed Member States, fundamental rights have created obligations to contract or general rights of access to physical property or social media platforms. The influence of fundamental rights on access restrictions is limited to the interpretation of the conditions under which the proprietor applies its positive right to property. The application of fundamental rights to private party agreements through open norms is controversial. As a principle, fundamental rights protect a private party from State intervention and, as such, have a vertical effect only. Therefore, requiring a proprietor to adhere directly to the fundamental rights protection of third parties diverts from the general functioning of these rights. Rather, the application of fundamental rights is indirectly imposed through the system of private law. In both Germany and the Netherlands, fundamental principles are used to fill in open norms in private law and to balance various interests in contractual relationships. This development is not new and is by no means a specific trend related to social media platforms: it is applied in the case law on physical access restrictions in both Member States equally and to the same extent as it occurs in the case law on social media platforms. Moreover, the inclusion of fundamental rights has not led to any *substantial* influence on the normative power that social media platforms can exert through their terms of service. Rather, fundamental rights are included to balance this power. The result of the latter is an increase in procedural safeguards.

Fundamental rights do not play a role in the assessment of fairness in the other two assessed Member States, but the influence of that difference seems negligible. The reference to fundamental rights can be omitted to reach the identical conclusion that increased procedural safeguards are needed to re-establish balance in the contractual relationship, as demonstrated by the Italian case law. Despite Germany and Italy's differing application of fundamental rights in their interpretation of the open norm of 'unfairness' in light of the Unfair Contract Terms Directive, an equal conclusion on the

karakteristiske for ejendomsretten og blot bestemmer denne som en almindelig beføjelse til at råde i enhver retning, hvor der ikke er hjemmel for særlige indskrænkninger til fordel for andre.'

unfairness of terms on social media platforms is reached based on identical argumentation. After balancing the fundamental rights of the platform and the users, the German *Bundesgerichtshof* concludes that user terms that allow unlimited discretionary powers to remove content or suspend users are unfair. The Italian Competition Authority reached that same conclusion without the inclusion of fundamental principles, concluding that without a provision of the reason(s) for termination or suspension, the users' right to defend themselves would be impaired as they would not have adequate possibilities to complain against the decision. The two systems result in the same procedural safeguards.

The inclusion of fundamental rights to fill in open norms makes visible which interests have been balanced in order to reach a conclusion on the open norm. That does not substantially change the position of a refused person but could procedurally help to challenge the decision. The above proves that the increased procedural obligations on social media platforms put forward in the DSA merely regulate the already existing practice in (some) Member States.

(iii) Public or social use rights could form a potential legal ground for an online right to access.

In Denmark, Italy, and the Netherlands, public and/or social use rights have been applied as a limitation to the proprietor's physical right to exclude. If the property fulfils a public function, falls in the public domain, or the user has an individual pressing need to access the property, the proprietor's possibility to deny access to the property is limited. The interest of the public to access the property outweighs the property right of the proprietor. Consequently, the latter is obliged to contract or offer open access. Despite the lacking system of public or social use rights, the German system has developed a similar system through case law. The German system is based on the proprietor's house right and has clear requirements to include types of property. The system of house rules applies to all properties that have been opened to the general public. If the property is open to the general public and a refusal would have an impact on the refused person's social life, a general right of use exists.

The Member States differ in their application of the public interest limitation, mainly regarding the types of property that fall within the scope. Danish legislation provides an exhaustive list of property to which access can be demanded on the basis of public interest. The inclusion of other types of property (social media platforms) requires legislative intervention. In the Netherlands, the requirements to decide whether a property serves a social function are unclear. The existing types of property (nursing homes, houses of worship, football stadium) have been marked as such in the case law, but any general requirements or arguments for the decisions on those qualifications do not follow from the case law. Italy offers the broadest scope and the most viable ground to potentially include social media platforms. In Italy, any (private) property placed in the public domain can be subject to public use rights. Private property falls within the public domain when the proprietor has allowed the property to be used by an indeterminate group of persons, and this use serves a general public interest. In several cases, Italian courts have concluded that a social media platform is able to reach an indeterminate number of persons, hinting that the property fulfils the first requirement. However, whether the platform fulfils a general public interest depends on the qualification of the service offered by social media platforms. The latter seems unlikely to be the case. The idea that a specific social media platform plays a role that is essential to society has been rejected in the examined Member States.

All Member States legal systems allow for the choice to include online platforms in the scope of public interest property. The Member States, however, have unanimously rejected the idea that social media platforms offer anything substantially different from a general contractual service. Social media platforms' lock-in effect can have a significant effect on users' intercommunication opportunities, but it does not render communication impossible. Even when sharing ideas and information on one platform is fully excluded, then there are other alternatives available – both offline and on the internet. In the reasoning of the Member States, that renders forced access to social media platforms superfluous, at least currently.[246]

246. This conclusion only reflects the findings of the comparative study. The possibilities to claim access to social media platforms is discussed in §5.5.

CHAPTER 3

The Elements of a Roadmap on Access Restrictions

3.1 IDENTIFYING THE ELEMENTS OF ACCESS RESTRICTIONS

Building upon the conclusions from the comparative study in the previous chapter, the elements to be included in a roadmap on access restrictions take form. The identification, framing and sorting of the roadmap's elements is the central point of focus of this chapter. 'Elements' in this sense is to be understood as the 'building blocks' of the roadmap and cover the various types of access restrictions included, as well as the legal framework used to address these types of restrictions. To strive for a technology-neutral roadmap, only elements that were observed in both the physical and the online world will be included. As the comparative study solely included restrictions that were imposed by a professional party onto a consumer, the blueprint of the roadmap outlined in this chapter does not take into consideration business-to-business relationships.

Access restrictions and content moderation decisions concern different fundamental questions. To demonstrate this, the roadmap is divided into four layers in which various distinct discussions take place: the foundational layer (the legal basis), the access layer (*ex ante* access restrictions), the content layer (*ex post* restrictions), and the enforcement layer. The next paragraph introduces these four layers. It questions and reflects on whether the elements identified in the case law and as used by the national courts pose a good starting point for a future roadmap for access restrictions on social media platforms. Where the answer is positive, the elements are included in the roadmap. Simultaneously, the various legal orders applicable to access restrictions are sorted in their respective layer. These two steps – the division into layers and the allocation of the legal orders – create the roadmap's blueprint. This chapter does not address the various layers in detail. The aim of this introduction is to provide an overview of the interaction between the different layers and to define the overarching blueprint. Following this 'horizontal exploration of the ocean', the second part of the book explores the different layers vertically.[247] An analysis of the individual layers, tailored to the characteristics of social media platforms, takes place in Chapter 4 (foundational layer), Chapter 5 (access layer), Chapter 6 (content layer), and Chapter 7 (enforcement layer).

3.2 FOUR LAYERS TO DISCUSS ACCESS RESTRICTIONS

From the case law in the examined Member States, it follows that the discussion on how to address access restrictions and moderation decisions takes place on different levels (*see* Figure 3.1). The difference depends on which legal aspect is the centre point of the (legal) debate. In short, these levels cover, first, the legal basis to impose access restrictions; second, the access restrictions that can be imposed on the basis of the legal foundation; third, the scope of the terms of service; and lastly, the enforcement of the terms of service. Starting from the top, the *foundational* layer covers the (constitutional) basis for imposing access restrictions. Building upon this foundation, the case law exposed four types of access limitations to private property. These access restrictions have been collected in an *access* layer. The content of the terms of service used to define the conditions to access are addressed in the third layer. As this layer focuses on the content of these terms, the layer has been named the *content* layer. Lastly, the elements concerning the execution of contractual sanctions for a breach of the terms of service are included in the *enforcement* layer.

Figure 3.1 Four Layers of Legal Discussions on Physical and Online Access and Moderation Decisions

Foundational layer	the legal basis for access restrictions
Access layer	the control over the access to private property
Content layer	the formation and validity of the terms of service
Enforcement layer	the execution of sanctions for breaching the terms of service

247. However, keeping in mind the differences between a surfer and a diver-study: '[surfers] also use their binoculars for vertically scanning downwards to see what threads of the ocean are most relevant to the connections they've made. The problem is binoculars can't see that far down. This is where the scuba gear comes in handy. When relevant threads are found, the surfer pauses their journey, throws on the scuba gear and does some diving. However, they don't go as deep as the diver. They go as far as they need to, gaining relevant information, resurfacing, and then continuing to surf.', Pandya (n. 37).

3.2.1 The Foundational Layer: Access Restrictions as a Property-Problem

The first layer of discussion covers the legal basis on which a proprietor can base an access or a moderation restriction. This layer is referred to as the *foundational layer*. The legal practice in the four examined Member States shows that national courts predominantly address and resolve access problems with reference to the right to property and its positive and negative rights to either allow or exclude access. Courts either refer to the right to property as such or to its positive element – the proprietor's freedom of contract. For online access problems, national courts stick closely to this legal framework for physical access restrictions.

Addressing access and moderation problems on social media platforms on the basis of the platform's right to property is the only effective way to reach an answer to the law currently applicable in the European Union. However, scholars have argued that various other legal fields would be better suited to address these types of access and moderation issues. In the legal literature, studies have focused on the (limits of the) contractual basis of the relationship between the platform and the user and the need for procedural rules on the enforcement of the contract,[248] though predominantly, the focus lies with social media platform's private governance power and the effect of that power on users' right to freedom of expression.[249] To achieve a more balanced relationship between platform and user, scholars have departed from various fields of law. First, some have argued that platforms should be obliged to adhere to international human rights law (IHRL), which laws could then serve as a starting point to address moderation issues.[250] Similarly, others argue that the private governance power of social media platforms can only be balanced by introducing constitutional norms into the framework.[251] These approaches are well-intended but do not help

248. Marco Almada and others, 'Opportunities and Limits of European Social Network Regulation' (2022) 62 Demokratie und Öffentlichkeit im 21. Jahrhundert – zur Macht des Digitalen 327; Palka (n. 34); Caterina Raffaele, 'Cyberspazio, Social Network e Teoria Generale Del Contratto' (2011) 20 AIDA. Annali italiani del diritto d'autore, della cultura e dello spettacolo 93. New procedural rules on the enforcement of terms of service also follow from newer European legislative acts, such as the Digital Services Act and the Directive (EU) 2019/770 on certain aspects concerning contracts for the supply of digital content and digital services.

249. *See, e.g.*, Balkin's triangulation of speech regulation in Balkin (n. 11). *See also* Kaye (n. 6); Belli and Venturini (n. 6); Venturini and others (n. 6); Bassini (n. 6); Monti (n. 6); Karanicolas (n. 6). Kettemann argues that platform power has shaped a 'normative order' on the internet: Kettemann (n. 6).

250. *See* on the limitations of the IHRL approach: Evelyn Douek, 'The Limits of International Law in Content Moderation' (Social Science Research Network 2020) SSRN Scholarly Paper ID 3709566 https://papers.ssrn.com/abstract=3709566 (accessed 24 February 2021).

251. There is a specific field of scholarship extending and applying this approach to a general trend of 'digital constitutionalism': Nicolas Suzor, 'Digital Constitutionalism: Using the Rule of Law to Evaluate the Legitimacy of Governance by Platforms' (2018) 4 Social Media + Society https://doi.org/10.1177/2056305118787812 (accessed 5 March 2021); Giovanni De Gregorio, 'The Rise of Digital Constitutionalism in the European Union' (2021) 19 International Journal of Constitutional Law 41; Giovanni De Gregorio, *Digital Constitutionalism in Europe: Reframing Rights and Powers in the Algorithmic Society* (Cambridge University Press 2022) https://www.cambridge.org/core/books/digital-constitutionalism-in-europe/A3F61C6368D17D953457234B8A59C502 (accessed 6 July 2022). There has also been criticism on the scholarship

reach an interpretation of the applicable law (*lex lata*). Including norms from IHRL and/or fundamental rights is necessary to guide the application of particular content moderation practices, but they neither (sufficiently) take into consideration the platform's right to property and the effect thereon,[252] nor do they form a legally just starting point to discuss the existence of access and moderation restrictions that originate in private law.[253] Furthermore, it is unclear how the rules of IHRL would apply to social media platform's content moderation practices.[254] As such, at maximum, IHRL standards could form an inspiration for how the law should develop over the coming years (*lex ferenda*), but they form an unsuitable starting point to adjudicate content moderation problems here and now.

The argument to oblige social media platforms to public law norms is invoked as a counterbalance for the powerful role of social media platforms in society and their private governance power over the communication possibilities of their users, but such rebalancing can be perfectly dealt with by private law. As a matter of fact, private law has done so for decades when dealing with physical access restrictions, as shown by the numerous examples in the comparative study in the previous chapter.[255] Scholars' criticism of private law's capability to deal with content moderation follows from a misunderstanding of the scope of property and contract law and displays merely a subjective favouring of IHRL or constitutional norms over property rights.[256] It also

referring to 'digital constitutionalism': Rachel Griffin, 'A Progressive View of Digital Constitutionalism – The Digital Constitutionalist' (14 June 2022) https://digi-con.org/a-progressive-view-of-digital-constitutionalism/ (accessed 28 January 2023); Róisín Á Costello, 'Faux Ami? Interrogating the Normative Coherence of "Digital Constitutionalism"' [2023] Global Constitutionalism 1. *See* on the need to introduce fundamental rights protection to balance platform power also: Rott (n. 87).

252. Ross Grantham, 'The Legitimacy of the Company as a Source of (Private) Power' in Kit Barker, Simone Degeling and Karen Fairweather (eds), *Private law and power* (Hart Publishing 2017) 239.
253. Costello (n. 251).
254. Douek (n. 250), p. 72.
255. These examples span a broad field of physical property types, covering the access to bars, restaurants, thermal baths, sports stadiums, nursing homes, airports, hotels, private shopping malls, and individual stores.
256. *See, e.g.*, João Pedro Quintais, Naomi Appelman and Ronan Fahy, 'Using Terms and Conditions to Apply Fundamental Rights to Content Moderation' (25 November 2022) https://papers.ssrn.com/abstract=4286147 (accessed 31 January 2023): 'Moreover, the contractual nature of T&Cs implies that the law conceptualizes the relationship between intermediary service providers and users as an equal one. Service providers, as private companies, have the right to offer their services on their own terms and, for their part, users are free to enter into this contract, negotiate other terms, or find an alternative provider. From this perspective, the provider's ability to set its own terms of service can be seen as a direct extension of its fundamental right to property and freedom of contract. However, this legal abstraction of two equal contractual parties does not hold in practice.' The conclusion that a contractual relationship implies an equal relationship between the parties is a misunderstanding of the functioning of contracts. For example, the entire field of consumer law is based on the assumption that the contracting parties are unequal. Subsequently that misunderstanding is used to disregard the use of property law and the freedom of contract. The latter is especially problematic, since the argument is made in relation to Art. 14 DSA, which the European legislator has explicitly formulated as an exception to the freedom of contract, *see* recitals (45) and (47) DSA.

overestimates the effects of such an obligation on the practice of content moderation. The general subject of fundamental rights obligations is states. Fundamental rights law does not (generally)[257] create obligations between private parties. The right to freedom of expression, therefore, forms an unsuitable starting point to address moderation problems. First, the right to freedom of expression does not have horizontal direct effect.[258] This means that a user cannot directly invoke these rights against a social media platform to either gain access to the platform or get content reinstated. The right solely restricts the regulatory freedom of a state and can solely indirectly find its way to contractual relationships through open norms. Apart from refraining from infringements of the right itself, the state must guarantee that all persons have an opportunity to freely express their opinions and to impart information. The threshold for this positive obligation to make sure that individuals have an effective opportunity to voice their opinions is high.[259] Only when the behaviour of private companies – such as access restrictions – has the effect of 'preventing any effective exercise of freedom of expression or the essence of the right is destroyed' does the state's positive obligation kick in.[260]

Scholars have argued that social media platforms wield significant influence over users' communication options to the point where they possess a state-like power over users' freedom of expression. As a result, there have been calls to impose greater fundamental rights obligations on these platforms.[261] Likewise, some argue that social media platforms have become so crucial for interpersonal communication that users would struggle to communicate effectively without them.[262] Such claims are unfounded. Social media platforms are not essential facilities,[263] nor are their services

257. Apart from those situations where fundamental rights are found to have horizontal direct effect. *See* for a full analysis of whether and when fundamental rights can be horizontally invoked §5.5.3 below. *See also* previously addressing this issue: Amélie Heldt, 'Content Moderation and Freedom of Expression – Digital Society Blog' (*HIIG*, 18 January 2023) https://www.hiig.de/en/content-moderation-on-digital-platforms/ (accessed 19 January 2023).
258. *See* for full analysis and argumentation supra §5.5.3.3.
259. Smed Larsen (n. 17).
260. *Appleby and Others v. United Kingdom* (n. 188), §47. Given the open infrastructure of the internet, it seems highly unlikely that users, when they have been excluded from one platform, can argue that they have been deprived from any effective exercise of their freedom. Most likely, they will be able to sign-up for another platform. Similarly, national courts have included various media in the physical world (newspapers, flyers, posters) in the assessment of whether 'any effective exercise' exists (*see* on this especially the practice in the Netherlands, *supra* §2.2.3.2). However, a different conclusion might be reached when all social media platforms would adopt a single strategy to exclude certain types of legal content. If an individual would like to voice a perhaps unpopular opinion and *all online platforms* have restricted the dissemination of that type of content, one could wonder how much of an effective alternative the media in the physical world offer for this individual. This dilemma will be discussed more thoroughly later in Chapter 6 when discussing the indirect application of the freedom of expression.
261. Susan Benesch (n. 31); Burkell and others (n. 27); Helberger, Pierson and Poell (n. 31); McCartney (n. 27); Schäfer (n. 28); Castells (n. 28); Telegen (n. 29).
262. McMullan (n. 33); Morris and Sarapin (n. 27); Heldt, 'Merging the "Social" and the "Public"' (n. 29); Bruns and Highfield (n. 30).
263. *See* for an analysis §5.5.5.2 below. *See* for a reflection on the regulation of social media platforms as public utilities §9.2.2.

indispensable for users to express their views and share their ideas. While one may argue that the *entire social media system* is crucial for communication in the digital age, this does not constitute a compelling rationale to restrict an *individual* platform's fundamental right to property. Moreover, some argue that the increase in (European) legislation, such as obligations for social media companies to remove illegal content, has indirectly limited the scope of the protection under the right to freedom of expression in a way that has not been seen before these social media platforms emerged.[264] However, these types of regulations have not limited the scope of the users' freedom of expression. Rather, they solely pertain to the enforcement of pre-existing laws.[265] The burden of enforcement is transferred to these social media platforms, but that in itself does not affect the *substantial* scope of the right. The scope of the right to freedom of expression never included these types of illegal content, to begin with.[266]

The transfer of the enforcement burden upon private actors could lead to *procedural* problems. As a means to avoid potential liability, platforms may choose to turn to overblocking questionable content.[267] Overblocking content does not limit the substantial scope of the freedom of expression, though, in practice, it can limit users' scope of expression on these services. Since overblocking may lead to a breach of contract, these issues are best dealt with by contract law. Challenging moderation decisions on the basis of contract law is increasingly (and successfully) taking place in the examined Member States.[268]

Scholars call to rely on IHRL or constitutional norms to govern content moderation practices and focus on the effects rather than the source of the problem. These approaches also oversee the limitations to the right to property as a means in itself to constrain platforms' private governance power.[269] Starting from the right to property does not mean that the right to property is placed above other fundamental rights or is/should be valued higher. Rather, with every layer that builds upon the right to

264. Balkin (n. 11).
265. The types of illegal content that must be removed is equally illegal in a physical context, such as for example terrorist and hate speech content, or trademark and copyright infringements.
266. *See, e.g.*, the recent case of the Tribunale di Roma (5 December 2022), n. 17909/2022, where the court reached the conclusion that Meta (Facebook) was allowed to suspend the account of the far-right association Casapound for its dissemination of hate speech content. The court concludes, in short, that hate speech does not fall within the freedom of expression, and as such, it was within the competences of Meta to decide to remove the content. Opposingly, the court points towards Meta's interest to remove such content to avoid any liability (in line with Art. 14 e-Commerce Directive).
267. *See* specifically on the risk of overblocking due to (indirect) state influence §6.2.1.
268. In Italy, users have been awarded non-material damages of up to EUR 14,000 for 'overblocking'. Overblocking is, in a contractual perspective, better referred to as a 'wrongful moderation decision', since the blocking in most cases also goes against the platforms' own user terms.
269. *See* Ugo Mattei and Alessandra Quarta, *The Turning Point in Private Law: Ecology, Technology and the Commons* (Edward Elgar Publishing 2019), p. 12: 'limits to the powers of the owner [proprietor] are diffuse and generally accepted by everyone as a necessary condition of relational life. For this reason, exceptions to the owner's right to exclude unwanted interferences with her property exist in every legal system.'

property, the right is further limited. By first defining the exact scope of the platform's power to govern the freedom of expression of the users on their platform (*lex lata*), one can subsequently criticise whether this scope should be increased or decreased (*lex ferenda*). That process can best be addressed starting from the origin of the platform power: the right to property. The right to freedom of expression is an element that comes into play when assessing the effects of content moderation but is not suitable as the starting point to address access restrictions and content moderation.[270] Fundamentally, the right to freedom of expression and the right to property differ in their scope of application. The right to freedom of expression applies between the state and its nationals. By contrast, the scope of the right to property can be invoked against the state and *directly against third parties* due to the nature of the right to property.[271] The right to property gives the proprietor a positive right to enter into an agreement with a third party to regulate the use of the property and a negative right to exclude another party from entering the property.[272] This third-party application of the right to property has been explicitly recognised by three of the examined Member States (Germany, Italy, and the Netherlands) through codification in national legislation and can, by deduction, also be transposed to the fourth (Denmark).[273] The right to property, therefore, forms the only viable starting point for defining the applicable law, as it is capable of including the rights and interests of *all parties*, not solely the platforms' users. It also addresses *all the layers of discussion* on access restrictions.

Consequently, the roadmap's foundational layer starts from the proprietor's right to property, from which two lines emerge (*see* Figure 3.2). These two lines reflect, respectively, the freedom to use the property as pleased and the right to exclude (*ius excludendi*). Additionally, as will be shown later in §4.3, the freedom to conduct a business supports the rights of the proprietor to the extent that it also protects its economic interests. Starting from the right to property allows the roadmap to stay within the existing legal framework in the Member States.

---

270. *See* this line of argumentation also in: Palka (n. 34); Alessandro Morelli and Oreste Pollicino, 'Metaphors, Judicial Frames and Fundamental Rights in Cyberspace' (2019) https://papers.ssrn.com/abstract=3422946 (accessed 29 September 2022).
271. *Frank Steinhoff and Others v. European Central Bank* (2019) Cúirt Ghinearálta Case T-107/17, §96; *Ledra Advertising and Others v. Commission* (2016) ECLI:EC:C:2016:701, §66: 'That provision, which states that everyone has the right to own his or her lawfully acquired possessions, is a rule of law intended to confer rights on individuals.' However, whether Charter provisions can at all confer direct horizontal effect is point of debate. *See* on this debate further §5.5.3.1.
272. With some going as far as to argue that the law of exclusion is the dominant approach to property: Mattei and Quarta (n. 269) 13.
273. In Denmark, only the freedom of contract is generally recognised. Though, if one can conclude a contract in which the use of property is regulated, there must be a negative side of that freedom. That negative side is the choice to not enter into an agreement on the use of the property, which corresponds to the negative right to exclude other persons from using it. *See* for a similar conclusion on the overlap between the freedom of contract and the right to property: Norbert Reich, *General Principles of EU Civil Law* (Intersentia 2014), p. 24.

Figure 3.2 The Foundational Layer on the Basis of the Right to Property

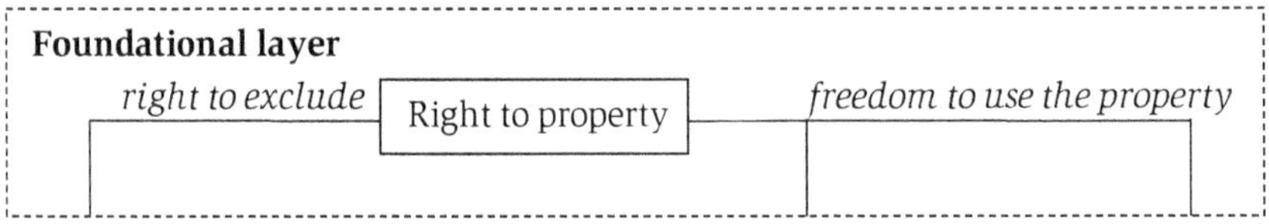

The above conclusion does not mean any intent to exclude IHRL and fundamental rights from the *entire* discussion on access and moderation issues. Their role is of significant importance in reaching a final conclusion. Their value comes into play (indirectly) in the access layer of the roadmap. Its protection is also used to interpret open norms in the content layer and must simultaneously be observed when enforcing user terms as a direct consequence of the Digital Services Act's Article 14. For the problem of overblocking, the right to freedom of expression will prove a helpful counterbalance to interpreting open norms and defining the scope of content moderation policies. Platforms can opt to moderate access and content in a way that goes beyond what is prescribed by law. This type of private governance over speech is not due to the indirect influence of the state over social media platforms but is the consequence of the social media platform's freedom of contract that allows such limitations to the permissible scope of interaction on its service. Those motives are just as much economical (creating an attractive space for advertisers) as they are political (supporting certain world views) and intended to eliminate legal risks (potential fines for secondary liability or fines for hosting illegal content). It is the normative choice of the platform that limits users' ability to interact on the platform within the full scope under the right to freedom of expression, but this normative choice is neither influenced nor connected - neither directly nor indirectly - to the state.

3.2.2 The Access Layer: Open, Forced, and Conditional Access

The second layer covers the outcome of the application of the property rights allocated in the foundational layer. The access layer concerns users' possibility to access property, or opposingly, to what extent a proprietor can exclude (certain groups of) people from accessing the platform's service (*see* Figure 3.3). From the comparative study, it follows that three distinct types of access can be distinguished: *forced, open,* and *conditional* access. Additionally, there is one type of absolute refusal based on the proprietor's right to exclude, which is referred to as *denied* access. A proprietor can decide to restrict access to its property, resulting in denied access. It can also decide to offer anyone access with or without imposing specific access conditions. Access problems that are discussed as part of the *access layer* always concern *ex ante* restrictions, meaning that they are imposed before the user has had access to the property or the service offered.[274]

274. The difference between *ex ante* and *ex post* restrictions and the (legal) effects of this difference on users is discussed in more detail below in §5.3.

Figure 3.3 The Access Layer on the Basis of the Right to Property

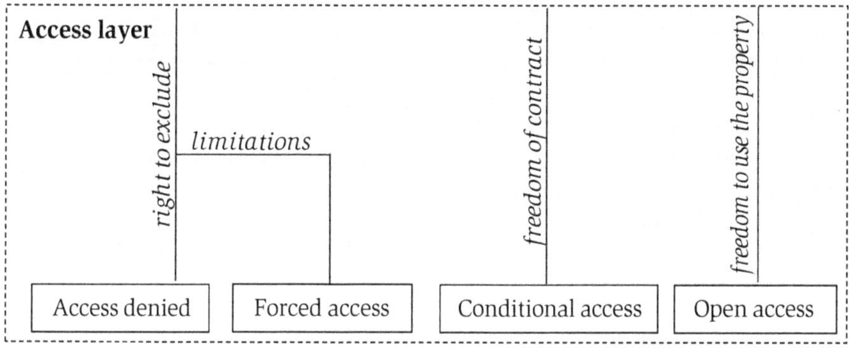

The choice between an access denial, open access, and conditional access falls within the proprietor's right to property. To start with the latter, denied access covers the situation where third parties are denied access to the property in full.[275] It does not distinguish between individual parties – *all* third parties' access or *all members* of a certain group's access is refused. From the point of view of the right to property, this is the purest application of the right to exclude. However, the right to exclude is not absolute. Under certain circumstances, the proprietor has an obligation to contract third parties. The latter leads to forced access. Following the results of the comparative study, third parties' forced access can be imposed on the basis of competition law, equality laws and anti-discrimination legislation, and by specific national legislation on public and social use rights.[276] Whether or not the claim is successful depends on the qualification of the proprietor's service, the societal interest, or the personal interests of the person who was denied access.

On the other side of the access layer is the proprietor's choice to allow access. This choice can lead to either open or conditional access. Open access concerns properties that have been opened for or services that are offered to the general public without any restrictions. Potential customers do not need to accept any terms of service before entering. In the physical world, these cover, for example, supermarkets and other generally accessible places. In the online world, platforms offering this type of access are scarce, but they do exist.[277] If a proprietor decides to provide access under certain house rules or terms of service, the access to the property is considered conditional. Only if a third party fulfils and accepts the conditions set by the proprietor,

275. Examples of current social media platforms that apply either one of the four different access restrictions can be found in §5.4.
276. For social media platforms, more limitations can be identified. *See* for the discussion on the various limitations to the platform's right to exclude and a full analysis of their application §5.5 below.
277. For example, the open camera chatbox *Chatroulette*, which does not apply any general terms of conditions, apart from a (vague and non-binding) choice of jurisdiction. *See* https://chatroulette.com/terms (accessed 26 September 2022). *See* more examples and the requirements of open access-platforms below in §5.4.1.

the person can access the property. For such conditional access, the contract between a platform and its users determines the platform's obligations to offer its services and, therewith, the scope to access and use the property. Examples of such a platform are generally well-known social media platforms such as Meta's Facebook and Instagram, Twitter, or TikTok.[278] In the physical world, these types of access cover the access to, for example, hotels, restaurants, or football stadiums.

For *ex ante* restrictions in the access layer, only the limitations to proprietor's *ius excludendi* serve as possible grounds to object to an access refusal. Since there is no agreement between the user and the proprietor yet, there are no contractual redress mechanisms to invoke.

3.2.3 The Content Layer: Defining the Conditions of Conditional Access

When a person has been given access through one of the three access types, the person 'lands' in the content layer. The content layer concerns the rules applicable to define the scope of the terms of service and the measures applicable to open access-property. It also outlines the measures of legal redress that persons can invoke to oppose access and moderation limitations that are imposed *ex post*. Opposed to the *ex ante* restrictions in the access layer, the content layer solely concerns *ex post* restrictions, meaning that the third party has (had) access to the service. Consequently, access and moderation decisions in the content layer are subject to the contractual internal redress mechanisms and to the legal remedies in national law.[279]

Following the results of the comparative study, the content layer is divided into two separate streams: the open access-stream and the contract-stream. The first concerns open access-property. If any restriction is imposed on the access or the use of open access-property, it must be based on an objective reason. The latter is to be defined by the indirect effect of fundamental rights or through general principles of private law.[280] The contract-stream stems from conditional and forced access. Deciding on the legitimacy of access and content restrictions in the contract-stream is more complicated than the system for open access-property. The assessment requires, first, to determine whether the agreement between the parties is valid and enforceable. To determine whether the agreement is valid, the agreement between the third party and the proprietor must fulfil the basic principles of contract law. To define whether the agreement is valid and enforceable, the requirements for the formation of a contract and the validity of the contractual terms are assessed. Mandatory rules of public policy can dictate specific rules that cannot be derogated from by an agreement – even if the parties agree on it. These cover, for example, rules on consumer protection, such as the

278. *See* further on the characteristics and requirements to qualify as a conditional platform §5.4.2. below.
279. Internal complaints mechanisms will become mandatory when the DSA comes into force. *See* on this §7.4.1.1.
280. The functioning of the general right of use is discussed in §6.3.

black and grey lists on unfair terms[281] or specific national rules on the removal of access (e.g., the German Network Enforcement Act). Moreover, all examined Member States in Chapter 2 have open norms through which the agreement between proprietor and third party must be reviewed. For Denmark, that is the unfairness test in §36 of the Agreement Act. Similar are the German test of reasonableness in §307 (for standard terms), the Dutch *redelijkheid en billijkheid* in Article 6:248, and the Italian *buona fede* in Article 1375 of the Italian Civil Code. In Germany and the Netherlands, and arguably Italy,[282] to interpret these norms, the interests (including the fundamental rights) of all parties involved are weighed and balanced. The assessment of the mandatory rules of public policy and the interpretation of the open norms of private law can lead to two conclusions. The user term(s) are valid and enforceable or invalid and unenforceable (*see* Figure 3.4).

Figure 3.4 The Content and the Enforcement Layer Based on the Right to Property

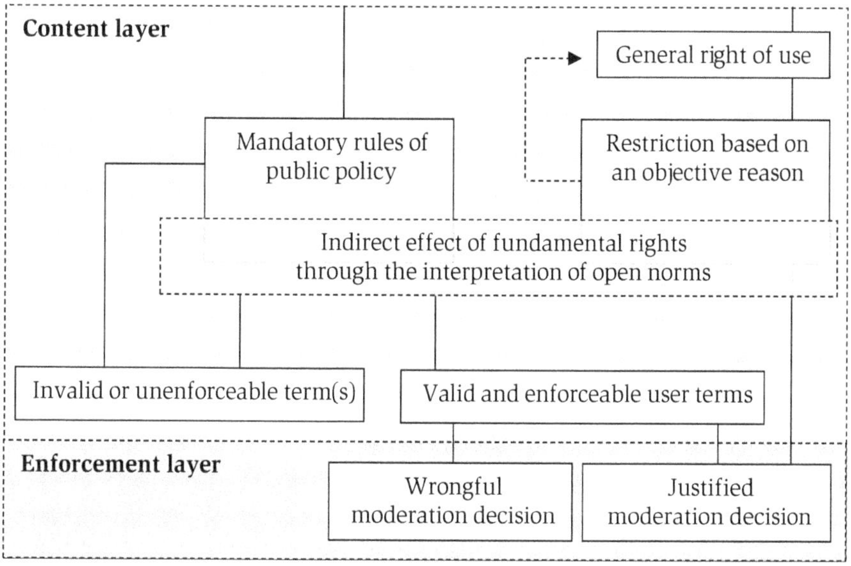

The latter is a final conclusion – user terms that are unenforceable do not have any legal effect, and as such, an access decision based on an unenforceable user term

281. Following from the Council Directive 93/13/EEC of 5 April 1993 on unfair terms in consumer contracts.

282. The effect of fundamental rights did not show from the comparative study on access restrictions, but has been argued in relation to other case law by Chantal Mak in *Fundamental Rights in European Contract Law: A Comparison of the Impact of Fundamental Rights on Contractual Relationships in Germany, the Netherlands, Italy, and England* (Kluwer Law International; sold and distributed in North, Central, and South America by Aspen 2008). Consequently, also in Italy, fundamental rights can come into play to fill the open norms of private law.

is null or void. If the user term is enforceable, it forms a valid part of the agreement, has legal effect, and can form the basis for an access decision. Supposedly, for forced access cases, invalidity of the terms will spark a new obligation to contract.[283] If the agreement lives up to the basic principles of contract law, the agreement between the two parties is, in principle, a valid agreement. The parties are bound by the obligations in the agreement. A breach of those obligations can be enforced.

3.2.4 The Enforcement Layer: Consequences of Breaching the Terms

The fourth and last layer concerns (the specific obligations for) the execution of contractual sanctions in case of a breach of the terms of service and the contractual and legal remedies available to oppose these sanctions. Following the new rules in Article 14 DSA, imposing restrictions on social media platforms is subjected to increased procedural rules. Furthermore, imposing sanctions for breaching house rules can lead to wrongful moderation decisions, even though the access or moderation decision has been based on a valid contractual term. These types of decisions cover the situation where a bouncer decides to refuse access on the basis of a wrong interpretation of a property's house rule. It also concerns situations where an online platform's algorithm wrongly flags and deletes content for breaching the user terms when, in fact, it does not, or a decision is taken without sending a necessary warning. These wrongful moderation decisions constitute a breach of contract and should be dealt with as such. The proprietor has offered to provide a service and does not live up to that promise. However, in the national case law, differences have been observed in applying the traditional contract remedies to the sphere of social media platforms.[284]

3.3 CONCLUSION: COMBINING THE ELEMENTS AND LAYERS OF THE ROADMAP

The above allows for an answer to the second sub-question: *Based on the findings of the comparative study, which elements can be used as the building blocks of the roadmap?*

First, the framework of the roadmap is made up of four layers, covering the legal foundation, the access to the property, the control over the behaviour/content within the property, and the enforcement of terms and services, respectively. Within each of these layers, specific elements make up the building blocks of the roadmap. The foundational layer includes the starting point, which is the right to property, and the

283. This discussion is named '*the infinity loop of forced access*' and is addressed in §5.4.4.1.
284. Compare for example the differences in awarding (immaterial) damages for the deletion of content and/or the suspension of user accounts, which practice varies greatly between the different Member States. The underlying cause seems to be the court's normative interpretation of 'damage' in the sphere of platforms, varying from views that deny all damages since 'posts on social media platforms do not have value' to the extreme on the contrary where large sums are awarded for wrongful moderation decisions. These discussions pose for interesting further research, where one could question whether and how these systems can be harmonised better and whether users can forum-shop to claim most damages.

two rights emerging from that starting point: the right to exclude (*ius excludendi*) and the freedom to use the property. Extending these lines into the access layer leads to the following elements: the four types of access (open, forced, conditional and denied access). The fourth type - denied access - marks an endpoint in the roadmap. After a valid decision to exclude all access, a person cannot take any legal steps to oppose that decision. For the other three types, the content layer further outlines their scope. For open access, the important elements within the content layer are formed by the general right of access and the restriction based on an objective reason, which together define whether a person can legally oppose an access or moderation decision. The elements for conditional and forced access are merged in the content layer and concern the validity of the terms of service that are applied for these types of access. The elements in this layer consist of the terms' compliance with the basic principles of contract law, the mandatory rules of public policy and the indirect effect of fundamental rights through the interpretation of open norms. The content layer includes one more endpoint of the roadmap: (an) invalid and/or unenforceable user term(s). Opposingly, terms that fulfil the basic principles of contract law and live up to the mandatory rules of public policy are valid and enforceable. The enforcement of that last category is addressed in the fourth layer. The enforcement layer includes two possible outcomes of moderation decisions: wrongful moderation decisions and justified moderation decisions.

The elements identified for the roadmap in this chapter are applicable to both physical and online property. However, to effectively use the roadmap to resolve access and moderation issues on social media platforms, the individual elements must be further deepened to reflect and address the specific characteristics of these types of properties, as well as current discussions in the literature. The tailoring of the individual layers to fit the characteristics of social media platforms forms the focus point of the second part of this book.

PART II Creating a Roadmap Fit for Social Media Platforms

CHAPTER 4
The Foundational Layer: Access Restrictions as a Property Problem

4.1 DIGGING INTO THE RIGHT TO PROPERTY'S (ONLINE) APPLICATION

This chapter marks the beginning of the book's second part. The second part focuses on interpreting the different elements of the roadmap to fit the specific problems on social media platforms. The results of the comparative study show that national courts predominantly address online access problems by applying the right to property. Contrary to this national practice, it has been argued in the legal literature that these problems would be best or better addressed from a constitutional or international human rights law starting point. The previous chapter has shown that, despite these opposing views in the literature, the right to property forms the actual starting point for courts to address access and moderation problems on social media platforms. Following this conclusion, an outline for a roadmap on online access problems was developed on the basis of the right to property. For the roadmap to function effectively, its elements must be adjusted to fit the specific circumstances of social media platforms.

Referring back to *the content square based on Balkin's speech triangle* outlined in the introduction, this research addresses two of the lines indicated by the content square: the private governance line between the social media platform and the speaker and the infrastructure regulation between the state and the social media platform. This chapter concerns the latter. The restrictions that are (or can be) imposed by states on social media platforms define the freedom that social media platforms have to exclude persons from accessing their services. This chapter's aim is, therefore, to outline the exact scope of the right to property as it applies to social media platforms. In the analysis of this chapter, the scope of the right to property as defined by Article 17 of the European Charter of Fundamental Rights and Article P1-1 ECHR is followed.

The chapter first outlines the right's scope and the object of the protection. This is followed by an outline of the proprietor's exclusive rights. Third, the right to property's interaction with the freedom to conduct a business is addressed. The CJEU regularly invokes the freedom to conduct business in Article 16 of the Charter, in addition to the right to property,[285] even though it seemingly does not have any individual value to add to the realm of social media platforms. Nonetheless, the CJEU's practice has been picked up as a new view for internet regulation.[286] The chapter concludes with an answer to the third sub-question.

4.2 THE RIGHT TO PROPERTY'S OBJECT OF PROTECTION

To effectively apply the roadmap to the realm of social media platforms, it is necessary to conclude whether access to social media platforms and their 'online space' falls within the scope of the right to property.[287] However, 'property' is not necessarily equally interpreted according to the national legal systems in Member States. A European property law does not exist – despite attempts to reach a European Civil Code or arguments for a European law of property.[288] In addition to, and as a consequence of,[289] the variations in the national systems, there is no unanimity on whether *virtual property* and *virtual spaces* should be granted equal rights as physical property. This book does not offer a stance on what a potential European property law could or should look like. The analysis included below does not reflect the various differences in the interpretation of the right to property in the national legal systems of the Member States, nor would that be necessary. European law poses a vast source of influence for the interpretation of 'property' in the national systems. The European Single Market and the freedoms of goods, persons, services, and capital cover aspects that interfere with national property laws.[290] The differences in the interpretations and definitions of property in the Member States do not necessarily affect the practical application of the roadmap. On the basis of the results of the comparative study it shows that national courts have addressed social media platforms' restrictive measures through a lens of access – whether or not they explicitly refer to the positive and negative elements of the

285. *See, e.g.*, *Case C-200/96 (Metronome Musik)* (CJEU), §21; *Case C-265/87 (Schräder)* (1989) ECLI:EU:C:1989:303 (CJEU), §15; *Case C-210/03 (Swedish Match)* (2004) ECLI:EU:C:2004:802 (CJEU), §72.
286. Oreste Pollicino, 'Internet Regulation: Not a Matter of Freedom of Speech, but Freedom to Conduct Business' (*Help Net Security*, 26 January 2021) https://www.helpnetsecurity.com/2021/01/26/internet-regulation-freedom/ (accessed 8 February 2021).
287. *See* on the difficulties to define property within virtual spaces: Alessandra Quarta, 'La Dicotomia Bene-Servizio Alla Prova Del Supporto Digitale'.
288. *See, e.g.*, a study on the common elements of European countries' property laws: Christian von Bar, *Gemeineuropäisches Sachenrecht* (CH Beck 2015).
289. The German Civil Code (§90) defines property rights as the most complete right a person can have on a *physical* object. This excludes by definition the equal recognition of virtual property. Other European Member States have a less stringent interpretation of 'property' and therefore the discussion on virtual property can have a different outcome.
290. Eveline Ramaekers, *European Union Property Law: From Fragments to a System* (Intersentia; Metro 2013). Sjef Van Erp, 'European Property Law as New Private Law?' (*Property*, 12 July 2016) https://property.jotwell.com/european-property-law-as-new-private-law/ (accessed 27 February 2023).

right to property. Furthermore, the European Charter of Fundamental Rights and the European Convention on Human Rights outline the minimum protection that must necessarily be offered by the Member States.[291] All Member States must safeguard the protection offered by Article 17 of the Charter. Moreover, the scope of 'possessions' in ECHR Article P1-1 has an autonomous meaning, superseding the legal categorisation of property in domestic law.[292] As such, despite the national differences, Articles 17 and P1-1 can serve as a base for the interpretation of property for the application of the roadmap.

This paragraph starts with outlining the objects that are protected under the right to property in the Charter and the ECHR. Following this assessment of the scope of Article 17 Charter and Article P1-1 ECHR, the discussions on *virtual* property rights in the literature are addressed in more detail, followed by a final take on the inclusion of social media platforms' assets and 'virtual space' within the scope of property rights.

4.2.1 The Object of Protection under the Right to Property

The right to property is protected under Article 17(1) of the Charter.[293] Article 17(2) equals the above protection to *intellectual* property. The object of the protection of Article 17(1) is a 'possession', which term must be interpreted autonomously and confers a broad scope.[294] It is settled case law that the scope of 'possessions' is broader than mere physical goods.[295] However, the exact scope of the term 'possession' cannot be deducted from a textual interpretation of Article 17 nor of Article P1-1 ECHR. Defining 'possession' or 'property' is therefore left to the interpretation of the CJEU and the ECtHR.[296]

First, possessions do not necessarily have to consist of material goods,[297] but they must have an economic value in order to fall within the scope of Article 17 and Article

291. Article 17(1) Charter corresponds to Art. 1 of the Protocol to the ECHR and therefore, Art. 17(1) may not provide a lesser protection than the protection offered by equivalent provision in the ECHR, *see* Art. 52(3) of the Charter. Consequently, limitations to Art. 17 may not reduce the scope of protection above what would be allowed under Art. P1-1 ECHR. Both the case law of the CJEU and the ECtHR are therefore to be taken into consideration to define the scope of protection of the right to property.
292. ECHR, 'Guide on Article 1 of Protocol No. 1 – Protection of Property' (August 2022) 89.
293. Article 17(1) Charter: 'Everyone has the right to own, use, dispose of and bequeath his or her lawfully acquired possessions. No one may be deprived of his or her possessions, except in the public interest and in the cases and under the conditions provided for by law, subject to fair compensation being paid in good time for their loss. The use of property may be regulated by law in so far as is necessary for the general interest.'
294. *Gasus Dosier-und Fördertechnik GmbH v. the Netherlands* (1995) ECtHR 15375/89, §53.
295. *Ibid.*
296. Sabrina Praduroux, 'Property and Expropriation: Two Concepts Revisited in the Light of the Case Law of the European Court of Human Rights and the European Court of Justice' (2019) 8 European Property Law Journal 172, DOI: https://doi.org/10.1515/eplj-2019-0012.
297. *Appl. No. 46470/11 (Parrillo/Italy)* (ECtHR), §211; *Gasus Dosier-und Fördertechnik GmbH v. the Netherlands* (1995) ECtHR 15375/89, §53.

P1-1.[298] The inherent risks of entrepreneurship are not protected by the right to property. As a result of those risks, some property does not have any economic value under certain circumstances, for example, infected livestock or fish.[299] Second, possessions can be economic assets, including claims (on assets), given that such (monetary) claims are an established right that can be legally claimed.[300] Commercial interests or opportunities are not protected.[301] The CJEU, taking into consideration the ECtHR's case law on the right to property in Article P1-1, recalls that an agreement can fall within the scope of the right to property if the agreement has 'an asset value creating an established legal position under the legal system, enabling the holder to exercise those rights autonomously and for his or her own benefit', and second, unless income 'has already been earned, it is definitely payable or there are specific circumstances that can cause the person concerned to entertain a legitimate expectation of obtaining an asset', future income falls outside the scope of the right to property.[302] Third, the right to property does not protect the acquisition of property, nor does it protect the profitability of the property.[303] Only *acquired* possessions are protected. Lastly, a restriction imposing an (indirect) economic burden does not impair the substance of the right to property, as such restrictions merely regulate the exercise of the right to property.[304] In sum, the right to property safeguards against unwarranted interference with already owned assets or the continued utilisation of such assets. However, it does not safeguard the acquisition of future assets or guarantee the profitability of asset exploitation.

---

298. *Parrillo v. Italy* (ECtHR), §215. In *Parrillo v. Italy*, the ECtHR found that 'having regard to the economic and pecuniary scope of that Article, human embryos cannot be reduced to "possessions" within the meaning of that provision.' *See* on the conclusion that the use of registered internet domains as property rights: *Paeffgen Gmbh v. Germany (dec)* [2007] ECtHR 25379/04, 21688/05, 21722/05, 21770/05.
299. *Booker Aquacultur Ltd (C-20/00) and Hydro Seafood GSP Ltd (C-64/00) v. The Scottish Ministers* [2003] ECJ Joined cases C-20/00 and C-64/00; Case C-579/19 (*Cleveland Meat Company/Food Standard Agency*) (2021) ECLI:EC:C:2021:665.
300. *See* ECHR (n. 292). and the case law cited: *Pressos Compania Naviera S.A. and Others v. Belgium*, §31; *J.A. Pye (Oxford) Ltd and J.A. Pye (Oxford) Land Ltd v. the United Kingdom [GC]*, §61; *Von Maltzan and Others v. Germany (dec.) [GC]*, §74 (c); *Kopecký v. Slovakia [GC]*, §35 (c).
301. *Inuit Tapiriit Kanatami and Others v. European Commission* [2015] ECJ Case C-398/13 P.
302. *Joined Cases C-798/18 and C-799/18: Judgment of the Court (Fifth Chamber) of 15 April 2021, Federazione nazionale delle imprese elettrotecniche ed elettroniche (Anie) and Others (C-798/18), Athesia Energy Srl and Others (C-799/18) v. Ministero dello Sviluppo economico and Gestore dei servizi energetici (GSE)* (ECJ).
303. van der Donk, 'The Freedom to Conduct a Business as a Counterargument to Limit Platform Users' Freedom of Expression' (n. 10).
304. *Liselotte Hauer v. Land Rheinland-Pfalz* [1979] ECJ Case 44/79; *Ralf-Herbert Kühn v. Landwirtschaftskammer Weser-Ems* [1992] ECJ Case C-177/90; *The Queen v. The Licensing Authority established by the Medicines Act 1968 (acting by The Medicines Control Agency), ex parte Generics (UK) Ltd, The Wellcome Foundation Ltd and Glaxo Operations UK Ltd and Others* [1998] ECJ Case C-368/96; *The Queen v. Secretary of State for the Environment and Ministry of Agriculture, Fisheries and Food, ex parte HA Standley and Others and DGD Metson and Others* [1999] ECJ Case C-293/97; *Booker Aquacultur Ltd (C-20/00) and Hydro Seafood GSP Ltd (C-64/00) v. The Scottish Ministers* (n. 299); *Case C-393/19 (Plovdiv)* (2021) ECLI:EU:C:2021:8 (CJEU); These cases have previously been discussed in: van der Donk, 'The Freedom to Conduct a Business as a Counterargument to Limit Platform Users' Freedom of Expression' (n. 10).

4.2.2 Discussions on Allocating Property Rights to Virtual Spaces

For social media platforms, the scope of the right to property has led to discussions in the literature as to what property rights social media platforms own and, more specifically, *which elements* of a social media platform business (physical servers, virtual space) fall within the scope of the right to property. Following the definition of a possession outlined above, social media platforms' servers, software, technical infrastructure, and databases are protected under the right to property. Some qualify because they are material goods (servers and other hardware), whereas others are autonomous rights that have an economic value (database rights, technical infrastructure). Contrarily, whether the data on the servers, including the personal data harvested from the platform's users and content created by the users, falls within the scope of protection of the right to property is far from clear. The latest version of the Council of Europe's Guide on Article P1-1 (August 2022) does not mention virtual property, nor has the subject been the object of a case before the ECtHR or CJEU.

These digital types of property challenge the existing scope of property. In the legal literature, the discussion on how to treat digital or virtual property is divided and has been ongoing for the last decades. Two debates exist on the qualification of 'virtual property'. The first discussion concerns the existence of property rights *within* online worlds, such as a property right on a virtual sword in an online game or the protection of trademarks in the Metaverse.[305] Within this discussion, one could address the potential property rights on content created and shared on social media platforms and whether a user account falls within the right to property of the platform's user or forms property in the form of data on the platform's server.[306] As the content created by users of social media platforms is mostly captured by the laws on intellectual property, this first discussion is not further addressed here. The second discussion, however, is highly relevant and concerns property rights for the *creation* of virtual spaces. As opposed to virtual property rights within virtual worlds, this second discussion concerns property rights of the virtual world itself. That discussion is necessary to address here, because in case a virtual space is the object of a property right, the owner (here the platform operator) can make use of its *ius excludendi* to deny access to it. Similarly, denied persons can invoke the limitations to the *ius excludendi* as grounds to claim access. The discussion in the legal literature relates mainly to whether these new types of spaces can and/or should be included in the physical, immaterial, or a new third category of property rights or whether they do not qualify as property at all.

305. These discussions are far from new. In the early 2000's, the rise of virtual worlds like Second Life already gave rise to a first wave of legal scholarship on virtual property rights. Facebook's Metaverse has now sparked a second wave of scholarship.

306. Joshua Fairfield, 'Virtual Property' 85 Boston University Law Review 56, refers as 'virtual property' to, amongst others, domain names/IP addresses, e-mail accounts and user accounts, as these are 'rivalrous, persistent, and interconnected', pp. 1055 ff. Przemyslaw Palka, 'Virtual Property: Towards a General Theory' (Thesis, 2017) https://cadmus.eui.eu/handle/1814/49664 (accessed 15 November 2022), refers to 'domain names, copies of literary works, files in the cloud, and virtual items', but also bitcoin – together he calls these '*digital objects*'.

The opponents of virtual property rights argue that these virtual spaces simply do not fit within the system of property rights as their characteristics are too different from their physical counterparts. In the German literature, it has been argued that something created by software can never be qualified as 'physical' property and that a qualification of the server as physical property would lead to an impossible situation.[307] Piras states that *if* the server would be qualified as property, then any change to a file stored on the server would lead to an infringement of §1004 BGB. Arguably, even accessing a website would require changes in the server's data, which could be prohibited as an infringement of §1004. However, Piras takes the server as a physical object as a starting point and concludes on the basis thereof that an online space (e.g., a social media platform) cannot be property as it solely consists of data *inside* actual property: the server. A server is not a 'space' but an 'object' that cannot be entered.[308] Contrarily, other scholars have argued that an online space is a virtual representation of a physical space and, as such, fulfils the 'physical' requirement.[309] A similar discussion took place before German courts.[310] The discussion in German literature is constrained by the fact that the German Civil Code has a stringent interpretation of 'property' (referring only to physical objects). This textual interpretation obstructs the allocation of rights to reward the development of a virtual infrastructure in which users can communicate.[311]

Those in favour of allocating property rights refer to the effort necessary to create these virtual spaces as an argument to allocate property rights. The investment in time and money should be awarded legal protection.[312] The general opinion evolved from

307. Piras (n. 120). Piras discusses the decision of the LG Bonn (p. 55) where the court found basis in the software to allocate property rights for an online chat box. Piras critiques this approach by referencing the lacking 'materiality' of software and the existing discussion in the literature (pp. 58 ff).
308. '*Software cannot be perceived and distinguished with the human eye, even when looking at the inside of the storage medium with a microscope*', *ibid.*, p. 60.
309. Schulze (n. 120). Elsaß, Labusga and Tichy (n. 120); Feldmann and Heidrich (n. 120).
310. In 1999, in *Virtuelles Hausrecht*, the *LG Bonn* compared an online chat box directly to a physical place and confirmed the existence of a virtual house right. The software underlying the virtual space was equated with the brick and mortar of a physical building. This was confirmed in several cases that followed, *see Oberlandesgericht Köln (Virtuelles Hausrecht bei einem Chat-Forum)* (2000) 19 U 2/00; *Landsgericht Hamburg (Virtuelles elektronisches Hausverbot)* (2006) 327 O 272/06; *Landsgericht München (Internetforum)* (2006) 2 O 310/18, ECLI:DE:LGMUEN1:2006:1025.30O11973.05.0A; *Oberlandesgericht Hamburg (Sperrung einer IP-Nummer)* (2007) 4 U 99/07. In more recent case law (*Virtuelles Hausrecht II* in 2018), the *LG Offenburg* concluded likewise that a virtual house right for online platforms exists, though it cannot be invoked to overrule the agreement between the parties. Opposingly, there is a stream of decisions rejecting the existence of a virtual house right: *Oberlandesgericht Frankfurt am Main* (2009) 6 U 221/08; *Oberlandesgericht Hamburg (Screen-Scraping)* (2009) 3 U 191/08; *Oberlandesgericht Hamburg (Screen Scraping II)* (2012) 5 U 38/10. Recently, in 2020, the *OLG München* rejected the existence of a virtual house right – an access restriction can only be invoked if foreseen by user terms, *see Oberlandesgericht München (Virtuelles Hausrecht bei Social-Media-Plattformen)* (2020) ECLI:DE:OLGMUEN:2020:0107.18U1491.19PRE.0A 18 U 149119.
311. However, the right to exclude can also be based on similar commercial rights or on the basis of a contractual relationship, *see* Piras pp. 162 ff. Through this alternate terminology, the German system would allow social media platforms to exercise a right to exclude.
312. Michaela MacDonald, 'The Case for Virtual Property' (2016).

viewing these digital assets through a lens of immaterial property rights[313] to the argument that digital assets share the qualities of physical property and should, therefore, be protected equally.[314] Others have argued that digital property does not seamlessly fit within the category of physical property or immaterial property and that updating the system is desirable.[315] In their view, digital objects differ significantly from tangible objects, most of which differences can be traced back to the digital objects' creation by code. Palka names, for example, the design choice to include or exclude rivalrous objects in a game, which possibility simply does not exist in the physical world. On the basis hereof, he concludes that the system of property rights lacks a third category to substitute material and immaterial property: *digital* property. In line with Palka's conclusions on digital property, the virtual *space* created by the platform becomes an independent object of protection under the right to property alongside the physical hardware and software.[316] To sustain this argument, he dissects this virtual space from the actions performed by the platform to create and sustain this space (maintaining the servers, updating software, etc.) and argues that these virtual spaces differ significantly from previous mediums used for communication. For example, a telephone provides a means for communication between person A and person B, whereas person A and person B interact on many more levels in a digital space on a platform. Within the latter, person A and person B have (digital) rights, including ownership over digital goods (e.g., the ownership over a digital sword in an online game), something that is impossible 'within' other mediums of communication. Following Palka, the code applied by platforms to sustain their virtual space is similar to private parties building a high fence around a private park and placing guards at the entrance. Users' *digital presence* creates a legal relationship to the digital space, similar as *physical presence* creates relationships between a person and the physical world.

313. Molly Stephens, 'Sales of In-Game Assets: An Illustration of the Continuing Failure of Intellectual Property Law to Protect Digital-Content Creators' (2002) 80.
314. Fairfield (n. 306); Greg Lastowka and Dan Hunter, 'The Laws of the Virtual Worlds' (29 May 2003) https://papers.ssrn.com/abstract=402860 (accessed 15 November 2022).
315. Przemyslaw Palka, 'Virtual Property: Towards a General Theory' (Thesis, 2017) https://cadmus.eui.eu/handle/1814/49664 (accessed 15 November 2022), pp. 107, 176. Palka distinguishes between two categories of digital property: virtual items on the one hand – encompassing digital copies (of copyrighted works), cryptocurrencies, and objects in online platforms and services – and user accounts on the other. Virtual items are then subsequently characterised by six features of digital objects, all of which constitute a property right: consumable or non-consumable items, functional or aesthetic, transferable or non-transferable, exchangeable or non-exchangeable, in-game earned or bought from the provider, and whether the objects are adaptable or non-adaptable, *see* p. 191. Palka argues also that the existence of digital property rights should lead to a 'positive obligation within the negative dimension of a property right – i.e. an obligation to keep sustaining the service'. *See* an equal conclusion on the need to create a third category of property: Quarta, 'La Dicotomia Bene-Servizio Alla Prova Del Supporto Digitale' (n. 287); Alessandra Quarta, 'Contenuti digitali e beni con elementi digitali: c'è ancora posto per la proprietà privata?' in Teresa Pasquino, Alberto Rizzo and Mauro Tescaro (eds), *Questioni attuali in tema di commercio elettronico* (Edizioni scientifiche italiane 2020); Justin Slaughter, 'Virtual Worlds: Between Contract and Property' [2008] Student Scholarship Papers https://openyls.law.yale.edu/handle/20.500.13051/5676 (accessed 27 February 2023).
316. *See* for a further discussion in a more recent work: Palka (n. 34), where he discusses whether the denial of access is a property or a contractual right (concluding on the former).

Therefore, in analogy to the property protection for physical spaces, these platform-owned digital spaces are best included within the scope of the right to property.[317] A similar outcome is reached by Quarta, though she bases that conclusion on access rights as a starting point for the definition of property.[318] Referring to the differences in the civil and common law's view on (physical) property, Mattei and Quarta summarise that the structure in both systems revolves around, first, the concentration of decision-making power about a certain thing in the hands of the owner, and second, the exclusion of any unwanted intrusion on the thing by a third party.[319] The right to exclude can then serve as a means through which property can be enjoyed, and third parties' 'power of access' forms an exemption to this means.[320] Access and non-access then form a starting point to define the object of property rights.[321]

The national case law in the comparative study in Chapter 2 revealed that the courts in the Member States predominantly apply the right to property to resolve access and moderation decisions, both to physical property and virtual spaces. Contextualising that practice with the arguments in the literature, three arguments can be made to include virtual spaces within the scope of the right to property. First, allocating property rights to virtual spaces seems to be the solution that safeguards the economic interests of social media platforms best. Through property rights, the operator/creator of the virtual space is able to deny access to that space, make use of the space in the way he/she pleases, and to regain the investment that was put into the creation of that space. Second, property rights offer the best opportunities for persons wishing to access these virtual spaces. Virtual spaces fulfil the two requirements set out by Mattei and Quarta, meaning that social media platforms, in principle, can deny access to their virtual space. Simultaneously, users gain access to the limitations of that right to exclude. That is a significant increase in the opportunities that the users have to contest access restrictions by platforms. In exchange for the allocation of property rights, platform proprietors have to accept that third parties, under certain circumstances, can access their space freely. Property rights, therefore, not only safeguard the economic interests of the platform operator but also increase the protection of (aspiring) users. Third, the allocation of property rights to virtual spaces seems to be most in line with the definition of property based on Article 17 of the Charter and with the case law of the

317. That is, until a better regulatory system can suit these exact problems, *see ibid.*, p. 161. This view is supported in the idea that virtual worlds (such as the one in online games) function differently from physical worlds and that property rights applicable in the physical world are not simply transferrable. The underlying code of the virtual world determines the boundaries of the property's characteristics. For example, the playing rules of some online games allow players to steal each other's assets. This significantly complicates the conclusion on property rights in these types of worlds. The full discussion on property rights in such online games that have rules that vary significantly from the physical world is omitted here, but *see* for a discussion of potential problems that can emerge: James Grimmelmann, 'Virtual Worlds as Comparative Law' (2004) New York Law School Law Review.
318. Alessandra Quarta, 'Ripensare la proprietà a partire dall'accesso' (2014) https://fair.unifg.it/retrieve/de2a638f-3e47-8577-e053-3705fe0aa5f3/Ripensare%20la%20 propriet%c3%a0_AQ.pdf.
319. Mattei and Quarta (n. 269) 14.
320. *Ibid.*, 42.
321. Quarta, 'Ripensare la proprietà a partire dall'accesso' (n. 318).

CJEU. Social media platforms can autonomously exercise their rights (to sell, to use, and to restrict the use) over the virtual space for their own benefit, fulfilling the requirements of possession under Article 17 of the Charter. Moreover, in *Slovak Telekom*, the CJEU notes that a company's telecom infrastructure and the use thereof fall within the scope of the right to property.[322] In line with the arguments put forward by Palka, virtual spaces like the ones created by social media platforms should arguably have *more* protection than traditional communication services, not less. As such, there is sufficient basis to conclude that also the *virtual space* created by the platform could be protected under their right to property.[323]

4.2.3 The Exclusive Rights of the Property Owner

The proprietor of an object that falls within the scope of the right to property can decide who should or should not be allowed to use and/or enter the property. Following a textual interpretation of Article 17(1) Charter, the proprietor has the right to own, use, dispose of and bequeath of lawfully acquired possessions. It consists of two main elements: the right to use the property and the right to collect the revenue from it.[324] According to Article 52(3) Charter, Article 17(1) may not provide a lesser protection than the protection offered by Article P1-1 ECHR. Article 52(4) adds thereto that Article 17 must be interpreted in light of and in harmony with the constitutional traditions common to the Member States. Following explicit references in the case law of the Netherlands[325] and German and Italian law,[326] the right to *use* the property according to their traditions encompasses both a positive right to use the property and a negative right to refrain from such use.[327] Social media platforms can invoke the latter right of exclusion against third parties to control access to their virtual space. The platform can rely on the right to freely *use* its lawfully acquired possession – and, in line with Palka, it can govern access to the digital space the platform governs. For social media platforms, this will mean controlling the access to the tangible servers on which the data is stored. When dealing with access restrictions on social media platforms, it thus

322. *See* for a conclusion on property and the restriction of access for competitors to a company's own infrastructure: *Case C-165/19 P: Appeal brought on 22 February 2019 by Slovak Telekom, as against the judgment of the General Court (Ninth Chamber, Extended Coslmposition) delivered on 13 December 2018 in Case T-851/14: Slovak Telekom v. Commission* (ECJ), §46.
323. Przemyslaw Palka, 'Virtual Property: Towards a General Theory' (Thesis, 2017) https://cadmus.eui.eu/handle/1814/49664 (accessed 15 November 2022).
324. Case C-235/17 (European Commission/Hungary) (2019) ECLI:EU:C:2019:432, §81.
325. In *Stadionverbod Vitesse*, a stadium owner had invoked its 'house right' as a legal basis to issue a stadium ban against any third party. In the case on the lawfulness of the stadium ban, the court confirms the existence of the house right and elaborates that '[the stadium owner] can derive from the right to property the power to deny third parties' access to the premises or to impose restrictions on the permission to access. It must be assumed that Vitesse can invoke this house right in principle as an independent ground for a stadium ban', *Stadionverbod Vitesse* (n. 165), §4.2.
326. §903 German Civil Code; Art. 841 Italian Civil Code.
327. Even without explicit reference, such as the Danish system, one can argue that the freedom of contract as flows from the right to property as a positive right, as without it the 'protection of property would be very seriously lacking if contractual engagements undertaken in relation to property were not respected', *see* Reich (n. 273), p. 28.

follows from the scope of application of the right to property that, in principle, a platform can deny access to its property.

However, the protection of the right to property is not absolute (*see* Figure 4.1).[328] Article 17 controls two forms of interference: expropriation and the control of the use of the property.[329] According to the third sentence of Article 17, the use of the property can be regulated by law if such restrictions are necessary in the general interest. Various objectives have proven suitable to genuinely fulfil objectives of general interest.[330] The protection of the rights and freedoms of others (explicitly the right to freedom of expression) is recognised as an aim of general interest,[331] as well as equality and non-discrimination laws and the doctrine of essential facilities under competition law. These limitations to the free use of the right to property do not form part of the foundational layer in the roadmap and are therefore not discussed in-depth at this point. They will be thoroughly discussed as part of the access layer in Chapter 5.

Figure 4.1 Exclusive Rights under the Right to Property

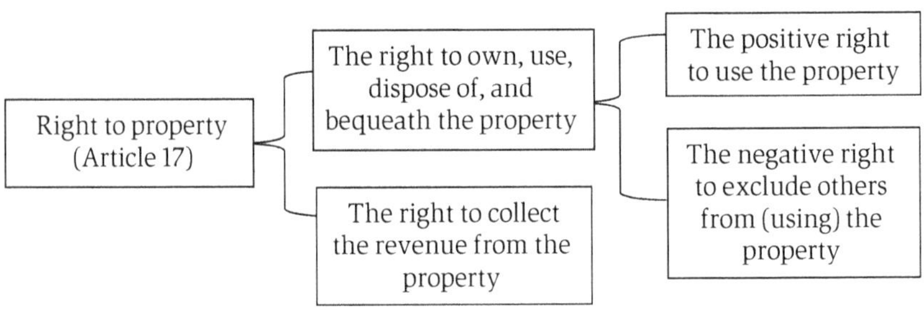

328. 'In that regard, it must be noted, first, that freedom to conduct a business and the right to property are not absolute rights but must be considered in relation to their social function', *see Deutsches Weintor eG v. Land Rheinland-Pfalz* [2012] ECJ Case C-544/10, §54; *Denise McDonagh v. Ryanair Ltd* [2013] ECJ Case C–12/11, §60; *Rectification order of 6 October 2021 Irish Ferries Ltd v. National Transport Authority Rectification of judgment Case C-570/19* (ECJ), §170.

329. The regulation of the use of the property by the government can serve to safeguard other rights, such as the freedom of expression, *see, e.g., Appl. Nos 39343/98, 39651/98, 43147/98 and 46664/99 (Kleyn and others v. The Netherlands)* [2003] ECLI:CE:ECHR:2003:0506JUD0039 34398 (ECtHR), where the access to property was limited in favour of the freedom of expression, because without this intervention, the nationals had no option to express their opinions.

330. Such as a restriction to plant vines on one's vineyard, obligations to kill and dispose of (infected) fish, or measures that limit how often cows can be milked, *see Case C-44/79 (Hauer/Land Rheinland-Pfalz)* (CJEU); *Case C-20/00 (Booker Aquaculture)* (2003) ECLI:EU: C:2003:397 (CJEU); *Case C-177/90 (Ralf-Herbert Kühn/Landwirtschaftskammer Weser-Ems)* (CJEU).

331. *Sky Österreich GmbH v. Österreichischer Rundfunk* [2013] ECJ Case C–283/11, §52: 'The safeguarding of the freedoms protected under Article 11 of the Charter undoubtedly constitutes a legitimate aim in the general interest'. An in-depth discussion of the effects hereof on the restrictions of the right to property is included below in the chapter on the access layer.

Restrictions that have the effect of depriving an owner of its property infringe the owner's right to property unless the restrictions follow the strict requirements for expropriation. The requirements for expropriation are outlined in the second sentence of Article 17.[332] The line between expropriation and the control of use can be hard to define. The decisive factor for solely 'controlling use' is whether the proprietor remains the owner of the property and to what extent the power to take formal decisions regarding the property is retained by the proprietor (e.g., selling the property).[333] As such, a temporary and reversible measure does not constitute expropriation of the right to property[334] but can nonetheless lead to an infringement of the right if the measure does not fairly balance the protection of the right to property and the requirement of a general interest.[335] In light of the discussion above on the inclusion of users' personal data in the scope of the platforms' right to property, *if* this data falls within the scope of the right to property, it does not mean that the use of users' personal data for economic gains cannot be (substantially) restricted. A measure that, as a result, would severely restrict the profitability of the sale and/or use of personal data does not expropriate the data, but since it nonetheless governs the use of the property, the measure must be necessary in the general interest. If the regulation is aimed at increasing consumer protection, even a substantial negative economic consequence for the proprietor can be justifiable.[336]

Social media platforms will not be able to oppose (increasing) measures on the deletion of illegal content. The support for the latter argument can be found in the joined CJEU cases of *Booker Aquaculture* and *Hydro Seafood GSP,*[337] where the concerned property shared similar characteristics. In both cases, the dispute concerned the legal obligation to destroy fish infected with epidemic diseases. The proprietors objected to the legal obligation as it would unjustly hinder the use of their property (the fish). The CJEU recalls that such measures do not fall within the scope of expropriation.[338] The CJEU's conclusion on the interference with the use of the property consists of two arguments. First, any business carries commercial risks. The occurrence of diseases in fish is one of them. Loss of such property is, therefore, inherently connected to running a business. Second, the infected fish had no 'marketable value', nor was it possible to determine the value of other fish that were not (yet) showing signs of disease because these fish might also have been infected. These two factors can be equally applied to the presence of illegal content on social media platforms. First,

332. Article 17(1) Charter, Case C-235/17 (European Commission/Hungary) (2019) ECLI:EU:C:2019:432, §87.
333. *Appl. No. 12033/86 (Fredin v. Sweden)* 18 February 1991 (ECtHR).
334. Case T-245/15 (Oleksandr Viktorovych Klymenko/Council of the European Union) (2017) ECLI:EU:T:2017:792 (CJEU), §208. Case C-352/20 (HOLD Alapkezelő Befektetési Alapkezelő Zrt.) ECLI:EU:C:2022:606, §78.
335. *Appl. No. 7151/75 (Sporrong and Lonnroth v. Sweden)* 23 September 1982 (ECtHR).
336. Case C-579/19 (Cleveland Meat Company/Food Standards Agency) (2021) ECLI:EU:C:2021:665, §97.
337. *Booker Aquacultur Ltd (C-20/00) and Hydro Seafood GSP Ltd (C-64/00) v. The Scottish Ministers* (n. 299).
338. §80: 'The measures referred to do not deprive farm owners of the use of their fish farms but enable them to continue to carry on their activities there.'

running a social media platform means that millions of people share information in an online space. Similar to the occurrence of epidemic diseases in livestock and fish, such presence results in an inherent risk of illegal activity. As such, the appearance of illegal content poses a business risk equal to that of the appearance of disease in livestock. Furthermore, the illegal content does not have any marketable value. Social media platforms cannot contractually agree with their users to disseminate illegal content, and by law, these platforms are furthermore obliged to delete illegal content as soon as they become aware of its presence. The illegal content is, therefore, unlawfully hosted on the platform's server. One could imagine that the fish without signs of disease could, in fact, still be sold. In those circumstances, the fish presumably has not yet lost all its market value. Similarly, one could argue that illegal content has value in attracting certain users to the platform (e.g., the business model of the Pirate Bay). In his opinion of the case, Advocate General Mischo states on the underlying reasoning of the rule to destroy the fish that 'no one would think of denying that everything that is dangerous ought to be eliminated, and that this constitutes one of the tasks of the State'.[339] He continues with a comparison of the infected fish to property infected with asbestos, neither of which would trigger a right to compensation because these properties form a danger to all others in society. Equally, illegal content is illegal for a reason: the legislator has deemed these types of content to pose a danger to society and has prohibited its dissemination. Despite its potential market value in practice, a platform would, therefore, not be able to invoke the right to property to oppose a measure obliging the deletion of illegal content.

4.3 THE INFLUENCE OF THE FREEDOM TO CONDUCT A BUSINESS

The right to property forms the basis for social media platform access and moderation decisions. Its scope is not absolute and can be limited by legislative measures that control the use of the property. In addition to the right to property, the Charter offers another freedom that is frequently invoked by the CJEU to increase the scope of protection of a proprietor: the freedom to conduct a business. Following a study of the case law of the CJEU, the freedom to conduct a business protects the freedom to exercise an economic activity, meaning that legislative measures limiting the normative power of social media platforms may not lead to the platforms' bankruptcy.[340] Consequently, the freedom to conduct a business potentially increases social media platforms' possibilities to oppose legislative measures that control the use of its property.

The freedom to conduct a business did not show up as an element of the roadmap in the first part, as it did not appear in any of the national courts in their cases on

339. Opinion to C-20/00 – Booker Aquaculture and Hydro Seafood (20 September 2001) ECLI:EU:C:2001:469, §92.
340. The conclusion on the scope of Art. 16's freedom to conduct a business and Art. 17's right to property of the Charter draws from a previous study mapping the CJEU's case law between, respectively, 1974 and 1979 until 2020. The results of this study have been published in: Van der Donk, 'The Freedom to Conduct a Business as a Counterargument to Limit Platform Users' Freedom of Expression' (n. 10).

(online) access restrictions. Presumably, this is due to the freedom's unclear scope of application. The unclear scope makes it hard to define whether the freedom to conduct a business has (or should have) any effect in a given case. That unclarity results in confusion on whether and to what extent freedom can be invoked by social media platforms or to what extent the freedom should be taken into consideration when balancing the parties' interests. This paragraph, therefore, examines whether the freedom to conduct a business can increase social media platforms' power over their property.

4.3.1 Interpreting the Scope of the Freedom to Conduct a Business

A textual interpretation of Article 16 does not provide any substantial basis for protection, as the full text of the article is condensed and rather cryptically formulated.[341] Contrary to the right to property, the freedom to conduct a business does not have any equivalent right in the ECHR.[342] Its scope is, therefore, to be defined by the text of the Charter and the CJEU. The case law of the CJEU, however, does not add any immediate interpretational value for the freedom either. Rather, 'the judgments in which the Court has had occasion to rule in this area have gone no further than either referring to the right to property or simply citing the provisions of Article 16 of the Charter'.[343] The only settled part seems to be that neither the right to property nor the freedom to conduct a business guarantees the *acquisition* of possessions, nor do they protect the *profitability* of the exploitation of owned possessions.[344]

As a consequence of mainly the CJEU's habit of frequently mentioning the freedom to conduct a business in conjugation with the right to property without making a difference between either of the rights, various opinions exist in the legal literature on the necessity to distinguish between the two rights at all. It has been argued that the freedom to conduct a business does not add any independent value as opposed to the right to property[345] and that including the freedom in the Charter has merely been housekeeping rather than a wish to create an increased scope of

341. 'The freedom to conduct a business in accordance with Union law and national laws and practices is recognized.'
342. It has been argued that the scope of Art. P1-1 ECHR can be expanded to include a similar right to economic initiative, *see* an overview of the applicable ECtHR cases in Dalia Vasariene and Lyra Jakulevičienė, 'Freedom to Conduct Business During the Covid-19 Pandemic' (2021) 26 Tilburg Law Review 16, DOI: https://doi.org/10.5334/tilr.246.
343. *Opinion of AG Cruz-Villalón to Case C-426/11 (Alemo-Herron and Others)* (CJEU), §49.
344. *Case C-398/13P (Inuit Tapiriit Kanatami and Others/Commission)* (2015) ECLI:EU:C:2015:535 (CJEU), §60. The uncertainty of profitability is inextricably linked to the economic activity of an undertaking and therefore, one cannot claim to be protected from such uncertainty, according to the CJEU in *J Nold, Kohlen- und Baustoffgroßhandlung v. Commission of the European Communities* [1974] ECJ Case 4-73, §14.
345. Peter Oliver, 'What Purpose Does Article 16 of the Charter Serve?', *General principles of EU law and European private law* (Kluwer Law International 2013); Xavier Groussot, Gunnar Thor Petursson and Justin Pierce, 'Weak Right, Strong Court – The Freedom to Conduct Business and the EU Charter of Fundamental Rights' (Social Science Research Network 2014) SSRN Scholarly Paper ID 2428181 https://papers.ssrn.com/abstract=2428181 (accessed 10 November 2020); *Opinion of AG Cruz-Villalón(Alemo-Herron and Others)* (n. 343).

protection.[346] Opposingly, it has been argued that the scope of the freedom to conduct a business is of a different nature than the right to property because Article 16 has an intrinsic 'performative' character which covers the economic opportunity to participate in the European market, rather than the protection of property itself.[347] The latter would mean that the introduction of the freedom to conduct a business in the Charter has expanded the scope of protection from the sole protection of possessions under the right to property to also include a broader economic right to participate in the market.[348]

As such, whether legal intervention interferes with the freedom to conduct a business or the right to property depends on the *effect* said measure has on either the existing property of the platform or the ability to choose how to allocate the assets of the platform for economic use. For example, an obligation to increase the types of content that are hosted on a social media platform ('must-carry obligation') forms a measure that interferes solely with the freedom to conduct a business. Such an obligation increases the amount of data on the platform's servers. The right to property does not protect the acquisition of assets or future assets - it only protects already *acquired* possessions. An obligation to host, therefore, falls outside the scope of Article 17. However, since such a measure does regulate how the platforms conduct their business - namely, how they allocate their resources and how they formulate their user terms - a must-carry obligation would interfere with the freedom to conduct a business. According to the explanatory memorandum to the Charter, the freedom to conduct a business consists of several sub-freedoms.[349] These sub-freedoms have been established in the case law of the CJEU, respectively, in the 1974 case of *Nold* and the 1979 case of *Sukkerfabriken Nykøbing*.[350] The freedom of contract, in turn, consists of two more elements: the freedom to decide whom to do business with and the freedom to determine the price of a service.[351] The CJEU consistently mentions these two sub-freedoms in their recent case law as parts of the protection under Article 16.[352] Arguably, and based on the more recent case law of the CJEU, the freedom of contract does not solely refer to these two recognised sub-freedoms but encompasses a broader protection. For example, the freedom to determine the *price* of a service arguably

346. Groussot, Petursson and Pierce (n. 345), p. 4.
347. Michele Everson and Rui Correia Gonçalves, 'Article 16', *The EU Charter of Fundamental Rights: A Commentary* (Hart Publishing 2014), at 16.04. Similar: *Opinion of AG Cruz-Villalón (Alemo-Herron and Others)* (n. 343).
348. *See* on this: FRA - European Union Agency for Fundamental Rights, 'Freedom to Conduct a Business: Exploring the Dimensions of a Fundamental Right'.
349. European Commission, 'Explanations Relating to the Charter of Fundamental Rights' (2007), on Art. 16; *see also Sky Österreich GmbH v. Österreichischer Rundfunk* (n. 331), §42. The third sub-freedom that was recognised by the Commission in 2007 covers the 'free competition' and is based on Art. 119(1) TFEU, rather than on the case law of the CJEU.
350. European Commission (n. 349); *J Nold, Kohlen- und Baustoffgroßhandlung v. Commission of the European Communities* (n. 344); *Sukkerfabriken Nykøbing Limiteret v. Ministry of Agriculture* [1979] ECJ Case 151/78.
351. *Case C-90/90 (Neu)* (1991) ECLI:EU:C:1991:303 (CJEU), §13; and *Case C-437/04 (Commission/Belgium)* (2007) ECLI:EU:C:2007:178 (CJEU), §51. Later confirmed in *Case C-283/11 (Sky Österreich)* (2013) ECLI:EU:C:2013:28 (CJEU), §43.
352. *Polkomtel sp z oo v. Prezes Urzędu Komunikacji Elektronicznej* [2017] ECJ Case C-277/16; *Joined Cases C-798/18 and C-799/18* (n. 302), §57.

extends its protection to the full determination of all the terms of the service. Additionally, the CJEU has developed in its case law a third sub-freedom concerning an undertaking's free allocation of the available resources. The freedom to determine the terms of service and the right to freely use the available resources do not (yet) form part of settled case law. However, they have been referred to by the CJEU in a way that allows for a substantiation of these sub-elements.[353] Since their application has a significant impact on the service of social media platforms, they are included in the assessment below (*see* Figure 4.2).

Figure 4.2 The Elements of the Freedom to Conduct a Business

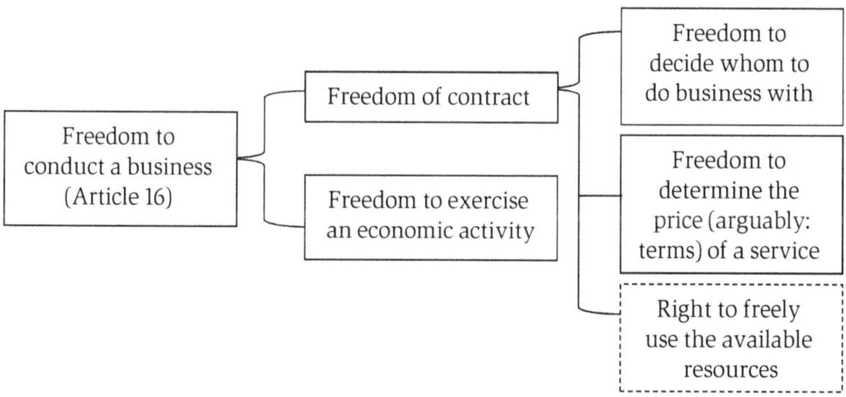

The following paragraphs discuss the individual sub-freedoms in more detail and illustrate the ways in which their protection is applicable to the service offered by social media platforms. Overarchingly for all these sub-freedoms is the fact that they 'may be subject to a broad range of interventions on the part of public authorities which may limit the exercise of economic activity in the public interest'.[354] The objective can also be rooted in the protection of the rights and freedoms of others, such as the right to freedom of expression or data protection.[355] The implications of how this broad permissible scope for limitations plays out for the different sub-freedoms are also included in the coming paragraphs. As a consequence of the influence of the freedom to conduct business on access restrictions on social media platforms, the roadmap's foundational layer will be expanded to reflect these additional sources of protection for social media platforms.

353. Compare §57 and §58 of the *Joined Cases C-798/18 and C-799/18* (n. 302).
354. *Sky Österreich GmbH v. Österreichischer Rundfunk* (n. 331), §46.
355. *Ibid.*, §66: 'the European Union legislature was entitled to adopt rules (...) which limit the freedom to conduct a business, and to give priority, in the necessary balancing of the rights and interests at issue, to public access to information over contractual freedom'.

4.3.2 The Freedom to Exercise an Economic or Commercial Activity

The freedom to exercise an economic or commercial activity protects a proprietor's free choice on how to exploit the property. The essence of this sub-freedom only protects the *continuation* of economic activity.[356] The latter means that if, as a result of a legislative measure, the undertaking goes bankrupt, the measure *directly* infringes on Article 16 of the Charter. That situation is rare. In the last fifty years, only one case before the CJEU was found to infringe on the essence of the freedom to exercise an economic activity.[357] Measures that regulate the exploitation but do not cause the end of the exploitation per se can be justifiable. A measure is justifiable if it is suitable for the attainment of the objective pursued and does not go beyond what is necessary in order to attain that objective.[358]

The list of justifiable objectives is long. It includes labelling restrictions on alcohol products (public health),[359] the regulation of the amount of hours truck drivers can work (road safety),[360] and regulating the number of bananas that can be imported into the European Union (securing a common agricultural policy).[361] A measure, in general, does not pass the necessity test if a less intrusive measure exists which is capable of achieving the same objective or goal.[362] Consequently, in principle, an undertaking must be free to dispose of and use its resources in the way it pleases. The control over the exploitation should be limited to dictating the objective or aim without prescribing how the undertaking must allocate its resources to reach that aim. This is especially the case for costly measures, such as filtering obligations.[363] A platform can be obliged to search for infringing content, though the exact measure to reach that aim cannot be prescribed as this would unduly limit the free choice on how to exercise the economic activity.[364]

In that way, the freedom to exercise an economic activity supplements the protection of the proprietor's positive right to property. This first sub-freedom protects against measures that do not fall within the scope of expropriation but nonetheless

356. van der Donk, 'The Freedom to Conduct a Business as a Counterargument to Limit Platform Users' Freedom of Expression' (n. 10).
357. *Finančné riaditeľstvo Slovenskej republiky v. BB construct sro* [2017] ECJ Case C-534/16, §41. In BB Construct, a Slovak company was subjected to an obligatory tax guarantee with a maximum of EUR 500,000. The CJEU concluded that: '(...) the provision of a guarantee – having regard to the fact that it is for a significant amount – would deprive, without justification, the company concerned of its resources from the moment of its creation and would prevent it from developing its economic activities, that guarantee is a manifestly disproportionate interference with the freedom to conduct a business.'
358. *Case C-55/94 (Gebhard)* (1995) ECLI:EU:C:1995:411 (CJEU), §37, where the CJEU mentioned the necessity test for the first time.
359. *Deutsches Weintor eG v. Land Rheinland-Pfalz* [2012] ECJ Case C-544/10, §57.
360. *Kingdom of Spain (C-184/02) and Republic of Finland (C-223/02) v. European Parliament and Council of the European Union* [2004] ECJ Joined cases C-184/02 and C-223/02, §54.
361. *Federal Republic of Germany v. Council of the European Union* [1994] ECJ Case C-280/93, §87.
362. *See* for a further discussion on the *Gebhard* test also Reich (n. 273), p. 157.
363. *Belgische Vereniging van Auteurs, Componisten en Uitgevers CVBA (SABAM) v. Netlog NV* [2012] ECJ Case C-360/10.
364. *UPC Telekabel Wien GmbH v. Constantin Film Verleih GmbH and Wega Filmproduktionsgesellschaft mbH* [2014] ECJ Case C–314/12.

would mean the economic end of the activity for which the property is used. In case a legislative measure creates significant costs for a proprietor, which potentially causes the end of the economic activity pursued with the use of the property, the right to property does not offer any protection. As concluded above, measures affecting the use of property are allowed if they are necessary in the general interest. As long as the ownership rights of the property (e.g., the power to sell) are not affected, the right to property does not protect against such a measure. Contrarily, such a measure would affect the essence of the freedom to exercise an economic activity. In short, the latter codifies the free choice to use the property for economic gain and protects the proprietor against severe economic interference that renders the economic use of the property impossible. It applies in situations where the proprietor remains the owner of the property, but exploitation is made difficult or impossible.

In the realm of social media platforms, the example of filtering policies demonstrates this difference in the scope of protection clearly. Taking as a starting point the right to property, the imposition of costly filtering obligations on social media platforms does not cause an interference with the essence of the right to property. The social media platform is not stripped from its property (it maintains the right to sell), so expropriation is ruled out. The measure does govern the use of the property. The measure must, therefore, fulfil the requirement of a general interest, which will presumably be the protection of the (intellectual property) rights of others. Thus, seemingly, a filtering measure limiting the right to property is justifiable. The imposition of these filtering obligations becomes more problematic from the point of view of the freedom to exercise an economic activity, as such a measure puts a significant economic burden on the platform's resources. If the measure renders the economic activity offered by the social media platform *fully* impossible, the platform can invoke the freedom to exercise an economic activity to oppose the measure. For the latter situation, it does not matter that the platform remains the owner of the property; what matters is the fact that the economic opportunity to exploit the property has been destroyed by the imposed matter.

Figure 4.3 The Foundational Layer of Access Restrictions on Social Media Platforms

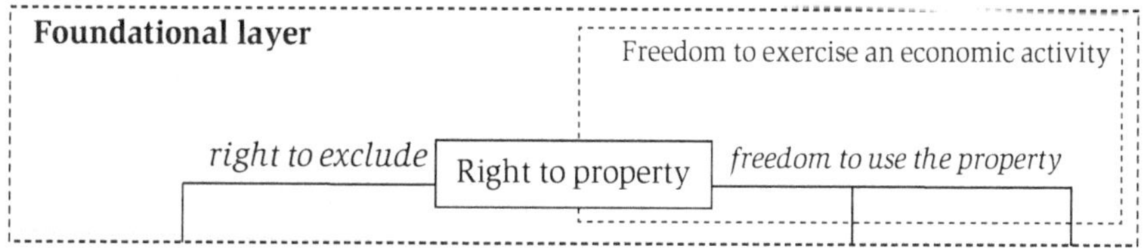

Consequently, in the application of the roadmap to the realm of social media platforms, the freedom to exercise an economic activity is included as a background protection of the positive right to property (*see* Figure 4.3). It does not extend its protection to the negative right because when exercising the right of exclusion, the proprietor has implicitly chosen not to make use of the property to exercise an economic activity but rather to exclude other parties from accessing or making use of the property. It is debatable whether the freedom to exercise an economic or commercial activity would extend to the limitations on the negative right to property (obligations to contract in the general interest). Arguably, since these obligations to offer the service do not constitute any free choice to exploit the property for economic or commercial activity, the application of this sub-freedom of the freedom to conduct a business does not extend its protection to this aspect of the right to property.

4.3.3 The Freedom of Contract

The second sub-freedom of the freedom to conduct a business is the freedom of contract. In 1979, the existence of a general principle of contractual freedom was recognised by the CJEU in *Sukkerfabrikken Nykøbing.*[365] Its scope has been deepened in the CJEU's case law before being explicitly recognised as a sub-freedom of the freedom to conduct a business by the European Commission in 2007 in its explanations relating to the Charter of Fundamental Rights.[366] The freedom of contract consists, in turn, of several sub-freedoms. For access restrictions on social media platforms, the following sub-freedoms will be discussed below: the freedom to decide with whom to do business, the freedom to decide on the terms of the contract, and the right to freely use the available resources.

4.3.3.1 The Freedom to Decide Whom to Do Business With

The CJEU first referred to what is now known as the freedom to decide whom to do business with in the 1991 case of *Neu.*[367] The freedom protects against measures that would adversely affect the free choice of a contractual partner. In *Neu*, the imposed measure did not limit the decision on whom to do business with explicitly, though the measure negatively affected the dairy producer in case the producer would switch from one purchaser to another. Indirectly, that meant that, due to the imposed measure, the dairy producer would be better off remaining with the same purchaser. As such, the measure was found contrary to the freedom to decide whom to do business with as it indirectly impaired the dairy producer's freedom to choose its contractual partner. The measure was deemed inappropriate to reach the intended aim (ensuring the quantity of milk in the Community) and therefore formed an unjustifiable interference with the freedom to conduct a business.

The case of *Neu* highlights the difficulty in distinguishing between the right to property and the freedom to conduct a business, and apart from *Neu*, there have unfortunately not been any cases before the CJEU that focus on this specific sub-freedom. Seemingly, if the milk supplier had invoked the right to freely use the property (the milk) on the basis of Article 17, an equal conclusion would have been reached. The

365. *Sukkerfabriken Nykøbing Limiteret v. Ministry of Agriculture* [1979] ECJ Case 151/78.
366. European Commission (n. 349).
367. *Jean Neu and others v. Secrétaire d'Etat à l'Agriculture et à la Viticulture* [1991] ECJ Joined cases C-90/90 and C-91/90.

free use of the property can only be restricted to serve a general interest, and as such, the measure would have been found not to be proportionate to achieve the aim. As such, the freedom to decide whom to do business with seemingly does not have an effect on access restrictions in a way that diverts from the protection offered by the right to property. It is, therefore, not specifically included in the roadmap. The proprietor's use of the property could already be limited on various grounds – including on grounds of general interest and, indirectly, the protection of the freedoms and rights of others. As such, the freedom to decide whom to do business with does not expand the scope of protection already awarded under the right to property as the latter already covers a free choice to deny access to the property, which limitation must serve a general interest.

4.3.3.2 The Freedom to Decide on the Terms of the Contract

The freedom of contract furthermore includes the 'freedom of the parties to arrange their own affairs'.[368] The exact scope of the latter freedom is debatable. In *Alemo-Herron*, the CJEU provided a general clarification on the scope of protection, namely that 'the transferee must be able to assert its interests effectively in a contractual process to which it is a party and to negotiate the aspects (...) with a view to its future economic activity'.[369] Subsequently, the CJEU has included in its scope the right of the parties to amend the contract,[370] to negotiate the different aspects of the contract,[371] the freedom to determine the price of the service,[372] and the freedom to enter into obligations with others.[373] The freedom to decide on the *terms* of the contract does not follow explicitly from the case law. In the periphery of the previous conclusions of the CJEU, however, lies an overarching need to safeguard the negotiation process of the obligations that are included in the agreement between the parties. If a party wants to effectively assert its interests in a contractual process, negotiate its aspects, and decide on the obligations to be included in the contract, the scope must necessarily include the freedom to define the terms. Throughout the years, the freedom of contract's scope has been more precisely defined by the CJEU. Referring back to the inclusion of the freedom of the parties to arrange their own affairs in *Spain v. Commission*, one can observe in the more recent case of *STEB* that the CJEU has extended its interpretation to include that the contracting parties' – subject to the mandatory rules of public policy

368. *Case C-240/97 (Spain/Commission)* (1999) ECLI:EU:C:1999:479 (CJEU), §99; *Arnold und Johann Harms als Gesellschaft bürgerlichen Rechts v. Freerk Heidinga* [2010] ECJ Case C-434/08, §36.
369. *Case C-426/11 (Alemo-Herron and Others)* (2013) ECLI:EU:C:2013:521 (CJEU), §33; and later confirmed in *Anonymi Geniki Etairia Tsimenton Iraklis (AGET Iraklis) v. Ypourgos Ergasias, Koinonikis Asfalisis kai Koinonikis Allilengyis* [2016] ECJ Case C-201/15, §87.
370. *Case C-240/97 (Spain/Commission)* (1999) ECLI:EU:C:1999:479 (CJEU), §99.
371. *Mark Alemo-Herron and Others v. Parkwood Leisure Ltd* [2013] ECJ Case C-426/11, §33.
372. *Commission of the European Communities v. Kingdom of Belgium* [2007] ECJ Case C-437/04, §51; *Sky Österreich GmbH v. Österreichischer Rundfunk* (n. 331), §43.
373. *Arnold und Johann Harms als Gesellschaft bürgerlichen Rechts v. Freerk Heidinga* [2010] ECJ Case C-434/08, §36.

– are free to define the terms of their legal relationship.[374] The latter indicates the inclusion of the freedom to decide on *all terms* to form a part of the freedom of contract. As such, despite not being recognised (consistently) as such, the freedom to decide on the terms is to be included as a sub-freedom of the freedom of contract.[375]

The possibility to define the terms of the contract can be limited in full, though in those situations, the economic interests the undertaking would have had when exploiting their property freely must be weighed against the legitimate aim in the general interest that the measure seeks to fulfil. That means that, under certain circumstances, social media platforms' freedom to decide on (or rather dictate) the terms of their service agreements can be significantly limited by the State. Recalling Article 52(1) of the Charter, such limitations must serve a genuine objective of general interest or must be necessary to protect the rights and freedoms of others. Safeguarding democracy and pluralism have previously been invoked as pressing general interests,[376] but also safeguarding the right to freedom of expression and to impart information or the right to data protection could serve as legitimate aims. The latter can (significantly) affect the current business models of social media platforms.[377] However, even when aimed at protecting the rights of others, such measures may not cause the end of the economic exploitation of the data. Recalling the essence of the freedom to conduct a business as defined above (the continuation of economic activity), a social media platform can oppose a measure causing the economic end of the commercial activity. Thus, despite safeguarding the rights of others, a measure that would *fully* limit the exploitation of data does not respect the essence of the freedom to conduct a business in Article 16 and is therefore not justifiable, regardless of whether data falls within the scope of a 'possession' under the right to property. Contrarily, it would only constitute a limitation of the free use of property under the right to property in Article 17 if data is considered a 'possession'. These potential interferences with the right to property could be justifiable, whereas interferences with the essence of the freedom to conduct a business cannot be justifiable.

This latter example demonstrates again the influence of (the sub-freedoms of) the freedom to conduct a business on (the business models of) social media platforms.

374. *Case C-277/05 (STEB)* (2007) ECLI:EU:C:2007:440 (CJEU), §28.
375. *Sky Österreich GmbH v. Österreichischer Rundfunk* (n. 331), §64.
376. *Ibid.*, §52.
377. As demonstrated for example by the practice of Meta's Facebook, which had formulated its user terms in a way that defines their core-business as the supply of a *personalised* service, *see* Meta Platforms, Facebook. Terms of Service. *1. The services we provide: 'Provide a personalised experience for you: Your experience on Facebook is unlike anyone else's: from the Posts, Stories, events, ads and other content that you see in Facebook News Feed or our video platform to the Facebook Pages that you follow and other features you might use, such as Facebook Marketplace and search. For example, we use data about the connections you make, the choices and settings you select, and what you share and do on and off our Products to personalise your experience.', see* https://www.facebook.com/terms.php (accessed 17 November 2022). Following a binding decision of the European Data Protection Board (6 December 2022, accessible at: https://edpb.europa.eu/news/news/2022/edpb-adopts-art-65-dispute-resolution-binding-decisions-regarding-facebook-instagram_en), the Irish Data Protection Commission fined Meta Ireland for breaching the rules in the GDPR when applying this practice of 'personalised service', indicating a strict(er) reading of the GDPR. This case is further discussed below in more detail in §6.4.3.4.

Whereas the permissible restrictions on the use of the property (collected data) would be plentiful under the right to property, the freedom to conduct a business protects the economic exploitation of the property beyond the scope of Article 17, leading to a significantly different set of potential remedies on the side of social media platforms.

4.3.3.3 *The Right to Freely Use the Available Resources*

Following the CJEU case of *UPC Telekabel*, the freedom of contract has a third distinct sub-element: the right to freely use the economic, technical, and financial resources available to the proprietor.[378] The origin of this sub-right is unclear. Prior to the conclusion of the CJEU in *UPC Telekabel*, the right to freely use the available resources was not mentioned, neither by Advocate General Cruz Villalón in his opinion of the case of *UPC Telekabel* nor in other prior case law or legislative documents. Before 2007, when the European Commission issued its explanation to the Charter, the sub-freedom seemingly did not yet exist as it is not mentioned in the explanation in Article 16. Since then, there has not been any other new (European) legislation from which this sub-freedom could have been inspired or distilled, or at least the latter does not follow from the considerations and argumentation of the Court. The creation of the right to freely use the available resources is solely based on the CJEU judges' interpretation of the freedom to conduct a business. The existence of the right to freely use the available resources is based on a (normative) conclusion of the Court. Nevertheless, the right has, since its first emergence, been reaffirmed by the CJEU on several occasions.[379]

The right to freely use the available resources protects against measures that oblige an undertaking to allocate (a considerable amount of its) resources in order to achieve a certain aim as set by the legislator.[380] An example of a measure that was found to limit the free use of the available resources was the imposition of a broad-scoped filtering injunction on the basis of the European copyright directive because, as a consequence of the injunction, an internet service provider would be obliged to take costly measures. The latter would restrict the right to freely use its resources.[381] Similarly, a labelling obligation for the retail of poultry meat was found to affect this freedom.[382] A measure can only form a limitation if it affects the *available* resources. If the measure solely limits an economic incentive that was not yet due, and the undertaking cannot legitimately expect to benefit from it in the future, the measure

378. *Case C-314/12 (UPC-Telekabel)* (2014) ECLI:EU:C:2014:192 (CJEU), §49.
379. *Case C-134/15 (Lidl)* (2016) ECLI:EU:C:2016:498, §26; *Case C-798/18 (Anie & Others)* (2021) ECLI:EU:C:2021:280, §62; *Case C-124/20 (Bank Melli Iran)* (2021) ECLI:EU:C:2021:1035, §78; *Joined Cases C-798/18 and C-799/18 (Athesia Energy)* (2021) ECLI:EU:C:2021:280, §63.
380. According to the case law, restrictions of this right to freely use the available resources exist in case of an 'obligation to take measures which may represent a significant cost for an economic operator, have a considerable impact on the organisation of his or her activities, or require difficult and complex technical solutions.', *Joined Cases C-798/18 and C-799/18 (Athesia Energy)* (2021) ECLI:EU:C:2021:280, §63; and *UPC Telekabel Wien GmbH v. Constantin Film Verleih GmbH and Wega Filmproduktionsgesellschaft mbH* (n. 364), §50.
381. *UPC Telekabel Wien GmbH v. Constantin Film Verleih GmbH and Wega Filmproduktionsgesellschaft mbH* (n. 364), §§48-50.
382. *Lidl* (n. 379), §29.

does not affect this right. In that case, the measure neither affects 'possessions' included in the definition of the right to property.[383] As a consequence, such measures fall outside the scope of protection.

The right to freely use the available resources is, like all the other sub-freedoms of the freedom to conduct a business, not absolute. Measures that limit the free use of the resources can be justifiable. The CJEU, after concluding that a measure infringes on the right, continues its argumentation by recalling that a measure that limits the right to freely use the available resources does not infringe the very substance (the essence) of the freedom to conduct a business[384] since the latter would only be the case if the measure obstructs all economic activity. Additionally, the obligation must be foreseen by law and meet a genuine objective of general interest, for example, the protection of the rights and freedoms of others.[385] Obligations are presumed proportionate if they leave the undertaking to freely determine the measures to reach the imposed aim. In *UPC Telekabel*, this meant, for example, that the addressee of the imposed injunction was free to determine the specific measures to be taken to live up to the injunction. The latter line was more recently confirmed in *Poland v. Parliament and Council.*[386]

For social media platforms, the right to freely use the available resources mainly comes into play when assessing the scope of the mandatory rules of public policy that limit the scope of the freedom to decide on the terms of the contract. As such, the right to freely use the available resources compliments the protection of the freedom to decide on the terms of the contract. Take the example of a (national) law that obliges social media platforms to guarantee an internal complaints mechanism that deals with content moderation issues within 48 hours.[387] Such a limitation would, first, restrict the platforms' freedom to decide on the terms of the contract because it imposes an involuntary obligation to which the platform is subjected. If the measure is necessary and serves a genuine objective in the general interest, the restriction does not form an unjustified interference with that sub-freedom. Second, the right to freely use the available resources allows the platform to challenge such an obligation. If the obligation poses a significant cost for the platform, has a considerable impact on the

383. *Joined Cases C-798/18 and C-799/18* (n. 302), §64.
384. *UPC Telekabel Wien GmbH v. Constantin Film Verleih GmbH and Wega Filmproduktionsgesellschaft mbH* (n. 364), §51; *Lidl* (n. 379), §32.
385. *See*, respectively, *UPC Telekabel Wien GmbH v. Constantin Film Verleih GmbH and Wega Filmproduktionsgesellschaft mbH* (n. 4); *Lidl* (n. 379).
386. *Republic of Poland v. European Parliament and Council of the European Union* [2022] ECJ Case C-401/19, §75: '(...) in order to respect the freedom of those service providers to conduct a business, guaranteed in Article 16 of the Charter, and to respect the fair balance between that freedom, the right to freedom of expression and information of the users of their services, enshrined in Article 11 of the Charter, and the right to intellectual property of the rightholders, protected in Article 17(2) of the Charter – to leave those service providers to determine the specific measures to be taken in order to achieve the result sought; accordingly, they can choose to put in place the measures which are best adapted to the resources and abilities available to them and which are compatible with the other obligations and challenges which they will encounter in the exercise of their activity.'
387. The obligation to offer an internal complaints mechanism is put forward in the Digital Services Act and is discussed below in §7.4.1.1. The timeframe of 48 hours is fictional and does not follow from the obligations in the DSA but is used here as an example of an obligation that would require significant resources.

organisation of the service, or requires difficult and complex technical solutions, the obligation restricts this right. One could imagine that an internal complaints mechanism could potentially be handled in 48 hours, but a full dispute resolution service would be very costly to offer within 48 hours. The outcome of whether the imposed measure puts too much of a burden on the available resources of the platform varies from case to case and from platform to platform because what might be an undue burden on one can be easily implemented by another, more resourceful platform.

In that sense, this sub-right mitigates the resource-power in the market. Whereas a large-scale global player presumably will be able to fulfil a certain duty, that same duty can negatively affect the economic viability of a smaller player in a way that is unjustifiable. In that way, the right to freely use the available resources inextricably links back to the essence of the freedom to conduct a business: the economic continuation of the exploitation of property. The right to freely use the available resources is a protection the platform can invoke against too burdensome (national) legislation, and it, therefore, plays an indirect role in the content layer where the (legal) limitations of the contractual conditions are put into place.

However, the right to freely use the available resources is a measure that can be invoked by platforms against legislation. As such, it does not influence the opportunities for users to oppose access decisions. Its influence on these latter restrictions is of an indirect nature, and as such, it does not form a part of the roadmap on access restrictions. Nonetheless, its influence must be kept in mind when defining which mandatory rules of public policy should be taken into consideration.

4.3.4 The Additional Value of the Freedom to Conduct a Business

The sub-freedoms of the freedom to conduct a business overlap considerably with the protection offered by the right to property. Specifically, the freedom to conduct a business clarifies, and perhaps even codifies, certain aspects of the right to property. For example, the freedom of contract, which has been recognised as a sub-freedom of Article 16, corresponds to the positive right under the right to property. Similarly, its sub-element of the freedom to decide with whom to do business corresponds to the choice a proprietor has between the negative and positive right to property. Adding thereto that an equivalent to the freedom to conduct a business was omitted in the ECHR because, arguably, the right to property already encompasses these freedoms, then it would be most logical to follow the conclusion posed by Groussot, Petursson and Pierce that the inclusion of the freedom to conduct a business in the Charter is housekeeping rather than an increase of the scope of protection for private undertakings.[388] However, the freedom to conduct a business also offers elements that are not (explicitly) included in the scope of the right to property and as such pose, Article 16 offers an additional valuable source of protection for social media platforms.

First, the freedom to determine the terms of the contract does not explicitly nor implicitly follow from the right to property. The freedom to determine the terms of the

388. Groussot, Petursson and Pierce (n. 345).

contract, however, can have significant implications for the private governance power of social media platforms, as it can be used as a counterweight against measures increasing the platform's obligations in favour of other parties' interests. This becomes especially relevant when assessing the upcoming DSA's balancing test of interests when enforcing terms of service.[389] Second, the freedom to exercise an economic activity offers protection that goes beyond the scope of the right to property. Whereas the right to property's essence solely protects against expropriation, the freedom to exercise an economic activity protects a proprietor against bankruptcy caused by measures that limit the use of its property. In those circumstances, the proprietor's property right would be untouched as the proprietor remains the owner of the property. The use of the property, however, could be limited to such an extent that it cannot be used in an economically viable way. When combining that sub-freedom with the (rather newly established) right to freely use the available resources, then the freedom to conduct a business suddenly steers away from mere housekeeping and forms a solid extension of the protection of a proprietor's effective economic use of the property.

As such, various elements of the freedom to conduct a business come (indirectly) into play in the roadmap. Those that have a direct effect on the discussions on access and moderation issues have been explicitly included. The freedom to exercise an economic activity is included in the foundational layer of the roadmap since it significantly extends the protection that a social media platform can invoke against state measures that obstruct the economic use of the property. The freedom to decide on the terms plays a significant role in the discussion on the conditions for forced access and also forms the starting point for the scope of the terms of service in general. It can be invoked as a counterweight for restricting measures in the interest of consumers and plays a role in deciding whether the agreement lives up to the basic principles of contract law. As such, the freedom to decide on the terms of the contract has been included as an interpretative building block around these two elements (basic principles of contract law and the mandatory rules of public policy). Indirectly, the right to freely use the available resources must be kept in mind throughout the application of the roadmap's elements. For example, when examining mandatory rules of public policy, these rules must be interpreted within the right of the platform to freely choose how to allocate its resources. As such, a measure may demand an outcome (less infringing content, balancing of rights) but may not prescribe costly measures to do so. As the protection under the right to freely use the available resources only comes into play when such measures are proposed, it has not been included as an explicit building block of the roadmap. Similarly, since the freedom to decide whom to do business with corresponds directly to the choice between the negative and positive right to freedom, neither this sub-freedom has been included as a building block. However, the case law on this sub-freedom of Article 16 must be included when examining existing or drawing up new measures that touch the negative or positive right to property.

389. *See* this discussion further on in §7.3.3.

4.4 CONCLUSION ON THE FOUNDATIONAL BASIS OF THE ROADMAP

The study of the scope of the right to property and the assessment of the additional value of the freedom to conduct a business lead to the answer to the third sub-question: *which fundamental rights form the foundational basis for access restrictions on social media platforms and what is their scope of application*

The foundational starting point for access decisions on social media platforms can be traced back to the right to property, despite arguments against the inclusion of *virtual spaces* within the (national) definitions of property. Based on the right to property in the Charter and the ECHR, a proprietor has the right to own, use and dispose of all their lawfully acquired possessions. The term 'possessions' includes any material or immaterial assets that represent an economic value. Following the legal literature and the scope of possessions defined by the CJEU and ECtHR, this includes social media platforms' technical infrastructure, their intellectual property, and, more important, their *virtual spaces*. To make use of the property, the platform can directly invoke two types of rights against other parties: the right to use the property and the right to collect revenue from it. In light of the traditions in the Member States, the right to *use* the property encompasses both a positive right to use the property and a negative right to exclude others from such use.

Additionally, the freedom to conduct a business in Article 16 of the Charter supplements the protection of the right to property in several ways. This additional protection corresponds to the freedom's three sub-freedoms. First, the freedom to conduct a business' first sub-freedom – the freedom to exercise an economic activity – increases the scope of unjustifiable measures for social media platforms. The essence of the right to property protects only against expropriation. Measures that restrict the use of the property can be justifiable if they are necessary and genuinely aim to meet an objective in the general interest. However, this does not protect against measures that, through restricting the use of the property, obstruct or render impossible the economic exploitation of the property. Contrarily, the freedom to exercise an economic activity protects the continuation of the economic exploitation of the platform. (Legislative) measures that render economic use of the property impossible are incompatible with Article 16 of the Charter. The second sub-freedom of the freedom to conduct a business concerns the drafting of the terms of the platform's user terms. Social media platforms must be able to participate in the negotiation process on the contractual terms, also when the agreement comes about as a consequence of an obligation to contract. The platform must, under all circumstances, be able to effectively assert its own (economic) interests. Third, under the freedom to conduct a business, social media platforms have a right to freely use their available resources. To guarantee this right, the platform must be let as free as possible in deciding how to allocate its assets. In principle, any measure (e.g., a filtering obligation to detect infringing content) can be justifiable if proportionate and does not lead to the economic end of the service.

Neither the right to property nor the freedom to conduct a business are absolute. Whether legal intervention interferes with the freedom to conduct a business or the right to property depends on the effect said measure has on either the existing property of the platform or the ability to choose how to allocate the assets of the platform for economic use. For the freedom to conduct a business, it is settled in CJEU case law that the freedom can be subjected to a broad range of interventions as long as they are necessary and serve a genuine objective in the general interest. The protection of the rights and freedoms of others – such as the right to freedom of expression or data protection – forms such objectives. The protection of democracy and safeguarding (media) pluralism have also been successfully invoked to limit the freedom to conduct a business. However, even when the measure serves an aim in the general interest, such measures may not cause the end of the economic exploitation of the social media platform's property as the essence of the freedom to conduct a business protects the continuation of economic activity. As such, a social media platform can oppose any measure that would mean the economic end of the commercial activity despite the limitation of fulfilling an aim in the general interest. However, the measure must cause the *end* of economic business – a decrease in profitability is *not* protected under the freedom to conduct a business since the latter forms an inherent risk of entrepreneurship. Measures that limit the use of property interfere with the right to property in Article 17. Though contrarily, nearly all interferences with the right to property can be justifiable because the essence of the right to property solely protects against expropriation.

In conclusion, social media platforms can invoke their exclusive rights under the right to property to limit access to their service. The right also provides a basis to allow access to (use) the property, whether by means of a contract (terms of service) or through open access. The right to property protects against (national) legislative measures that unjustly interfere with these rights. The freedom to exercise an economic activity protects the economic continuation of the use of the property. The exact scope of application of the positive and negative right to property to the realm of social media platforms forms the focus point of the following chapter. This includes an overview of the different ways a platform can decide to allow access (positive right), and it covers the situations in which the right to exclusion (negative right) can be limited.

CHAPTER 5

The Access Layer: Open, Forced, and Conditional Access

5.1 THE RIGHT TO PROPERTY AS AN ACCESS REGULATOR

Whereas the previous chapter focused on the scope of the foundational basis of access restrictions, this chapter concerns the first interference with this right from the point of view of the users. As discussed in the previous chapter, based on the right to property, social media platforms can exercise certain exclusive rights. Specifically, these platforms can choose to (conditionally) allow access and can choose to exclude (certain groups) from accessing. This chapter outlines these possible avenues to access a social media platform.

Due to the absolute nature of the internet's technical interface, accessibility in an online world cannot be fully equalled to accessibility in the physical world. This chapter, therefore, starts with a reflection on these differences and their impact on addressing online access problems. Second, the four types of access restrictions applied by social media platforms are closely examined. Social media platforms can restrict access to their platform either *ex ante* and *ex post*, respectively before the user has ever entered the platform and as a sanction after the user has had access. The differences between these two types of access restrictions impact the user's redress possibilities. Third, equal to the elements distilled in Chapter 3, platforms have four ways to *ex ante* restrict access to their platforms (open, forced, conditional, and forced access). All of these types of access restrictions will be looked into and illustrated with examples from current social media platforms. Lastly, the various limitations to social media platforms' right of exclusion are discussed. These cover the protection of the rights and freedoms of others, the direct effect of fundamental rights, public and/or social interest rights, and competition law (services of general economic interest, universal services, and essential facilities). The chapter concludes with a reflection on users' ability to access a social media platform and their options in case access is refused *ex ante* and an answer to the fourth sub-question.

5.2 ACCESSIBILITY AS A BENCH MARK FOR ONLINE PRESENCE?

In the physical world, the accessibility of a property is determined by whether or not one can physically enter it. Physical constraints that prevent access to the property can be natural, such as oceans and mountains, as well as human-made locks, gates, and walls.[390] As a default, physical property is accessible unless access has explicitly been obstructed. Legislation and terms of service only regulate the consequences of accessing private property rather than obstructing access itself. For example, entering a private building without permission may be forbidden and accessing it could have legal or personal consequences, such as trespassing or facing a different treatment by the proprietor in the future. That fact might deter the person from entering, but it does not *obstruct* access to the property. A person could still enter if willing to face the (legal) consequences. The proprietor would have to call the police to enforce the law and cannot remove a person with force from the premises. Therefore, only physical obstructions can completely obstruct access in the physical world, while legal regulations merely influence a user's access decision.

Lessig describes how technical characteristics of the internet create access obstructions.[391] The online space functions differently from the physical world due to the internet's infrastructure. In the first place, internet users must obtain an internet connection to access any online services offered. Without a connection, the person cannot access the internet.[392] Second, online services can be either fully closed off (private servers, intranet), open (most websites, some platforms), or conditionally restricted (paid news sites, most social media platforms). As such, default accessibility does not exist online since all access is controlled. Unlike the physical world where a person could accept the legal and social consequences of trespassing, an online user will not be able to enter the technical infrastructure, even if willing to accept the consequences.[393] Third, the terms of service further obstruct access in a way that cannot be achieved in the physical world. These terms, combined with the technical interface of the internet, function as automatically enforceable locks and gates. As opposed to the physical proprietor who must call the police to enforce a house rule, a breach of a platform's (normative) terms, in combination with the use of automated

390. Although not all human-made obstructions obstruct access equally, as demonstrated by the example of the bridges built by Robert Moses as discussed in: Robert A Caro, *The Power Broker: Robert Moses and the Fall of New York* (Vintage Books Edition September 1975, Vintage 1975). The low-hanging infrastructure of the bridges made it impossible for buses to pass underneath, obstructing passage for lower-class Americans. Whether or not these bridges were intentionally built that way is disputed, *see, e.g.*, Thomas J. Campanella, Robert Moses and His Racist Parkway, Explained, 9 July 2017 Bloomberg, https://www.bloomberg.com/news/articles/2017-07-09/robert-moses-and-his-racist-parkway-explained (accessed 7 December 2022).
391. Lessig (n. 69).
392. Albeit technically possible, accessing without an ISP-subscription is nearly impossible due to economical and legal constraints.
393. 'Hacking' a way into a closed off platform would result in accessibility despite the technical interface. However, for the general internet user, hacking poses the same alternative to access as picking a lock of a house in the physical world. This technical interface therefore resembles a human-made obstruction, rather than the acceptance of a (legal) consequence for entering a house without any obstructions.

content moderation, leads to automated enforcement of the restriction.[394] As such, in the online space, all access is restricted unless explicitly allowed. The default access is standardly obstructed by the technical interface with an intertwined, automatic enforcement tool.

In contrast to the physical world, where accessibility serves as a measure of whether one can enter a property or not, online access is inherently restricted. The proprietor of the server or the company offering the service designs the technical infrastructure that functions as an obstacle that cannot be bypassed. This obstacle determines whether a user can enter or not. As a result, focusing on the *types of access restrictions* imposed by social media platforms provides a better foundation for addressing access issues on these platforms than simply examining the ability of users to access or not access a service.

5.3 *EX ANTE* VERSUS *EX POST* ACCESS RESTRICTIONS

Access can be denied to a user at two different points in time. First, an access restriction can be imposed before ever accessing the platform (*ex ante*) or, second, when a user has been able to use the service on the platform but further use has been (permanently) suspended or terminated (*ex post*).[395] *Ex ante* access restrictions can be based on various reasons, targeting specific groups, reflecting advertiser preferences, or following from jurisdictional limitations.[396] *Ex post* restrictions can be imposed either arbitrarily or due to a triggering event, such as a breach of terms, harm to a third party, or illegal activity. In the case of *ex post* restrictions on social media platforms, the relationship between the user and the social media platform is governed by the agreement between the parties, and it is the content of this agreement that (mostly) leads to the restriction of access to the service. In the next chapter in which the content layer is discussed, *ex post* restrictions are outlined in detail. As the current layer focuses on the (denial of) first access to a social media platform, only *ex ante* restrictions are discussed at this point.

The consequence of both an *ex ante* and an *ex post* restriction is exclusion from access to the service. *Ex ante* restrictions are further reaching and more problematic for potential users than *ex post* restrictions because an *ex ante* restriction is more difficult to challenge. *Ex ante* refused persons cannot access the platforms' internal redress

394. *See* similar: João Pedro Quintais, Giovanni De Gregorio and João C Magalhães, 'How Platforms Govern Users' Copyright-Protected Content: Exploring the Power of Private Ordering and Its Implications' (2023) 48 Computer Law & Security Review 105792. point 2, DOI: https://doi.org/10.1016/j.clsr.2023.105792: 'Platforms can enforce contractual clauses directly without the need to rely on a public mechanism, such as a judicial order or the intervention of law enforcement authorities.'

395. This distinction between *ex ante* and *ex post* restrictions has previously been addressed in: van der Donk, 'Ex-Ante and Ex-Post Access Restrictions in Online Marketplace's Terms of Service' (n. 8).

396. *See, e.g.*, former president of the United States Donald Trump's social media platform *Truth Social* when accessing the page from the European Union: 'At the moment, Truth Social is available for U.S. users only, but rest assured, we are working hard to make it available in your country' (https://truthsocial.com/ (accessed 20 December 2022)).

mechanisms. Those mechanisms are defined in the terms of service, which are only applicable in case the user has a contractual relationship with the platform at the time of the access restriction. As such, *ex ante* restrictions cannot be challenged internally. Equally, the increased rules on transparency and redress that are put forward in the Digital Services Act do not apply to *ex ante* access restrictions.[397] An *ex ante* access restriction can only be challenged in national courts as an unjustified refusal of contract. Whether or not a refused user can claim access to the platform depends on the type of *ex ante* restriction applied.

5.4 CONTEXTUALISING THE FOUR TYPES OF *EX ANTE* ACCESS RESTRICTIONS

Equal to access to physical property, access to social media platforms can be divided into three types: open access, conditional access, and denied access. Additionally, obligations to contract on social media platforms form a fourth type: forced access. Whereas open access-platforms and conditional platforms form an expression of the platforms' positive aspect of the right to property, forced and denied access follow from the platform's right to exclude (the negative aspect of the right to property). For the former, the proprietor chooses to provide access, either based on certain conditions or fully open to the general public.[398] In the latter situation, the proprietor chooses actively to exclude other persons from accessing its property. When access is denied, there are nonetheless situations under which users can claim (forced) access, resulting in an obligation to contract on the side of the platform.[399]

To contextualise the access layer, the four different types of access (*see* Figure 5.1), including their characteristics, are discussed in more detail below. The platforms that apply open access and conditional access are referred to as, respectively, open access-platforms and conditional platforms. Platforms that fully deny access are referred to as private platforms. Forced access is not a choice of application of specific types of platforms but a consequence of balancing the interests of users against the platform's right to exclude.

397. The rules in Art. 17 DSA ('statement of reasons') only apply to 'recipients of the service', which *ex ante* refused persons are not. The same applies for the internal complaint-handling system in Art. 20, with the exception of notifiers that have made use of the notice-and-action mechanism outlined in Art. 16.
398. *See* a similar distinction between 'websites that select access' and 'websites that do not select access' in Alessandra Quarta, 'Beyond Assimilation: Are Terms of Use Really Contracts?' 134.
399. Note that these categories of access only apply to the definition of social media platforms as used in this book, meaning a service where at least two consumer parties – of which none of the two is the proprietor of the service – can intercommunicate. It does not cover other types of online (platform) services, such as search engines, and third-party vendors on online marketplaces. Therefore, these four types of access are not automatically by analogy applicable to the *entire* internet.

Figure 5.1 The Access Layer with Its Four Access Restrictions and Its Relation to the Foundational Layer's Proprietor Rights

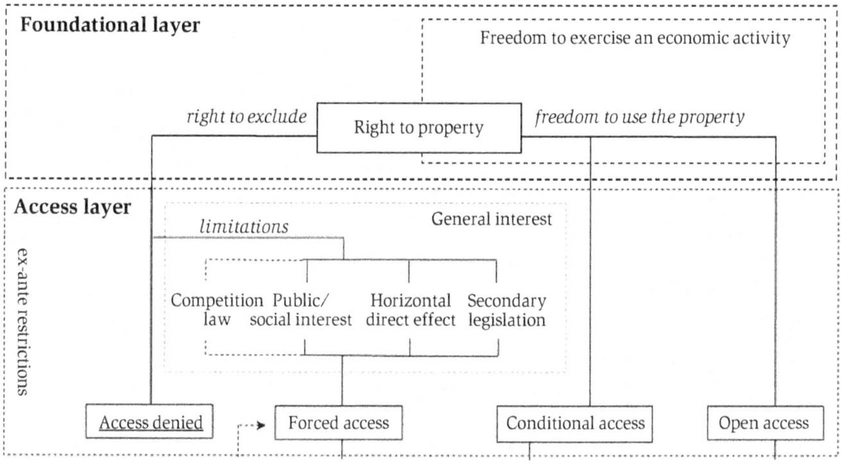

5.4.1 Open Access

Social media platforms with open access are rare. Most social media platforms that are aimed at offering services to a broader audience require the user to sign up before accessing the platform's service. However, there are also social media platforms which one can simply 'enter' and use straight away. It is these platforms that make up the group of open access-platforms. Open access-platforms do not necessarily omit the use of terms of service, but the consequences of those terms differ significantly from those on conditional platforms. Those limited consequences form one of the overlapping characteristics that distinguish open access-platforms from conditional platforms. Distinguishing these two types of platforms is important, as users of open access-platforms have a general right of access, and any moderation decision interfering with general access may only be taken on the basis of an objective reason.[400] This paragraph starts with existing examples of this type of platform, followed by the three characteristics to identify an open access-platform.

5.4.1.1 Examples of Open Access-Platforms

The traditional open access-model is that of an online chat box. A person enters a web address in a browser, enters the service, sometimes chooses a temporary user name, and can then use the service immediately after. Currently, *7strangers.com* and *Chatroulette* seem to be the only two services that offer such a service fully open and

400. The interpretation and application of the general right of access will be discussed as part of the content layer, *see* §6.3 below.

without (indirectly) applying normative user terms limiting the scope of the information that can be shared. On both platforms, the users can use the service right away (*7strangers*) or after turning on their camera (*Chatroulette*) before being connected to a random other person on the internet. Neither one of these two platforms has specified *any* restrictions on content in their terms.[401] Most other open access-services have some restrictions on the content to be shared, which usually follow (national) law in relation to illegal content, age restrictions, and/or unwanted behaviour such as spam and sexually explicit content. This is, for example, the case of *Omegle*, an anonymous worldwide chat box that connects users with another person who speaks their chosen language. Whereas *Chatroulette* has approximately 1.5 million visitors a month, with an average visit duration of two and a half minutes,[402] *7strangers* attracts little under 100,000 visitors a month with an average time of 10 seconds. The short duration of the latter service could be due to the inability of the website to create a stable connection between two users.[403] *Omegle* attracts 67 million visitors a month, with an average duration of six and a half minutes.[404] Lastly, a more elaborate example of an open access-platform is the online communication platform *4chan*. The online forum allows people to anonymously access the platform and post messages on one of the boards. A sign-up is not required. Before entering a specific board, visitors are shown a disclaimer with the service's rules, which have to be accepted before entering. *4chan*'s rules are elaborate.[405] The consequences of not following the rules of the platform are substantial.

5.4.1.2 *Three Characteristics to Identify an Open Access-Platform*

An open access-platform's service is of a temporary nature, a breach of the terms has limited consequences for the subject, and the service is not limited by general access restrictions. These three characteristics to identify an open access-platform are interconnected. The first requirement, the temporary nature of the service, creates the foundation for the limited consequences of a breach of the terms and makes sure that these types of platforms, in principle, do not apply any access restrictions. The three characteristics are discussed in more detail below.

401. 7strangers: https://7strangers.com/rules (accessed 9 December 2022). Chatroulette: https://chatroulette.com/terms/ (accessed 9 December 2022).
402. *See* https://www.similarweb.com/website/chatroulette.com/#traffic (accessed 21 December 2022).
403. That was at least the problem the author has faced on numerous occasions trying to use the service during November and December 2022. For the statistics, *see* https://www.similarweb.com/website/7strangers.com/#overview (accessed 21 December 2022).
404. *See* https://www.similarweb.com/website/omegle.com/#overview (accessed 21 December 2022).
405. *See* https://www.4chan.org/rules (accessed 13 December 2022). The rules include rules on the 'quality of the post' (prohibiting gibberish and indecipherable text, amongst other types of speech) and an elaborate sectioning of their communication board (specific posts can only be posted in specific threads).

(i) The temporary nature of the service offered

The first distinction between an open access-platform and a conditional platform relates to the service the platforms are offering and the effect of the service's nature on the contractual relationship with and the position of the user. Identifying and defining this first characteristic of open access-platforms has been based on analogy to the definition of open access physical property. Recalling the latter's definition that followed from the results of the comparative study in Chapter 3, the requirement for physical property to be open access does not depend on whether or not the proprietor applies user terms. It first and foremost depends on whether the service is open to the general public without entering into a (continuous) contractual relationship. The service offered by open access-platforms mimics these criteria for open access physical property. Open access-platforms offer a temporary service – a brief service that, after closing the browser or shutting down the computer, stops existing.[406] It means simultaneously that any content (text, video, other data) that is shared through the service, is not retained for a future visit of the user. Consequently, the potential dissemination of any illegal or unwanted behaviour through the service is confined to the period in which the user has an active session on the platform. On the contrary, platforms that apply a conditional access-model provide a continuous agreement, as will be further detailed below. When a user closes an active session on a conditional platform, the user's relationship with the conditional platform does not stop. As such, when the user returns to the platform at a later point, the technical structure of a conditional platform allows the user to take off where it left during the last session. The relationship between the platform and the user is not dependent on the single active session initiated by the user, which is the case for open access-platforms – the relationship is continuous in nature for conditional platforms, whereas the relationship has a temporary nature for open access-platforms.

(ii) A breach of the user terms has limited individual consequences

The second characteristic of an open access-platform is the lack of long-term individual consequences that a breach of the terms during one active session can have on future access to the platform. A lack of access restrictions does not mean that an open access-platform does not impose any rules on their service. The open character of these platforms does not rule out the application of user terms per se. An open access-platform might apply user terms, but as opposed to conditional platforms, the terms of open platforms do not govern the access of the user to the website. As such, an open access-platform can make use of terms that prohibit the posting of certain types of content and dictate that breaching that term leads to suspension or termination from the service. However, the consequences hereof are negligible for the users of the service. Terminating an individual's session does not have any concrete effect on

406. For some services, one can simply close the tab in the internet browser to end the service. Other types of online services make use of cookies to save the active session until a user actively logs off, which is the case on for example talk.chat. Though, all services have in common that after closing the active session, data from that session cannot be retrieved again at a later point in time.

accessing the service at a later point in time. If a user of an open access-platform shares content that is not allowed based on the user terms of the service, solely that content is removed, and potentially, the ongoing active session of the user is ended. The individual's use of the service and the relationship between the user and the platform ends, just as would be the case when the user closes the tab in the internet browser. The user can then simply access the service again in the same way as the user had started the previous session.

The breach of the user terms only has an effect on the single temporary service relationship between platform and user. Since neither of the individual sessions is intertwined in a continuous relationship, the expulsion of one session does not create any burden for a following session. The user of an open access-service does not lose any stored content, nor does the individual lose any connections in a way that is different from the normal practice. The service does not retain data, and therefore, the effect of a termination of an active session is negligible as opposed to the consequences of a conditional service. One could imagine that the termination of a user account on Twitter, TikTok, or Facebook would have a greater impact as the user would lose the invested time over the continuous period in which the person had used the service. Moreover, a user who wishes to share content that falls outside the scope of the platform or a user who does not agree with any normative rules imposed on the service can simply move to the next online chat box. Since there is no data stored on a long-term basis, there is no risk of a lock-in effect, as observed in conditional platforms. If the user switches from one conditional platform to another, the user will lose all the connections and data connected to that specific user account. The temporary nature of open access-services prevents lock-ins.

(iii) The service is not limited by general access restrictions

The third and last characteristic refers to the existence of access restrictions to the service. This requirement can similarly be observed in the case law on physical access restrictions, for example, in Germany, where courts were held to define 'open access-property'.[407] A platform that offers conditional access makes access conditional to accepting a set of terms and conditions. Without explicitly accepting these terms, one cannot technically enter the platform. An open access-platform differs from a conditional access-platform because access is not conditional to creating a user account

407. *See, e.g., Bundesverfassungsgericht (Fraport)* (n. 78). Not open are in any case: buildings used for administrative purposes, enclosed facilities, public swimming pools, and hospitals (§65). In addition to 'open to the general public', the Court refers to 'places open to general traffic' (§66) and 'public fora' (§70), including predominantly *public street space*. These places are used by the people to 'exchange information and views and cultivate their personal contact'. (§67) and are 'characterised by the fact that it can be used to pursue a variety of different activities and concerns leading to the development of a varied and open communications network' (§70). If the place serves only one or mainly one purpose, the place should not be included in this definition. The Court continues its reasoning and expands the historical definition of public spaces to include shopping centres, shopping malls, or other meeting places, irrespective of whether these places are publicly or privately owned, whether they are connected to public or private infrastructure, and whether they are indoors or outdoors. If an individual assessment is carried out (safety check for passengers in an airport, ticket sale in public swimming pool), then the place is not open to the general public.

or accepting a set of user terms.[408] Inherently to the nature of a temporary service, an open access-platform does not offer a continuous relation, and as such, a sign-up for a user account is not necessary. The service is open without any restrictions on access, which means that anyone visiting the website can start using the service – sometimes only after freely choosing a (nick)name for the active session.

Some terms of service applied on open access-platforms may appear to impose access restrictions. A general applied practice on online access-platforms is the requirement of a minimum age to access the services (for example, either 13+ or 18+ restrictions can be observed in the user terms[409]). These terms mainly seek to avoid the dissemination of content to minors and any potential liability following therefrom and do not, as such, form an enforceable obstacle to entering the service. These are formal restrictions (some of which follow directly from national law) rather than substantive access restrictions. Second, one could argue whether access restrictions confined to the boundaries of jurisdictions fall within or outside this scope. If a platform is solely offered to users in a certain part of the world, they do de facto impose an access restriction for potential users from outside this jurisdiction.[410] If a platform applies territorial restrictions, then arguably, the platform's nature remains open access for the territory the platform operates in. It qualifies merely as an unavailable service outside that jurisdiction. The imposition of a jurisdiction restriction, therefore, does not change the platform into a conditional platform since users in the blocked jurisdiction have no means to comply with the restriction. Lastly, there are open access-platforms that make use of temporary and/or permanent bans from their service, which could effectively pose a restriction of access. For some platforms, the scope to issue such a ban is unilateral and unlimited.[411] Additionally, some platforms have added thereto that any circumvention of an imposed ban is prohibited.[412] The enforceability of these terms is limited,[413] and therefore, they do not pose an actual access restriction for users. The

408. Quarta goes as far as to say that open access-platforms cannot restrict the access to these goods, in parallel to the physical world. *See* Quarta, 'Beyond Assimilation: Are Terms of Use Really Contracts?' (n. 398), p. 134.

409. Such as for example the services offered by Chatous (https://chatous.com/terms) and Omegle (https://www.omegle.com/static/terms.html).

410. This is the case for United States Donald Trump's social media platform *Truth Social* which is limited to use in the United States only: 'At the moment, Truth Social is available for U.S. users only, but rest assured, we are working hard to make it available in your country.' (https://truthsocial.com/ (accessed 20 December 2022)).

411. Omegle Community Guidelines (2021-06-01): 'Omegle reserves the right to ban (temporarily or permanently) or take other appropriate action with or without notice with respect to any user that engages in conduct that Omegle determines, in its sole discretion, to be inappropriate or harmful, whether or not such conduct is identified below.' Available at: https://www.omegle.com/static/guidelines.html (accessed 9 December 2022). 7strangers Rules: 'We may terminate or suspend your access immediately, without prior notice or liability, for any reason whatsoever, including without limitation if you breach the Terms. Upon termination, your right to use the Service will immediately cease.' Available at: https://7strangers.com/rules (accessed 9 December 2022).

412. *Ibid.*, 'Ban Circumvention. Any attempt to circumvent a ban, whether temporary or permanent, is prohibited.'

413. The terms include an unlimited discretionary power, which has previously been deemed unfair by Italian courts, *see* §2.2.2.2.

sole effect of these measures is the termination of the active session, which, in line with the second characteristic, has limited individual consequences.

5.4.2 Conditional Access

As opposed to open access-platforms, conditional platforms offer a continuous service. As a consequence of the service's nature, conditional platforms make access to their service conditional to either a general sign-up process and/or an acceptance of their (layered)[414] terms of service. That, in turn, makes it possible for these platforms to exert (great) normative power over the (behaviour of the) users of their service. Like the previous one, this paragraph starts with examples of conditional access-platforms, followed by these platforms' characteristics.

5.4.2.1 Examples of Conditional Access-Platforms

Conditional access-platforms are usually meant when referring to 'social media platforms'. These are any platforms that have a continuous nature and have the possibility to apply normative terms of service to govern their platform. Examples of these are Meta's *Facebook* and *Instagram*, *X*, Google's *YouTube*, and ByteDance's *TikTok*, but also forums such as *Reddit* and former president of the United States Donald Trump's *Truth Social*.

5.4.2.2 Three Characteristics to Identify a Conditional Access-Platform

(i) The continuous nature of the service

The nature of the service offered by conditional access-platforms aims at establishing a long-term contractual relationship between the user and the platform. These types of services offer predominantly communication channels, reflected by different options to connect (becoming friends/followers/subscribers, etc.). To offer a service that can be retrieved at a later point in time, these platforms make use of sign-up processes. Before entering, prospective users must make a user account and accept the terms of service.

Directive 2019/770 defines the *continuous manner of supply* of a service as a digital service that is, first, available to consumers for a fixed or indefinite period of time. It refers thereby explicitly to '*an indefinite social media platform membership*' as falling within the scope of that definition. Second, it refers to the availability of the service, which is dependent on a contractual relationship – whether for a (short) fixed time or an indefinite period. When the contract ends, the availability of the service automatically ends. During the contractual relationship supported by the account

414. Some platforms use more than one intertwined set of terms of service that are layered upon each other, where one mostly outlines the contractual obligations and other define the normative scope of behaviour allowed on the service. The latter are often referred to as Community Guidelines or Platform Rules.

infrastructure, the user can retrieve data at a later point. That means that the service is not limited to one single active session, as is the case for open access-platforms. On conditional access-platforms, a user can log in and resume the session even after having closed a previous active session.

(ii) A user account is necessary to interact on the service

As opposed to platforms like *4chan*, where anyone instantly can post content and reply to other's posts, conditional platforms require users to create a user account. Interaction on the platform subsequently happens through these user accounts. This second characteristic must not be confused with the *accessibility* of the platform. Some conditional platforms are freely accessible (e.g., YouTube), but the *interaction* requires a user account.

(iii) The power to exercise normative power

The continuous nature of the service affects the consequences for users in case of a breach of the terms. In case of a breach, users face suspension or termination of their user account, which means that their options to access the service in the future (under that account or user name) are restricted. Opposed to open access-platforms, the consequences of these restrictions can be severe for individuals. The latter would be able to create a new user account[415] but would not be able to regain access to the data stored in the user account. That means any content, connections, or other information stored in the blocked user account is (temporarily) inaccessible, which poses a social and economic risk.[416] Moreover, users cannot simply export their data from one account to another or to another service. As such, users are dependent on the platform to stay connected to their online (social) connections. The latter creates a lock-in effect on these types of platforms. The combination of the potentially significant consequences for users and their inability to advert these risks by switching from one platform to another gives platforms that offer these services a powerful position. For users, the only possibility to prevent the risk of losing access to the data stored in the user account, is to comply with the terms dictated by the platform. Therefore, these types of platforms can exert great normative power over the scope of their service and, consequently, over the information that can be shared between their users and the individual scope of the freedom of expression of individual users.

415. That is, if the platform allows one person to have multiple accounts and to circumvent a ban in that way. For example, on Twitter, one can rather easily create a new user account. Only the e-mail address used for the initial blocked account cannot be reused, which requirement can easily be circumvented. On Meta's Facebook, however, the account name on a Facebook profile must be identical to one that appears in an identification document as indicated by Facebook's terms, which means that once that person has been permanently banned from their service, they cannot easily sign-up again. *See* for the terms: https://www.facebook.com/help/229715077154790/?helpref=uf_share (accessed 9 December 2022).

416. According to the Italian Consumer Authority, a loss of data that can have a significant impact on the consumer, *see* §2.2.2.2 and *Provvedimento n 29818 – CV195 – Dropbox* (n. 150); *Provvedimento n. 26729 – CV157 – App Pokemon GO* (n. 150), §44.

5.4.3 Denied Access

Contrary to the choice to (conditionally) open the platform for users, platforms can also offer a service that is fully closed off from the general public. Just as a proprietor in the physical world, an online proprietor can use its right of exclusion (*ius excludendi*) to deny access. These types of *private platforms* are, for example, used internally in companies, for example, as an intranet or extranet. These private platforms are generally unproblematic as access is not intended to include people from outside the target group.

In addition to these private platforms, there are other – more problematic – instances of denied access. In these cases, the proprietor denies access to certain (groups of) people. This would also be the case for private platforms, though, in these instances, the platform itself is not intended to function as a private platform for a limited target group only. The platform offers a general service available to the public but excludes groups on the basis of a normative choice rather than on an objective reason. Public platforms that exclude groups of people are not necessarily problematic in nature, but they can be. A platform can aim its scope to a group of people with a similar identification (think of an LGBTQI+ platform that excludes heterosexual, cisgender users or a forum that only allows one to register if they own a dog), but access restrictions can also be used to silence or exclude marginalised groups from large-scale social media platforms.[417]

The exclusions of certain groups' presence on social media platforms can come about either as an exercise of the proprietor's right to exclude or as a very strict condition imposed by the proprietor as a prerequisite to access a platform conditionally. They can also be the consequence of the use of algorithms to determine the order of content on the platform.[418] If the exclusion of access prevents a user from entering the platform altogether, meaning the user has never been able to become a part of the platform, the issue is framed as a consequence of the proprietor's right to exclude. If the exclusion is a consequence of strict user terms or of the functioning of the technical interface or algorithms, the issue is treated as a content problem. The latter will be addressed in the next chapter. Whether or not a proprietor can invoke its *ius excludendi* to limit the target group of users depends on whether one of the limitations to the right to exclude applies.

417. *See* on the relation between access exclusion and the effect on marginalised groups (mainly LGBTI people, disabled people, and migrants): World Economic Forum, 'The digital divide is silencing groups of LGBTI people, those with disabilities and forced migrants – this is how we ensure they're heard', 28 February 2020, https://www.weforum.org/agenda/2020/02/data-exclusion-marginalized-groups-lgbti-disabled-migrants/ (accessed 12 December 2022).

418. Which was the case for content depicting violence against the Rohingya people in Myanmar in 2017, which content was spread exponentially by Meta's algorithms. However, these did not lead to 'access problems' to the platform – this issue is rather a consequence of the platform's rules and practices in the content-layer.

5.4.4 Forced Access

The proprietor's right to exclude is not absolute. Following the conclusions of the comparative study in the first part, the right is subject to limitations on the basis of competition law, equality laws, and (individual) public/social rights. Adding thereto the results of the foundational law study in Chapter 4, the proprietor's *ius excludendi* can also be restricted to protect additional rights and freedoms of others.

The legal consequence of a limitation of the right to exclude is an obligation to contract. The platform operator can no longer freely decide to deny access - the pressing grounds that limit the right to exclude lead to forced access. This is the case, for example, if a decision to exclude a (group of) person(s) leads to discrimination or restricts access to a space essential to exercise the right to freedom of expression. In those situations, the refused persons can force the platform to provide access to the service. The latter claim is based on these restrictions to the platform operator's *ius excludendi* and forms the legal basis for access rights.

All of these limitations, however, have to serve an aim in the general interest.[419] Without an aim in the general interest, a limitation forms an unjustified interference with the proprietor's right to property. In the roadmap, to indicate that all the limitations to the right to exclude must serve an aim in the general interest, they are individually included but all together placed within a box of 'general interest' (*see* Figure 5.2). It follows from the case law of the CJEU that all the limitations that followed from the national case law and the study in Chapter 4 (protection of the rights of others, horizontal direct effect, public/social interest, and competition law) fulfil the requirement of serving an aim in the general interest.[420]

Figure 5.2 The Access Layer Including the Box of 'General Interest'

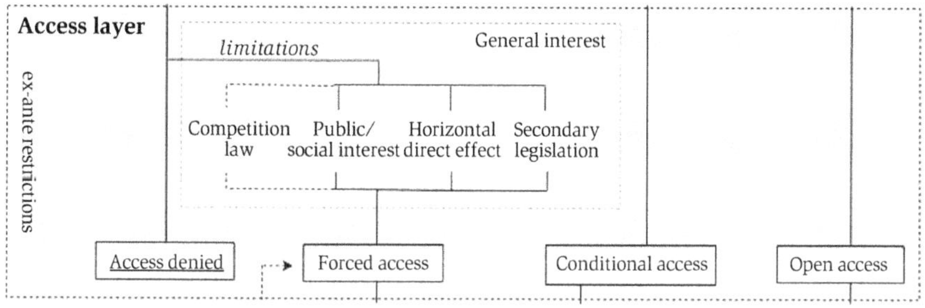

One could imagine that in case the platform operator is obliged to provide access to the service, the proprietor could simply offer access to the platform on the basis of

419. *See* the conclusion above in §4.2.3 and the case law cited there: 'According to the third sentence of article 17, the use of the property can be regulated by law if such restrictions are necessary in the general interest.'

420. *See* an in-depth assessment of all the individual limitations in §5.5.

very strict terms. That would result in a de facto denial of access for the user, as those terms are inacceptable. Whether or not the proprietor has the right to freely decide on the user terms in a case of forced access is addressed as the *infinity loop of forced access*.

5.4.4.1 *The* 'Infinity Loop of Forced *Access*'

The freedom of contract can be divided into two aspects: the freedom to conclude the contract (e.g., deciding with whom to enter into an agreement) and the freedom to decide the terms (the content of the agreement). A social media platform's obligation to enter into an agreement with a person does not necessarily mean that the platform loses its freedom to decide the content of the terms. To effectively assert its own economic interests, the platform must be able to refuse to contract with a third party on terms that are detrimental. An obligation to contract does not include an obligation to offer the service under all circumstances and on all terms.[421] However, an obligation to contract based on one of the grounds included in Figure 5.2 must lead to effective access to the platform. If not, the general aim to limit the platform's right of exclusion will not be fulfilled. In those situations where the user has de facto not gained access to the platform, an infinite problem arises for cases of forced access. A platform can, in principle, deny access on the basis of its right to exclude. When a person claims access on the basis of a limitation to that right to exclude, the platform is obliged to contract that person. If the platform then decides to only offer the service on the basis of restrictive terms, the access claim of the user has not been met, and equally, the obligation to contract remains to be fulfilled. This problem is infinite, as the person's interest to access the platform remains unfulfilled as long as the platform applies overly strict access terms. In the roadmap (*see* Figure 5.3), this process is referred to as *the infinity loop*. As the loop stretches over the access and content layer, it is reflected as such in the roadmap.

Figure 5.3 The Infinity Loop of Forced Access (Highlighted in Dark Grey)

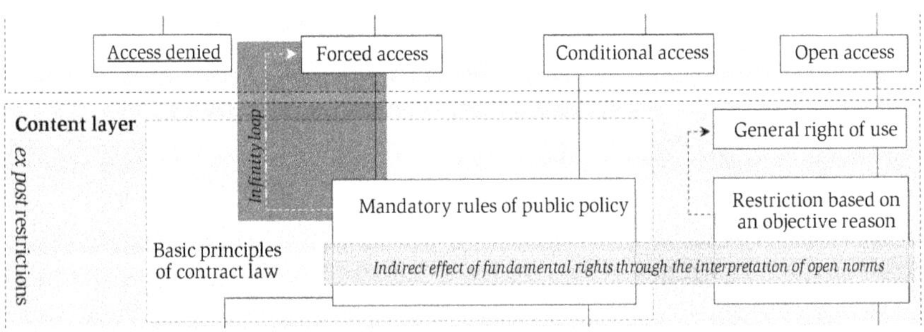

421. By analogy (in relation to insurance companies), *see* Ivan Sørensen, *Forsikringsselskabers kontraheringspligt i Danmark, Sverige, Norge, England og Tyskland* (Djøf 2014), pp. 23-25.

Breaking the infinity loop is difficult because the platform's freedom of contract is protected under the freedom to conduct a business and must be balanced against the interest of the users. The freedom of contract can be limited, but measures dictating the (outcome of the) terms form a severe restriction. The CJEU concluded in *Polkomtel* that the very essence of the freedom of contract is not affected if measures solely outline the negotiation process and include obligations on the formation of the terms. Those measures solely prescribe a contracting framework.[422] This line of reasoning equals the Court's earlier argumentation in *AGET Iraklis*.[423] That would mean that legislative measures can prescribe *how* the contractual terms should be negotiated but not *which* terms should be included in the agreement.

In practice, the number of persons ending up in the infinity loop will be rare. Presumably, the problem will mainly arise when a previously permanently terminated user tries to re-enter the service.[424] The discussion then relates to whether and on which terms that person should be allowed to re-access the service. In these situations, a person previously had a user account to access a social media platform's service but, due to (repetitive) breaches of the terms of service has had his/her user account permanently terminated.[425] In those situations, one could imagine that the platform has an interest in, first, not allowing that person to re-access the service as it might lead to new infringing activity. Second, to prevent further unwanted behaviour, the platform could have an interest in applying stricter terms for these re-entrees than for first-time entrees. It is here that the infinity loop becomes a reality. How the interests of both parties should be reconciled is unclear, not only in this specific situation on social media platforms but in general when dealing with obligations to contract.[426] Without legal clarity on the scope of the terms that can be imposed, an obligation to contract is merely a toothless bulldog. Research on the exact scope of the terms permissible in these situations is highly necessary, both for obligations to contract in general and especially in relation to obligations that apply to big tech giants. Unfortunately, this is not the right place to address that issue in full. Addressing the scope of the freedom to decide on the terms in a situation where the contract emerges from an obligation to contract rather than the free wish of both parties to be bound by the

422. *Case C-277/16 (Polkomtel)* (2017) ECLI:EU:C:2017:989 (CJEU), §52.
423. *Case C-201/15 (AGET Iraklis)* (2016) ECLI:EU:C:2016:972 (CJEU).
424. Despite the current limited scope, the occurrence of the dilemma of the infinity loop could play an increasing role if either a general right of access to (certain types of) social media or the regulation of these platforms as some form of public utility becomes reality.
425. Compare here also Art. 23 DSA, that only obliges online platforms to suspend the access to their service *for a reasonable period of time* when dealing with repeated infringers. The proportionality of a permanent termination should be weighed against the interests of the user as per Art. 14(3) DSA.
426. The scarce literature on the topic mainly focuses on the obligation to *enter into* a contract, rather than the content of the contract that must be concluded. *See, e.g.*, Verena Klappstein, 'The Obligation to Contract in British Law' (2014) 3 Journal of Governance and Regulation 15; Ilhan Helvacı, 'Obligation to Contract' in Ilhan Helvacı (ed.), *Turkish Contract Law* (Springer International Publishing 2017) https://doi.org/10.1007/978-3-319-60061-1_7 (accessed 21 January 2023); Joachim Wiemann, 'Obligation to Contract and the German General Act on Equal Treatment (Allgemeines Gleichbehandlungsgesetz)' (2019) 11 German Law Journal 1131, DOI: https://doi.org/10.1016/j.clsr.2023.105792.

agreement contains in itself an analysis of the size of this book. However, some reflections on a possible solution to the problem can be made here. General principles of (European) private law can be applied to fill in gaps that emerge 'when the dispersed rules of European private law do not contain an answer'.[427] To interpret, balance and limit the scope of the freedom of contract, a solution could be found by looking at the principles of good faith and the protection of the weaker party.[428]

The principle of good faith includes the prohibition of an abuse of a right in a contractual process.[429] When the platform applies excessively strict terms of service when obliged to contract, one could assess whether that practice constitutes an abuse of rights, especially in those cases where the terms of service that are used for cases of forced access are significantly stricter than terms applied by similar terms of services for conditional access. Following the CJEU's conclusion in *Messner*, the principle of good faith obstructs behaviour that goes beyond what is necessary to effectively exercise a right or freedom. It adds thereto in *Synergy Hellas* that 'an abuse of rights consists in exercising a right in a manner that manifestly exceeds the limits of the normal exercise of that right by a person exercising all due care.'[430] In that line, it can be argued that the use of excessively strict terms of service that deviate from the general practice goes beyond the necessity to effectively protect the economic interests of the platform but rather forms an intentional obstruction to the person's right to access the platform on the basis of one of the limitation grounds. This is especially the case when the platform deviates (significantly) from the general conditions that it applies to first-time entrees without substantial reasoning to do so. In those circumstances, an abuse of rights can be assumed.

427. Hans-W Micklitz, *The Politics of Justice in European Private Law* (Cambridge University Press 2020), pp. 359-360. *See* similar: Thomas MJ Mollers, 'Working with Legal Principles – Demonstrated Using Private Autonomy and Freedom of Contract as Examples' (2018) 14 European review of contract law: ERCL 101, who builds upon the theories of Esser and Dworkin that principles are norms that can be used as arguments to reach a conclusion on individual rights. The recognition of principles' interpretation and review function follows directly from Art. 51(1) of the Charter, *see* on this: Reich (n. 273), p. 8. According to the latter, these general principles are framed autonomy, protection of the weaker party, non-discrimination, effectiveness, balancing, proportionality, and good faith.

428. *See* for a discussion on the existence of a principle of good faith: Reich (n. 273), p. 190 ff. The principle also exists in fairly all Member States' national systems, e.g., *redelijkheid en billijkheid* in the Dutch Civil Code, *Treu und Glauben* in Germany, the Danish *loyalitetsplikt*, and the Italian *buona fede*. The CJEU has referred to the principle in CJEU Case C-489/07 *Messner* (3 September 2009) ECLI:EU:C:2009:502, and as such, this paragraph will continue in line with that affirmation.

429. CJEU Case T-271/04, *Cytimo v. Commission* (8 May 2007) ECLI:EU:T:2007:128, §106: 'In view of the criteria identified by the case law, it is necessary first to determine whether the breaches claimed by the applicant relate to rules of law conferring rights on individuals. On this point it must be observed that the plea of abuse of a right resulting from the circumstances of the abandonment of the lease and the termination of the pre-contract negotiations has, in the applicant's arguments, no significance independent of the complaint of a breach of the principle of good faith. Therefore the plea of an abuse of rights is indistinguishable from the latter complaint.'

430. CJEU Case T-106/13 *Synergy Hellas* (18 November 2015), ECLI:EU:T:2015:860, §73, drawing from the decision of the Cour de Cassation, 16 November 2007, AR nr C.06.0349.F.1.

The principle of the protection of the weaker party comes into play when there is an inequality of power between the contracting parties, and as a consequence of that inequality, the parties do not have an equal opportunity to negotiate the components of the contract.[431] However, this inequality is inherent to consumer contracts between a social media platform and its user. The problem of unequal contracting parties is well-known and thoroughly addressed through consumer protection law. After the re-entree accepts the (restrictive) terms of service, redress is available. If the platform applies overly strict terms that deviate significantly from the ordinary course of business, those terms are most likely unfair and can be challenged as such even after the conclusion of the contract. One could wonder whether such *ex post* measures are sufficient to rebalance the party's contracting power. Users will have to initiate litigation, which can be a burden on users. The problem of including stricter terms than usual could be addressed by including that practice in the list of unfair commercial practices or by qualifying those terms as unfair contract terms.[432] Moreover, the existing consumer protection rules do not rule out any new consumer protection measures that address the contracting phase between unbalanced parties. Such *ex ante* consumer protection rules could potentially better safeguard the protection of the weaker party when facing an infinity loop.

5.5 THE LIMITATIONS TO A SOCIAL MEDIA PLATFORM'S *IUS EXCLUDENDI*

The limitations to the proprietor's *ius excludendi* form the grounds on which a denied user potentially can claim access to a platform. The limitations discussed in the following paragraphs cover limitations based on various grounds. This part starts by addressing the general requirements to restrict the right to property. Following Articles 17 and 52 of the Charter, only necessary measures that serve an aim for the general interest are justifiable. Safeguarding the rights and freedoms of others forms such an aim in the general interest. Therefore, following a general introduction on the necessity of the general interest, two examples are given of restrictions that serve to safeguard the rights of others: the European equality laws Council Directive 2000/43/EC and Council Directive 2004/113/EC, and the discussion on a positive state obligation to further regulate the right to property to safeguard the freedom of expression and information. Second, under certain circumstances, fundamental rights can be directly and horizontally invoked against other third parties. The potential of direct horizontal effect as a countermeasure against the platform's right to exclude is discussed in light of two Charter rights: the right to non-discrimination and the right to freedom of

431. Mollers (n. 427), p. 120. Reich (n. 273) 39.
432. See a similar call from Loos and Luzak to update consumer protection legislation to reflect the digital era: Marco Loos and Joasia Luzak, 'Update the Unfair Contract Terms Directive for Digital Services' https://www.europarl.europa.eu/RegData/etudes/STUD/2021/676006/IPOL_STU(2021)676006_EN.pdf (accessed 26 February 2021).

expression and information. Third, a limitation that followed from the comparative analysis of the practice in the Member States' national systems is discussed: the public and/or social interest as a basis for access claims to private property. Lastly, different doctrines in the field of competition law will be discussed as a limitation to the right to exclude.

5.5.1 Permissible Restrictions of the Right to Property

A state can only impose legislative measures that limit the platforms' right to property if such measures live up to the requirements of Article 52 (1) of the Charter. That means that if a state wants to regulate access rights to social media platforms, it will have to take into consideration the right to property (and the freedom to conduct a business) of the platform and the limitations that are made must be necessary in the general interest. From the analysis in Chapter 4, it follows that the protection of the right to property is not absolute. According to the third sentence of Article 17 of the Charter, the use of property can be regulated by law only if such restrictions are necessary for the general interest. A limitation to the right to property that does not serve to meet an objective of general interest does not live up to the requirements in Article 17 nor the requirements of Article 52 (1) of the Charter. In those situations, the proprietor can oppose legislation that unjustifiably limits its right to property. The case law of the CJEU on limitations to Article 17's right to property outlines numerous objectives that limit the right to property in the general interest. These include the protection of investors,[433] ensuring the stability of the banking and financial system and preventing a systemic risk,[434] avoiding the distortion of competition,[435] and protecting the rights and freedoms of others,[436] which includes explicitly the right to freedom of expression,[437] the protection of the environment,[438] consumer protection,[439] the protection of health,[440] the protection of the right to information and the aim to ensure access by the public to television coverage of events of major importance.[441]

433. CJEU Case C-352/20, ECLI:EU:C:2022:606 (1 August 2022), §80.
434. CJEU Case C-686/18, ECLI:EU:C:2020:567 (16 July 2020), §92; CJEU Case T-570/17, ECLI:EU:T:2022:314 (1 June 2022), §405.
435. CJEU Case T-362/04, ECLI:EU:T:2007:25 (31 January 2007), §93.
436. 'The need to protect the rights and freedoms of others' also follows directly from the scope of Art. 52(1) of the Charter.
437. *Sky Österreich GmbH v. Österreichischer Rundfunk* (n. 331), §52: 'The safeguarding of the freedoms protected under Article 11 of the Charter undoubtedly constitutes a legitimate aim in the general interest'.
438. CJEU Case C-234/20, ECLI:EU:C:2022:56 (27 January 2022), §64: '*First, it follows from settled case-law of the Court that protection of the environment is one of those objectives of general interest (see, to that effect, judgment of 9 March 2010, ERG and Others, C-379/08 and C-380/08, EU:C:2010:127, paragraph 81 and the case-law cited). Protection of the environment is therefore capable of justifying a restriction on the use of the right to property (judgment of 15 January 2013, Križan and Others, C-416/10, EU:C:2013:8, paragraph 114 and the case-law cited).*'
439. CJEU Case C-12/11, ECLI:EU:C:2013:43 (31 January 2013), §63.
440. CJEU Case C-210/03, ECLI:EU:C:2004:802 (14 December 2004), §74.
441. CJEU Case C-201/11 P, ECLI:EU:C:2013:519 (18 July 2013), §102.

The restrictions must not only serve an aim for the general interest, but they must also be *necessary* to meet that aim.[442] Recalling the conclusion in §4.3.2, in principle, a measure does not pass the necessity test if a less intrusive measure exists which is capable of achieving the same objective or goal.[443] For social media platforms, that means that an obligation to contract must be necessary for the general interest and that the aim cannot be obtained in any other way that is less infringing on the right to property. Since an obligation to contract is a direct limitation of a fundamental right, it should be avoided if possible. If, for example, achieving the aim (granting fair and equal access to the service) could be sufficiently safeguarded by requiring interoperability,[444] then an obligation to provide the platform service to all people would constitute a disproportionate interference with the platforms' own fundamental right to property.

5.5.2 Limitations to Safeguard the Rights and Freedoms of Others

It follows from the text of Article 52(1) Charter that the protection of the rights and freedoms of others can serve as a base for limitations to fundamental rights. Moreover, it is settled case law that regulation of the use of the property can serve to achieve that aim.[445] The European directives on equal treatment are an example of European legislation that aims to protect of rights and freedoms of others by limiting the right to property. Moreover, discussions exist to what extent states *should* take regulatory measures to fulfil their positive obligation to safeguard the right to freedom of expression.

5.5.2.1 The European Directives on Equal Treatment

Equality laws can play a defining role in accessing social media platforms, as has been demonstrated by the German and Danish case law in the first part.[446] At a European level, two directives on equal treatment apply directly to the supply of services by

442. *Republic of Poland v. European Parliament and Council of the European Union* (n. 386), §65: 'As regards observance of the principle of proportionality, that principle requires that the limitations which may, in particular, be imposed by acts of EU law on rights and freedoms enshrined in the Charter do not exceed the limits of what is appropriate and necessary in order to meet the legitimate objectives pursued or the need to protect the rights and freedoms of others; where there is a choice between several appropriate measures, recourse must be had to the least onerous, and the disadvantages caused must not be disproportionate to the aims pursued.' Similar: judgments of 13 March 2019, *Poland v. Parliament and Council*, C-128/17, EU:C:2019:194, §94; 17 December 2020, Centraal Israëlitisch Consistorie van België and Others, C-336/19, EU:C:2020:1031, §64.
443. *See* for a further discussion also Reich (n. 273), p. 157.
444. Which is for example required under the new rules in the Digital Markets Act, *see* Arts 6 and 7.
445. *See, e.g.*: *Sky Österreich GmbH v. Österreichischer Rundfunk* (n. 331); *UPC Telekabel Wien GmbH v. Constantin Film Verleih GmbH and Wega Filmproduktionsgesellschaft mbH* (n. 364); *Lidl* (n. 379).
446. *See* respectively §2.2.1.2 and §2.2.4.2.

private parties – also in an online context.[447] These are first, the Council Directive 2000/43/EC (Racial Equality Directive), and second, the Council Directive 2004/113/EC (Gender Goods and Services Directive).[448] The directives form the legal basis to oppose discriminating access restrictions in situations where these directives apply. Discrimination on the basis of gender, racial or ethnic grounds when accessing goods or services offered to the general public is prohibited. Both directives lay down minimum requirements. It is, therefore, possible that European Member States have implemented more favourable provisions.[449] Less favourable measures are explicitly forbidden.[450]

The provisions of the directives apply to parties that provide goods and services to the general public.[451] This covers goods and services that are offered 'irrespective of the person concerned, which are offered outside the area of private and family life'.[452] An offer of access to a social media platform falls within this scope.[453] Both directives differentiate between *direct* and *indirect* discrimination. Direct discrimination refers to terms that explicitly differentiate on the basis of gender (Directive 2004/113) or on grounds of racial or ethnic origin (Directive 2000/43). That would be the case if a platform is restricted to one gender or (excludes) a specific ethnic group.[454] Indirect discrimination occurs when terms are apparently neutral, but as an effect, persons of

447. It follows from national case law that the supply of services includes the access to private property, such as the access to bars, restaurants and night clubs, and shops, *see* FRA, Handbook on European non-discrimination law (2018), p. 134 and the national case law cited. The extension to online services can deducted from Directive (EU) 2019/770 on certain aspects concerning contracts for the supply of digital content and digital services.
448. In addition to these two directives, more European directives exist in the field of non-discrimination and equal treatment, but since their scope of application is limited to employment issues, occupation, and work environments, they do not apply to the issues related to accessing social media platforms and are therefore not included in this analysis. *See* for a full list of the non-discrimination and equality legislation at European level: European Commission, 'Non-discrimination', https://commission.europa.eu/aid-development-cooperation-fundamental-rights/your-rights-eu/know-your-rights/equality/non-discrimination_en (accessed 14 December 2022).
449. For example, Denmark has extended the scope of its gender equality laws substantially in December 2022, which now include (amongst other categories) sexual orientation and gender identity. *See* §2.2.4.2.
450. Directive 2000/43, Art. 6 and directive 2004/113/EC, Art. 7.
451. Directive 2000/43/EC, Art. 3(1)(h); Directive 2004/113/EC, Art. 3(1).
452. Directive 2004/113/EC, Art. 3(1).
453. *See* on this Directive (EU) 2019/770 on certain aspects concerning contracts for the supply of digital content and digital services, which includes in the definition of the supply of digital content and digital services the *access to the use of social media* (preamble 19).
454. Here the legal consequences of the choice for a minimum harmonisation become pressing. In Denmark, direct discrimination on the basis of sex includes direct discrimination on the basis of gender identity and sexual orientation, whereas that outcome is not guaranteed in other Member States. This is problematic when dealing with cross-border online services that apply predominantly one set of terms for the entire Union. For example, excluding LGBT content in the terms of service of a social media platform would fall within the scope of direct discrimination under the Danish implementation of Directive 2004/113/EC. The rise of anti-LGBT legislation (such as Hungary's Act LXXIX of 2021 on taking more severe action against paedophile offenders and amending certain Acts for the protection of children) can give rise to serious conflicts of laws within the Union, which minefield will have to be closely navigated by social media platforms to prevent legal consequences.

one sex or persons of a racial or ethnic origin are put at a particular disadvantage. This situation would, for example, occur when terms of a social media platform would exclude any portrayal or discussion of childbirth. Even though the term is formulated as neutral – all childbirth content is prohibited – it would negatively affect women more than men.

Direct discrimination on the basis of racial or ethnic origin is always prohibited, whereas direct discrimination on the basis of gender can be justifiable. Indirect discrimination can be justifiable for both categories. An indirect discriminative access restriction on either ground or a direct restriction on the basis of gender in the terms of service can be justifiable if the term is objectively justified by a legitimate aim and the means of achieving that aim are appropriate and necessary.[455] As such, when offering access to a social media platform, the terms of service can, under no circumstances, *directly* discriminate on the basis of racial or ethnic origin. It is possible, however, to offer a male or a female-only platform or to create sub-sections of a platform that are only available to one gender – though only if such a restriction serves a legitimate aim and is appropriate and necessary. As such, the 'female nipple prohibition' can survive the test if it serves a legitimate aim, whereas restricting content on the basis of skin colour is, under no means or circumstances, justifiable.

The discussion on what constitutes a legitimate aim is unsettled.[456] Balancing the interests of the proprietor on the one side and the prospected customers on the other has proven difficult. The choice to limit the scope of a platform's service falls within the proprietor's freedom to conduct a business in Article 16, and as such, a choice to limit the scope to a certain group could constitute a legitimate aim in itself.[457] Satisfying the platforms' advertisers, creating a platform that is welcoming and open to users, or a simple normative preference could form reasons for a platform to restrict the supply of its service. The test to define whether a measure is appropriate and necessary to fulfil the requirement of a legitimate aim is strict.[458] It depends on a case-by-case basis whether a specific measure fulfils the requirement. The discriminating measure must be objectively justifiable, meaning that the proprietor has a genuine need to impose the restriction. From the CJEU's case law, it follows that two elements can be used to demonstrate a genuine need. First, the rights and legitimate wishes of the (other) users of the service[459] – though only when those wishes are not in itself based on

455. For indirect discrimination: Directive 2000/43/EC, Art. 2(2)(b); Directive 2004/113/EC, Art. 2(b). For direct discrimination on the basis of sex: Directive 2004/113/EC, Art. 4(5).
456. The discussion is not limited to European law. The discussion between a proprietor's freedom to decide the scope of its service and the right to non-discrimination was the main point in the US case *Masterpiece Cakeshop v. Colorado Civil Rights Commission*, 584 U.S. Supreme Court (2018), and the UK case *Lee v. Ashers Baking Company Ltd and others* (2018) Supreme Court of the United Kingdom 49. The latter case was appealed to the ECtHR, which appeal was dismissed in December 2021: ECtHR Application No. 18860/19.
457. CJEU Case C-157-/15, *Achbita* (14 March 2017), ECLI:EU:C:2017:203, §§37-38 – in relation to restrictive rules in an employment contract on the basis of religious beliefs.
458. CJEU Case C-83/14, *CHEZ Razpredelenie Bulgaria* (16 July 2015) ECLI:EU:C:2015:480, §112.
459. CJEU Joined Cases C-341/19 and C-804/18, *MH Müller* (15 July 2021), ECLI:EU:C:2021:594, §65.

discriminatory grounds.[460] Second, the discrimination could be objectively justifiable if, in the absence of such a policy, the freedom to conduct a business is undermined. That is the case if 'given the nature of its activities or the context in which they are carried out, [the service] would suffer adverse consequences'.[461] In light of employment restrictions, the CJEU has concluded that a wish to offer a neutral service to customers or the prevention of social conflict were seen as legitimate aims to indirectly discriminate on the basis of religious beliefs.[462] Whether that practice also extends to the general supply of goods and services is unclear. The CJEU cases of *Achbita*, *Bougnaoui* and *MH Müller* concerned employment cases. In those situations, Council Directive 2000/78/EC of 27 November 2000 establishing a general framework for equal treatment in employment and occupation applies, which has a broader scope than the two directives addressed above.[463] This broader scope of rules does not apply to the general supply of goods and services.

5.5.2.2 The Protection of the Right to Freedom of Expression

According to the CJEU in *Sky Österreich*, it follows that 'the safeguarding of the freedoms protected under Article 11 of the Charter undoubtedly constitutes a legitimate aim in the general interest, the importance of which in a democratic and pluralistic society must be stressed in particular'.[464] Consequently, a state can limit the right of exclusion under the right to property if such a limitation is necessary to protect the right to freedom of expression and information. Currently, no legislation (whether national or European) provides a right to claim access to a social media platform. Under certain circumstances, states have a positive obligation to take measures to make sure that nationals' rights are protected and ensured. The positive obligation of a state to effectively protect the freedom of expression could mean that access to private property under certain circumstances must be regulated to safeguard the right to freedom of expression.

460. CJEU Case C-188/15, *Bougnaoui and ADDH* (14 March 2017) ECLI:EU:C:2017:204. For example, a platform that offers a discussion forum for persons with afro-textured hair could restrict the participation of people from ethnic groups that do not possess afro-textured hair and in that sense, indirectly discriminate on the basis of ethnic or racial origin. This discrimination is indirectly, because the term is neutral ('only discussions on afro-textured hair'), but as an effect that term puts persons of a racial or ethnic origin at a particular disadvantage. Though, the choice to limit the scope conveys a wish from the community of users on the platform, namely to discuss the specific characteristics of afro-textured hair. That wish is not based on discrimination (excluding a certain group of persons) but is founded on an objective point of interest, and thus it demonstrates a legitimate interest in discussing a topic that only concerns a limited group of persons.
461. CJEU Joined Cases C-341/19 and C-804/18, *MH Müller* (15 July 2021), ECLI:EU:C:2021:594, §67.
462. *Ibid.*, §76.
463. Council Directive 2000/78/EC, Art. 1: The purpose of this Directive is to lay down a general framework for combating discrimination on the grounds of *religion or belief, disability, age or sexual orientation* as regards employment and occupation, with a view to putting into effect in the Member States the principle of equal treatment. (underlining by the author).
464. *Sky Österreich GmbH v. Österreichischer Rundfunk* (n. 331), §52.

The dilemma of balancing the freedom of expression and the right to property has previously been addressed by the ECtHR in the case of *Appleby*.[465] In this case, the owner of a shopping mall refused a group of persons to campaign in the privately owned shopping mall. However, the refused people had other possibilities to express themselves (e.g., demonstrating on public grounds or through the media). Without state intervention, the nationals had thus other options to express themselves. The ECtHR concludes that a general right of access to private property cannot be inferred from Article 10. Only in case the refusal of access to private property prevents 'any effective exercise of freedom of expression or it can be said that the essence of the right has been destroyed, [then] a positive obligation could arise for the State to protect the enjoyment of the Convention rights by regulating property rights'.[466] The latter does not seem to be the case for social media platforms.[467] If access to one platform is denied, one can simply join another one.[468] The essence of the right to freedom of expression will not be destroyed by a refusal of access to a particular social media platform, and as such, states do not have a positive obligation to regulate the proprietor's *ius excludendi* to the extent that all persons can demand access to the service on the basis of the freedom of expression, simply because the users' essence to express themselves will not be destroyed by a refusal of access to a social media platform.

5.5.3 Direct Effect of Fundamental Rights

The conclusion that it is settled case law that regulation of the use of the property can serve to safeguard the rights and freedoms of the users merely applies to cases where a *state* regulates the use of private property. There is a difference between a state regulating the access to private property and a private party drawing up the scope of the service it offers and, as a consequence, limiting the access to private property. This difference is particularly important and exemplified by the fundamental principle of direct effect under European law and its differences in *vertical* and *horizontal* direct effects.

If a state has not explicitly provided a right to access a social media platform (under certain circumstances), then the platform is, in principle, free to make use of its private property and to exclude (groups of) persons from accessing their property. The proprietor can make unlimited use of its right to exclude. Other parties' fundamental rights do not automatically create obligations between two private parties. In principle, users can, therefore, not directly claim access to a platform by invoking their right to freedom of expression. The ECtHR in *Appleby* highlights that the right to freedom of

465. *Appleby and Others v. United Kingdom* (n. 188), 24 September 2003.
466. *Ibid.*, §47.
467. *See* for an equal conclusion: Smed Larsen (n. 17).
468. *See* on this also the argumentation later on regarding essential facilities, explaining why the refusal of access to one social media platform does not rule out the possibility to join another platform and express oneself.

expression 'does not bestow any freedom of forum for the exercise of that right'.[469] A person cannot simply choose the means to express an opinion but has to choose from the accessible available options. Private parties only have to observe the obligations under fundamental rights in case the provisions have horizontal direct effect.[470] If a provision falls within the latter category, a social media platform must take the fundamental right protection of the other party into consideration when drawing up the access criteria to the platform. However, deciding exactly when a fundamental rights provision has horizontal direct effect has proven a tough debate.

5.5.3.1 Horizontal Direct Effect of the European Charter's Provisions

Direct effect can be invoked vertically against the state or, under certain circumstances, horizontally against another private party. Whether the provisions – and in case, which provisions – of the Charter have horizontal direct effect is unclear.[471] Primary European law can, in principle, be invoked horizontally by private parties,[472] though only in case the provision fulfils the requirements for direct effect as stipulated in the case of *Van Gend & Loos*. That means that a provision has direct effect only if it is clear, unconditional, sufficiently precise, and does not require any further implementing measures.[473] Following Article 6(1) TEU, the Charter has the character of primary European law. It should, thus, in principle, be horizontally invocable if a provision lives up to the requirements in *Van Gend & Loos*. However, to make matters more difficult, the Charter has an ingrained limitation that seemingly restricts its scope to *vertical* direct effect only. Article 51 outlines the Charter's field of application. The article limits the Charter's addressees to the institutions, bodies, offices and agencies of the Union' and to the Member States when they act in the scope of the EU law[474] or when they implement EU law.[475] Private parties are not explicitly included as addressees of the Charter. The latter argument, however, would bypass the CJEU's earlier decision in *Defrenne v. Sabena*, where the horizontal direct effect was applied despite the disputed article not being formally addressed to private parties.[476] Following a clear

469. *Appleby case*, §47.
470. This is irrespective of any possible consequences to the private parties' contractual relationship imposed by national courts, which can use fundamental rights to interpret open norms in private law in disputes between the parties. This indirect effect of fundamental rights is separately addressed as part of the content layer in the next chapter.
471. Nuria Bermejo, 'Fundamental Rights and Horizontal Direct Effect Under the Charter' in Cristina Izquierdo-Sans, Carmen Martínez-Capdevila and Magdalena Nogueira-Guastavino (eds), *Fundamental Rights Challenges: Horizontal Effectiveness, Rule of Law and Margin of National Appreciation* (Springer International Publishing 2021) https://doi.org/10.1007/978-3-030-727 98-7_5 (accessed 13 December 2022).
472. Case C-43/75, *Defrenne v. Sabena* (No 2) [1976] ECR 455, *see also* Eleni Frantziou, 'The Horizontal Effect of the Charter of Fundamental Rights of the EU: Rediscovering the Reasons for Horizontality' (2015) 21 European Law Journal 657.
473. CJEU Case C-26/62, ECLI:EU:C:1963:1 (5 February 1963) (*Van Gend & Loos*).
474. CJEU Case C-5/88, ECLI:EU:C:1989:321 (13 July 1989) (Wachauf).
475. CJEU Case C-292/97, ECLI:EU:C:2000:202 (13 April 2000) (Kjell Karlsson).
476. Frantziou (n. 472).

statement of Advocate General Bot in the Joined cases of *Bauer and Willmeroth*,[477] the CJEU provided more clarity on the discussion in the case of *Shimizu*:

> although Article 51(1) of the Charter states that the provisions thereof are addressed to the institutions, bodies, offices and agencies of the European Union with due regard for the principle of subsidiarity and to the Member States only when they are implementing EU law, article 51(1) does not, however, address the question whether those individuals may, where appropriate, be directly required to comply with certain provisions of the Charter and cannot, accordingly, be interpreted as meaning that it would systematically preclude such a possibility.[478]

That conclusion by the CJEU seems to read between the lines that Article 51(1) does not explicitly *preclude* the horizontal direct effect of the Charter's rights between individuals, even though the text, in any case, does not explicitly *include* such a possibility. A full discussion on whether the CJEU has overstepped its competence or whether this conclusion is the right way forward falls outside the scope of this book, though this conclusion of the CJEU is, to say the least, based on a shaky foundation. Following the developments in the CJEU's case law, the debate has moved into (somewhat) calmer waters, and the general understanding seems to be that a horizontal direct effect of the provisions in the European Charter is possible. That is true, at least for some of the provisions, as not all Charter provisions are directly horizontally invocable. As outlined by Frantziou, recalling the decision in *Van Gend & Loos:* 'Charter provisions that are framed in a mandatory and unconditional manner can in principle be invoked [directly], both vertically and horizontally.'[479] There are currently three rights that have been affirmed by the CJEU to have horizontal direct effect: Article 21 (the right to non-discrimination),[480] Article 31 (the right to fair working conditions),[481] and Article 47 (the right to effective judicial protection).[482] There are also several rights that were found *not* to have horizontal direct effect. These include Article 26 (integration of persons with disabilities), Article 27 (worker's right to information), and Article 38 (consumer protection).[483]

477. The CJEU referenced this opinion of the AG's later in the case of *Shiminzu* (§77): *'First of all, as noted by the Advocate General in point 78 of his Opinion in Joined Cases Bauer and Willmeroth (C-569/16 and C-570/16, EU:C:2018:337), the fact that certain provisions of primary law are addressed principally to the Member States does not preclude their application to relations between individuals.'*
478. *Max-Planck-Gesellschaft zur Förderung der Wissenschaften eV v. Tetsuji Shimizu* [2018] ECJ Case C-684/16, §76.
479. *See* Eleni Frantziou, 'The Horizontal Effect of the Charter: Towards an Understanding of Horizontality as a Structural Constitutional Principle' (2020) 22 Cambridge Yearbook of European Legal Studies 208, and the case law cited under III.
480. CJEU Case C-414/16 (*Egenberger*), ECLI:EU:C:2018:257 (17 April 2018).
481. *Shimizu*, supra.
482. *Egenberger*, supra.
483. *See* Frantziou (n. 472), 208, and the case law cited under II. These cover respectively for Arts 26, 27, and 38: CJEU Case C-356/12 (*Glatzel*), ECLI:EU:C:2014:350 (22 May 2014), CJEU Case C-176/12 (*Association de Médiation Sociale*), ECLI:EU:C:2014:2 (15 January 2014), and CJEU Case C-122/17 (*Smith*), ECLI:EU:C:2018:631 (7 August 2018).

In line with the requirements on horizontal direct effect stipulated in the CJEU case law, the right to property in Article 17 seemingly fulfils these and, therefore, presumably has horizontal direct effect against other private parties. The right is clear, unconditional, sufficiently precise, and does not require any further implementing measures, which can be demonstrated by the mere fact that the national law of several Member States has codified the (near) identical text in their civil codes.[484] Furthermore, in several decisions, the CJEU has consistently held that the provision 'which states that everyone has the right to own his or her lawfully acquired possessions, is a rule of law intended to confer rights on individuals'.[485] As such, the right to property forms a solid basis for the proprietor of a platform to deny access directly to another private party (the user).[486] That means that, in principle, since the right to property can thus be invoked horizontally against other private parties, platforms are free to decide on who can or cannot enter.

To what extent platforms can freely draw up terms that govern other circumstances than access and thereby limit other private parties' fundamental rights protection is unclear. In relation to the right to freedom of thought, conscience, and religion (Article 10 of the Charter), the CJEU has previously held in *Achbita* that the freedom of contract (Article 16) can serve as a basis even for contractual terms that, as an effect, limit other parties' Charter freedoms.[487] Exactly to what extent Charter rights can be directly invoked against such a denial of access on the basis of Article 16 is unsettled.[488] One could imagine that other Charter rights have the potential to be directly invoked against the platform's choice to limit access to the platform if these individual provisions have horizontal direct effect. When discussing a potential right to access a social media platform on the basis of a fundamental right in the Charter, naturally, a few articles prove interesting to dive further into. These consist of, first, the right to non-discrimination in Article 21, which can serve as a basis to oppose restrictive terms that distinguish on the basis of protected grounds that are not explicitly regulated by the two directives discussed above. Second, access restrictions have a limiting effect on the right to freedom of expression's protection. Horizontal direct effect of the article could lead to an obligation on other private parties – including social media platforms. Therefore, also the right to freedom of expression should be considered.

484. Art. 832 Italian Civil Code, Art. 5:1(2) Dutch Civil Code, §903 German Civil Code.
485. *Frank Steinhoff and Others v. European Central Bank* (2019) Cúirt Ghinearálta Case T-107/17, §96; *Ledra Advertising and Others v. Commission* (2016) ECLI:EC:C:2016:701, §66: 'That provision, which states that everyone has the right to own his or her lawfully acquired possessions, is a rule of law intended to confer rights on individuals.'
486. *See also* the previous conclusion in §3.2.1.
487. Case C-157/15 (*Achbita*), ECLI:EU:C:2017:203 (14 March 2017), §§38-40.
488. For example, a preliminary ruling is pending that discusses whether terms of services limiting the fundamental freedom of equal treatment, which terms are based on Art. 16's freedom of contract, are justifiable or whether Art. 10 of the Charter can be taken into consideration in the examination of the justifiability of such terms, *see* the request for a preliminary ruling from the Bundesarbeitsgericht (Germany) lodged on 30 April 2019 – *MH Müller Handels GmbH v. MJ* (Case C-341/19).

5.5.3.2 *The Horizontal Effect of the Right to Non-discrimination*

The two directives covered above in §5.5.2.1 only stipulate rules for discrimination when accessing goods and services on the basis of gender and racial or ethnic origin. What conclusion does this leave for the other protected categories that are included in both Article 19 TFEU and Article 21 of the Charter? These other categories – religion or belief, disability, age, or sexual orientation[489] – are not explicitly addressed in European legislation applicable to the sphere of accessing goods and services.[490] Due to lacking specific legislation that protects the other grounds of discrimination through secondary legislation, the question of whether these grounds can be used to restrict access when offering social media services depends, first, on the national legislation and implementation of the directives in the Member States,[491] and second, on the horizontal direct effect of Article 21 Charter and Article 14 ECHR. Regarding the latter, the CJEU recalls in *Egenberger* its previous line of case law and concludes that 'as regards its mandatory effect, Article 21 of the Charter is no different, in principle, from the various provisions of the founding Treaties prohibiting discrimination on various grounds, even where the discrimination derives from contracts between individuals.[492] Article 21(1) has horizontal direct effect, as 'the prohibition, which is laid down in Article 21(1) of the Charter, is sufficient in itself to confer on individuals a right which they may rely on as such in disputes between them in a field covered by EU law'.[493]

However, the circumstances in the cases discussed by the CJEU, in which Article 21 of the Charter was given direct effect, were specific employment cases in which situations had been explicitly regulated by the European legislator through various directives. On online marketplaces, private persons who use the platform's service as

489. The scope of Art. 21 of the Charter is broader than the terminology in Art. 19 of the TFEU. In addition to the latter, Art. 21 Charter also mentions: genetic features, language, political or any other opinion, membership of a national minority, property, and birth. A further point of discussion is whether these traditional classifications of protected groups are sufficient in the digital age. Wachter has pointed out that artificial intelligence moderation creates new, non-traditional groups, that can lead to significant discriminatory outcomes. *See* on this: Sandra Wachter, 'The Theory of Artificial Immutability: Protecting Algorithmic Groups under Anti-Discrimination Law' (15 February 2022) https://papers.ssrn.com/abstract=4099100 (accessed 14 December 2022).
490. They are included in the directives against discrimination and equal treatment in employment situations, where the same requirement is applied ('an objectively justified legitimate aim which is appropriate and necessary'), *see, e.g.*, Council Directive 2000/78/EC of 27 November 2000 establishing a general framework for equal treatment in employment and occupation.
491. Due to the scope of this research, an in-depth study into the differences in all European Member States has not been included here.
492. CJEU Case C-416/16 *Egenberger* (17 April 2018), ECLI:EU:C:2018:257, §77, recalling the conclusions in CJEU Case-C53/75 (8 April 1976) *Defrenne*, ECLI:EU:C:1976:56, §39; CJEU Case C-281/98 (6 June 2000) *Angonese*, ECLI:EU:C:2000:296, §§33-36; CJEU Case C-411/98 (3 October 2000) *Ferlini*, ECLI:EU:C:2000:530, §50; and CJEU Case C-438/05 (11 December 2007) *International Transport Workers' Federation and Finnish Seamen's Union*, ECLI:EU:C:2007:772, §§57-61.
493. CJEU Case C-416/16 *Egenberger*, §76.

self-employed workers may not be refused on any of the grounds in Article 21.[494] However, it remains unclear whether the CJEU would reach a similar conclusion *outside* the scope of employment matters. The equality directives that deal with *employment situations* include all potential discriminatory grounds mentioned in the Charter, whereas the directives that cover the access and supply to goods and services are limited to gender, racial and ethnic origin. It seems, therefore, most in line with the reasoning of the European legislator that the other grounds in Article 21 do not apply horizontally between private parties when offering goods and services to the public, but that conclusion cannot be drawn with certainty. There does not seem to be a specific reason as to why discrimination on the basis of gender and ethnic origin when accessing services has been regulated directly and the other grounds of Article 21 Charter have been left out.[495] One of the reasons could be the lack of necessity to address the other discriminatory grounds since these grounds mostly pose a theoretical problem as opposed to an existing problem in practice when accessing private property such as social media platforms. Potentially discriminative access restricting terms that do not concern race or gender are rarely enforced when accessing social media platforms. *See*, for example, the situation on the (American) online dating website *FarmersOnly.com*, which, according to its terms of service, offers a platform 'oriented towards allowing single farmers, ranchers, cowboys, cowgirls, and other rural and country folk to create Profiles in order to meet each other online'.[496] However, the possibility to create an account on the platform is not limited to people who fall within that category only. The same argument can be made for dating application *Jswipe*, which is the self-proclaimed '#1 Jewish Dating App'. Though the words 'jew', 'Jewish', or 'Judaism' do not appear at all in the platform's terms of service.[497]

Specific cases on the conflict between the freedom to conduct a business and the right to non-discrimination when supplying goods and services to the general public have not been (successfully) brought before the CJEU or the ECtHR. In case law from other jurisdictions, only restrictive measures that affect the supply of the goods to third parties were found to infringe the right to non-discrimination.[498] The right does not extend to an obligation to supply certain goods or services. The US case *Masterpiece Cakeshop v. Colorado Civil Rights Commission* and the UK case *Lee v. Ashers Baking Company Ltd and others* concerned, respectively, the refusal of a wedding cake for a gay marriage and the refusal of a cake with pro-gay messages. The courts in both cases ruled in favour of the business owners, concluding that they cannot be obliged to

494. *See* a confirmation of this recently in the CJEU's decision in C-356/21 (12 January 2023), ECLI:EU:C:2023:9, on the refusal to conclude a contract with a self-employed worker on the basis of sexual orientation.
495. Outside the scope of employment, it has been argued that from a German perspective, the laws on equal treatment (specifically §21 AGG) should be applicable outside the scope of employment matters and can lead to an obligation to contract, *see* Wiemann (n. 426).
496. Farmersonly.com, Terms of Service (9 July 2016), https://www.farmersonly.com/pages/terms-and-conditions (accessed 22 December 2022).
497. Jswipe, Terms of use agreement (30 March 2022), https://jswipeapp.com/terms-of-service (accessed 22 December 2022).
498. *Masterpiece Cakeshop v. Colorado Civil Rights Commission*, 584 U.S. Supreme Court (2018); *Lee v. Ashers Baking Company Ltd and others* (2018) Supreme Court of the United Kingdom 49.

support opinions that they profoundly disagree with or simply do not hold. In *Lee v. Ashers Baking Company Ltd and others*, the refusal of service did not discriminate based on sexual orientation since the persons were not rejected to be supplied with goods (regular cakes). The refusal related 'to the message and not to any particular person or persons'.[499] In *Masterpiece Cakeshop*, the protection of the freedom of religion was found to outweigh the interests of the customers.[500] Following the reasoning in these cases, a proprietor cannot distinguish to whom it wishes to supply the goods, but it can refuse to supply certain goods that contravene its personal beliefs. Whether that stance will be followed by the ECtHR and the CJEU remains unclear. The UK case was brought before the ECtHR but was dismissed without a substantial assessment of the case.[501] The applicant had not invoked its right to non-discrimination under Article 14 ECHR before the national court. Whether that article can be directly invoked and would have led to a different output 'is highly fact-sensitive and to date no similar issue has been addressed by the [ECtHR]. By relying solely on domestic law, the applicant deprived the domestic courts of the opportunity to address this important issue themselves before he lodged his application with the [ECtHR]'.[502] The ECtHR highlights that the balancing of the interests of the proprietor and the prospected customer depends on a case-by-case assessment. Referring to the US case, the ECtHR concludes that '*these disputes must be resolved with tolerance, without undue disrespect to sincere religious beliefs, and without subjecting gay persons to indignities when they seek goods and services in an open market*' and must take due regard to the local (political) situation.[503]

Presumably, since equal treatment forms a general principle, courts can apply the legislative framework applicable to employment matters to fill this gap.[504] However, that would pose a problem since the two directives do not apply the same test for cases of direct discrimination. For direct discrimination on the basis of ethnic or racial origin, an absolute prohibition exists, whereas an objective justification test for direct discrimination on the basis of gender is applied. If the other grounds in Article 21(1) were to be treated similarly to the framework in the Racial Equality Directive, then a specific religious platform, an LGBT+ platform, or any age limitations in the access restrictions on social media platforms would be directly challengeable by those that have been rejected. These access restrictions would be directly discriminating on the basis of religion, sexual orientation, and age. That does not seem to be a desirable

499. *Lee v. Ashers Baking Company Ltd and others* (2018) Supreme Court of the United Kingdom 49, §22, §34, §47.
500. 'While it is unexceptional that Colorado law can protect gay persons in acquiring products and services on the same terms and conditions as are offered to other members of the public, the law must be applied in a manner that is neutral toward religion.', *Masterpiece Cakeshop v. Colorado Civil Rights Commission*, 584 U.S. Supreme Court (2018).
501. *Lee v. the United Kingdom (dec)* [2021] ECtHR 18860/19.
502. *Ibid.*, §74.
503. *Ibid.*, §75. The Court notes further that: 'It is clear from the impassioned third-party interventions in this case (*see* paragraphs 58-67 above) that this balancing exercise is a matter of great import and sensitivity to both LGBTIQ communities and to faith communities.'
504. By analogy: CJEU Joined Cases C-528 and C-619/10, *Nelson et al v. Lufthansa et al* (6 September 2012) ECLI:EU:C:2012:531, *see* on this Reich (n. 273), pp. 8-9.

outcome. The framework, as applied to restrictions on the basis of gender, seems more suitable.[505] In those cases, access restrictions that directly discriminate on either of the protected grounds are allowed if the restriction serves a legitimate aim and is appropriate and necessary. If a platform with sexually explicit content restricts access for minors, such an access restriction on the basis of age would pass the test of the legitimate aim (shielding minors from sexually explicit content). The restriction is appropriate (only targets minors) and necessary to achieve that aim. A similar argument can be made for an LGBTQI+ platform when the legitimate aim for the restriction is to create a safe space to discuss certain topics, free from interference.

The discussion on the horizontal effect of the right to non-discrimination when accessing a social media platform's service could increase in importance over the coming years. In the DSA, Recital 47 stipulates that 'when designing (...) restrictions, providers of intermediary services should act in a non-arbitrary and non-discriminatory manner', therewith seemingly implying a direct effect of the right to non-discrimination when accessing a social media platform.[506] If the terms are drawn up in a way that excludes (certain groups of) persons on the basis of a discriminative ground, then the platform's terms do not live up to the requirement of a non-discriminatory design of restrictions. The exact effects of these new standards in the DSA are unclear.[507]

5.5.3.3 The Horizontal Effect of the Right to Freedom of Expression

Following the conclusions above on limitations to a proprietor's right to exclude to protect the right to freedom of expression, there is currently no European secondary legislation explicitly providing a provision to claim access to a platform and neither do states have a positive obligation to enact such acts since users are not deprived of effective means to express themselves. In the CJEU case of *Sky Österreich*, the discussion revolved around legislation that limited a broadcaster's freedom to conduct a business in Article 16 in favour of the right to freedom of expression and to impart information protected under Article 11. As such, the question was not whether Article 11 can be invoked horizontally to claim access but rather whether the legislation was striking the right balance between the different fundamental rights. It did not address the horizontal effect of the right to freedom of expression.

Regardless, it seems unlikely that the right to freedom of expression would be able to be invoked horizontally between private parties. The right to freedom of

505. Sexual orientation is since December 2022 included in the Danish implementation of the Gender Goods and Services Directive. It will be interesting to follow any cases brought before the Danish Equality Board that follow from this expansion to observe whether this would in- or decrease the number of legal issues.
506. The implication of the direct effect on the design of the terms of service is unclear. The recital includes in its scope the 'design, application, and enforcement', whereas the corresponding Art. 14 only includes 'application' and 'enforcement'.
507. Whether these restrictions apply to access restrictions or solely to content restrictions, and whether such clauses are subsequently contractually enforceable by the user, can be debated. *See* the discussion in §6.4.3.1.

expression in Article 11 does not fulfil the requirements set out in *Van Gend & Loos*. From the text of Article 11 of the Charter, it follows that the freedom of expression, at a maximum, provides vertical direct effect. The text in the second sentence of the provision limits the scope of potential interference with public authority.[508] That rules out the possibility of demanding access to a platform based on the horizontal direct effect of the right to freedom of expression since the scope of the article itself is limited to interference by the state rather than interference with the right by another private party. As such, it would be a stretch to conclude that the right to freedom of expression can be used to claim access to a social media platform, at least up until the point that the users have *any other effective* way to express themselves. Since there are numerous online ways to express an opinion and/or to impart information online, there is no risk that the refusal of access to one social media platform will destroy the essence of the right to freedom of expression of a single user. Even in those cases, the lack of any effective way to express oneself would most likely trigger a positive state obligation to regulate access to social media platforms rather than horizontal direct effect. Additionally, contrary to the argument made on the basis of Recital 47 DSA concerning the horizontal effect of the right to non-discrimination when designing the terms of service, there is only a reference in the DSA that the freedom of expression must 'be taken into account'.[509] That seems far less reaching than the instigation on platforms to 'act in a non-discriminatory manner'. That means that for *ex ante* access refusals, the right to freedom of expression does not prove helpful to refused persons.

Potentially, the *radiating effect* described by Frantziou can broaden the scope of the (horizontal) direct effect of fundamental rights in a way that can aid users at a later stage to oppose *ex post* access restrictions. Through this radiating effect, which effectively refers to the discussion on indirect effect of Charter rights in disputes between private parties,[510] the CJEU can interpret existing secondary legislation in the light of fundamental rights protection to ensure effective protection. The right to freedom of expression could play a role in assessing and balancing the contractual relationship between a social media platform and a user, but in those circumstances, the user has already gained access to the platform at the moment the right to freedom

508. 'This right shall include freedom to hold opinions and to receive and impart information and ideas without interference by public authority' (cursive highlight added by the author). An identical conclusion on the lack of a horizontal direct effect of the freedom of expression in the realm of artificial intelligence follows from Maja Brkan, 'Freedom of Expression and Artificial Intelligence: On Personalisation, Disinformation and (Lack Of) Horizontal Effect of the Charter' (17 March 2019) https://papers.ssrn.com/abstract=3354180 (accessed 13 December 2022). However, Brkan continues and concludes later in her paper that the CJEU *might nonetheless* conclude on a creative teleological interpretation of Art. 11 of the Charter and reach a conclusion that the article holds horizontal direct effect. What the final conclusion on the matter will be, is to be seen in the future.

509. Recital 47 DSA: 'When *designing*, applying and enforcing those restrictions, providers of intermediary services should act in a non-arbitrary and non-discriminatory manner and *take into account* the rights and legitimate interests of the recipients of the service, including *fundamental rights as enshrined in the Charter*. For example, providers of very large online platforms should in particular pay due regard to freedom of expression and of information, including media freedom and pluralism.'

510. In analogy to the effect of Arts 7 and 8 in *Google Spain*, Frantziou (n. 472), under IV.A.

of expression is invoked. These latter indirect effects of the right to freedom of expression on the contractual relationship are therefore further discussed in the next chapter as part of the content layer in §6.4.3.3.

5.5.4 Access Claims on the Basis of Public and Social Interest

The third limitation to the proprietor's ius excludendi follows from the refused person's possibility to invoke public or social interests as a legal ground for an obligation to contract. This limitation follows from the practice in the Member States, as observed in the comparative study in Chapter 2. Claims on the basis of public and social interest are (to varying degrees) observed in Italy, Denmark, and the Netherlands. The legislation in Denmark is confined to access to specifically defined physical properties, which rules out the possibility of an application by analogy to social media platforms. Contrarily, the claims to access private property on the basis of public and/or social interest, as observed in Italy and the Netherlands, pose a useful and applicable potential for a right to access social media platforms. The practice observed in these two Member States could serve as an inspiration for future European or national legislation regulating access rights to essential communication spaces such as social media platforms.

In Italy, the origin of public and social use rights can be traced back to constitutional law. The Italian constitution's Article 42 distinguishes private property from public property. It also explicitly recognises the need to limit the use of private property rights 'in order to ensure its social function and to make it accessible to all'. Specific limitations can be found in the Italian Civil Code.[511] If a private property has a *public function*, access to it by other persons must be allowed. This is the case when a private property functions as a public domain, meaning that the proprietor has allowed the property to be used by an indeterminate group of persons and the use of the property serves a general public interest. Whether or not the proprietor had the intention to open the property for general use is irrelevant; if the conduct shows the intention that a group of indetermined persons can use the property for a public cause automatically renders the property available to the general public. Furthermore, the property must be accessible to the service of the community, without reservations or limitations, voluntary, unlimited, and free of charge. By analogy to this legal framework for physical property, the argumentation proves equally useful to *ex ante* access restrictions on social media platforms. First, starting with the argument that the service offered on social media platforms serves a public function and is available to the general public, Italian courts have concluded on numerous occasions that the service of social media platforms is offered to an indeterminate group of persons in light of

511. *See* for specific examples and references the analysis of the Italian legal system in §2.2.2 above. The summary below on the Italian system also follows from the case law analysis above in §2.2.2.

Italian law.[512] Second, social media platforms arguably serve a general public interest, namely the provision of users' interpersonal and political communication and the dissemination of information to large groups in a society. According to the ECtHR in 2015, 'the internet has now become one of the principal means by which individuals exercise their right to freedom of expression and information'.[513] In the more recent case of *Facebook Poland*, the CJEU has expanded this to also include the role of *social media platforms*, focusing on these platforms' roles in enhancing the public's access to information.[514] As such, the argument to limit a proprietor's right to impose *ex ante* access restrictions on social media platforms similar to the way public use rights apply to physical property would closely mirror the argumentation as applied to physical private property under Italian law.

In the Netherlands, the use of public/social interest to lift restrictions on private property follows solely from national case law. As such, the Dutch system differs from the Italian system to the extent that the constitutional basis is lacking. However, the application, scope, and final outcome of the Dutch case law on the 'societal role' of private property resembles the Italian system closely. On several occasions, Dutch courts have ruled that certain proprietors are not at liberty to define their house rules or to (arbitrarily) refuse access to their property. This is the case if a property is publicly accessible and fulfils a 'societal role' (*maatschappelijke functie*). The Dutch case law does not provide guidance or criteria to define which (types of) property fulfil such a societal role. Examples include a football stadium,[515] a nursing home,[516] and a house of worship.[517] Interestingly, an underlying, identical stream of thought supports the limitation to exclude visitors from these seemingly diverse types of private property. Neither one of these places is a one-of-a-kind property – there are other football stadiums, nursing homes, and houses of worship that can be visited instead of the specific property to which access has been denied. However, neither one of these places is visited for the characteristics of the property itself. When one visits a football stadium, one visits that exact property to cheer for the team playing on the field.

---

512. Tribunale di Pavia, sez. III, 14/03/2019, n. 468, and later confirmed in Tribunale di Firenze, sez. II, 13/07/2021, n. 1916; Tribunale di Cassino, 09/07/2021, n. 506; and Tribunale di Vicenza, 03/05/2021, n. 426. The same conclusion has been reached in German case law:

> social media platforms 'offer [their service] to an unlimited number of people without regard to the person and which, for a considerable part of those affected, determine to a considerable extent their participation in social life', *Bundesgerichtshof (Inhaltesperrung)* (n. 23), §§78-79.

513. ECtHR, *Cengiz and Others v. Turkey* (1 December 2015) CE:ECHR:2015:1201JUD004822610, §52, and ECtHR, *Vladimir Kharitonov v. Russia* (23 June 2020) CE:ECHR:2020:0623JUD0010 79514, §33.
514. *Republic of Poland v. European Parliament and Council of the European Union* (n. 386), §46: 'In the light of their accessibility and their capacity to store and communicate vast amounts of information, internet sites, and in particular online content-sharing platforms, play an important role in enhancing the public's access to news and facilitating the dissemination of information in general, with user-generated expressive activity on the internet providing an unprecedented platform for the exercise of freedom of expression.'
515. *Stadionverbod Vitesse* (n. 165), §4.2.
516. *Nursing home* (n. 170), §4.7.
517. *Refusal of entry to a mosque* (n. 173).

Equally, one visits a certain nursing home because a specific person is taken care of in said property, just as one visits a house of worship due to the connection with the (religious) group related to that specific property. As such, these places become unique properties due to the visitors' *aim of visiting*. Another football stadium, nursing home, or house of worship would simply not suffice as an alternative to that specific private property they wish to access. Consequently, a proprietor of a private property with a societal role may not, without reasonable justification, deny access to the property.[518] Users of social media platforms decide to sign up for a specific platform in a similar way as people decide to visit these specific types of property. A user chooses a specific platform because friends, family, or other like-minded groups are present on the platform or because there is specific information or content to be found. There is a specific *aim of visiting*, which cannot be substituted by joining another platform (yet[519]). As such, in both the Italian and the Dutch systems, *ex ante* access restrictions to publicly available social media platforms should be opposable on the basis of public and social interest. This should be the case, at least for those platforms that fulfil a public or social function. That in turn, corresponds to the reasoning by the German *Bundesgerichtshof* on the direct effect of the principle of equal treatment. The principle of equal treatment has a third-party effect if access restrictions in terms of service of publicly offered services have a significant effect on a person's social life'.[520] Social media platforms were found to have a significant effect on their users' social life – especially young persons.[521]

An interpretation and combination of the case law in Italy and the Netherlands lead to the following two requirements to sustain an *ex ante* access claim to a social media platform. First, the service must be offered to an indeterminate group of persons. In principle, this criterion is fulfilled by most large-scale social media platforms since, in principle, anyone is free to sign up for these services. Second, the person claiming access to the platform's service must have an aim of visiting that specific platform that cannot be sufficiently substituted by another social media platform. This latter requirement takes into consideration the Dutch 'social function' as well as the Italian requirement of a property's 'public function'. By analogy, that means that social media platforms that are publicly accessible – meaning that they are not aimed at or (technically) limited to a specific group of persons – and which fulfil a societal role should adhere to a duty of care to safeguard public access to their service or to guarantee an alternative to achieve the aim of visiting.

However, the above conclusion does not entail an unlimited free pass to access a platform's service on the terms the user pleases. Solely *access* to the platform's service

518. *Nursing home* (n. 170), §4.7.
519. Platform interoperability might be able to solve this problem created by exclusivity. If users of one platform can reach users on another platform, there is no longer a need to be a member of a certain social media platform. Whether this will adequately solve the problem will be proven in the next years, as the newly adopted Digital Markets Act (Regulation (EU) 2022/1925) stipulates interoperability obligations for (certain) gatekeepers of communications services in Art. 7.
520. *Bundesverfassungsgericht (Stadionverbot II)* (n. 90); *see also* a confirmation in *Bundesgerichtshof (Therme)* (n. 77).
521. *Bundesgerichtshof (Inhaltesperrung)* (n. 23), §78.

can be imposed on the basis of social or public interest. The platform remains free, within its scope of the freedom of contract, to dictate the terms that apply to the service.[522] In practice, claims based on public and social use would be most impactful for persons who have previously had their user accounts permanently terminated and wish to re-enter the platform at a later point in time. The claim under a public and social use right can, in those circumstances, be used to oppose the permanent nature of an access restriction in those cases where access to the property is open to anyone and the refusal would lead to social exclusion or other adverse personal effects on the refused person.

5.5.5 Competition Law

Competition law forms the fourth category of limitations to the proprietor's *ius excludendi*. The ECtHR and the CJEU concluded that social media platforms form important tools for disseminating opinions and imparting information.[523] Similar views have been expressed in relation to the field of competition law. This has sparked a debate concerning the necessity to regulate these social media platforms similar to electronic communications networks. The latter were regulated as a universal service in the early 2000s.[524] In the literature, two main views exist on the necessity to regulate social media platforms as public infrastructures: those that interpret the increase of social media platforms' role for general communications purposes as an argument to regulate social media platforms as a communication infrastructure and those against that interpretation.[525] Those against argue mainly that the market is fully capable of

522. *See* a similar discussion above on the *infinity loop of forced access* in §5.4.4.1.
523. ECtHR, *Cengiz and Others v. Turkey* (1 December 2015) CE:ECHR:2015:1201JUD004822610, §52, and ECtHR, *Vladimir Kharitonov v. Russia* (23 June 2020) CE:ECHR:2020:0623JUD001079514, §33; *Republic of Poland v. European Parliament and Council of the European Union* (n. 386), §46.
524. *See* Directive 2002/22/EC of the European Parliament and of the Council of 7 March 2002 on universal service and users' rights relating to electronic communications networks and services (Universal Service Directive), more recently repealed by Directive (EU) 2018/1972 of the European Parliament and of the Council of 11 December 2018 establishing the European Electronic Communications Code. *See* a comparison between this regulation and social media platforms in Graef (n. 9).
525. Van Dijck et al. argue that platforms, and especially the 'Big Five' (Alphabet-Google, Apple, Meta-Facebook, Amazon, and Microsoft), have slowly turned into a network of strategic infrastructural platforms. José van Dijck, Thomas Poell and Martijn de Waal, *The Platform Society: Public Values in a Connective World* (Oxford University Press 2018), In a later reflection, Van Dijck interprets Mark Zuckerberg's words – stating that Facebook aims to become a social infrastructure – and links this directly to the notion of public utilities – van Dijck (n. 35). Earlier, Thierer has argued against this trend. He points out that those in favour of qualifying social media platforms as public utilities frequently point towards an increase of fairness, privacy, and protection from reputational harm. Going over the available academic literature in favour of social media platforms as public utilities, he concludes that the overarching argument of scholars boils down to the belief that social media platforms are increasingly becoming the equivalent of 'social utilities' or 'social commons', and are essential for one's social existence. He argues strongly against this, stating that social media platforms are not public utilities in the traditional sense of the word, and regulators should avoid regulating them as such, as public utility regulation will lead to a decrease in consumer welfare,

satisfying the infrastructural needs and that market forces will naturally require societal changes from social media platforms. Otherwise, users will move elsewhere.

For a meaningful discussion on the use of competition law in the sphere of social media platforms, some terminological errors, (legal) inconsistencies, and linguistic confusion on the difference between public utilities, services of general (economic) interest, essential facilities, and universal services must be resolved.

5.5.5.1 *Resolving Terminological Confusion*

Confusion is indispensably connected to the similar terms of public utilities, services of general interest, and universal services within competition law. The confusion is understandable. From a linguistical point of view, these different terms seem to cover similar or equal situations. From a practical point of view, the terminology overlaps at times and can include identical services (train tracks are covered by public utilities and essential facilities, and telecommunications are covered by public utilities and universal services), making its application complex. From a legal point of view, they all share the commonality of belonging to the field of competition law. However, these terms cover different situations within competition law and should, therefore, not be used intertwined in the debate on the necessity to regulate social media access.

Public utilities or *public services* are overarching terms covering both *universal services* and *services of general interest.*[526] Public utilities always have a 'state component': a European Member State or the European legislator must be (indirectly) involved with the service to fall within this category. In some Member States, *public utility* or *public interest* equals the definition of a service of general economic interest.[527]

Services of general (economic) interest (SGI/SGEI) are services assigned (to certain undertakings) by a Member State. Under normal conditions, the undertakings offering services under these circumstances would be subject to European competition rules on state aid.[528] As part of assigning the status of SGI to a service, specific public service obligations are imposed on the actor providing the services. There are three

as it will harm innovation and competition: Adam Thierer, 'The Perils of Classifying Social Media Platforms as Public Utilities' (2013) 21 CommLaw Conspectus: Journal of Communications Law and Technology Policy (1993-2015) 249.

526. 'EUR-Lex – Public_service – EN – EUR-Lex' https://eur-lex.europa.eu/EN/legal-content/glossary/public-service.html (accessed 5 March 2023).
527. 'Public Undertakings/Services in the EU: Summary – Part 2 (DG4 Study ECON W21) – Public Undertakings and Public Services in the European Union: Summary – Part 2' https://www.europarl.europa.eu/workingpapers/econ/w21/sum-2_en.htm (accessed 5 March 2023).
528. However, Art. 106(2) TFEU exempts SGEI from the rules in the European Treaties as far as these rules would obstruct the performance of the tasks they have been assigned. Art. 14 of the TFEU recognises the Union's and national Member States' necessity to respect SGEI. At European level, the European institutions have the competence for European services necessary to achieve the objectives of the Union outside the competence of the Member States, *see* Art. 14 TFEU; *Case T-289/03 (BUPA and others/Commission)* (2008) ECLI:EU:T:2008:29 (General Court); *Case T-565/08 (Corsica Ferries/European Commission)* (2012) ECLI:EU:T:2012:415 (CJEU); Communication from the Commission – Services of general interest in Europe 2001; CESI Europe Academy, 'Providing High-Quality Public Services in Europe Based

types of SGI: Services of general *economic* interest (SGEI), non-economic services, and social services of general interest.[529] If social media platforms would fall within either of these categories, it would be within SGEI. The access to SGEI is explicitly recognised in Article 36 of the Charter of Fundamental Rights of the European Union – and is in scope and application a copy of Article 14 of the TFEU.[530] The qualification of a service as an SGEI is decided at Member State level and can, therefore, differ between the different Member States of the European Union.[531]

Defining the scope of services that fall within the scope of SGEI is difficult. In numerous decisions, the CJEU has recalled that 'European Union law does not provide a precise definition of the concept of services of general economic interest.'[532] However, an interpretation can be deducted from looking at the applications of Article 106(2) TFEU, which excludes SGEI from the rules of competition law in specific situations, and the CJEU's case law on the topic. In *Altmark*, the CJEU laid down four conditions to be met to fall within the scope of Article 106(2) TFEU, which excludes SGEI from the scope of (illegal) state aid. Of these four conditions, the first condition is relevant for the definition of whether an undertaking falls within the scope of an SGEI. The CJEU concludes that an undertaking 'must actually have public service obligations to discharge, and these obligations must be clearly defined'.[533] According to the conclusion in *Corsica Ferries*, the public service obligation to be discharged must fulfil an actual societal need and fulfil an objective in the public interest.[534] A public service

on the Values of Protocol 26 TFEU' (2012) https://www.cesi.org/wp-content/uploads/2012/10/121129_ Brochure-Protocole26-2-EN_DEF.pdf.

529. The European Commission applies the following terminologies for these three categories (*see* https://commission.europa.eu/topics/single-market/services-general-interest_en (accessed 16 December 2022)): *Services of general economic interest,* which are basic services that are carried out in return for payment, such as postal services. These services are subject to European internal market and competition rules. However, there may be derogations to these rules if necessary to protect citizens' access to basic services. *Non-economic services,* such as the police, justice, and statutory social security schemes, are not subject to specific European legislation or to internal market and competition rules. *Social services of general interest* are those that respond to the needs of vulnerable citizens and are based on the principles of solidarity and equal access. They can be both of an economic or non-economic nature. Examples include social security schemes, employment services and social housing.

530. European Commission (n. 349). Protocol 26 to the TFEU dictates that Member States must ensure that SGEI offer a high level of quality, safety, and affordability. They must secure equal treatment, and they must promote universal access and user rights. These are referred to as 'the six values'. The first three are relative ('high level') and do not create an absolute obligation for the Member States. The fourth one – equal treatment – is absolute and cannot be limited, whereas the fifth and sixth values are objectives rather than obligations.

531. 'EUR-Lex – Services_general_economic_interest – EN – EUR-Lex' https://eur-lex.europa.eu/EN/legal-content/glossary/services-of-general-economic-interest.html (accessed 5 March 2023).

532. *Corsica Ferries v. European Commission* (n. 528); *BUPA and others v. Commission* (n. 528); *Case T-17/02 (Olsen/Commission)* (2005) ECLI:EU:T:2005:218 (CJEU).

533. *Case C-280/00 (Altmark)* (2003) ECLI:EU:C:2003:415 (CJEU). Member States are in principle free to define these services to be discharged and can thus define their own services of general interest. Only in case of a manifest error by the Member State, the Commission can question the appointment of an SGEI, *see* Art. 14 TFEU; *Corsica Ferries v. European Commission* (n. 528); Communication from the Commission – Services of general interest in Europe; CESI Europe Academy (n. 528).

534. *Corsica Ferries v. European Commission* (n. 528).

is necessary when the objective, both concerning qualitative and quantitative criteria, cannot be ensured by private actors alone.[535] The involvement of a state is to be limited to those situations where it would not otherwise be possible for the undertaking to perform the tasks entrusted to it.[536] The service must furthermore exert an interest that has a special characteristic ('particular task') as compared to the exploitation of regular economic services in a society.[537] Following clarification on the interpretation and application of Article 106(2) TFEU by the EC, the services must serve the interest of society or be addressed to citizens directly, irrespective of whether the service is carried out by private or public undertakings.[538] The exact scope of which services qualify as SGEI is non-static. The inclusion of services depends on the needs of citizens, the technological and market developments, and the social and political preferences in the given Member State. The 'particular task', as referred to in Article 106(2) TFEU, 'implies the supply of services which, if it were considering its own commercial interest, an undertaking would not assume or would not assume to the same extent or under the same conditions'.[539] It continues: 'it would not be appropriate to attach specific public service obligations to an activity which is already provided or can be provided satisfactorily and under conditions, such as price, objective quality characteristics, continuity and access to the service, consistent with the public interest, as defined by the State, by undertakings operating under normal market conditions'. That means that if the service is or can be adequately offered by an undertaking under normal market conditions, it should not be included in the scope of SGEI. In sectors where there are adequate private investors which have established the infrastructure and are offering competitive services – such as the broadcasting sector – newly emerging parallel infrastructures should neither be qualified as SGEI.[540]

Universal services refer to a group of services deemed so essential that they should be offered to anyone at any given time.[541] Universal services are to provide 'a safety net to ensure that a set of at least the minimum services is available to all end-users and at an affordable price to consumers, where a risk of social exclusion arising from the lack of such access prevents citizens from full social and economic participation in society'.[542] Their aim is to ensure access to quality services at an affordable price throughout the European Union.[543]As opposed to SGEI, universal services are therefore decided at the European level to prevent differences in the Member States. The legislative basis can be found in Article 169. Without specific regulation from the European Union, a service might still be of outmost importance to all Europeans, though it does not qualify as a universal service. Legislation puts an

535. *Ibid.*; *Olsen v. Commission* (n. 532).
536. *Joined Cases T-568/08 & T-573/08 (Métropole télévision)* (2010) ECLI:EU:T:2010:272 (CJEU).
537. *Case C-179/90 (Merci Convenzionali Porto di Genova)* (1991) ECLI:EU:C:1991:464 (CJEU).
538. Communication from the Commission on the application of the European Union State aid rules to compensation granted for the provision of services of general economic interest 2012.
539. *Ibid.*
540. *Ibid.*
541. 'EUR-Lex – Universal_service – EN – EUR-Lex' https://eur-lex.europa.eu/EN/legal-content/glossary/universal-service.html (accessed 5 March 2023).
542. Directive (EU) 2018/1972 on the European Electronic Communications Code.
543. 'EUR-Lex – Universal_service – EN – EUR-Lex' (n. 541).

obligation on Member States to ensure that all citizens, also in remote areas and with low incomes, can access these universal services. In that sense, rules on universal services dictate what a Member State would otherwise be free to decide under the SGEI rules. Examples of such legislation concern telecommunications services[544] and broadband internet.[545]

As opposed to public utilities, the *essential facilities doctrine* is a doctrine developed in the CJEU's case law and could apply irrespective of any influence of a Member State or European instance. It concerns facilities which, due to geographical or legal limitations, are unable to be multiplied (harbours, train tracks). When an undertaking controlling an essential facility refuses to grant access to a dependent party (refuse of contract), this could constitute an abuse of a dominant position under the essential facilities doctrine. In light of the discussion on the regulation of digital services, the doctrine might see a revival in Europe.[546] Building upon the CJEU case law on the *refusal to supply*, the first European references to an essential facilities doctrine can be found in two cases from the 1990s, in which the European Commission referred to the refusal to grant access to an essential facility: *British Midland v. Aer Lingus* and *Sea Containers v. Stena Sealink.*[547] Following these decisions, a dominant player offering access to an essential facility may not differentiate between the terms on which it provides access to its own service.[548] There is a high threshold to successfully claim access to another undertaking's facility. Too easy access would decrease the incentive

544. In the late 1990s, the telecom sector was liberalised to create better competition, which eventually had to lead to better access, quality, and prices for consumers. To make sure that every European citizen would keep access to telecommunication services, universal service rules were laid down to ensure these basic services were delivered, also to those users the market usually wouldn't service, for example because of high costs due to people living in very remote areas. This led to the Directive 2002/22/EC of the European Parliament and of the Council of 7 March 2002 on universal service and users' rights relating to electronic communications networks and services (Universal Service Directive).
545. *See, e.g.*: Press Release of 25 September 2008, Broadband Internet for all Europeans: Commission launches debate on future of universal service, IP/08/1397, available at: https://ec.europa.eu/commission/presscorner/detail/en/IP_08_1397 (accessed 14 September 2021). This led to the European Electronic Communications Code, which was established by Directive (EU) 2018/1972 of the European Parliament and of the Council of 11 December 2018 establishing the European Electronic Communications Code [OJ L 321] at the end of 2018.
546. The essential facilities doctrine derives from US antitrust laws. Under the essential facilities doctrine, the refusal to deal can lead to a violation of the Sherman Act. The doctrine's (indirect) starting point is United States v. Terminal Railroad Ass'n, 224 U.S. 383 (1912). *See* for a discussion for example James R Ratner, 'Should There Be an Essential Facility Doctrine' (1987) 21 U.C. Davis Law Review 327; Gregory J Werden, 'The Law and Economics of the Essential Facility Doctrine' (1987) 32 Saint Louis University Law Journal 433. The Appeals Court refers to this case when defining the doctrine in Hecht v. Pro-Football, Inc., 570 F.2d 982, 992-93 (D.C. Cir. 1977), 993, n. 44. It was subsequently indirectly referred to in several cases, before it was explicitly formulated in the case of *Hecht v. Pro-Football, Inc.* by the United States Court of Appeal D.C. Circuit. In Europe, the doctrine's role is rather vague and has not been used in recent times. *See* on the discussion on its revival: Graef (n. 25).
547. *Commission Decision (British Midland/Aer Lingus)* (1992) OJ L 96; *Commission Decision (Sea Containers/Stena Sealink)* (1994) OJ L 15.
548. In *Sea Containers v. Stena Sealink*, Sea Containers complained about Sealink's abusive behaviour, consisting in refusing to provide access to an essential facility or infrastructure without objective justification, namely providing access to the harbour. The Commission concludes that Sealink, being the port authority, has a dominant position in the provision of an

for innovation and investments. Following the *Magill* judgment,[549] the refusal of service must likely eliminate all competition and must not be objectively justifiable. The CJEU adds to these requirements in the *Bronner* case that '*the service in itself must be indispensable to carrying on that person's business, inasmuch as there is no actual or potential substitute in existence for that [service].*'[550] It does not matter whether it is less advantageous for the competitor to develop its own facility - technical, legal, or economic obstacles capable of making it impossible or unreasonable difficult must exist in order for a service to be qualified as an essential facility. Train tracks and harbours form examples of essential facilities because it is undesirable to have ten sets of train tracks around a city, and geographical characteristics make it impossible to endlessly build harbours.

Following the CJEU case law defining the requirements for an essential facility, essential facilities are, first, to be exploited by a dominant player in the market. Second, access to the facility must be indispensable for the exercise of one's profession or undertaking, and third, it must be impossible or unreasonably difficult to create a substitute for the service. Social media platforms do not live up to these requirements. First, the general users of social media platforms - apart from influencers and other business accounts - are persons who use the service without economic incentive. They are therewith not competitors of the platform. A refusal of access to a private end-user can, therefore, not lead to a distortion of competition.[551] Second, if the essential facilities doctrine *were* applicable to social media platforms, these platforms would not live up to the requirements for a service to be qualified as an essential facility. One of the requirements is the lack of any actual or potential substitute in existence for that service. According to the above-cited CJEU case law, there must be obstacles that hinder a competitor from creating a competing service. This requirement is simply not met by social media platforms. The mere fact that multiple large-scale platforms exist, in combination with a large supply of (smaller scale) platforms, such as blogs and forums where users can express their opinions, demonstrates that social media platforms do not lack actual or potential substitutes. Additionally, once again, the rise of new social media platforms provides further evidence of the existence of adequate competition opportunities, as can be observed in the video streaming market. Before the emergence of new players like TikTok and Snapchat, YouTube was the dominant player in the world of video streaming. The quick overtake in market share of these new players shows the existence of both current (actual) substitutes and the potential for new substitutes to be quickly developed in the future. The erroneous qualification of social media platforms as essential facilities is understandable when looking at 'the

essential facility, which it defines as 'a facility or infrastructure, without access to which competitors cannot provide services to their customers', *ibid.*, §65.

549. *Joined Cases C-241/91 P and 242/91 P (RTE/ITP)* (1995) ECLI:EU:C:1995:98 (CJEU).

550. *Case C-7/97 (Bronner)* (1998) ECLI:EU:C:1998:569 (CJEU).

551. The outcome would be different for business users. For example, Art. 6(12) of Regulation (EU) 2022/1925 of the European Parliament and of the Council of 14 September 2022 on contestable and fair markets in the digital sector and amending Directives (EU) 2019/1937 and (EU) 2020/1828 (Digital Markets Act) obliges software application stores to 'apply fair, reasonable, and non-discriminatory general conditions of access'.

infrastructure of social media platforms as a whole' – meaning all platforms together and at the same time. The combined system of platforms plays an important role in users' daily lives, as also concluded by the CJEU in *Facebook Poland*. However, individual platforms are not irreplaceable nor limited by any geographical or legal constraints. A brand-new social media platform can be created any day. Therefore, social media platforms do not fall within the scope of the essential facilities definition as developed in the case law of the CJEU.

5.5.5.2 *Using Competition Law to Claim Access Rights*

Social media platforms have not been regulated as public utilities (SGEI or universal services). This means that users who wish to access a social media platform cannot currently turn to competition law to claim access to a social media platform's service. Scholars have argued to include social media platforms in the scope of public utilities,[552] but that discussion does not concern the positive law to adjudicate access and moderation decisions on social media platforms. Furthermore, doing so would not solve the problems related to access and moderation decisions.[553] Competition law has, therefore, not been completely removed from the scope of the roadmap as the political choice to regulate access to (social media) platforms as public utilities remains an option. The line to 'competition law' as a limitation of the proprietor's *ius excludendi* is included in the roadmap with a dotted line.

5.6 CONCLUSION ON USERS' RIGHTS TO ACCESS SOCIAL MEDIA PLATFORMS

Following the conclusions above, the fourth sub-question can be answered: *which types of access restrictions are imposed by social media platforms, and what possibilities do users have to oppose them?*

On the basis of their right to property, social media platforms can choose to allow access to their platform and can choose to exclude (certain groups) from accessing their service. Access restrictions can be imposed both *ex ante* and *ex post*. Social media platforms have three options: to provide, refuse, or restrict access to their platform. Equal to the restrictions physical proprietors can impose on access to their physical property, social media platforms can offer open access, conditional access, or fully deny access. Only the platform's decision to deny access can be opposed. In case of open access or conditional access, the person is allowed to access the platform (on the terms dictated by the platform). That means that those forms of access do not lead to absolute access problems. Whether or not the terms on which the person can enter the platform under open or conditional access are fair is a discussion that is resolved in the

552. Thierer (n. 525); Rahman (n. 24); Bagnoli (n. 24); Busch (n. 24).
553. *See* for a reflection on the possibility to regulate social media platforms as public utilities in §9.2.2 below, where I argue that, first, social media platforms do not fall within the scope of services to be regulated by public utility regulation, and that doing so would in any case not solve the problems related to access and moderation decisions.

content layer. A social media platform's power to deny access is not absolute. A fourth access category is therefore formed by the limitations to this right to exclude: forced access. This category applies when refused persons successfully oppose the platform's decision to deny access. When a person has a right to forced access, the social media platform is obliged to contract the person. Limitations can be made to the platform's right to exclude if such limitations are necessary for the general interest. This can include secondary legislation with an aim to protect the rights of others, equality and non-discrimination laws, the users' public and social interest, the horizontal direct effect of fundamental rights, and competition law form potential limitations to the right to exclude on which basis refused persons could claim access to the platform.

First, a state can opt to restrict the platform's right to exclude with the aim of protecting the rights and freedoms of others. In the case of equality and non-discrimination, the European legislator has regulated access to goods and services in two directives. These apply equally to matters of access to social media platforms. It follows from the Racial Equality Directive that access restrictions may never be directly discriminating on the basis of race or ethnic origin. Both direct and indirect discrimination on the basis of gender, as well as indirect discrimination on the basis of race and ethnic origin, can be justifiable if the term is objectively justified by a legitimate aim and the means of achieving that aim are appropriate and necessary. Secondary legislation limiting the right to exclude in favour of the right to freedom of expression does not exist, nor do states seemingly have a positive obligation to do so. The state is only obliged to step in when the user has been deprived of all possibilities to express an opinion. In an online ecosystem with multiple social media platforms and other means to express oneself, that requirement is not fulfilled. Second, refused persons could have an opportunity to claim access to a refused service on the basis of direct horizontal effect of fundamental rights. The right to freedom of expression does not fulfil the requirements for horizontal direct effect. Opposingly, it is settled case law that the right to non-discrimination can be invoked directly between private parties – though the exact balancing of this right against the platform's freedom to conduct a business remains unclear. Third, access claims based on public and social use pose a potentially impactful tool to oppose access restrictions that lead to social exclusion or other adverse personal effects for the refused person. The foundational basis of public and social use follows from the case law of the Member States discussed in the internal comparative study in Chapter 2. There are two requirements that can lead to an obligation to contract based on public and social use: the service must be offered to an indeterminate group of persons, and the person claiming access to the platform's service must have a unique aim of visiting that specific platform that cannot be sufficiently substituted by another social media platform. Lastly, access rights to social media platforms based on the rules for public utilities under competition law do not exist, nor will they likely be enacted. When viewing accessibility in absolute terms, access to these platforms is not technically impossible. Access and quality problems on social media platforms are caused by the extensive normative power of these platforms to dictate the requirements on which users can enter their services. As such, access problems are not infrastructural problems that can be resolved by public utility regulation. Furthermore, there are adequate investors in the market, there is a functioning infrastructure with (conditional) access to all European citizens, and there are numerous competing services. Social media platforms do, therefore, not fulfil the requirement of indispensability, which renders intervention to guarantee the existence of the service superfluous.

CHAPTER 6

The Content Layer: The Conditions for Conditional Access

6.1 THE CONTENT OF TERMS OF SERVICE IN THEORY AND PRACTICE

In the access layer discussed in the previous chapter, one end point in the roadmap was reached: the full denial of access. If a platform owner decides to fully deny access to its service and none of the limitations to the proprietor's right to exclude apply, then the decision to deny access is final. Persons who were denied access under those circumstances cannot oppose that decision.

The current chapter outlines the remaining avenues following from the other three types of access: open access, forced access, and conditional access. The aim is to examine to what extent a proprietor can restrict either one of these offers of access through restrictive terms of service. This chapter's focus lies therefore, predominantly with the assessment of the validity of the terms that are imposed by social media platforms.

Figure 6.1 An Overview of the Content Layer after Accessing the Platform

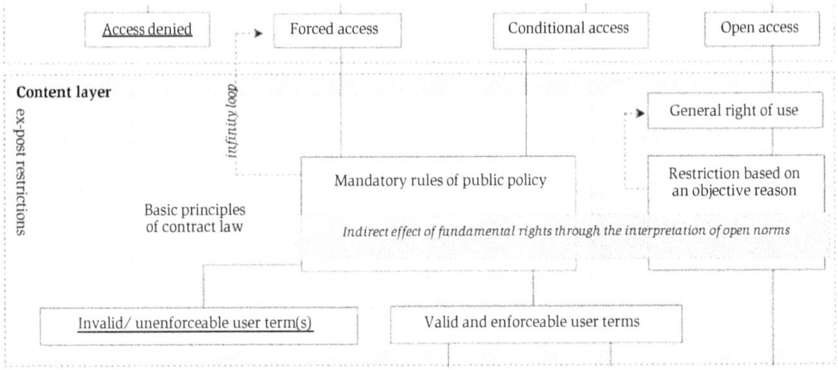

The chapter starts with an explanation of three different types of moderation decisions: mandatory, normative, and wrongful moderation decisions. These three different types of decisions to moderate content on a platform can be observed in all platforms (and physical places that apply house rules for access), irrespective of whether the access to the platform was based on open, conditional, or forced access (*see* Figure 6.1). As observed in the comparative study in Chapter 2, these different types of moderation decisions trigger different legal consequences, and therefore, it is important to have a clear demarcation between the three types. After this clarification, the general right of use on open access-platforms is discussed. Starting from a general discussion on the general right of use in the online sphere, the requirement of an 'objective reason' is outlined.

After the practice on open access-platforms has been discussed, the rules on forced and conditional access are addressed. Within the content layer, forced and conditional access are both defined by the terms imposed by the proprietor. Their application is therefore identical and they are therefore discussed together. The discussion on forced and conditional access relies predominantly on the validity of the terms imposed by the platform. This part therefore, starts by, first, addressing discussions in the literature on the general validity of terms of service as contracts. After concluding that terms of service are indeed contracts, the requirements for the formation of a contract and the validity of the contractual terms are discussed. Lastly, the (difficulty of the) interpretation of social media platforms' terms of service is further examined.

The answer to sub-question five depends on the combination of conclusion of the content layer included in this chapter and the enforcement layer included in Chapter 7. That means that Chapter 6 will be concluded by an *interim* conclusion on the content layer. The answer to sub-question five follows at the end of Chapter 7.

6.2 MANDATORY, NORMATIVE, AND WRONGFUL MODERATION DECISIONS

A distinction must be made between three types of moderation carried out by social media platforms: mandatory, normative, and wrongful moderation. These three types of moderation decisions do not only apply to moderation in the online sphere, but they also apply equally to and have been observed in the case law of access to physical property. Distinction between these different types of moderation decisions is necessary because the distinction determines which (if any) legal redress mechanisms are available to users that were subjected to a moderation decision.

6.2.1 Mandatory Moderation Decisions

The first category - mandatory moderation - concerns decisions to remove content which the platform itself has not (freely) decided on. The decision that the content's scope is illegal does not follow internally from the platforms' policy. The illegality of the content is prescribed by law. Obligations to remove illegal content from social media platforms can be explicit or can be incentivized through potential liability for hosting illegal content of third parties. Examples under European law are terrorist content,[554] child sexual abuse material,[555] copyright-infringing content,[556] and illegal goods and services.[557] Similarly, at Member State level, national legislation exists that imposes mandatory removal obligations on social media platforms. Presumably the most known example is the German Act to Improve Enforcement of the Law in Social Networks (Network Enforcement Act, or NetzDG).[558] To what extent the legislator can demand platforms to collaborate in deleting content that is illegal varies. Keller points to three types of governmental influence on social media platforms' moderation decisions: direct regulation, indirect pressure, and cross-border influence.[559]

6.2.1.1 Governmental Influence Through Direct Regulation

The first one, direct regulation, refers to the practice outlined above and includes legislative measures that declare certain types of content illegal. In that line, the European legislator has chosen time again to apply a definition of 'illegality' that

554. Regulation (EU) 2021/784 of the European Parliament and of the Council of 29 April 2021 on addressing the dissemination of terrorist content online.
555. Regulation (EU) 2021/1232 of the European Parliament and of the Council of 14 July 2021 on a temporary derogation from certain provisions of Directive 2002/58/EC as regards the use of technologies by providers of number-independent interpersonal communications services for the processing of personal and other data for the purpose of combating online child sexual abuse.
556. Directive (EU) 2019/790 of the European Parliament and of the Council of 17 April 2019 on copyright and related rights in the Digital Single Market and amending Directives 96/9/EC and 2001/29/EC [OJ L 136].
557. Regulation (EU) 2022/2065 (Digital Services Act), preamble 12, and Art. 7 (indirectly).
558. Gesetz zur Verbesserung der Rechtsdurchsetzung in sozialen Netzwerken (Netzwerkdurchsetzungsgesetz - NetzDG) 2017.
559. Keller, 'Who Do You Sue? State and Platform Hybrid Power Over Online Speech' (n. 19), pp. 3ff.

reflects the situation in the offline world.[560] Direct regulation is a national legislative process and as a consequence thereof, new categories of illegal content emerge constantly. For example, in January 2023, the Dutch regulator proposed to forbid the dissemination of content with 'suffering dogs and cats' on social media.[561] If this proposal becomes reality, it means that posting a video or photo of a pug or a Scottish Fold cat becomes illegal – even if that dog or cat is one's own. Removing such content constitutes a mandatory moderation decision since the legal basis is positive law rather than a normative choice of the platform.[562]

The risks of direct regulation consist, first, as also pointed out by Keller, the risk of *overblocking*. This occurs when a social media platform decides to remove questionable content that might be illegal to prevent any legal consequences, such as fines, or to evade a potential risk of (secondary) liability. The risk of overblocking in the case of direct regulation is not easily prevented. On the one hand, governments need social media platforms to stop the dissemination of illegal content through their service since these platforms are the ones closest to the infringing activity. Moreover, platforms have the technical means to remove the content. Without a (legal) incentive, platforms will unlikely allocate a large sum of resources to the detection, removal, and prevention of illegal content. On the other hand, as demonstrated by the varying argumentations and conclusions in the national case law in Chapter 2, taking a decision on whether content is illegal is not easy. Social media platforms are private companies offering a service. They are not members of the judiciary. Placing a risk of hefty fines or liability on these platforms incites them to take down more content than necessary because taking down too much content is not as harshly punished as leaving illegal content online. As will be shown and elaborated further upon in §6.2.3, mandatory moderation decisions can

560. Referring to a *principle* of 'what is illegal offline should also be illegal online', *see* latest the European Declaration on Digital Rights and Principles (15 December 2022), https://digital-strategy.ec.europa.eu/en/library/european-declaration-digital-rights-and-principles, but *see also* previously: the DSA, preamble (12); the European Commission Communication on Tackling Illegal Content Online (28 September 2017) COM(2017) 555 final, preamble (2), and the European Commission Communication on 2030 Digital Compass: the European way for the Digital Decade (9 March 2021) COM(2021) 118 final/2, under 3.

561. 'Suffering dogs and cats' refers to dogs and cats 'with extreme external features that create consistent suffering or increased risk of suffering, such as cats with folded ears or extremely short-snouted dogs'. Piet Adema (Minister of Agriculture, Nature, and Food Quality), 'Aanpak gezelschapsdieren met schadelijke uiterlijke kenmerken' (*Tackling pet animals with harmful external features*, translation by the author) 20 January 2023, accessible at: https://www.tweedekamer.nl/kamerstukken/brieven_regering/detail?id=2023Z00672&did=2023D01592 (accessed 22 January 2023). This letter solely displays the intention of the minister to look into the possibilities for such a ban, the actual proposal has not been formulated yet. The letter shows the intent to ban the use of suffering cats and dogs in advertisements, commercials, by influencers and celebrities, but also refers to a general 'social media-ban'. The breeding of these animals has been forbidden in the Netherlands since 2014. *See* for more information on this: NVWA, Fokken met gezelschapsdieren, ken de regels, accessible at: https://www.nvwa.nl/documenten/dier/dierenwelzijn/welzijn/publicaties/fokken-met-gezelschapsdieren-ken-de-regels (accessed 22 January 2023).

562. However, the enforcement of such a ban is difficult. Other European Member States do not have a similar ban, meaning that the content remains available in those jurisdictions. Furthermore, Member States may not ask social media platforms to search for infringing content, as that would fall within the scope of the general monitoring prohibition in Art. 15 of the e-Commerce Directive (equally Art. 8 DSA).

result in *wrongful* moderation decisions. Overblocking falls within this category of wrongful moderation, and users have a solid set of legal redress mechanisms to fight overblocking,[563] including by collective redress and representation.[564]

The second risk of relying on direct regulation as a foundation for mandatory moderation decisions refers to the legitimacy of the removal requests based on national legislative acts - especially in restrictive authoritarian and totalitarian regimes. Examples cover the Vietnamese law against 'content opposing the Communist Party and the Government of Vietnam'[565] and the Russian laws prohibiting the dissemination of 'false information', which includes (fact-checked, objective) information on the Russian war on Ukraine.[566] Discussions on the legitimacy of totalitarian regimes are not isolated to the sphere of content moderation or social media platforms, and resolving this issue goes beyond the scope of this book. The discussion on whether or not social media platforms must comply with requests from governments based on (democratically) questionable laws is a highly complicated one. Broadly, two arguments can be outlined. Either a platform decides to abide by the governmental power - whether legitimately acquired or not - or the platform decides to externalise its own norms to the situation and disregard national laws.[567] The latter includes social media platforms that refrain from taking down certain content with reference to IHRL, which has been argued to be an effective solution to deal with the matter.[568] A conclusion on the best approach to these oppressive regimes is yet to be reached.[569]

6.2.1.2 *Governmental Influence Through Indirect Pressure*

The second one, indirect pressure, refers to governmental coercion to 'voluntarily' take measures to safeguard moderation decisions' legitimacy. The European Union has

563. Most effectively, through a claim for non-material damages for wrongfully removed content as observed in the Italian case law. This conclusion is in line with the observation of Keller (p.4) based on arguments of human rights scholars.
564. Article 86 DSA and Directive (EU) 2020/1828 of the European Parliament and of the Council of 25 November 2020 on representative actions for the protection of the collective interests of consumers and repealing Directive 2009/22/EC.
565. Following Facebook's transparency report, hundreds of posts were removed at the request of the Vietnamese government after the coming into force of the anti-communist party content-legislation.
566. State Duma, Amendments on liability for fakes about the work of state bodies of the Russian Federation abroad have been adopted, 22 March 2022, http://duma.gov.ru/news/53773/ (accessed 4 January 2023).
567. Facebook argued, for example, that non-compliance with the requests from the Vietnamese regime would have led to Facebook becoming unavailable in full in Vietnam, creating even bigger risks for freedom of expression and the access to information and communication tools in the country, according to: The Washington Post, 'The case against Mark Zuckerberg: Insiders say Facebook's CEO chose growth over safety', 25 October 2021, https://www.washingtonpost.com/technology/2021/10/25/mark-zuckerberg-facebook-whistleblower/ (accessed 4 January 2023).
568. Douek (n. 250).
569. *Ibid.*, p. 72.

increasingly turned to these mechanisms, mainly through codes of practice and general codes of conduct.[570] The Union's competence to enact legal acts and codes of conduct follows from the same legal basis in the TFEU.[571] This increasing role and the overall legitimacy of using codes of conduct as a legislative instrument have been questioned.[572] Vander Maelen points out that private companies are, first, obliged to participate in the codes of conduct. Social media platforms cannot simply refuse to sign these codes since the refusal by a social media platform to adhere to a specific code of conduct can have severe legal consequences.[573] Second, codes of conduct, as prescribed in the DSA, do not live up to the traditional character of a code as a tool to offer private actors discretion in how to achieve certain goals. The use of codes of conduct to instigate social media platforms to increase their voluntary measures can lead to a risky balancing game on the border between an unlawful monitoring obligation and lawful attempts to increase voluntary action. For European Member States, the Digital Services Act's Article 8 – which is a direct copy of its predecessor in Article 15 eCD – prohibits Member States from imposing an obligation on platforms to monitor their service and actively seek facts and circumstances that indicate illegal activity. Social media platforms that wish to carry out such tasks voluntarily can do so if they act diligently and in good faith (Article 7 DSA).

570. For example, the Commission's 2018 Code of Practice on Disinformation and its 2022 Strengthened Code of Practice Disinformation, https://digital-strategy.ec.europa.eu/en/library/2022-strengthened-code-practice-disinformation (accessed 5 January 2023); The Memorandum of Understanding on the sale of counterfeit goods on the internet, https://single-market-economy.ec.europa.eu/industry/strategy/intellectual-property/enforcement-intellectual-property-rights/memorandum-understanding-sale-counterfeit-goods-internet_en#:~:text=The%20Memorandum%20of%20understanding%20(MoU,from%20appearing%20in%20online%20marketplaces. (accessed 5 January 2023); the EU Code of Conduct on countering illegal hate speech online, https://commission.europa.eu/strategy-and-policy/policies/justice-and-fundamental-rights/combatting-discrimination-0/racism-and-xenophobia/eu-code-conduct-countering-illegal-hate-speech-online_en (accessed 5 January 2023). New codes are on their ways, *see*, *e.g.*, the proposal for a 'EU code of conduct on age-appropriate design' in the Commission's Communication on A Digital Decade for children and youth: the new European strategy for a better internet for kids (BIK+) (2022) COM/2022/212/final.

   See for a full historical overview: Carl Vander Maelen, 'Hardly Law or Hard Law? Investigating the Dimensions of Functionality and Legalisation of Codes of Conduct in Recent EU Legislation and the Normative Repercussions Thereof' (2022) 47 European Law Review 752.

571. Both follow from the legislative power in Art. 288 TFEU, *see ibid.*, p. 756. According to Vander Maelen, codes of conducts fall within the same category at recommendations and resolutions.

572. *Ibid.*, Vander Maelen (2022). Vander Maelen argues that codes of conduct with private parties hardly fit the common general purpose of code of conducts as 'steering instruments' used to achieve closer cooperation between the parties. He highlights three dimensions in which codes of conducts have slowly 'hardened' from soft law instruments into binding norms, *see* pp. 757-759.

573. Not signing a code of conduct can lead to a potential infringement of the obligations under the DSA, *see* DSA preamble (104): '(...) The refusal without proper explanations by a provider of an online platform or of an online search engine of the Commission's invitation to participate in the application of such a code of conduct could be taken into account, where relevant, when determining whether the online platform or the online search engine has infringed the obligations laid down by this Regulation.'

These 'voluntary' measures cause a shift in the legal basis for moderation decisions.[574] Keller points out that online platforms, as a result of the codes of conduct on countering illegal hate speech online, remove hate speech on the basis of their own terms of service rather than on the basis of legislation.[575] Social media platforms agreed in the code of conduct to include the removal of certain types of hate speech in their terms of service.[576] That practice goes directly against the spirit of the monitoring prohibition, which is strange since the EC expressly sustained the Member States' monitoring prohibition when adopting the Digital Services Act. Seemingly, the EC found an option to circumvent the prohibition, and that practice has proven contagious. The first Member State has initiated its own national code of conduct inspired by the EC's approach: the *Netherlands Code of Conduct Transparency Online Political Advertisements.*[577]

The removal of hate speech on the basis of the platforms' own terms as opposed to the law affects users' protection under the right to freedom of expression, as well as their redress mechanisms to oppose moderation decisions. First, a state measure to increase the scope of content to be removed from social media platforms triggers vertical direct effect of the fundamental right to freedom of expression, meaning that the state has to live up to the safeguards provided for by Article 11 Charter and Article 10 ECHR. However, when a state transfers the decision to remove certain types of content from a legal provision to the agreement between the platform and the user, the right to freedom of expression has been superseded. Simply put, social media platforms have the freedom to limit the scope of their service and to eliminate the dissemination of content they deem unwanted (*see* §6.2.2 below). Governments cannot do that without taking the fundamental rights of the users into consideration. By dictating that the removal of certain types of content must be included in platforms' terms of service, governments have found a way to circumvent that obligation. Argument could be

574. Niva Elkin-Koren, 'Government-Platform Synergy and Its Perils' in Edoardo Celeste, Amélie Heldt and Clara Iglesias Keller (eds), *Constitutionalising Social Media* (Bloomsbury Publishing Plc 2022) 178 http://ebookcentral.proquest.com/lib/kbdk/detail.action?docID=7027117 (accessed 7 February 2023). Referring to the practice of governments to flag harmful content through the internal mechanisms of platforms rather than legally enforcing it. Previously coined by her and Michael Birnhack as the 'invisible handshake': Michael Birnhack and Niva Elkin-Koren, 'The Invisible Handshake: The Reemergence of the State in the Digital Environment' (10 April 2003) https://papers.ssrn.com/abstract=381020 (accessed 9 February 2023).
575. Keller, 'Who Do You Sue? State and Platform Hybrid Power Over Online Speech' (n. 19), p. 6.
576. 'The IT Companies (...) have agreed with the European Commission on a code of conduct setting the following public commitments: The IT Companies to have in place clear and effective processes to review notifications regarding illegal hate speech on their services so they can remove or disable access to such content. *The IT companies to have in place Rules or Community Guidelines clarifying that they prohibit the promotion of incitement to violence and hateful conduct.*' Code of Conduct on countering illegal hate speech online.
577. Ministry of the Interior and Kingdom Relations and International Institute for Democracy and Electoral Assistance, 'Dutch Code of Conduct Transparency Online Political Advertisements' (2021) https://www.idea.int/sites/default/files/news/news-pdfs/Dutch-Code-of-Conduct-transparency-online-political-advertisements-EN.pdf (accessed 5 January 2023).

made that a user who is a national of a Member State imposing such codes of conduct could make a case against the Member State invoking an (indirect) infringement of its right to freedom of expression. The conduct (social media platforms removing certain types of content) can be traced back directly to the agreement between the state and the platform (the code of conduct). Through codes of conduct, the state circumvents the obligation to adhere to the requirements in Article 11 Charter and Article 10 ECHR.[578]

Additionally, following the code of conduct approach by the EC can cause grave risk for social media platforms. By taking moderation decisions on the basis of the code of conduct, social media platforms lose their liability protection under Article 7 DSA. According to the latter, searching for illegal activity on a voluntary basis secures access to the liability exemption for hosting providers in Article 6 DSA. However, these voluntary investigations must be carried out at the platform's *own initiative*, must serve to stop *illegal content*, or be necessary to comply with Union or national law.[579] Neither of those requirements is met when following indirect orders through a code of conduct. The content is not illegal nor does the obligation follow from Union or national law. One could furthermore argue whether platforms 'voluntarily' have entered into these codes of conduct, given the risks outlined above. Moreover, the investigations are, in any case, not carried out on the platforms' own initiative – the incentive follows from the code of conduct. This leads to high risks on the side of platforms, as they risk losing the liability exemption for the availability and dissemination of content on their service that is mentioned in the code of conduct.

The seemingly problematic use of codes of conduct to 'voluntarily' tackle types of illegal content is exacerbated by the fact that Article 45 DSA further encourages the use of codes of conduct to 'contribute to the proper application of [the] Regulation'. As such, an increase in the use of codes of conduct aimed specifically, though not exclusively, at tackling illegal content and to curb systemic risks is to be expected.

6.2.1.3 *Governmental Influence Through Cross-Border Influence*

The third and last governmental influence concerns cross-border influence, meaning the (un)intentional influence by a state on the content that can be hosted in other jurisdictions. This could be the case if legislation demands that certain user accounts or certain types of content be blocked on a worldwide scale. The consequence of the latter 'regulatory race to the bottom' in speech regulation is that the strictest law will

578. Whether states can lawfully do so, and what potential consequences of that practice are, is unclear. Further research clarifying this issue would be welcomed, especially given the increase in the use of codes of conducts.
579. *See* Art. 7 DSA: 'Providers of intermediary services shall not be deemed ineligible for the exemptions from liability referred to in Arts 4, 5 and 6 solely because they, in good faith and in a diligent manner, carry out *voluntary* own-initiative investigations into, or take other measures aimed at detecting, identifying and removing, or disabling access to, illegal content, or take the necessary measures to comply with the requirements of Union law and national law in compliance with Union law, including the requirements set out in this Regulation.' (emphasis by the author)

eventually dominate the online playing field.[580] Since this book solely concerns platforms' access and moderation decisions and users' redress mechanisms in the European Union, cross-border influence is not of direct relevance to the outcome of the project. Though reflections on the extent to which cross-border influence should (be able to) effect (especially normative) moderation decisions are to be made both in general and in light of a potential *Brussels*-effect[581] of the rules in the DSA and the case law of the CJEU.[582]

Generally, the effect of legislation (should) end(s) at a state's jurisdictional border.[583] This territorial effect poses problems for moderation decisions and the effective prevention of re-emerging content. The internet is not bound by borders. There is no territorial internet – apart from attempts of states (e.g., Russia and China) to restrict access to the worldwide web. As such, if the effect of legislation is solely to be confined within the borders of a state, the measure does not achieve the intended aim of preventing access to certain content. If the content remains available in other parts of the world, users can access that content by using technological circumventions such as VPN systems. Therefore, states can have an 'interest in regulating a certain matter with extraterritorial effect', which in turn 'becomes the crucial factor in determining its prescriptive jurisdiction'.[584] Opposingly, an arguably worse scenario would be to allow states to initiate legislative measures in jurisdictions where they do not have legislative power, leading to the above-highlighted regulatory race to the bottom. The latter would mean that, in the end, users' ability to express their opinions online will be reduced to a hollow shell.

A choice will have to be made between these two scenarios. Either to sustain the idea that the internet is a global phenomenon and must be treated as such, inherently accepting the risks that states can dictate rules with effect outside the borders of their jurisdiction or alternatively, the idea of a global internet must be revisited, allowing for national governance of the online space where states accept the inherent fact that they cannot prevent that their nationals can reach nationally prohibited content by circumventing geo-blocking rules. An answer as to how to address the extraterritoriality of

580. Problems arising from the extraterritorial effect of legislation are not confined to social media platforms. *See* for a theoretical overview and a case-study on extraterritorial effect of legislation in the field of international shipping: Maxim Usynin, 'Sailing in All Winds: Extraterritorial Regulation as a Trigger for Self-Regulatory Practices in the Shipping Industry' (2020) 26 JIML.
581. The term Brussels-effect was coined by Bradford (n. 41) and refers to the de facto cross-border effect and influence of European Union legislation, such as for example happened after the enactment of the GDPR. By law, not all actors have to comply with European law all the time, but due to the optimalisation of processes, it is often easier for companies to apply the strictest norm to their entire business model.
582. In 2019, the CJEU found that the e-Commerce Directive's Art. 15 (general monitoring prohibition) did not preclude a court to issue an injunction that requires the *worldwide removal* of information on a social media platform, *see Eva Glawischnig-Piesczek v. Facebook Ireland Limited* [2019] ECJ Case C-18/18.
583. Usynin (n. 580), p. 340.
584. In relation to international shipping: *ibid.*, p. 342.

content moderation rules is subject to ongoing debate,[585] and a final answer exceeds the scope of this book.[586]

6.2.2 Normative Moderation Decisions

The second category concerns moderation decisions of the platforms' own volition. These moderation decisions go beyond the scope of the law and reflect a normative preference of the platform. These normative moderation decisions are a consequence of the freedom of contract between the two parties involved: the platform and the user. The parties can decide together on the scope of the service, although in practice, the user does not have any power to oppose normative moderation clauses in the terms of service of social media platforms. Mostly,[587] a user's choice is limited to a take-it-or-leave-it option. For social media platforms, the terms of service indicate which types of content are prohibited on the service. This can include content that falls within the scope of the right to freedom of expression and which would have otherwise been legal to share. Normative moderation also includes restrictions on content that does not fit the aim intended by the platform (or its advertisers), such as sexually explicit content, or content that would decrease the user experience on the platform, such as spam content. More examples of normative moderation decisions are the prohibition of anonymous accounts or the requirement to only allow sign-ups with a person's legal name.[588]

Apart from these rather harmless choices, normative moderation choices have the potential to facilitate the externalisation of norms from one state to another, as was the case for euthanasia content and content depicting Dutch 'Black Pete' on Facebook in 2020.[589] On 11 August 2020, Facebook increased the scope of its rules on hate speech in its terms of service, explicitly prohibiting to upload content containing harmful

585. Especially after the CJEU's decision in *Eva Glawischnig-Piesczek v. Facebook Ireland Limited* (n. 582); *see* for a discussion on the extraterritorial enforcement of injunctions to remove content: Valentina Golunova, 'In Tech We Trust? Fixing the Evolutionary Interpretation by the Court of Justice of the Prohibition of General Monitoring in the Era of Automated Content Moderation' in Evangelia Psychogiopoulou and Susana de la Sierra, *Digital Media Governance and Supranational Courts* (Edward Elgar Publishing 2022) https://www.elgaronline.com/display/book/9781802203004/book-part-9781802203004-8.xml (accessed 6 March 2023).

586. To reach an answer in the future, the field of international private law and the examples of international shipping form a perfect source of inspiration to address the issue of extraterritoriality in content moderation legislation. As highlighted by Usynin, international shipping has faced regulatory challenges because of the process of globalisation and 'questions relating to the exercise of regulatory powers by states beyond their territorial borders (meaning, with extraterritorial effect) have been traditionally popular in international law scholarship', *see* Usynin (n. 580). p. 338.

587. This is not always the case, as demonstrated by the immense backlash of users on *OnlyFans* after the platform's decision to restrict sexually explicit content in mid-2021, which led to the platform overturning their normative decision.

588. *See* for example the 'name policy' of Meta's Facebook: 'Names Allowed on Facebook | Facebook Help Centre' https://www.facebook.com/help/112146705538576 (accessed 6 March 2023).

589. These examples of normative moderation decisions on Facebook have previously been discussed in van der Donk, 'The Freedom to Conduct a Business as a Counterargument to Limit Platform Users' Freedom of Expression' (n. 10).

stereotypes. In Facebook's definition, such harmful stereotypes include antisemitic claims relating to Jewish people controlling the world and content that includes any form of blackfacing.[590] This amendment to Facebook's Community Guidelines had immediate consequences in the Netherlands. Due to the amendment, sharing content portraying the original version[591] of the national tradition of *Sinterklaas* and his helper, Black Pete (*Zwarte Piet* in Dutch), fell within the scope of the new restriction on blackfacing, and consequently, Facebook began to remove Black Pete-related content from their platform. With regard to euthanasia, in September 2020, French pro-euthanasia activist Alain Cocq wished to stream his personal suffering on the platform. In his eyes, his suffering was caused by a lack of access to active euthanasia in France and streaming his suffering would, therefore, contribute to the discussion on legalising euthanasia. Facebook prohibited and blocked his live streaming, as according to Facebook, allowing Cocq to stream his death would go against its Community Guidelines, which prohibit portrayals of suicide.[592] It did not matter that Cocq's actions constituted a political protest: a distinction between suicide and euthanasia did not exist at the time in the Community Guidelines. Despite the fact that there is no consensus on the legality of euthanasia worldwide, Facebook regulated the matter privately and consequently applied a unified rule to its 2.9 billion users worldwide. Another example of a normative restriction can be observed in the service of Google Maps. The latter does not show Palestine as an independent region or country despite being recognised by 138 out of 193 Member States of the United Nations. Kosovo, instead, is included as an independent region despite only being recognised by 101 UN Member States.[593] This difference indicates a normative choice leading to a difference that (seemingly) cannot be objectively justified.

The basis for taking normative moderation decisions is the terms of service that are accepted when signing up for a platform service. The power to make normative moderation decisions is not absolute. First, increasing procedural requirements are imposed to safeguard users against arbitrary normative moderation decisions. In the DSA, the necessity for such safeguards has been explicitly included in Article 14, and its importance is highlighted under Recital 45:

> Whilst the freedom of contract of providers of intermediary services should in principle be respected, it is appropriate to set certain rules on the content,

590. Facebook Community Guidelines, August 2020 Policy Rationale (III: Objectionable Content), https://www.facebook.com/communitystandards/recentupdates/hate_speech/ (accessed 5 January 2023).
591. The last years the tradition has been subject to mayor revision. Different 'Petes' have emerged, such as colourful and cookie ones. From 2022 onwards, only sooty Petes are featured on the state broadcasting channels.
592. The terms applicable to the Facebook platform have since been changed. According to the latest version of the terms, euthanasia content can be shared with persons over 18 years of age, though the content will be placed behind a sensitivity screen. *See* 'Suicide and Self-Injury | Transparency Centre' https://transparency.fb.com/en-gb/policies/community-standards/suicide-self-injury/ (accessed 6 March 2023).
593. The United States is one of 101 countries that has recognised Kosovo, whereas the United States does not form a part of the 138 countries that have recognised Palestine as a state. Whether or not this has been an argument supporting this diverging approach in their service is unclear.

> application and enforcement of the terms and conditions of those providers in the interests of transparency, the protection of recipients of the service and the avoidance of unfair or arbitrary outcomes. Providers of the intermediary services should clearly indicate and maintain up-to-date in their terms and conditions the information as to the grounds on the basis of which they may restrict the provision of their services. In particular, they should include information on any policies, procedures, measures and tools used for the purpose of content moderation, including algorithmic decision-making and human review, as well as the rules of procedure of their internal complaint-handling system. They should also provide easily accessible information on the right to terminate the use of the service.[594]

This indicates a codification of the shift in approach as was already observed in the Member States' case law assessed in Chapter 2. Following the comparative analysis in Chapter 2, national judges in the assessed Member States (indirectly) used fundamental rights to impose such procedural requirements. The DSA paves a unified front against inexplainable, untransparent, and unjustified limitations of the scope of a platform's service. These new procedural standards do not limit social media platforms' power to make normative decisions – they solely force platforms to take such measures in a transparent, non-discriminative, and proportionate manner. This discussion will be further addressed in §7.3.1 below.

6.2.3 Wrongful Moderation Decisions

In essence, a wrongful moderation decision entails that the decision to remove content or suspend an account has either been based on wrong facts or data, is the result of a wrong interpretation of the law or the platform's own terms of service, or the moderation decision has simply been a mistake, including wrongful flagging by algorithmic systems. As such, wrongful moderation decisions occur both when taking mandatory moderation and normative moderation decisions. A wrongful moderation decision constitutes a breach of contract on the side of the platform, and the user can act against that breach (*see* §7.4).

Wrongful moderation decisions are observed mainly when interpreting national law or when a platform has overseen that their worldwide terms of service apply differently in a national context. The most illustrative example follows from the Italian case before the *Corte d'appello dell'Aquila* where a social media platform, in its terms of service, had excluded content that was *'contrary to the law, misleading, discriminatory or fraudulent'* and, on that basis, had removed (varying degrees of) fascist content. Similar cases where the removal was tested against the platform's own terms of service can also be observed in Germany and the Netherlands.[595] The platform presumed the

594. Recital (45). Underlining by the author.

595. The content restore claim was rejected in the German case before the *Landgericht Frankfurt am Main (Restore claim)* (n. 102), as well as in *Microsoft OneDrive* (n. 199). In both cases, the user had shared child exploitative images. In the third case, *Microsoft OneDrive II* (n. 199), the removal base was identical to the first two (child exploitative images), but the user had successfully argued that the person in the photo was not a minor, *inter alia*, by bringing the person as a witness. The latter led to a reinstatement, as the initial removal was found to be wrongful.

content to be contrary to Italian law.[596] The national court assessed that provision in light of Italian law and concluded that (some of) the shared posts were not, in fact, violating Italian law and ordered the platform to pay damages for the time the content had not been hosted.[597] Facebook's counterargument that such regulation would render it impossible to offer a worldwide service was explicitly dismissed by the Italian Competition Authority when examining the potential unfairness of the user terms applied to Meta's WhatsApp service:

> No correlation exists between the opportunity/need to provide a 'single and uniform service, widespread and available throughout the world' and the need to regulate it everywhere in the same way. The provision of a service that is technically usable by consumers all over the world does not seem in any way incompatible with the adaptation of the Terms of Use to the different legal contexts of the countries where the Professional's service is offered, least of all if this practice results in limitations for the users.[598]

The choice to offer a worldwide service is the free choice of the platform operator. Using that same argument to contest the application of the national law of the country where the operator has freely decided to offer its service is struck down by the court and the Italian Consumer Authority. The platform is not forced to apply one set of terms for all the jurisdictions where they offer their service. If they wish to do so, it is up to the platform to align those terms with national laws.

Wrongful moderation decisions can also occur because of the enormous volume of content posted daily rather than the wrong interpretation of the platform's own playing rules. To curb the dissemination of illegal and unwanted content in the stream of millions of posts daily, social media platforms increasingly (and predominantly) use detection software based on (some type of) image and speech recognition machine learning tools.[599] While necessary to filter out the most harmful posts, these systems are negatively affecting the freedom of expression of users,[600] increase harmful

596. *Corte appello L'Aquila (Correggiari)* (n. 21). *See* for a more extensive discussion of the case, supra §2.2.2.2 on the online access restrictions in Italy.
597. *See* point 10.2: The unjustified removals and temporary suspension of the user profile form 'an unjustified limitation of the interpersonal relations and private communications of the plaintiff'. This 'represents conduct capable of producing harmful consequences both in terms of personal suffering and in terms of preventing to sustain the relationships on the platform which formed the very reason to subscribe'. (...) 'taking into account the duration (approximately three months) and the fact that the period was not continuous, and the fact that the plaintiff in that period was unable to cultivate his relationship with his contacts (approximately 2.500 of them) (...) In view of all these elements, it is considered appropriate to estimate, on an equitable basis, the damage suffered at an amount of €3,000'.
598. *Provvedimento n. 26596 – CV154 – WhatsApp* (n. 143), §61.
599. Robert Gorwa, Reuben Binns and Christian Katzenbach, 'Algorithmic Content Moderation: Technical and Political Challenges in the Automation of Platform Governance' (2020) 7 Big Data & Society. However, where the latter conclude that the use of these automated content moderation systems exacerbate existing problems, newer research suggests that these systems, in fact, deter users' rule-breaking behavior: Manoel Horta Ribeiro, Justin Cheng and Robert West, 'Automated Content Moderation Increases Adherence to Community Guidelines' (arXiv, 19 October 2022) http://arxiv.org/abs/2210.10454 (accessed 8 January 2023).
600. Emma J Llansó, 'No Amount of "AI" in Content Moderation Will Solve Filtering's Prior-Restraint Problem' (2020) 7 Big Data & Society 2053951720920686.

stereotypes,[601] and simply can lead to mis-flagging content that does not breach the terms of service or the law. This practice is increased by the platform's interest to avoid hefty fines and liability, resulting in a system that favours overblocking questionable content (*see* above on overblocking, §6.2.1.1).

With the DSA, wrongful moderation decisions are challengeable in three ways.[602] First, social media platforms must offer an internal complaints mechanism. Article 20 specifies the exact requirements of the internal complaint-handling system, which must be free of charge and available for at least six months following the moderation decision. The procedural rules for this internal complaint-handling system must be outlined in the terms of service.[603] Second, social media platforms must facilitate the option to challenge a moderation decision in an out-of-court dispute settlement made up of 'certified bodies that have the requisite independence, means and expertise to carry out their activities in a fair, swift and cost-effective manner.'[604] Third, Member States are urged to ensure that their legal systems allow the challenging of such wrongful decisions through a 'content restore'-claim.[605] The denial of the former can infringe the users' right to an effective remedy and a fair trial ensured in Article 47 of the Charter. The user's legal redress options are further addressed in the enforcement layer in §7.4.

6.3 THE GENERAL RIGHT OF USE ON OPEN ACCESS-PLATFORMS

Having made a distinction between the different types of moderation decisions and outcomes (mandatory, normative, and wrongful), this paragraph will lead back to the discussion of the roadmap's elements, starting with the path generated by a proprietor's access decision to offer an open platform (*see* Figure 6.2). Recalling the requirements for an open access-platform defined in §5.4.1.2, a social media platform falls within this category if the service offered is of a temporary nature, a breach of the user terms has limited individual consequences, and the service is not limited by general access restrictions.

601. Christina Dinar, 'The State of Content Moderation for the LGBTIQA + Community and the Role of the EU Digital Services Act'.
602. DSA preamble (59): 'Recipients of the service should be able to choose between the internal complaint mechanism, an out-of-court dispute settlement and the possibility to initiate, at any stage, judicial proceedings.'
603. DSA Art. 14(1) and preamble (45).
604. DSA Art. 21 and preamble (59).
605. DSA preamble (39): 'when applying this Regulation Member States should respect the fundamental right to an effective judicial remedy and to a fair trial as provided for in Article 47 of the Charter. This Regulation should therefore not prevent the relevant national judicial or administrative authorities from issuing, on the basis of the applicable Union or national law, an order to restore content, where such content was in compliance with the terms and conditions of the provider of the intermediary service but has been erroneously considered as illegal by that provider and has been removed'.

Figure 6.2 The Open Access-Platforms' Pathway of Access and Moderation (Highlighted in Dark Grey)

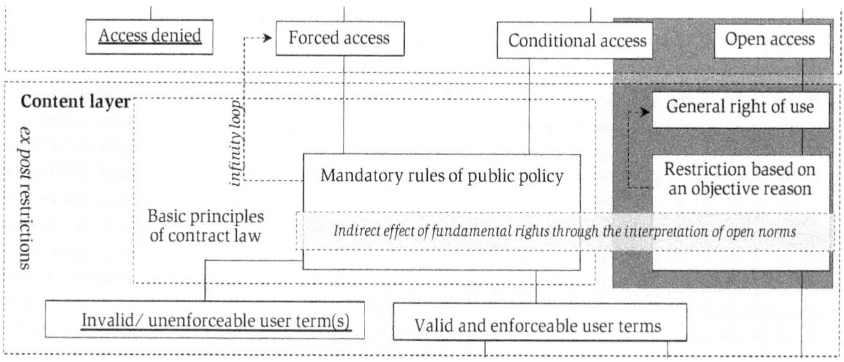

The relationship between an open access-platform and its users is not contractual in nature, nor is there specific legislation that covers these types of platforms. That makes addressing access and moderation issues difficult despite the pressing problems of illegal and harmful content on these platforms.[606] A solution on how to address these issues is therefore needed. Therefore, inspiration has been sought in the elaborate doctrine on house rights in Germany and the rules following the Italian RD 635/1940.

Due to the distinct nature of open access-platforms have their own individual, separated paths for moderation decisions. This paragraph discusses the three elements of that path. First, as a result of the proprietor's decision to offer open access, and by analogy to the German doctrine on open access-property in the physical world, the users of an open access-platform acquire a *general right of use*. This general right of use is far-reaching but not absolute. Since the relationship between the user and the operator is not a contractual one,[607] the scope and application of the doctrine of a general right of use are the determining factors to assess whether a platform operator's moderation decision was taken justly.

6.3.1 The General Right of Use: From the Physical to the Online Sphere

Both the German legal system and the Italian legal system refer to a general right of use for (certain types of) openly accessible property. In Italy, whether the general right of use extends to open access social media platforms is unclear. Recalling the conclusion in §2.2.2.1, physical property without formal access restrictions that offers a service to

606. *See* more on this topic and a discussion in §9.2.4.
607. The general principles of contract law (formation, substance, interpretability) are not fulfilled, *see* more on the requirements for a valid contract §6.4 below.

the public '*may not, without a legitimate reason, refuse the services of their establishment to anyone who requests them and pays for them*'.[608] This covers, for example, the free access to service in restaurants and bars. The scope of the 'legitimate reason to refuse service' is unsettled due to lacking legislation and case law, as is a final conclusion on whether this provision could equally apply to social media platforms. The applicable law (RD 635/1940) dates from before the second world war, meaning that the legislator by no means would have been able to foresee the current dilemma of access restrictions on social media platforms. A textual interpretation of the article does not explicitly exclude the application of Article 187 RD 635/1940 to online retailers:

> Salvo quanto dispongono gli articoli 689 e 691 del codice penale, *gli esercenti* non possono, senza un legittimo motivo, rifiutare *le prestazioni del proprio esercizio* a chiunque le domandi e ne corrisponda il prezzo.
>
> Without prejudice to the provisions of Articles 689 and 691 of the Criminal Code, [*gli esercenti*] may not, without a legitimate reason, refuse the performance of their services to anyone who requests them and pays the price.

The interpretation boils down to the scope of the word *esercente* and whether this term inextricably links to a physical property or should be interpreted more broadly to also encompass the performance of a service by online parties. *Treccani*[609] outlines the meaning of *esercente* as: 'one who carries out a business activity on his own ≈ trader, manager, shopkeeper, retailer, seller'.[610] Note the inclusion of the 'almost equal to' sign when aiming at defining the exact scope of *esercente* – seemingly, the scope is flexible and includes any business activity carried out by a proprietor. Thus, it seems most in line with the intention of the law's underlying norm (to safeguard indiscriminative access to publicly offered services) to apply it in a similar manner to the service offered on an open access-platform, but that conclusion cannot be made explicitly, due to the age of the law and the context in which it was enacted.

In Germany, however, there is a rich case law on the *generellen Nutzungsbefugnis* (general right of use), which has been equally applied to online open access-platforms.[611] In *Virtuelles Hausrecht bei Social-Media-Plattformen*, the *Oberlandesgericht München* recalls in §83 that it is up to the platform to decide whether they want to open and advertise their platform as an '*open forum which does not serve the general exchange of information and opinions*'. If a platform is 'open' to any type of content, the restriction of a certain type of content requires an objective reason. Equally, a

608. Regio Decreto 6 maggio 1940, n. 635. Approvazione del regolamento per l'esecuzione del testo unico 18 giugno 1931-IX, n. 773, delle leggi di pubblica sicurezza. (040U0635). Service can only be refused in one of the situations mentioned in Arts 689 and 691 of the Criminal Code (respectively selling alcohol to minors and selling alcohol to persons clearly intoxicated).
609. The Italian Encyclopaedia of Sciences, Letters and Arts.
610. esercente /ezer'tʃɛnte/ s. m. e f. [part. pres. di esercire]. – (comm.) [chi svolge un'attività commerciale in proprio: libero e.] ≈ commerciante, gerente, gestore, negoziante, rivenditore, venditore, https://www.treccani.it/vocabolario/esercente/ (accessed 9 January 2023).
611. *See* the conclusion in §2.2.1.2 based on *Landsgericht Offenburg (Virtuelles Hausrecht II)* (n. 98), §34; *see* earlier: *Oberlandesgericht Köln (Virtuelles Hausrecht bei einem Chat-Forum)* (n. 310). A general right of access for conditional platforms has been explicitly rejected. The platform is free to select its contractual partners within the framework of the general prohibition of discrimination, *see Bundesgerichtshof (Inhaltesperrung)* (n. 23), §14.

virtual house right cannot be used to deny access to a free-of-charge publicly accessible platform without an objective reason.[612] This applies equally in case users have been previously expelled from the service. That means that the scope of the 'objective reason' determines whether a content restriction is permissible.

6.3.2 The 'Objective Reason' to Restrict the General Right of Use

Following the German case law, some requirements to define the scope of the objective reason can be formed. In relation to physical property, the *Bundesgerichtshof* concluded that 'an objective reason (...) exists if, based on objective facts, not because of mere subjective fears, future disturbances by the persons concerned are to be feared. Such a danger is regularly presumed in the case of previous unlawful disturbances but may also exist in the case of a first threatening disturbance'.[613] That means that a user of an open access-platform can be blocked from accessing the service in case an *objective fear* of disturbance exists, such as when a user has shared illegal content on an open access-platform. Specifically on online behaviour, the *Landsgericht Bonn* has added hereto that blocking a user because of insulting statements does not qualify as an objectively justified reason if the insulting statements are part of the usual behaviour amongst the chat forum users unless such behaviour is explicitly prohibited in valid terms of service.[614]

A restriction on an open access-platform cannot be based on the subjective ideas of the platform but must be based on objectifiable criteria.[615] Furthermore, in case the access restriction has *'a considerable impact on the ability of the person concerned to participate in social life,'*[616] then the restriction may not unjustly interfere with the user's fundamental rights. Following the German case law, this includes, in any case, the right to equal treatment in Article 3 of the German Basic Law.[617] The third-party effect of constitutional rights depends on several factors, such as the dominant position of the platform operator, the orientation of the platform, the degree of user dependence on the platform, and the affected interests of the platform operators and other third parties.[618] That limits the scope for moderation decisions on open access-platforms to those situations where a user of the service has breached the law, or the platform operator has an objective fear that such breaches could arise in the future. There must be objectively verifiable facts that prove (previous) unlawful conduct or that sustain the existing fear of future disturbances. Moreover, large-scale open access-platforms

612. *Landsgericht Bonn (Virtuelles Hausrecht)* (1999) 10 O 457/99.
613. *Bundesgerichtshof (Stadionverbot I)* (n. 82), §17.
614. Interestingly, the *Bundesgerichtshof* also found that the use of a pseudonym to circumvent the block is allowed, since everyone is free to use different pseudonyms according to the terms and conditions applicable to the platform, *Landsgericht Bonn (Virtuelles Hausrecht)* (n. 612).
615. *Ibid.*, §88.
616. *Bundesverfassungsgericht (Stadionverbot II)* (n. 90); *Bundesgerichtshof (Therme)* (n. 77).
617. *Ibid.*
618. *Bundesverfassungsgericht (der III. Weg)* (n. 117), §15, and later confirmed in *Bundesgerichtshof (Inhaltesperrung)* (n. 23) and *Bundesgerichtshof (Kontosperrung)* (n. 23).

will most likely have to take the right to non-discrimination into consideration. The latter conclusion is, however, unsettled.

The above criteria have been deducted from the case law in one Member State (Germany). In Italy, it is unclear whether the general access right to physical private property is transferable to open access-platforms, and in the other Member States that were assessed in the comparative study (Denmark and the Netherlands), neither a general right to access physical private property nor to online access-platforms was observed. This renders a conclusion on the general applicability of these criteria to all open access-platforms in the European Union impossible at this point. The requirement of an objective reason resembles the requirement of a 'legitimate aim' in the secondary European legislation on equal treatment.[619] To fulfil the requirement of a 'legitimate aim', a measure must, in any case, be objectively justifiable, meaning that the proprietor has a genuine need to impose the restriction. That resembles the requirement for an objective reason. Potentially, the scope of these two requirements could be aligned. However, as also outlined in the discussion on the equal treatment legislation, the exact scope of what constitutes a legitimate aim is unsettled. The developments in these discussions can most likely serve as a source of inspiration to settle the debate on 'objective reasons' to restrict access to open access-platforms and vice versa. Similarly, developments in the discussion on the horizontal direct effect of the right to non-discrimination (*see* §5.5.3.2 above) have the same potential.

6.4 SOCIAL MEDIA PLATFORMS' TERMS OF SERVICE AS CONTRACTS

As highlighted in the description of the content layer in §3.2.3, the content layer is divided into two separate streams: the open access-stream and the contract-stream. After discussing the open access-stream above, the contract-stream is the next point to address. This paragraph, therefore, focuses on social media platforms' terms of service from the perspective of contract law. When a user is given the opportunity to enter the platform's service conditionally or has a right to claim forced access to the platform, the user and the platform need to agree on the contractual terms under which the service will be provided. When doing so, the platform implicitly waives the further use of the right of exclusion. The agreement is an expression of the free will and interest of the platform, and therefore, the platform cannot subsequently invoke its rights of private autonomy, entrepreneurial freedom, or general property rights (including its house right) to deny the service that was agreed on in the agreement.[620] For an agreement between two parties to have legal effect, three things must be in place. First, the parties must have the capacity to conclude a contract concerning the given substance. Second, it must be assessed *whether* the parties have agreed to be bound by the agreement (formation of the contract), and if so, third, it must be determined *what* the content is

619. *See* §5.5.2.1 above.

620. Exceptionally, under certain circumstances, 'weighty factual reasons' can be invoked to end an existing agreement of service. *See* an example hereof in: *Bundesgerichtshof (Hausrecht des Hotelbetreibers)* (n. 77), §14.

of the contractual obligations the parties have consented to (validity and interpretation of the contract).[621] These requirements refer back to the basic principles that underpin the contractual relationship between the parties: private autonomy and mutual consent.[622]

The outline of this paragraph looks as follows. First, a distinction is made between substance that falls within and substance that falls outside the scope of the parties' private autonomy. Second, within the scope of private autonomy, the focus shifts to the question of reciprocity when dealing with social media platforms' terms of service. Can these terms of service be regarded as contracts, or are they merely one-sided promises? Third, the requirements for the formation of a contract are reviewed, with a specific focus on mutual consent and the requirements of transparency. The parties can only reach an agreement when both parties know what they say yes to.[623] Especially for the application of unilaterally imposed obligations by a trader on a consumer – which is the case for terms of services used on social media platforms – requirements on transparency and the provision of information follow from mandatory law.[624] Fourth, the validity of the contractual terms is examined in light of mandatory law. This part addresses the Unfair Contract Terms Directive's unfairness test. Based on the unfairness test, platforms cannot include terms that cause a significant imbalance in the parties' rights and obligations. This part theorises how this unfairness test should unfold when dealing with terms that restrict the protection of fundamental rights, with a specific focus on the freedom of expression and the protection of personal data. The last part of this paragraph addresses the (discussion on the) interpretation of the contractual terms.

6.4.1 Not Everything Can Form the Substance of a Contract

Contractual parties are, in principle, free to agree on contractual obligations between them, though this freedom is not absolute. The scope of the parties' private autonomy to enter into an agreement is bound by the law. Following the analysis (§4.3.3.2) of

621. Trevor C Hartley (ed.), 'Contracts: The Principle of Party Autonomy', *International Commercial Litigation: Text, Cases and Materials on Private International Law* (Cambridge University Press 2009) https://www.cambridge.org/core/books/international commercial-litigation/contracts-the-principle-of-party-autonomy/899C42C4D91C0736A2C823C97AC308B1 (accessed 25 January 2023).

622. Hansen, Ulfbeck and Petersen (n. 6) 337. The authors refer to 'party autonomy' rather than 'private autonomy'. I have opted for the latter to indicate a difference from the existing German literature on 'Parteiautonomie', which refers to the parties' choice over the governing law as opposed to 'Privatautonomie' which refers to the contractual freedom's three elements to (i) choose whether or not to enter into a contract, (ii) choose a contractual partner, and (iii) to decide on the content of the contract. *See* on the difference: Salvatore Patti, 'Contractual Autonomy and European Private Law' in Jacobien Rutgers and Pietro Sirena (eds), *Rules and Principles in European Contract Law* (Intersentia 2015) https://www.cambridge.org/core/books/rules-and-principles-in-european-contract-law/contractual-autonomy-and-european-private-law/3B9B01AFFDEA675CCF0840311EC0F19F (accessed 25 January 2023).

623. Mak, *Legal Pluralism in European Contract Law* (n. 65) 155.

624. For terms of service on social media platforms, the formal requirements on consent, information and transparency follow from the Unfair Contract Terms Directive (UCTD), from the DSA, and from the GDPR's rules on consent.

freedom of contract, the contracting parties are at liberty – subject to the mandatory rules of public policy – to define the terms of their legal relationship.[625] Rules can affect the formation of the contract or the substance of the contract. For example, national law can prohibit minors from legally entering into a contract (restriction on the formation) or prohibit the sale of endangered animals (restriction on the substance). For social media platforms and their users, excluded from their private autonomy are agreements including illegal activity, such as offering a platform for the sale of illegal goods or narcotics. The majority of the terms applying to services offered by platforms on the *dark web* are, therefore, invalid and unenforceable.

Two specific discussions related to the existence of a contractual relationship between a social media platform and its users are outlined below. First, the discussion as to what extent the obligation to 'pay with personal data' falls within the parties' private autonomy is addressed in light of the recent binding decision by the European Data Protection Board concerning Meta. Second, the argument that the terms of service do not fulfil the general principle under the doctrine of reciprocity that unless both parties are bound to perform, neither party is bound to perform. The question as to whether users can contractually waive other fundamental rights protection (especially the right to freedom of expression) is addressed later on in §§6.4.3.3-6.4.3.6.

6.4.1.1 The 'Payment' with Personal Data

Users' consent to supply personal data to the platform as a counter-performance for a communication platform is subject to strict rules on transparency.[626] Undertakings must have a valid processing ground when processing personal data. These follow from Articles 6 and 9, respectively, dealing with normal and sensitive personal data. One of the processing grounds consists of the users' consent (Article 6(1)(a)). The GDPR stipulates that users can only consent to the processing of their personal data if the consent has been given *freely*.[627] Consent is not considered freely given if the data subject's access to the provision of a service is conditional to giving consent for the processing of data, at least in those circumstances where the processing of the data is not necessary for the performance of a contract.[628] Equally, when the withdrawal of consent would lead to the eviction of the platform's service, the consent is not regarded as freely given.[629] The user of a social media platform cannot be forced to choose between using the platform's service by supplying personal data or not accessing the service at all. Especially when processing personal data for *behavioural advertisements*,[630] the information provided to the users must be extensive in order for them to

625. *STEB* (n. 374), §28.
626. Henrik Udsen, 'Personoplysninger som en modydelse', *Festskrift til Palle Bo Madsen* (Djøf 2021); Cosio (n. 12).
627. The requirement to freely consent to be bound by an obligation is also a general principle in contract law and a requirement for the formation of a contract. *See* on this also §6.4.2.
628. GDPR, Art. 7(4). *See also* Udsen (n. 626), p. 486.
629. GDPR, preamble (42).
630. A definition can be found in point 95 of the EDPB Binding Decision 3/2022: Behavioural advertisement consists of collecting data of individual users from numerous sources and

validly consent since that practice is especially invasive on the personal life of the users.[631]

The EDPB's binding decision on Meta proves helpful in deciding on the transparency obligations for consent in the GDPR. According to Meta, the parties agreed that Meta would supply the user with behavioural advertisements in exchange for the users' personal data. As such, Meta argued that the processing of personal data was necessary for the performance of a contract (Article 6(1)(b) GDPR). The EDPB rejected the argument that the processing of personal data was necessary for the performance of 'personalised services on social media platforms' as defined by Meta's terms of service for their Facebook platform. The mere fact that the social media platform itself had formulated its terms of service creatively to indicate that its core obligation is the supply of behavioural advertisement instead of offering a communication platform does not outweigh the users' interest in having their data protected. This is even more so when the users are unaware of giving up their protection and the platform is in a powerful position.[632] Based on an assessment of the terms of service applicable between the user and Meta, the EDPB concludes that Meta does not have any obligation to supply personalised advertisements to individual users. Whether or not Meta would have such an obligation on the basis of another contract with a third party (advertisers) does not alter that conclusion.[633] Rather, Meta has obliged itself to supply a service where users can communicate with one another.[634] The users had never voluntarily agreed to be bound by an agreement for behavioural advertisements – rather, the users wanted to gain access to a general communication platform. In that line, the EDPB concludes that a simple reference to those obligations is not enough since 'a reasonable user cannot expect that their personal data is being processed for behavioural advertising simply because Meta IE briefly refers to this processing in the Facebook Terms of Service'.[635] Moreover, 'the very brief and insufficient information that Meta provides about [behavioural advertising] in the Facebook Terms of Service and Data Policy, [makes it] extremely difficult to argue that an average user can fully grasp it, be aware of its consequences and impact on their rights to privacy and data protection, and reasonably expect it solely based on the Facebook Terms of Service'.[636]

linking 'these data with the user's Facebook account to enable advertisers to tailor their advertising to Facebook's individual users based on their consumer behaviour, interests, purchasing power and personal situation. This may also include the user's physical location to display content relevant to the user's location. Meta IE offers its services to its users free of charge and generates revenue through this personalised advertising that targets them, in addition to static advertising that is displayed to every user in the same way.'

631. EDPB Binding Decision 3/2022 (5 December 2022), point 123.
632. EDPB Binding Decision 3/2022, point 115-116.
633. *Ibid.*, point 118: 'The fact that the Facebook Terms of Service do not provide for any contractual obligation binding Meta IE to offer personalised advertising to the Facebook users and any contractual penalty if Meta IE fails to do so shows that, at least from the perspective of the Facebook user, this processing is not necessary to perform the contract. Providing personalised advertising to its users may be an obligation between Meta IE and the specific advertisers that pay for Meta IE's targeted display of their advertisements in the Facebook service to Facebook users, but it is not presented as an obligation towards the Facebook users.'
634. EDPB Binding Decision 3/2022, point 129.
635. EDPB Binding Decision 3/2022 (5 December 2022), point 123.
636. *Ibid.*

The EDPB concludes that Meta has, first, violated its transparency obligation in Article 5(1)(a) GDPR. Second, the contract is void as 'one of the parties is not provided with sufficient information to know that they are signing a contract'.

The economic and commercial interests of the platform do not outweigh the users' right to data protection. The EDPB is clear in that regard in its guideline to Article 6(1)(b): 'Even if the data subject can agree to the processing of personal data, they cannot trade away their fundamental rights through this agreement.' The latter means, in sum, that a user can agree to give up their protection partially, but that they cannot fully waive their right to data protection on the basis of the freedom of contract. Therefore, Meta cannot use the processing ground in Article 6(1)(b) GDPR to circumvent the protection of the GDPR. The latter would mean that the full protection of the users' right to data protection is compromised because users would solely be able to choose between using the service without effective protection or not using the service at all. Since parties only have private autonomy to decide on the obligations they wish to be bound by as long as those obligations do not conflict with mandatory rules of public policy, the private autonomy of the parties is subordinate to the data subject's right to data protection.

In Case C-252/21 (*Facebook and Others v. Bundeskartellamt*),[637] the CJEU addressed a similar preliminary question. On the validity of consent to exchange personal data for access to a dominant social media platform such as Facebook, AG Rantos concluded in his opinion to the case that in case a clear imbalance exists between the parties, consent cannot constitute a valid legal ground for processing.[638] On the note of the balancing of fundamental rights and the financial interests of the platform operator, the CJEU concludes that:

> Despite the fact that the services of an online social network such as Facebook are free of charge, the user of that network cannot reasonably expect that the operator of the social network will process that user's personal data, without his or her consent, for the purposes of personalised advertising. In those circumstances, it must be held that the interests and fundamental rights of such a user override the interest of that operator in such personalised advertising by which it finances its activity (...).[639]

The sole fact that a social media platform has a dominant position does not render the consent invalid but must be taken into consideration when assessing the validity of the consent.[640] Similarly, the EDPB put emphasis on the fact that social media platforms offer a '*take it or leave it*'-option and that there are few alternative services available in the market.[641] The CJEU continues in that line and concludes that a dominant position does not prevent valid consent, but it does constitute a factor to be weighed to assess whether the user had a free choice or was unable to refuse or

637. *Case C-252/21 (Facebook and Others v. Bundeskartellamt)* (2023) ECLI:EU:C:2023:537 (CJEU).
638. Opinion of Advocate General Rantos delivered on 20 September 2022 to Case C-252/21 (Meta platforms v. Bundeskartellamt), ECLI:EU:C:2022:704, §74.
639. *Ibid.*, §117.
640. *Ibid.*, §75.
641. EDPB Binding Decision 3/2022, point 127.

withdraw consent.[642] Users must have access to the platform (in the case of Facebook) without consenting to the processing of their personal data. If necessary, the platform operator may, to compensate, charge a fee for accessing the service or impose an equivalent alternative.[643] Moreover, the fact that the processing of personal data may be referenced in the contract or may be useful for the performance of the contract is irrelevant. The processing must be essential for the *proper performance* of the contract, and there must be no workable, less intrusive alternatives available.[644] It is up to the platform operator to prove that the main subject matter of the contract cannot be achieved without the processing of personal data.[645] Similarly, one could wonder whether a general limitation of other fundamental rights protected by the Charter in a contract between a powerful online platform and its users could be justifiable or whether the same test of *proper performance* could be applied. If the restriction of fundamental rights is not absolutely necessary, or less intrusive alternatives exist, the justification of the limitation is fragile.

Apart from the conclusion on whether the supply of personal data could (not) be qualified as a commodity, users of social media platforms' services should nonetheless have access to contractual remedies.[646] That marks the conclusion that even in case one would argue the obligation to supply personal data does not fall within the scope of the parties' private autonomy, then users are nonetheless entitled to contractual remedies. The agreement must then be assessed from the point of view of contract law. Furthermore, as opposed to the discussion above related to the processing of personal data for behavioural advertisements, social media platforms could opt to solely provide *contextual advertisements*, which are advertisements that are based on geography, language, and content, rather than personal data. The EDPB referred to this as a viable alternative for the performance of Meta's contractual obligations to supply a communication platform on the basis of personal data.[647] Since contextual advertisements do not involve users' personal data, the requirements for consent fall outside the scope of the GDPR. That means that when the contract fulfils the requirements of consent and stays within the borders of the law, then a contract that exchanges contextual advertisements for access to the platform is, in principle, valid. Another request for preliminary rulings on the same matter is currently pending before the CJEU.[648]

642. *Case C-252/21 (Facebook and Others v. Bundeskartellamt)* (2023) ECLI:EU:C:2023:537 (CJEU), §§147-148.
643. *Ibid.*, §150.
644. *Ibid.*, §99.
645. *Ibid.*, §98.
646. The Digital Goods and Services Directive, preamble (24): 'Digital content or digital services are often supplied also where the consumer does not pay a price but provides personal data to the trader. Such business models are used in different forms in a considerable part of the market. While fully recognising that the protection of personal data is a fundamental right and that therefore personal data cannot be considered as a commodity, this Directive should ensure that consumers are, in the context of such business models, entitled to contractual remedies.'
647. EDPB Binding Decision 3/2022, point 121.
648. CJEU Case C-446/21 (*Schrems v. Facebook Ireland*) lodged on 20 July 2021.

6.4.1.2 *The Doctrine of Reciprocity*

If the substance of the agreement falls within the private autonomy of the parties, they can, in principle, agree on the obligations they wish to be bound by. However, following the European Data Protection Board's (EDPB) binding decision limiting social media platform's business models to rely on users' personal data as a counter-performance, some scholars have highlighted that the agreement between a platform and a user lacks reciprocal obligations since the user does not supply anything.[649] The doctrine of reciprocity (also referred to as mutuality[650] or linked to the English doctrine of consideration[651]) entails the general principle that unless both parties are bound to perform, neither party is bound to perform. The inclusion of the principle of reciprocity in European and national Member State discussions on the validity of contracts has been critiqued.[652] Despite referring to the relevance of the discussion for some European Member States, Quarta refers to a 'huge misunderstanding' to invalidate terms of service on the basis of the exchange model included in the principle of reciprocity. Even in case the principle of reciprocity would be applicable, then it seems unlikely to sustain the argument that users do not supply anything in return for accessing the platform's service. Simply by using the service, the users create valuable data for the platform operator, whether the data consists of personal data or behavioural data. That data can, in turn, be used by the platform to sell advertisement space (*see* Figure 6.3).

Figure 6.3 The Creation of Value Without a User's Direct Obligation to Supply

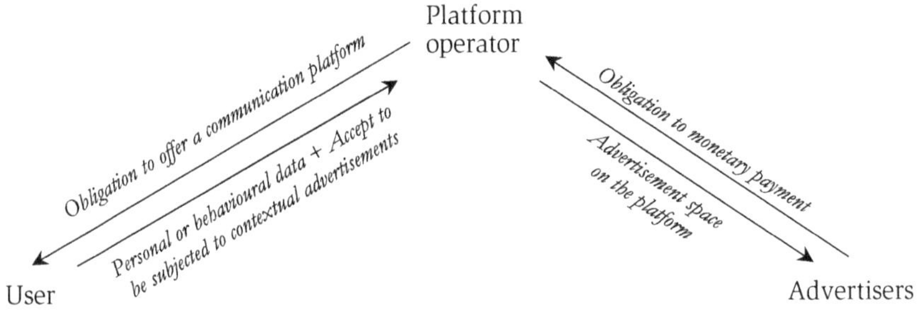

Based on the above situation, the contractual relationship between the platform operator and the user offers both parties value. The user accepts to be subjected to

649. *See* Cosio (n. 12), pp. 145-147, highlighting a discussion in (Italian) legal doctrine.
650. Hansen, Ulfbeck and Petersen (n. 6) 337.
651. Bénédicte Fauvarque-Cosson and Denis Mazeaud, *European Contract Law: Materials for a Common Frame of Reference: Terminology, Guiding Principles, Model Rules* (Walter de Gruyter 2009) 8.
652. The inclusion has been amplified by including out-of-context arguments from other jurisdictions (referring mainly to the United States), *see* Quarta, 'Beyond Assimilation: Are Terms of Use Really Contracts?' (n. 398), pp. 133-134.

contextual advertisements and the platform, in turn, is obliged to offer a communication platform in which, optionally, the community of users can choose to engage. A similar conclusion can be observed in the Commission's guidance on the interpretation of the UCTD in relation to social media platforms. Following the latter, the provision of payment for a good or service is not mandatory for users to be able to contest the unfairness of contractual terms. The CJEU concluded earlier that monetary consideration is not a requisite for the UCTD to be applicable.[653] The Commission concludes that 'also contracts between consumers and providers of social media services must be considered to be covered by the UCTD regardless of whether consumers have to pay certain amounts of money or whether the consideration for the services consists in consumer generated content and profiling'.[654] Therefore, the argument that the terms of service do not fulfil the general principle under the doctrine of reciprocity is insufficient to make the argument that there is no contract between the user and the platform operator.

6.4.2 Requirements for the Formation of a Contract

The parties can only reach an agreement when both parties know what they say yes to,[655] and therefore, the obligations must be presented in a transparent way. When transparency is lacking, it obstructs the party's free choice to be bound by the agreement, even more so when there is a power imbalance between the parties. The requirement that users know what they say yes to when signing up for a social media platform's service raises questions. One could question whether the platform operator's take-it or leave-it offer, providing users with the option to pick between agreeing to the terms or not accessing the service, obstructs the users' voluntariness to be bound. Does a user express a will to be bound by the contractual obligations stipulated in the terms of service by signing up to a platform's service by clicking 'I agree'? Does the user even know what contractual obligations are imposed when doing so?

There has been an ongoing discussion on the consequences of the *unreadability* of platforms' terms of service. As mentioned in the introduction, it has been empirically proven, time after time, that the terms of services as they are applied on social media platforms are unreadable and incomprehensible. With regard to the formal requirements, Venturini et al. concluded in 2016 that '*there is a lack of clear and specific information in the Terms of Service on which content is allowed or not in the platform.*'[656] Regarding the substantive requirements, Benoliel & Becher demonstrated empirically in 2019 that the user terms applied by the 500 most popular websites,

653. Cases C-74/15 *Dumitru Tarcău* (19 November 2015) ECLI:EU:C:2015:772; and C-534/15 *Dumitraş* (14 September 2016) ECLI:EU:C:2016:700.
654. Commission notice of 27 September 2019 – Guidance on the interpretation and application of Council Directive 93/13/EEC on unfair terms in consumer contracts, point 1.2.1.2.
655. Nancy S Kim, *Wrap Contracts: Foundations and Ramifications* (Oxford University Press 2013) 7.
656. Jamila Venturini and others, *Terms of Service and Human Rights: An Analysis of Online Platform Contracts* (Editora Revan 2016) http://bibliotecadigital.fgv.br/dspace/handle/10438/18231 (accessed 3 March 2021), p. 96.

online platforms included, are nearly all unreadable.[657] The latter was confirmed once again by the EDPB's decision on Meta discussed above, where 97.5% of the users who signed up to Meta's Facebook platform did not understand or had not been aware of the contractual obligations in the terms of service.[658] As a consequence, users do not know what they have clicked 'I agree' on when signing up for social media,[659] despite the benefits for both users and platform operators when increasing transparency.[660]

Transparency is a key element in determining whether the user has agreed to be bound by the terms of service. Transparency obligations in consumer protection law serve two purposes. It allows consumers to be able to access the relevant information needed to make an informed decision, and the information must be comprehensible to the 'average consumer'. Transparency requirements consist, therefore, of formal requirements (Has the information been included in the terms and did users have a chance to read the terms?) and substantive requirements (Did the users understand what was written in the terms?). The UCTD sets a broad, general standard for unilaterally imposed terms of service. Recently, the DSA has further increased the transparency obligations for social media platforms.[661] This sub-paragraph outlines these transparency obligations. First, the formal requirements in the UCTD and the DSA are outlined, followed by the substantive requirement on lingual clarity. Lastly, the German case law on specific transparency when dealing with social media platform terms of service is outlined as examples of national courts' conclusions on the transparency of the terms on social media platforms.

6.4.2.1 Transparency Requirements in the UCTD and the DSA

The DSA stipulates increased formal transparency requirements for the terms of service applied by social media platforms. First, Article 14(1) obliges social media platforms to include information on all restrictions that are imposed 'in relation to the use of their service in respect of information provided by the recipients of the service'. This rather cryptical description can be broken down as follows: any restrictions imposed by providers of intermediary services in relation to (i) the use of their service, (ii) in respect of information provided, (iii) by the recipients of the service. The definition of

657. Uri Benoliel & Shmuel I Becher, 'The Duty to Read the Unreadable' (2019) 60 Boston C.L. Rev.
658. *See* EDPB Binding Decision 3/2022 (5 December 2022), point 97. In the case, it was demonstrated that only 1.6%-2.5% of the questioned Facebook users was aware that they supplied personal data in exchange for 'a contractual right to personalised advertisement' on the platform's service. Users were generally unaware that they were subjected to behavioural advertisement as a consequence of accepting the terms of service. The research was carried out by the complainant and disputed by Meta and the Irish Data Protection Commissioner.
659. Quarta, 'Beyond Assimilation: Are Terms of Use Really Contracts?' (n. 398).
660. Giuseppe A Veltri and others, 'The Impact of Online Platform Transparency of Information on Consumers' Choices' (2023) 7 Behavioural Public Policy 55. The findings of the study suggest that 'greater online transparency has three effects: (1) it is important in decision-making; (2) it increases trust and confidence in the online environment; (3) and, all things being equal, it increases the probability of product selection.'
661. Mak, *Legal Pluralism in European Contract Law* (n. 65) 155. Vanessa Mak refers to this as the two-pronged transparency test in the UCTD.

a recipient of the service follows from Article 3(b).[662] That means that *ex ante* restrictions do not have to be outlined in the terms. Persons who have not yet been granted access to the platform's service are not considered recipients of the service. They have neither used the service nor provided any information. For *ex post* restrictions, Article 14(1) obliges the inclusion of 'any policies, procedures, measures and tools used for the purpose of content moderation, including algorithmic decision-making and human review, as well as the rules of procedure of their internal complaint handling system' to be included in the terms of service. Concretely, that means that information must be included in any interference with the content provided by the users of the service, referring mainly to content moderation. It does not solely include deletion of the content but also covers shadow-banning and down-ranking of content. The terms of service must also include information on the use of algorithmic decision-making and human review, and the terms must outline the procedural rules for the internal complaint-handling system, which is obligatory for online platform providers according to Article 20 DSA. In case a platform is applying a recommender system, it must include the main parameters of its use, as well as the options to modify or influence those parameters.[663] Providers of very large online platforms ('VLOPs') must provide their terms of service in all the languages of the Member States and must provide a summary of their terms of service in a concise, easily accessible, and machine-readable manner. The summary must include the available remedies and redress mechanisms.[664] Lastly, when the platform substantially changes the terms, it must inform the users.[665]

Seemingly, a strict interpretation of the text of Article 14(1) excludes the suspension and termination of user accounts, since these types of access restrictions do not concern restrictions *in respect of information provided.* A broader reading of the first sentence could potentially allow for the inclusion of account restrictions since a restriction of an account would lead to a restriction of the recipient's use of the service and ability to provide information. Similarly, the suspension or termination of an account is a consequence of the information posted and as such, those measures could be interpreted as restrictions imposed in respect of information provided by the user.[666] The broad reading finds support in Recital (45), which refers to '*the grounds on the basis of which [intermediary service providers] may restrict the provision of their services*'.

662. Article 3(b) DSA: 'recipient of the service' means any natural or legal person who uses an intermediary service, in particular for the purposes of seeking information or making it accessible'.
663. Article 27(1) DSA.
664. Article 14(5) and (6) DSA.
665. Article 14(2) DSA. Loos and Luzak have argued that not informing a user of a change with a reasonable notice should be put on an additional blacklist of unfair terms, *see* Loos and Luzak (n. 432) 50.
666. Especially for providers of hosting services, which includes social media platforms, this seems to be the case. The obligatory statement of reasons that must be sent to the affected users (Art. 17) includes explicitly under (c) the suspension or termination of the provision of the service in whole or in part, and (d) the suspension or termination of the recipient of the service's account.

Following the UCTD's transparency obligation, all of the above information that must be included in the terms of service on social media platforms must be drafted in plain, intelligible language when offered to consumers.[667] The DSA adds thereto the requirement that terms must be clear, user-friendly, unambiguous, and shall be publicly available in an easily accessible and machine-readable format.[668] To fulfil the requirement of plain and intelligible information, the trader must, first, ensure that the other party has the opportunity to get acquainted with the terms and conditions before the contract is concluded, and second, the terms must be written understandably for the (average) consumer.[669] The requirement of plain and intelligible language 'is to be understood as requiring not only that the relevant term should be grammatically intelligible to the consumer, but also that the contract should set out transparently the specific [obligation] (...) so that that consumer is in a position to evaluate, on the basis of clear, intelligible criteria, the economic consequences for him which derive from it'.[670] The conclusion on whether terms of service fulfil the formal and substantive transparency criteria is left to national courts.

6.4.2.2 Contractual Transparency: Lessons from German Case Law

Assessing whether terms of service on social media platforms are transparent enough for the user to validly consent can prove difficult in practice. The rich German case law proves helpful, as it has thoroughly addressed the numerous discussions related to social media platforms' terms of service and, as such, can serve as a source of inspiration. On the transparency review of platforms' user terms, the German case law has clarified the following. The mere fact that social media platforms make use of 'layered user terms' (linking from one set of user terms to another) does not, per default, make the user terms untransparent.[671] Furthermore, user terms can be unilaterally amended by the platform as long as the platform user – at some point – clicks 'I agree' and is made aware that clicking said button means that the user terms are updated.[672] The fact that the platform only grants the user the opportunity to agree

667. Articles 4(2) and 5 UCTD.
668. Article 14(1) DSA. Additionally, the DSA sets a higher barrier for services directed at minors in Art. 14(3) DSA: *Where an intermediary service is primarily directed at minors or is predominantly used by them, the provider of that intermediary service shall explain the conditions for, and any restrictions on, the use of the service in a way that minors can understand.* The specific rules for minors are not addressed further in this book.
669. Marco BM Loos, 'Transparency of Standard Terms under the Unfair Contract Terms Directive and the Proposal for a Common European Sales Law' (2015) 23 European Review of Private Law, DOI: https://doi.org/10.54648/erpl2015015; Loos and Luzak (n. 432), §1.1.2 'Transparency principle' and the summary of the CJEU's case law included there.
670. CJEU Case C-26/13 (Kásler), 30 April 2014, ECLI:EU:C:2014:282, §75.
671. *See* a thorough assessment of the validity of the 'normal practice' of social media platforms when updating their user terms: *Bundesgerichtshof (Inhaltesperrung)* (n. 23), §§46-51. *Oberlandesgericht Dresden (Unfair platform terms)* (n. 103), §13. Later confirmed in *Oberlandesgericht Schleswig* [2020] 9 U 12519, §39.
672. *Oberlandesgericht Dresden (Amended user terms)* [2019] 4 U 1471/19; *Oberlandesgericht Schleswig* (n. 671), §§30-32. The platform does not have a contractual obligation, neither when the platform fulfils a dominant role in society. The amendment of user terms cannot be

to the new terms or leave the platform does not change this. User terms are deemed transparent if the consequences are sufficiently clear to an objective user.[673] Lastly, the use of legal terms in a way that deviates from the law does not per se breach the requirement of transparency.[674]

6.4.2.3 Legal Redress for Lacking Transparency in the Terms

Within the scope of the UCTD, the consequence of non-compliance with either of the two elements of the transparency test in Article 5 of the UCTD is unfairness.[675] Users must be able to oppose untransparent terms, though the parties remain bound by the parts of the agreement that are not unfair, for as far as possible.[676] The Directive obliges Member States to ensure legal remedies against the continued use of unfair terms when implementing the directive into national law.[677] To what extent the legal consequences for transparency following the UCTD equally apply to the increased obligations of clarity, user-friendliness, unambiguity, public availability, and machine-readability in Article 14(1) DSA is unclear. Terms that do not stipulate mandatory information requirements are to be interpreted as most favourable or risk to be non-binding. This protection is absolute; derogation of the protection awarded in the UCTD is not possible.[678]

Analysing the legal consequences of a breach of the DSA's transparency obligations is difficult, as the DSA does not stipulate legal redress for users in case of a breach

---

subjected to the transparency and unfairness tests in §307, because the amendment is based on the user's declaration of intent. That declaration of intent is valid (in line with §138 (1) BGB) even if the user would otherwise be refused further access to the platform, *see Bundesgerichtshof (Inhaltesperrung)* (n. 23), §§56-60. For distorted intent on the user's side, the platform must have used its dominant position to gain an unfair advantage (for its own selfish motives), disregarding the legitimate interests of the user. This is not the case when the updated version of the user terms does not deviate significantly from the previous version or in case the updated version does not negatively affect the user (§§61-61). *See* further on the legitimacy of such unilateral variation clauses in contract law: Ole Hansen and Hamish George Ritchie, 'Unilateral Variation Clauses in Professional Platform-User Agreements' (2022) 6 European Review of Private Law, DOI: https://doi.org/10.54648/erpl2022050.

673. *See* for an in-depth assessment of transparency: *Oberlandesgericht Schleswig* (n. 671), §§40-43.
674. *See* on this also Gerald Spindler, 'Löschung und Sperrung von Inhalten aufgrund von Teilnahmebedingungen sozialer Netzwerke – Eine Untersuchung der zivil- und verfassungsrechtlichen Grundlagen' (2019) 35 Computer und Recht 238, 242.
675. This outcome can differ from Member State to Member State, as it does not directly follow from the UCTD. The interpretation that a breach of transparency leads to unfairness seems to be the current interpretation of Art. 5 UCTD in the literature after the CJEU's judgment in *Amazon* (C-191/15) and the previous decision in Kásler (C-26/13), *see* the analysis by Vanessa Mak, highlighting the unclarity on the legal effects in the UCTD and the resulting divergences in national Member States' implementation: Mak, *Legal Pluralism in European Contract Law* (n. 65), p. 157.
676. Article 6(1) UCTD. This is only possible if the essential parts of the contract remain upheld. If the main subject matter of the contract is unfair, the contract as a whole is rendered invalid.
677. Article 6(1) jo. 7(1) UCTD. The legal consequences for unfairness are also implemented differently in the Member States' national systems. For example, the Dutch implementation allows a user to claim annulment of the unfair term (Art. 6:233 BW) whereas unfair terms according to German law are invalid (§307BGB).
678. Article 6(2) UCTD.

of the provisions. The Regulation solely stipulates the Commission's power to adopt decisions and impose fines.[679] The UCTD allows users to file direct appeals for transparency breaches, but its scope is narrower than that of the DSA. The interaction of the two is, as is the case with multiple acts of consumer protection law, unclear.[680] The DSA does not explicitly define the interaction between the acts, apart from mentioning that the Regulation is without prejudice to Union law on consumer protection as set forward in, amongst others, the UCTD.[681] To resolve the interaction of plural legal orders in consumer protection law, Mak has previously focused on the overlap between the elements of the transparency assessment in the legal acts. Mak refers to the double-edged transparency sword in the UCTD as the *two-pronged transparency test* and highlights that the two elements (inclusion and comprehensibility) have not been included equally in all European consumer protection legislation.[682] However, both the UCTD and the DSA apply the same test, where the terms must first provide certain information, and second, that information is understandable. The exact assessment of transparency differs slightly. For example, the requirement of comprehensible terms is stricter in the DSA than in the UCTD. Whereas the UCTD solely refers to 'plain and intelligible language', the DSA includes in that scope 'clear, user-friendly, and ambiguous'. The transparency test of the DSA is, in that sense, a *lex specialis* of the general transparency test in the UCTD, but since both apply to the terms of service on social media platforms, users that face untransparent terms will likely be able to invoke either one of the tests.

Moreover, viewing the transparency test in the DSA as a *lex specialis* of the general transparency test in the UCTD would resolve the lack of user redress in the DSA. The latter seems in line with the legislator's intention on the breach of transparency in the DSA. Despite 'unfair' not being mentioned in any of the provisions of the DSA, the consequence of a breach of the transparency obligations has been implied in the recitals. Following Recital 45, rules on the content, application and enforcement of the terms are appropriate 'in the interest of transparency, the protection of recipients of the service and the avoidance of unfair or arbitrary outcomes'. The legislator there clearly indicates that the aim of restricting the freedom of contract of the parties in the DSA is to increase the protection of the user through transparency obligations, leading to a fair and non-arbitrary outcome. That would mean that the breach of either of the elements of transparency set out in the DSA (inclusion and comprehensibility) would lead to unfairness of the term equal to the unfairness test in the UCTD. Whether or not users can then claim redress on the basis of the national implementations of the UCTD is unclear (and makes a very good candidate for preliminary questions).

The legal effects of the UCTD can have serious implications for social media platforms, not the least because the directive allows third parties and consumer

679. Articles 73-74 DSA, resembling the *ex post* approach of competition law.
680. *See* extensively on this: Mak, *Legal Pluralism in European Contract Law* (n. 65) 154-159.
681. Recital (10) DSA.
682. Mak, *Legal Pluralism in European Contract Law* (n. 65) 158. Referring to the differences between the UCTD and the Consumer Credit Directive. The latter does not include a two-pronged transparency test, but only includes formal requirements (inclusion) in the assessment.

organisations to challenge the unfairness of the terms on behalf of the platforms' users.[683] Furthermore, the consumer protection authorities in Poland, Belgium, Italy, and the Netherlands can ex officio prohibit the use of non-negotiated standard contract terms that they deem unfair.[684] Therefore, explicit clarification on the consequence of breaching the transparency obligations in the DSA would be welcome. Similarly, scholars have called for an update of the UCTD to better outline the sanctions for unfair terms for digital service providers.[685] Despite the unclarity on the legal effects, the future prognosis for spotting and enforcing unfair terms is good due to the creation of automated tools that can be used to quickly and effectively spot unfairness in online terms of service.[686]

Moreover, the omission of the information requirements in the DSA on content moderation can lead to an infringement of the Unfair Commercial Practices Directive (UCPD). However, for the latter to apply, the average user's transactional decision must have been distorted. That could be the case if, as a consequence of the non-compliance with the information and transparency obligations, the user signs up for the platform and the average user cannot reasonably be expected to have done so if the restrictions on content were clear.[687]

6.4.3 The Validity of the Contractual Terms

To decide what exactly can be included in the terms of service, the restrictions in mandatory law must be outlined. These cover the (questionably applicable) requirements in the DSA on the design of the terms of service and the unfairness test in the Unfair Contract Terms Directive. Specifically, this part of the book aims to assess to what extent platforms can limit the fundamental rights protection of their users through their terms. Open norms in secondary European and national legislation have become increasingly important to answer such questions regarding the permissible scope of terms and service. Mainly through open norms in consumer protection ('unfair') and in national private law ('good faith' and 'reasonable'), the scope of the platform's freedom of contract is affected by the indirect horizontal effect (or 'spillover effect') of these rights.

This paragraph first addresses the (debatable) prohibition in the DSA to *design* restrictions arbitrary or discriminatory. Second, the unfairness test in the UCTD will be outlined, followed by a theorisation of the application of the unfairness test to the

683. Article 7(2) UCTD.
684. Commission Notice – Guidance on the interpretation and application of Directive 2005/29/EC of the European Parliament and of the Council concerning unfair business-to-consumer commercial practices in the internal market (Text with EEA relevance) 2021.
685. Loos and Luzak (n. 432), pp. 47 ff.
686. F Lagioia and others, 'AI in Search of Unfairness in Consumer Contracts: The Terms of Service Landscape' (2022) 45 Journal of consumer policy 481.
687. Article 7 UCPD. The UCPD applies to the relationship between social media platforms and their users, *see* Commission Notice – Guidance on the interpretation and application of Directive 2005/29/EC of the European Parliament and of the Council concerning unfair business-to-consumer commercial practices in the internal market (Text with EEA relevance) (n. 684), §4.2.5.

limitation of fundamental rights protection in social media platforms' terms of service. To reach a conclusion on the latter, inspiration is drawn from Dutch and German case law and other fields of law (data protection and immoral contracts).

6.4.3.1 Restrictions That Are **Designed** *Arbitrary or Discriminatory*

The Digital Services Act imposes on social media platforms several obligations related to their terms of service. Most of these cover transparency obligations (§6.4.2.1) or duties for the enforcement of the terms (Chapter 7, §7.3.3). The DSA does not explicitly control the validity of the terms of the agreement. The only reference to be found is included in the Regulation's recital. Under (47), the legislator has expressed the intention that the 'design' of restrictions in the terms of service may not be arbitrary and discriminatory and must be based on a fair balance of the legitimate interests, including the fundamental rights, of the recipients of the service. However, the actual provision corresponding to that recital does not refer to 'design' but solely imposes those obligations when applying and enforcing restrictive terms. The discrepancy between the text of Recital 47 (including 'design') and the corresponding operative provision in Article 14(4) (without 'design') can cause confusion on the exact scope of the provision. Moreover, not only is the substance of the obligation unclear, but the obligation itself differs.

The consequences of whether or not the design of the terms is included in the scope of Article 14(4) are far-reaching. In case the design is not included, a social media platform only has to outline the restrictions it imposes on its service (Article 14(1) DSA). That is a transparency obligation in line with the transparency requirements of the UCTD. However, if the obligation in Article 14(4) would also apply to the *design* of the terms, platforms will have to observe those obligations already when they define the scope of their service. According to Article 14(4), providers of intermediary services *shall act in a diligent, objective, and proportionate manner, with due regard to the rights and legitimate interests of all parties involved, including the fundamental rights of the recipients of the service.* The recital outlines, in turn, that those actors *should act in a non-arbitrary and non-discriminatory manner.* If these obligations apply to the design of the terms, it means that a social media platform must take the fundamental rights of *potential* consumers in mind when defining the service that it wishes to offer. That seems like a burdensome, if not impossible, task.

The omission of the word 'design' in the final text of the provision can be read as a means for the legislator to safeguard the platforms' freedom to conduct a business and the parties' freedom of contract. As such, there are arguments to make in favour of the omission of the obligations in Article 14(4) when drawing up the terms. Take the example of a platform that prohibits the dissemination of sexually explicit content in the terms of service. If that design choice falls within the scope of Article 14(4), the platform would have to take due regard to the limitation that this would pose for the right to freedom of expression of the users (which it would since users can no longer express themselves through sexually explicit content), or even the economic interests of potential sex workers, and should have to act diligently, objectively, and proportionately in deciding to include that limitation. Another clashing example would emerge when a social media platform decides to either allow or ban content that provides information on (medical) abortions. Both banning such content as well as allowing such content could limit the beliefs of certain groups and, therefore, form a problem for the right to freedom of expression and the right to freedom of thought, conscience, and religion.

Table 6.1 Differences in Wording in the DSA's Recital 47 and Article 14(4)

Recital 47	*Article 14(4)*
When ***designing,*** applying and enforcing those restrictions, providers of intermediary services ***should act in a non-arbitrary and non-discriminatory manner*** and take into account the rights and legitimate interests of the recipients of the service, including fundamental rights as enshrined in the Charter. For example, providers of very large online platforms should, in particular, pay due regard to freedom of expression and information, including media freedom and pluralism. All providers of intermediary services should also pay due regard to relevant international standards for the protection of human rights, such as the United Nations Guiding Principles on Business and Human Rights.	Providers of intermediary services shall act in a ***diligent, objective and proportionate*** manner in ***applying and enforcing*** the restrictions referred to in paragraph 1,[688] with due regard to the rights and legitimate interests of all parties involved, including the fundamental rights of the recipients of the service, such as the freedom of expression, freedom and pluralism of the media, and other fundamental rights and freedoms as enshrined in the Charter.

Furthermore, the requirement to act 'objectively' or 'proportionately' when designing the terms seems hard to fulfil. When would a contractual clause be objective or proportionate? Moreover, wouldn't the platform's own freedom to conduct a business to some extent allow the platform to subjectively decide the scope of the service it would like to offer? Subjecting the content of the agreement to the obligations in Article 14(4) would lead to more legal uncertainty – all the more since users already have the means to oppose excessively unbalanced terms. The latter would generally not pass the unfairness test of the Unfair Contract Terms Directive and will, therefore,

688. Article 14(1): Providers of intermediary services shall include information on any restrictions that they impose in relation to the use of their service in respect of information provided by the recipients of the service, in their terms and conditions. That information shall include information on any policies, procedures, measures and tools used for the purpose of content moderation, including algorithmic decision-making and human review, as well as the rules of procedure of their internal complaint-handling system. It shall be set out in clear, plain, intelligible, user-friendly and unambiguous language, and shall be publicly available in an easily accessible and machine-readable format.

not be binding on consumers. The differentiation between the text of Recital 47 and the actual provision in Article 14(4) must be characterised as the ugly duckling of the DSA and will, in time, create legal uncertainty as regards the obligations for intermediaries to design their terms.[689] As such, the *content* of the terms seems to be unaffected by the increased rules in Article 14(4) due to the omission of the word 'designing' in the text of the provision.[690]

6.4.3.2 *The Application of the Unfair Contract Terms Directive*

The Unfair Contract Terms Directive (UCTD) sets out a framework to determine whether terms in not-individually negotiated consumer contracts distort the balance between the parties and should therefore be deemed invalid. According to the preamble to the UCTD, 'acquirers of goods and services should be protected against the abuse of power by the seller or supplier, in particular against one-sided standard contracts and the unfair exclusion of essential rights in contracts'. Due to their generally lower level of knowledge, as opposed to the seller, and their lesser bargaining power, it is assumed that consumers are in a weaker position.[691] Due to this weaker position, the consumer can end up 'in a situation that leads to his agreeing to terms drawn up in advance by the seller or supplier without being able to influence the content of those terms'.[692] To counterweigh this weaker position, the consumer must be protected against terms that further increase this unfair distribution of power – the so-called unfair contract terms. Thus, the aim of the protection is to restore the weakened position of the consumer when entering into an agreement which contains terms that have not been individually negotiated.

For the UCTD to apply, there must be a contract concluded between a seller or supplier and a consumer where the contract terms have not been individually negotiated.[693] As touched upon in §6.4.1.2, whether that contract is subject to a (monetary) payment is irrelevant. The Commission clarified in 2019 that the UCTD is applicable to the terms of service on social media platforms, even where platforms'

689. *See* Quintais, Appelman and Fahy (n. 256), p. 15: 'First, it is stated that the obligation applies not just to the application and enforcement of restrictions, but also to its design' as a demonstration of opposed interpretations of the discrepancy between the provision and the recital.
690. *See* for an opposed reading of Art. 14: *ibid.*, p. 12, concluding that 'rules on T&Cs in the DSA will govern the contractual relationship between service providers and a "recipient of the service" – including individual users in the EU directly regulating the conditions under which intermediaries can offer their services. When applied to Big Tech platforms, Article 14 DSA has therefore the potential to shape the provision of what some authors consider to be their core service: content moderation.'
691. As confirmed by the CJEU in several cases. *See, e.g., Case C-92/11 (RWE Vertrieb)* (2013) ECLI:EU:C:2013:180 (CJEU), §41 and the case law cited there.
692. *Case C-26/13 (Kásler and Káslerné Rábai)* (2014) ECLI:EU:C:2014:282 (CJEU), §39, and the case law cited.
693. There are some exceptions, such as the exclusion of 'core terms' to the unfairness test, and the exclusion of contract terms which reflect mandatory statutory or regulatory provisions, which will be addressed further below in §6.4.3.2.

users do not pay for the use of the service.[694] A platform user can, therefore, rely on the (nationally implemented provisions of the) UCTD to seek protection against user terms on online platforms that do not withstand the unfairness test or that do not fulfil the obligation of transparency.

Prior to the discussion on the potential unfairness of the terms in online platforms' user terms, it must be noted that some contractual terms are excluded from the unfairness test. Article 4(2) excludes contract terms that define the main subject matter of the contract, and terms concerning the (adequacy of the) price and remuneration, though only when written in plain intelligible language. Article 4(2) must be applied autonomously and uniformly throughout the European Union, and the assessment of whether a term qualifies under 4(2) must reflect the purpose of the UCTD.[695] Multiple conclusions are possible under Article 4(2). The outcome depends on a combination of the content of the term (essential or not) and the readability. The following three outcomes are possible:

(1) the contract term is essential and formulated in plain, intelligible language. It is, therefore, excluded from the unfairness test; or
(2) the contract term is essential but *not* formulated in plain intelligible language. The exemption does not apply; or
(3) the contract term is *not* essential. The exemption does not apply.

In the example under b), the contract term would simultaneously be in breach of Article 5 UCTD, which dictates that all written contracts offered to consumers must be drafted in plain, intelligible language. In practice, only when the contract is comprehensible, the exemption for the main subject matter should come to discussion. Arguably, the terms of service on social media platforms will not pass the transparency test.[696] However, in case they would, it is thus of essence to define the main subject matter of the contract to determine which terms can be challenged for unfairness.

The main subject matter of the contract 'must be understood as being those that lay down the essential obligations of the contract and, as such, characterise it'.[697] The test of what falls within that scope is strict.[698] Ancillary terms that do not define the very essence of the contractual relationship fall outside the scope of the main subject matter and can be subjected to the unfairness test.[699] The conclusion on the assessment

694. Commission notice of 27 September 2019 – Guidance on the interpretation and application of Council Directive 93/13/EEC on unfair terms in consumer contracts [OJ C 323], §1.2.1.2.:

> (...) also contracts between consumers and providers of social media services must be considered to be covered by the UCTD regardless of whether consumers have to pay certain amounts of money or whether the consideration for the services consists in consumer generated content and profiling.

695. *Case C-143/13 (Matei & Matei)* (2015) ECLI:EU:C:2015:127 (CJEU), §50.
696. The general transparency obligation in Art. 5 is discussed in more detail above in §6.4.2.1.
697. *Árpád Kásler and Hajnalka Káslerné Rábai v. OTP Jelzálogbank Zrt* [2014] ECJ Case C-26/13, §49.
698. *Ibid.*
699. *Ibid.*, §50.

of the main subject matter of the contract depends on a case-by-case basis. As highlighted in the introduction, consensus on the role of social media platforms does not exist with regard to the function of their platform – and similarly, defining what the essential, characterising obligations of the contract are can be difficult. Fortunately, the EDPB recently carried out that assessment to reach a conclusion in its decision on Meta's data processing behaviour.[700] The EDPB concluded in that regard that the main purpose for which users sign-up to a social media platform's service (specifically, in this case, Meta's Facebook platform) is to communicate with others.[701] Given the fact that the assessment of the main subject matter must be given an autonomous and uniform interpretation throughout the European Union,[702] the conclusions of the EDPB can serve as a general starting point.

The assessment then turns to defining whether content moderation restrictions form an essential part that characterises the obligation to supply a communication platform or whether they are mere ancillary terms. The definition of the content to be hosted on a platform seems to fall in the former category and would, therefore, constitute the main subject matter of the agreement. If the platform's main contractual obligation is to host content of its users, then defining the content to be hosted forms an essential element of the contractual obligation. For example, if the terms of service outline that a social media platform will host content X but not content Y, then the platform does not have an obligation to host content Y. The core obligation of the platform is to host the content that the parties agreed on: content X. The DSA seems to confirm that reasoning in Recital 45:

> Providers should inform recipients of their service through appropriate means of significant changes made to terms and conditions, for instance when they modify the rules on information that is permitted on their service, or other such changes which could directly impact the ability of the recipients to make use of the service.

Following a textual interpretation, the 'rules on information that is permitted on their service' can directly impact 'the ability of the recipients to make use of the service'. Both sentences are united in causality through the choice of '*such* changes'. Thus, the clauses outlining the scope of permissible information seemingly dictate (partially) the main subject matter of the contract.

That would mean that a contractual term limiting the content that is hosted on the platform's servers cannot be subjected to the unfairness test as long as the terms are transparent and understandable. Since the conclusion on whether the content to be

700. EDPB Binding Decision 3/2022 (5 December 2022). Details of the case are extensively discussed below in §6.4.3.4.
701. EDPB Binding Decision 3/2022, §§117, 122-124. For example, specifically in §117: 'Meta IE presents its Facebook service in its landing website as a platform enabling users to "connect with friends and the world around you on Facebook" and at the beginning of its Facebook Terms of Service as being its mission "to give people the power to build community and bring the world closer together. To help advance this mission, we provide the Products and services described below to you: (...)" which include in consecutive headings "Connect you with people and organizations you care about: (...)"; "Empower you to express yourself and communicate about what matters to you: (...)" and "Help you discover content, products and services that may interest you: (...)".'
702. Judgment of 20 September 2017, Andriciuc and Others, C-186/16, EU:C:2017:703, para. 34.

hosted constitutes the main subject matter of the terms is merely a theorisation of the applicability of the exemption in 4(2) UCTD, there is a chance that the terms could be subjected to the unfairness test. Moreover, if the terms do not live up to the requirement of transparency, the terms can be equally subjected to the unfairness test. In case the terms of service applied on social media platforms do not fulfil the requirement of transparency or do not constitute the main subject matter of the contract, the unfairness test proves a useful tool to decide whether or not terms of service can limit fundamental rights protection.

6.4.3.3 Is Waiving Fundamental Rights Protection Unfair?

According to Article 3(1) of the UCTD, a contractual term is unfair if it causes a significant imbalance in the parties' rights and obligations arising under the contract – to the detriment of the consumer – and is contrary to the requirement of good faith. The UCTD contains an indicative, non-exhaustive list of unfair terms (the black and grey list). These lists cover neither, specifically, the exclusion of legal content nor, more generally, the limitation of fundamental rights protection.[703] Therefore, the assessment is left to the 'general' unfairness test consisting of an assessment of the good faith intention of the platform and the assessment of a significant imbalance. The assessment can, according to the Commission's guidance, be boiled down to two elements: the good faith assessment and the assessment of significant imbalance.[704] First, to assess the requirements of good faith, the national court must assess whether the seller could reasonably assume that the consumer would have accepted the contract term in a similar way if he had been given the chance to negotiate the term in question individually.[705] The outcome hereof depends strictly on the circumstances of the case. Second, the national court should assess in what position the consumer would have been if the questioned contract term had not existed. This analysis 'will enable the national court to evaluate whether and to what extent the contract term places the consumer in a legal situation less favourable than under the otherwise applicable contract law'.[706] The imbalance is significant if the impairment of the consumer's legal situation is sufficiently serious.

Some of the limitations imposed by platforms concern *awful but lawful* content. Other restrictions simply express a normative choice of the platform. Looking at these two different categories of lawful content excluded in the terms of service that limit the users' possibility to share content that would otherwise fall within the right to freedom of expression highlights the difference in the outcome of the unfairness test.

---

703. *See* for an interesting discussion on the necessity to extend the black and grey list to better suit online services: Loos and Luzak (n. 432).
704. This is however not undisputed. Advocate General Hogan suggests in C-34/18 (*Ottília Lovasné Tóth*) that good faith should not be treated as a separate requirement. *See* §3.4.1. of the Commission notice of 27 September 2019 (n. 654), and the references in footnote 215 of that paragraph.
705. §3.4.1. of the Commission notice of 27 September 2019 (n. 654).
706. *Ibid.*, §3.4.2.

First, in the category of *awful but lawful* content,[707] numerous platforms restrict the sharing of spam content.[708] Starting with the second question on the assessment of the significant imbalance, the user would be in a better position in relation to its right to freedom of expression if the clause limiting spam had not been there. As a consequence of the contractual clause, the content that can be shared by the user is limited as opposed to the general scope of the right to freedom of expression. Second, it is not unthinkable that the consumer would also have accepted the prohibition of spam content if the terms had been individually negotiated. As such, the inclusion of a conditional clause that limits the consumer's right to freedom of expression by excluding spam content from the permissible content to be shared on the platform would not be an unfair contract term.

When addressing other examples of the assessment of content that would otherwise be legal, the assessment of the unfairness becomes less clear. Looking at the contractual condition applied on some social media platforms that users must either use their real name,[709] or at least prohibit the use of *fake identities*,[710] then the outcome of both the good faith and the significant imbalance becomes questionable. Starting with the latter, is the user worse off by the imposed contractual clause? That depends. Without the contractual clause, users have more freedom in the way they would like to present themselves. It might also be beneficial to whistle-blowers, people that suffer from stalking, or could increase equality in debates. Users might also be harmed by the fact that anonymity could lead to more negative interactions since consequences are no longer linked directly to a person. These arguments, however, are pure speculation – whether or not the user is better off with or without the contractual prohibition to use a fake name is not as crystal clear as the prohibition of spam content, and a definite answer on the unfairness, therefore, requires more research into the consequences of such a condition on the behaviour of the community of users. In that same line, it is not possible to assess whether consumers would reasonably have accepted the condition if it was individually negotiated.

As another example, one could imagine that in case a large-scale social media platform would follow the proposal of the Dutch government to ban certain types of dogs and cats from social media. In January 2023, the Dutch regulator proposed to

707. Keller, 'Lawful but Awful?' (n. 5).

708. *See, e.g.*: 'Twitter's Platform Manipulation and Spam Policy | Twitter Help' https://help.twitter.com/en/rules-and-policies/platform-manipulation (accessed 27 January 2023); 'Managing Spam on Facebook | Facebook Help Centre' https://www.facebook.com/help/217854714899185 (accessed 27 January 2023); 'Avoid Fraudulent Message Attacks on TikTok | TikTok Help Center' https://support.tiktok.com/en/safety-hc/account-and-user-safety/avoid-fraudulent-message-attacks-on-tiktok (accessed 27 January 2023).

709. Facebook Terms of Service, '3. Your commitments to Facebook and our community': Provide for your account the same name that you use in everyday life, available at https://www.facebook.com/legal/terms?paipv = 0&eav = AfaWbdjExpNTwd2b_NDGQ3rUvhBEBUm3wjfFBlV6AOhU-A7KsL4pgm93Yuk1VhiFRn0&_rdr (accessed 27 January 2023).

710. 'Misleading and Deceptive Identities Policy' https://help.twitter.com/en/rules-and-policies/twitter-impersonation-and-deceptive-identities-policy (accessed 27 January 2023). 'Fake identities, which may use stolen or computer-generated photos and fabricated names to pose as a person or organization that doesn't exist, are also considered deceptive when they engage in disruptive or manipulative behavior.'

restrict the dissemination of content with 'suffering dogs and cats' on social media.[711] If following this regulation in the Netherlands, a social media platform would extend that ban to generally apply to its service and ban 'suffering dogs and cats' in all Member States of the European Union, then that would mean a limitation of the users' freedom of expression in those jurisdictions. In that case, users of the platform would be in a worse position with the contractual clause than without since it restricts the user's freedom to post content, including those animals, even in the cases where that animal would be the user's own pet. Here, the difference between State regulation and the private power of social media platforms through terms of service becomes clear. States are bound directly by fundamental rights. The proposed law by the Dutch legislator can be tested against the rights in the Charter.[712] Consequently, if the interference with the right to freedom of expression is not proportionate,[713] the proposal will fail. When a social media platform decides to apply the same restriction in its terms of service, it is not bound by the restrictions in Article 11 Charter, at least not directly.[714]

Social media platforms have powers to govern the interaction on their platform, similar to those of a state, but without the same safeguards. Platforms govern a (normative) private order through their terms of service.[715] To provide the same

711. 'Suffering dogs and cats' refers to dogs and cats 'with extreme external features that create consistent suffering or increased risk of suffering, such as cats with folded ears or extremely short-snouted dogs'. Piet Adema (Minister of Agriculture, Nature, and Food Quality), 'Aanpak gezelschapsdieren met schadelijke uiterlijke kenmerken' (*Tackling pet animals with harmful external features*, translation by the author) 20 January 2023, accessible at: https://www.tweedekamer.nl/kamerstukken/brieven_regering/detail?id = 2023Z00672&did = 2023D01592 (accessed 22 January 2023). This letter solely displays the intention of the minister to look into the possibilities for such a ban, the actual proposal has not been formulated yet. The letter shows the intent to ban the use of suffering cats and dogs in advertisements, commercials, by influencers and celebrities, but also refers to a general 'social media-ban'. The breeding of these animals has been forbidden in the Netherlands since 2014. *See* for more information on this: NVWA, Fokken met gezelschapsdieren, ken de regels, accessible at: https://www.nvwa.nl/documenten/dier/dierenwelzijn/welzijn/publicaties/fokken-met-gezelschapsdieren-ken-de-regels (accessed 22 January 2023).
712. Interestingly, proposals from the Dutch legislator cannot be validated against the Dutch Constitution. Art. 120 of the Dutch Constitution prohibits constitutional review. An attempt for Constitutional amendment stranded in 2018. The Constitution does, in turn, allow Dutch proposals to be reviewed against *international treaties*, including the European Charter of Fundamental Rights, which thus arguably has a higher ranking in the Dutch hierarchy. The proposal on suffering cats and dogs can therefore be reviewed against the Charter's right to freedom of expression in Art. 11, but not against the Dutch Constitution's own freedom of expression and censorship ban in Art. 7.
713. Meaning the proposal is necessary and meets an objective of general interest recognised by the Union or the need to protect the rights and freedoms of others (Art. 52(1) Charter). The protection of animal welfare would presumably be recognised as an objective in the general interest. The proportionality can be debated – I would argue that the prohibition to show these types of animals on social media is a severe infringement of the right to freedom of expression, especially for the owners of such animals. The objective could be reached in a less infringing way. Breeding these animals has been prohibited since 2014 in the Netherlands, but enforcement has been difficult. Since the aim of also this proposal has been to stop the breeding of these animals, then rather than a ban on social media depiction, forced sterilisation of young animals seems more effective to reach the aim.
714. *See* on the direct effect of the right to freedom of expression, §5.5.3.3.
715. Belli and Venturini (n. 6); Kettemann (n. 6); Belli (n. 7).

safeguards against this power, some scholars have argued that 'constitutionalisation'[716] of the terms of service is necessary to tackle the private power of social media,[717] while others have argued that the terms *themselves* already demonstrate constitutional elements[718] or that the European Union has already entered 'a new phase of *digital* constitutionalism'.[719] This mix-pot approach to constitutionalism has been criticised because it '*obscures the true nature of the governance architectures to which it is applied*'[720] and because it lacks a clear distinction between '*descriptive accounts of digital constitutionalism in current law and mainstream policy debates, and normative accounts of digital constitutionalism as an agenda for platform governance*'.[721] The application of constitutionalism, as argued by Griffin, can be used as a (political) *normative* argument to further restrain the private power of social media platforms, but it cannot be used as an absolute standard of legitimacy to do so.[722] As such, the introduction of regulation based on the values of constitutionalism – democracy and the principle of the rule of law[723] – is an expression of an ideological, legislative choice. Such an explicit legislative choice has been expressed through the rules on the enforcement of terms of service in the DSA, which rules demonstrate the decision to limit private contractual powers in favour of accountability. Arguably, limiting the private autonomy to decide on the contractual clauses in a contract between two private parties goes too far, as it would mean a disproportionate interference with the parties' right to freedom of contract. There are two reasons why such an interference does not seem proportionate. First, users of social media platforms are portrayed as fully incapable of grasping what social media platforms are doing, which is not the case. Protests of users have, in fact, led to changes in the user terms of social media

716. Here following the definition by Loughlin: 'Constitutionalisation is the term used for the attempt to subject the exercise of all types of public power, whatever the medium of its exercise, to the discipline of constitutional procedures and norms.', Martin Loughlin, 'What Is Constitutionalisation?' in Petra Dobner and Martin Loughlin (eds), *The Twilight of Constitutionalism?* (Oxford University Press 2010) https://doi.org/10.1093/acprof:oso/9780199585007.003.0003 (accessed 28 January 2023). Digital constitutionalism simply applies this idea to subject 'power in a networked society', Suzor (n. 251).
717. *See* a full overview of the development of the field of 'digital constitutionalism' in the literature (and criticism on the terminology of digital constitutionalism): Costello (n. 251).
718. Edoardo Celeste, 'Terms of Service and Bills of Rights: New Mechanisms of Constitutionalisation in the Social Media Environment?' (2019) 33 International Review of Law, Computers & Technology 122, pointing at the language used in terms of service that has started to mimic constitutional texts.
719. De Gregorio, 'The Rise of Digital Constitutionalism in the European Union' (n. 251).
720. The governance model on social media platforms is contractual. Calling it constitutional 'conflates the practical reality'. Róisín Á Costello, 'Faux Ami? Interrogating the Normative Coherence of "Digital Constitutionalism"' 2023 Global Constitutionalism.
721. Griffin (n. 251), suggesting a 'distinctively left-wing normative account of digital constitutionalism'.
722. This is the same conclusion as reached on the necessity to depart from the right to property in §3.2.1.
723. Both before and after *digital* was added to constitutionalism: Dieter Grimm, 'The Achievement of Constitutionalism and Its Prospects in a Changed World' in Petra Dobner and Martin Loughlin (eds), *The Twilight of Constitutionalism?* (Oxford University Press 2010) https://doi.org/10.1093/acprof:oso/9780199585007.003.0001 (accessed 28 January 2023); Suzor (n. 251).

platforms.[724] The problem lies in the technically obstructed interoperability of platforms, a discussion addressed as a final note of this book.[725] Users *would* switch platforms if their disagreement increases, though because of the lack of interoperability, these switches are limited.[726] Arguably, this could be the case because the consequences for switching are currently too high.[727] Second, alternative solutions already exist that interfere to a lesser extent with private autonomy and, therefore, form a more proportionate solution. In addition to the decision to regulate social media platforms in a way that reflects constitutional principles – which inherently challenges the underlying principle of private autonomy in contract law – the system of contract law itself allows for a balancing of power and for the inclusion of standards from fundamental rights law. The system of contract law is not as rigid as portrayed, but it must be kept in mind that the aim of contract law adjudication differs from constitutional law. In civil disputes between private parties, the aim of adjudication is not to minimise the interference with constitutional freedoms but rather to reconcile the freedom of one party with the freedom of the other, as opposed to the constitutional rights duty of the state to guarantee all individual rights and freedoms.[728] The increased focus in European legislation to protect the weaker party through consumer protection law reflects an aim to redistribute power and a strive towards social justice.[729] Through the system of open norms, such as the unfairness test addressed in this paragraph or the open norms in national law,[730] the ultimate balancing of different interests remains with the judiciary. In my view, leaving the balancing up to the national courts is favourable over the decision of the European legislator to put that task in the hands of

724. At the moment of writing a chapter on the normative limitations of social media platforms in 2021 (van der Donk, 'The Freedom to Conduct a Business as a Counterargument to Limit Platform Users' Freedom of Expression' (n. 10).), Facebook's terms of service prohibited the dissemination of euthanasia content. The terms at that point equalled euthanasia to suicide – and as a consequence, the livestream of pro-euthanasia protested Alain Cocq was blocked. Flash forward to 2023, the backlash of the normative choice of Meta to equal euthanasia and suicide have led to the Facebook terms of service no longer prohibiting euthanasia, but rather Meta includes a 'sensitivity screen' and restricts the content to persons over the age of 18.

725. *See* §9.2.3.

726. For example, the increase of Mastadon-users following Twitter's overtake by Musk: Matt Binder, 'Mastodon Has Gained Millions of New Users since Elon Musk Bought Twitter' (*Mashable*, 20 December 2022) https://mashable.com/article/mastodon-millions-users (accessed 29 January 2023). Problem lies in the fact that users lose access to all their earlier acquired connections, posts, and other data that lies in the service they leave.

727. The consequences of switching conditional platforms is outlined in §0.

728. The Germans even have a word for this civil balancing through open norms: *Praktische Konkordanz* ('practical concordance'). The *Bundesgerichtshof* has recently endorsed that practice for the adjudication of social media platform content issues: In *Inhaltesperrung* and *Kontosperrung*, the Court concludes that a private undertaking such as a social media platform is not directly bound by fundamental rights as a state would be and thus fundamental rights do not need to be directly included in the assessment of fairness. A social media platform does not overtake the communication function of the state as is the case for private telecommunication service providers. It cannot be compared to a state monopoly, nor a privatised equivalent. The court highlights that large-scale social media platform (in the case Facebook) offers a significant communication possibility on the internet but does not guarantee access to the internet as such.

729. Micklitz (n. 427).

730. Mak, *Fundamental Rights in European Contract Law* (n. 65).

social media giants, as will likely be the outcome of the increased enforcement obligations in the DSA.[731]

Where does the above lead us on the assessment of the unfairness of a contractual cause limiting the scope of the freedom of expression of users? Rather than applying principles from constitutional law, for example, through enhanced user participation (e.g., letting users participate in the decision to limit content), the system of open norms in contract law allows a fair balance of both the users' and society's interest in transparency and accountability when removing content, while allowing an undertaking to decide the scope of the service in accordance with its right to property and the freedom to conduct its business. In July 2021, the *Bundesgerichtshof* decided on two similar cases (*Inhaltesperrung* and *Kontosperrung*[732]), demonstrating how such a balancing act takes shape when dealing with content restrictions on social media platforms.[733]

The *Bundesgerichtshof* assessed the unfairness of the social media platform's terms. It concludes that the terms are transparent enough and moves to the assessment of whether the terms are unreasonably disadvantaging the user. Based on an assessment of the mutual interests, the goal, the nature of the agreement, and to what extent the agreement deviates from the law, the court concludes that social media platforms are, in principle, allowed to restrict content in its user terms that would otherwise be legal. Its conclusion follows previous decisions.[734] Earlier, *Oberlandesgericht* concluded that the freedom of expression cannot, without any further balancing, be invoked to oppose the deletion of content that would otherwise be protected by the freedom of expression. Similarly, *LG Heidelberg* found that limiting hate speech content in user terms is not unreasonably disadvantaging the user despite the effect such a restriction has on the freedom of expression. The users' right to freedom of expression must be weighed against the interest of the platform (Facebook in this case) to create a profitable communication platform. Consequently, the platform can make a decision to create an online environment without unwanted content as long as the decision is based on objective criteria, does not restrict one specific type of expression, and is foreseen in the user terms. *Landsgericht Heidelberg* formulates it clearly and precisely:

> An unreasonable disadvantage of the contractual partner of the [platform] within the meaning of §307 BGB is given if the [platform] abusively tries to enforce his own interests at the expense of his contractual partner by a unilateral drafting of the contract without sufficiently taking into account the interests from the [user] and without granting him an adequate compensation.'

As such, when restricting fundamental rights protection, platforms must adhere to procedural safeguards to guarantee that such restrictions are fair.[735] In line with the

731. *See* similar: Griffin (n. 251).
732. *Bundesgerichtshof (Inhaltesperrung)* (n. 23); *Bundesgerichtshof (Kontosperrung)* (n. 23).
733. These cases have also been discussed as a part of the German comparative study, *see* §2.2.1.2.
734. *Oberlandesgericht Dresden (Unfair platform terms)* (n. 103); *Landsgericht Heidelberg (Hate speech II)* (n. 107); *Landgericht Frankfurt am Main (Access blocks)* (n. 107).
735. These reflect the increased obligations on application and enforcement of terms of service in the DSA. Restrictions in the user terms that deviate from the law (e.g., the removal of legal content) are only fair if, first, there exists an objective reason to delete the content. That could

conclusion in the cases before the *Bundesgerichtshof*, a breach of the procedural criteria in Article 14 DSA will most likely lead to unfairness and, thus, invalidity. Interestingly, that conclusion only applies to the *enforcement* of the terms and does not limit the social media platform's power over the scope of the terms. Seemingly, the conclusion is that whatever platforms decide in their user terms is fair, as long as it has been clear to the user and the enforcement is not arbitrary and subjective. In light of the *Bundesgerichtshof* view on platforms,[736] that is understandable.

The above shows the difficulty (and normativity) of reaching an answer to the question of whether the contractual limitation of the freedom of expression is unfair. Its assessment depends on variabilities that are under the influence of change. Equally, it allows the court's assessment to take into consideration the current social perception of a given restriction. For example, considering the good faith assessment, it seems unlikely that currently, the average consumer could be reasonably expected to accept the restriction on suffering cats and dogs if that condition had been individually negotiated. However, this perception might change over time as the general societal acceptance of these types of dogs and cats decreases.[737] It also means that the outcome of the fairness test can differ significantly from Member State to Member State, creating a patchwork of permissible content in the European Union.[738] In addition to the German example, to gain an idea of how the answer on waiving fundamental rights protection potentially falls out, inspiration can be drawn from other fields of law. A judicial development towards a ban on *fully* waiving fundamental rights protection has been realised in the field of data protection law. Furthermore, there is a rich stream of Dutch case law on rental contracts, terms and conditions, satellite antennas, and the waiving of fundamental rights – these cases specifically concern the waiving of the right to freedom of expression in Article 10 ECHR. Combined with the scholarship on immoral contracts, national courts could draw inspiration from these examples in national case law and the practices in data protection in combination to reach a conclusion on the unfairness of fundamental rights waiving-contractual terms. After addressing these examples, a final reflection is made on contractually waiving fundamental rights protection.

be a breach of the terms of service, but it requires that the terms have been drafted sufficiently precise. Undefined and unobjective user terms do not reflect a fair balance. They are also unenforceable, *see* §7.3.3.

736. The *Bundesgerichsthof* concludes in both cases that a private undertaking such as a social media platform is not directly bound by fundamental rights as a state would be and thus fundamental rights do not need to be directly included in the assessment of fairness. *Inhaltesperrung*, §71 and idem *Kontosperrung*, §59: 'Neither does state-like binding follow from the market-dominant position of the platform in the area of social media platforms. The market power of the defendant cannot be equated with the monopoly position of state-owned companies in the field of public services, such as the postal service in the past.' A social media platform does not overtake the communication function of the state as is the case for private telecommunication service providers. It cannot be compared to a state monopoly, nor a privatised equivalent. The court highlights that large-scale social media platforms (in the case Facebook) offer a significant communication possibility on the internet, but they do not guarantee access to the internet as such.

737. Decreasing societal popularity of suffering dogs and cats is the aim of the Dutch law proposal.

738. Similarly highlighted by: Loos and Luzak (n. 432) 47.

6.4.3.4 *Drawing Inspiration from Data Protection Law*

Contractually waiving fundamental rights protection is not unlawful per se. When the contract is concluded in a way that is fair and strikes a balance between the commercial interests of the dominant party and the rights and expectations of the consumer, users can validly agree to (partially) waive their right to data protection.[739] A fair balance requires 'that personal data should not be processed in a way that is unjustifiably detrimental, unlawfully discriminatory, unexpected or misleading to the data subject'.[740] The terms of service applied by Meta to offer their Facebook service were found not to strike a fair balance. First, the users were not free to decide to waive their right to data protection. Rather, they had the option to: 'either contract away their right to freely determine the processing of their personal data and submit to its processing for the obscure and intrusive purpose of behavioural advertising, which they can neither expect nor fully understand based on the insufficient information Meta IE provides to them or, they may decline accepting the Facebook Terms of Service and thus be excluded from a service that enables them to communicate with millions of users and for which there are currently few realistic alternatives. This exclusion would thus also adversely affect their freedom of expression and information'.[741] The users were not given a choice to give up their right to data protection. Rather, Meta creatively drafted its user terms in a way that meant that users could choose between accessing the service and giving up their protection or not accessing the service at all. A choice that was not necessary because Meta could run the same service on the basis of contextual advertisements. Second, even if the users would have understood that they agreed to be supplied with behavioural advertisements in exchange for their personal data, then that agreement would nonetheless be unlawful. The freedom of contract cannot supersede an individual's protection of data protection. The law prevents the user from (permanently) giving up their protection by obstructing the possibility of deciding to trade away the right to data protection. The EDPB concluded that 'the GDPR, pursuant to EU primary law, treats personal data as a fundamental right inherent to a data subject and his/her dignity, and not as a commodity data subjects can trade away through a contract'.[742] It recalls the CJEU's conclusion in the *Google Spain*-judgment that 'the fundamental rights of data subjects to privacy and the protection of their personal data override, as a rule, a controller's economic interests'. A social media platform does not have the 'absolute discretion to choose the legal basis that suits better its commercial interests'.[743] Platforms are held to live up to the principles in the

739. EDPB Binding Decision 3/2022 (5 December 2022), point 223.
740. EDPB Guidelines 4/2019 on Art. 25 Data Protection by Design and by Default, Version 2, Adopted on 20 October 2020, §69. Referred to in EDPB Binding Decision 3/2022, point 221. The requirement of fairness stems directly from the Charter: 'Art. 8 EU Charter of Fundamental Rights states as follows: "1. Everyone has the right to the protection of personal data concerning him or her. 2. Such data must be processed *fairly* for specified purposes and on the basis of the consent of the person concerned or some other legitimate basis laid down by law" (emphasis added).'
741. EDPB Binding Decision 3/2022, point 130.
742. *Ibid.*, point 101.
743. *Ibid.*, point 104.

GDPR even when such application would be 'inconvenient or runs counter to the commercial interests [of the platform]'.[744]

Interestingly, the GDPR does not *explicitly* prohibit users to contractually waive all their rights to data protection and neither does the corresponding article in the Charter. The decision reached by the EDPB (based on the CJEU's decisions) limits the parties' private autonomy in order to preserve the fundamental rights protection of the weaker party. That argumentation resembles the underlying thought used to limit the private autonomy of contractual parties in *immoral contracts*. Under this category, certain types of contracts are prohibited, such as for example sex work contracts, surrogacy agreements, and contracts on the sale of organs. Tracing back the origins of the prohibition on immoral contracts in Roman law, Ciacchi puts forward that already in the second century, 'the notion of immorality was used to tackle abuses of private autonomy that resulted in excessive restrictions of what contemporary scholars would call fundamental rights and freedoms'.[745] However, applying the doctrine of immorality in contracts to the sphere of social media platforms to reach an answer proves difficult. Reaching a consensus on the interpretation of morality in contract law is far from easy, not the least because the European Member States' national systems differ greatly in their interpretation and application of morality in contract law. In an attempt to find a common approach to contractual morality, Mak revisits Dworkin's opposing views of legal positivism's separation thesis (law and morality are not necessarily connected) and highlights that 'in cases concerning the validity of a contract in light of good morals and public policy, a judge's task would be to identify the legal rights and duties of the parties against the background of a coherent legal system'.[746] For the adjudication of contract law cases, courts could then first identify the positive law applicable to the case and then interpret these rules in light of the moral principles of society.[747] Potentially, that could be applied as a two-step test to answer whether the private autonomy of users of social media platforms does not cover the capacity to waive fundamental rights protection. However, a standard of contractual morality does not exist on a European level and resolving this question would, therefore, be up to the national legislative systems.[748] Currently, a conclusion on the outcome in these Member States cannot be drawn. As put by Ciacchi in conclusion on the *common core* of the twelve case studies of morally dubious contracts in twenty-eight jurisdictions:[749]

744. *Ibid.*, point 105.
745. Aurelia Colombi Ciacchi, 'Immoral Contracts in Europe: The First Common Core' in Chantal Mak, Zeeshan Mansoor and Aurelia Colombi Ciacchi (eds), *Immoral Contracts in Europe* (Intersentia 2020) https://www.cambridge.org/core/books/immoral-contracts-in-europe/BA5381E5A2BE0A231DF703547888C1C9 (accessed 16 January 2023), pp. 4-5.
746. Chantal Mak, 'Immorality of Contracts in Europe: Four Approaches' in Aurelia Colombi Ciacchi, Chantal Mak and Zeeshan Mansoor (eds), *Immoral Contracts in Europe* (Intersentia 2020), p. 19.
747. *Ibid.*, 18.
748. *See* for an example the 12 case-studies in Aurelia Colombi Ciacchi, Chantal Mak and Zeeshan Mansoor (eds), *Immoral Contracts in Europe* (Intersentia 2020), for a very interesting insight into how national legal systems would deal with various questions of immorality in contract law and the sometimes greatly divergent conclusions are reached in different Member States.
749. The study included 26 European Member States plus England and Scotland.

> The degree of convergence between the national answers to the questionnaire's questions varies a lot from case to case. In some cases, the national answers only converge for what concerns the (in)validity or (un)enforceability of the contractual agreement, but not for what concerns the remedies ultimately available to the parties. Vice versa, in other cases, the national answers only converge to a certain extent for what concerns the remedies ultimately available, *while no consensus can be found for what concerns the validity of the contractual agreement: half of the countries would consider the agreement valid and enforceable; the other half would deem it invalid and/or unenforceable.*[750]

Despite the lack of consensus at a European level, national courts have the opportunity to resolve moderation issues on social media platforms through a lens of immoral contracts. The discrepancies in morality pose a challenge to legal certainty. Differences in the outcome of these disputes lead to (legal) inequality in regard to the content that users are allowed to post. The national interpretation of contractual terms can, therefore, lead to a patchwork of permissible content on platforms in the EU. Pointing back to the notion of Roman law included above, it is clear that the interaction between morality, abuse of power, and fundamental rights restrictions within the field of contract law proves a promising path for further research.

6.4.3.5 Drawing Inspiration from National Case Law

Other inspiration on the limitation of fundamental rights protection through contracts can be found in the case law on satellite antennas in the Netherlands and Germany. In these cases, tenants claim the necessity to mount a satellite antenna to their rental property to impart information, which clashes with the landlord's right to property and/or the rental agreement's terms.

The German case law focuses on the balancing between the landlord's right to property and the tenant's right to impart information.[751] In the 1994 case, the Bundesverfassungsgericht highlights that 'Everyone has the fundamental right to be informed freely from generally accessible sources, regardless of where they come from. If this right – as in the case of the installation of parabolic antennas in rented living space – collides with the interests of third parties protected by fundamental rights, a balancing exercise within the framework of civil law regulations is required.' A balance must thus be sought within the framework of civil law. Based on earlier case law, the Bundesverfassungsgericht recalls the principles to balance these rights. First, in case the landlord provides a cable connection, then usually that constitutes a relevant reason to refuse the mounting of a satellite antenna.[752] Second, the interest of

750. Aurelia Colombi Ciacchi, '28 Jurisdictions and 12 Types of Morally Dubious Contracts. To What Extent Is There a Common Core?' in Aurelia Colombi Ciacchi, Chantal Mak and Zeeshan Mansoor (eds), *Immoral Contracts in Europe* (Intersentia 2020), p. 717.

751. *Bundesverfassunigsgericht (Parabolantenne)* (1994) 1 BvR 1687/92, ECLI:DE:BVerfG:1994:rs19940209.1bvr168792; *Bundesverfassunigsgericht (Parabolantenne II)* (2005) 1 BvR 1908/01, ECLI:DE:BVerfG:2005:rk20050214.1bvr190801; *Bundesverfassunigsgericht (Parabolantenne III)* (2005) 1 BvR 42/03, ECLI:DE:BVerfG:2005:rk20050317.1bvr004203.

752. *Bundesverfassunigsgericht (Parabolantenne)* (n. 751). §26. According to the court, 'the owner's interest in preserving the appearance of his home is met by the fact that he can avoid the

foreigners living permanently in Germany in receiving radio programs from their home countries must be considered to balance the interests of the parties, as their interests are often insufficiently guaranteed by the supply of a cable connection.[753] In principle, a tenant's right to freely impart information outweighs the right to property only if they have a special legitimate information interest. Such a special legitimate information interest exists when the necessary information cannot be met via the general broadband cable network. That need cannot be based on the tenant's subjective interest,[754] nor does it entail that the information must be provided free of charge.[755] When an interest in receiving specific information is not demonstrated, the proprietor's right to property must prevail.[756]

In Dutch rental agreements, a landlord can restrict the renter's freedom to mount objects to the outside of the property. As opposed to Germany,[757] this competency is explicitly provided for by Dutch law.[758] This has led to a rich stream of case law on the mounting of satellite antennas to rental properties. The tenants, on the one hand, argue that a satellite antenna is necessary to make use of their right to freedom of expression and to impart information. The landlord, on the other hand, argues that mounting an antenna leads to a breach of contract and that, principally, such a clause is justifiable because it deters the risk of liability. The dilemma in these cases is that the rental contract provides the property's owner with the sole right to restrict the renters access to information (foreign TV channels), as the owner must consent to the mounting of a satellite antenna on the outside of the building. In most cases, the Dutch courts rule in favour of the landlord. In *Satellite Antenna*, the defendant was a (private) stock trader who wished to use the satellite antenna to gain access to real-time stock data. The court

installation of dish antennas by providing a cable connection. Conversely, in view of the range of programs that can be used via a cable connection, the impairment of the tenant's freedom of information, who is not allowed to set up a parabolic antenna, is not of major importance.'

753. *Ibid.*, §27: 'However, this consideration based on the typical average case does not take sufficient account of the special information interests of foreigners living permanently in Germany. As a rule, they are interested in receiving programs from their home country in order to learn about what is happening there and to be able to maintain cultural and linguistic connections. In view of the small number of foreign programs that are fed into the domestic cable networks, this possibility usually only exists by means of a satellite reception system.'
754. *Bundesverfassunigsgericht (Parabolantenne II)* (n. 751), §§12-13.
755. *Bundesverfassunigsgericht (Parabolantenne III)* (n. 751), §15.
756. *Bundesverfassunigsgericht (Parabolantenne II)* (n. 751), §12.
757. *Bundesverfassunigsgericht (Parabolantenne)* (n. 751), §18: 'There are no regulations in the BGB that expressly refer to the attachment of antennas to rented apartments. Rather, the civil courts regularly rely on the general provisions of §§535, 536, 242 BGB when deciding conflicts about the installation of reception systems.'
758. Dutch law dictates that a renter may make alterations to the rented property if the alterations can be undone and removed without significant cost at the end of the rental period. In these cases, consent of the property's owner is not needed (Art. 7:215 (1) Civil Code). However, for the outside of the building, the property owner may require consent (Art. 7:215 (6)). That means for satellite antennas the following: in case they are mounted on the *inside* of the apartment, no consent of the property's owner is needed. If such a consent requirement would be included in the (user terms to the) rental contract, the renter would be able to claim invalidity based on 6:233 (a) or 6:248, as it goes beyond the law. The owner's claim to remove an antenna that has been placed inside would consequently be unenforceable. If, however, the antenna is mounted on the *outside* of the building, the owner can demand prior consent in (the terms and conditions to) the rental agreement.

states first that the parties have validly agreed to the limiting clause, and 'by doing so, [the defendant], as a tenant in his private law relationship with [the landlord], subjected part of his freedom of expression to [the landlord's] consent and to that extent has waived unlimited access to obtain information'.[759] The court applies the principles underlying Article 10 ECHR horizontally to balance the interests of the parties.[760] The open norm of 'reasonableness and fairness' in Article 6:248 of the Dutch Civil Code can be interpreted by a direct application of fundamental rights such as Article 10 ECHR. According to Article 3:12, fundamental rights may be used to define the scope of the generally recognised legal principles and the fundamental concepts of law in the Netherlands and can, therefore, play an indirect role in the interpretation and application of contractual terms. The court finds that the landlord's interests must be favoured because the defendant could receive the information through other means than a satellite antenna.[761] This conclusion was upheld by the Supreme Court.[762] The same conclusion was reached in *Stichting Stadsgenoot* and *Stichting Woonstad Rotterdam*,[763] where the court concluded that the affected renters had other means than a satellite antenna to receive foreign news channels. In *Russian Old Lady*, the court reached a different outcome. The facts were equal to the cases included above, apart from the fact that the defendant was an old Russian lady suffering from numerous diseases, which made it impossible for her to access Russian news channels in any other way than using a satellite antenna. In §4.7, the Court states that 'it is unacceptable by standards of reasonableness and fairness for the landlord to rely on the fact that a tenant has waived, in advance, the rights granted by the ECHR'. The clause in the terms and conditions was found to be overly broad and unspecific. On that basis, a refusal which led to a limitation of the freedom to impart information was not justified without a solid argumentation. The court decides in favour of the defendant. she is allowed to keep her satellite antenna even without explicit permission from the landlord. Ordering its removal would constitute a disproportionate interference with her right to freedom of expression and to impart information. With that conclusion, the court dismisses the agreed contractual terms by referring to the reasonableness and fairness, which principle was interpreted considering the balancing of interests prescribed in Article 10 ECHR. A refusal to mount an antenna did not reflect a fair balancing of the interests at stake. To prevent unlimited power over the freedom of expression and the freedom to impart information, the court imposed a duty of care on the owner of the property: the owner must balance the interests of the renter and his own interests prior to taking a decision on the consent. If the renter has no other possibilities to impart information than by mounting a satellite antenna on the outside of the building, then a clause in the rental contract that limits such mounting is unfair - even if the law specifically foresees the possibility of imposing such a restriction.

759. *Satellite antenna* (n. 758), §8, underlining by the author.
760. In line with the ECtHR case: *Appl. No. 23883/06 (Khurshid Mustafa and Tarzibachi/Sweden)* (ECtHR).
761. *Ibid.*, §§9-15.
762. *Hoge Raad* (2012) ECLI:NL:HR:2012:BY2583.
763. *Gerechtshof Amsterdam (Stichting Stadsgenoot)* (2016) ECLI:NL:GHAMS:2016:227; *Rechtbank Rotterdam (Stichting Woonstad Rotterdam)* (2016) ECLI:NL:RBROT:2016:4345.

Renters cannot *fully* waive their protection under the right to freedom of expression through a rental contract.

Following these conclusions in the Dutch and German cases, a contractual obligation that limits a weaker party's right to freedom of expression and to impart information may only be enforced if that party has other alternatives to impart the information. However, to strike a fair balance between that right and the proprietor's right to property, access to that information must be objectively justifiable and may not be based on mere subjective preferences. In light of the latter, the proprietor must take into consideration any special interests that the weaker party may have to impart certain information.

6.4.3.6 Waiving the Right to Freedom of Expression Contractually

Drawing from the (German) application of the unfairness test in the UCTD, the limitations to the protection under the right to data protection, and the Dutch and German case law on waiving the freedom of expression-protection in rental contracts, the question as to whether the right to freedom of expression can be waived contractually can finally be answered. As a starting point, the private autonomy of the parties allows them to decide on the scope of the agreement as long as the substance of the agreement stays within the borders of the law. Consequently, in principle, parties can agree to waive their fundamental rights' protection, including their protection under the right to freedom of expression. However, when there is an imbalance in the power between the parties – which is the case when dealing with a social media platform and a user who is a consumer – the protection of the right may not be *fully impaired*. That conclusion is in line with the Dutch and German case law, the practice in data protection law, and the underlying idea of immoral contracts to tackle abuses of private autonomy that result in excessive restrictions of fundamental rights and freedoms. This standard equally follows the ECtHR's case law on the freedom of expression.[764]

Fairness of contract terms thus entails that a social media platform cannot fully limit the right to freedom of expression when dealing with consumers. In line with the case law of the ECtHR, a 'full impairment' of the right would destroy the essence of the right's protection. The discussion pointed out in the introduction on the necessity to qualify social media platforms (private, public, or quasi-public) is thus subordinate to reaching a conclusion in specific cases. The main requirement is to assess whether *actual alternatives* exist to communicate and impart information. It does not matter whether the more powerful contracting party is a social media platform or a privately owned physical library; both can end up in a situation where they are a powerful party able to fully impair the fundamental rights protection of the weaker party. The effect of a restriction on a social media platform could fully impair the freedom of expression in

764. *Appleby and Others v. United Kingdom* (n. 188), §47: 'Where, however, the bar on access to property has the effect of preventing any effective exercise of freedom of expression or it can be said that the essence of the right has been destroyed, the Court would not exclude that a positive obligation could arise for the State to protect the enjoyment of the Convention rights by regulating property rights.'

case it would be the only available platform. A restaurant would equally qualify as such if it were the only restaurant in a town, as would a library if it is the individual's only means to impart information. For social media platforms, the *Bundesgerichtshof* has listed the criteria to assess whether the platform has a decisive role over the scope of the users' fundamental rights protection in a way that would justify interference with private autonomy.[765] The conclusion on the latter depends on the degree of market dominance of the operator, the orientation of the platform, the degree of dependence of the users on the platform, and the interests of the platform operators and other third parties affected.[766] In those circumstances where the platform's interests do not outweigh the users, a contractual term that impairs the freedom of expression of the weaker party will not pass the fairness test in the UCTD.

6.4.4 The Interpretation of the Contractual Obligations

As a last prerequisite for contractual terms to be binding, the contractual obligations must be determinable. Terms that are incomprehensible (not written in plain, intelligible language) must be interpreted in the way that is most favourable to the consumer.[767] Where that is not possible, the incomprehensible terms are not binding on consumers.[768] For example, a social media platform's terms of service offer, 'to provide a safe platform', is undeterminable without further information on content that is deemed 'unsafe' or on the sanctions that can be taken in case of a breach.[769] Indeterminable and overly broad terms were found unfair in both Italy and Germany. In Germany, the *Oberlandesgericht München* concluded that terms of service that allow a platform to unilaterally decide which content breaches the 'community norms' are unreasonably disadvantaging the platform's users as it is unclear what is understood under that obligation.[770] In Italy, the Italian Consumer Authority (ICA) found that an overly broad termination clause that requires the platform's substantive interpretation is unfair and not binding on consumers. In *TikTok*, the first version[771] of the terms was

765. Arguably, there is nothing inherently related to social media platforms within these criteria, and therefore they could be equally applied to other types of property – whether in the online or the physical world.
766. *Bundesgerichtshof (Inhaltesperrung)* (n. 23), §76.
767. Article 5 UCTD.
768. Article 6(1) UCTD.
769. In Germany, indeterminability leads to unfairness, as the user would be left to the full subjective interpretation of the platform, *see Oberlandesgericht München (Content block)* (n. 108); *Oberlandesgericht Dresden (Unfair platform terms)* (n. 103).
770. *Oberlandesgericht München (Content block)* (n. 108); *Oberlandesgericht Dresden (Unfair platform terms)* (n. 103). In *Content Block*, the *Oberlandesgericht München* concluded that user terms that allow the platform to decide which content breaches the 'community norms', unreasonably disadvantages the platform's user (§307 (1) BGB). Subsequently, in *Unfair Platform Terms*, the *Oberlandesgericht Dresden* followed the *Content Block* decision and states that: 'the Terms of Use no longer link the removal of contributions and the other sanctions regulated therein – as the platform's provision still did [in Content Block] – to a unilateral right of determination by the platform, but to a breach of Facebook's terms of use, community standards and other conditions and guidelines and thus to criteria that can in principle be objectified.'
771. The issue concerns clauses 6, 7, and 11. Clause 6 (Termination) empowers the trader to suspend or close the consumer's account or to impose restrictions on the use of the services

found to be unfair, whereas the second[772] could withstand the unfairness test because 'the reasons for the disabling (temporary or definitive) of the account and the limitation of access to content appear to be formulated in a sufficiently precise manner, while considering the operating requirements of the Platform; moreover, they are not left to the mere discretion of the professional, constituting "just cause" and "justifiable reasons indicated in the contract itself" within the meaning of Article 33(2)(h) and (m) of the Italian Consumer Code'.[773] A similar outcome was reached in *Google Drive*, where the ICA concludes that Google no longer exerts absolute discretionary power over suspension and termination but instead sends a decision to terminate the account by e-mail seven days prior to enforcement and offers the user a complaint mechanism. Furthermore, Google specifies the exact circumstances under which it can potentially suspend or terminate an account, apart from the situation where there is an imminent danger of criminal behaviour.[774]

Moreover, social media platforms operate globally, though their terms are applicable nationally. The platform's terms of service will be interpreted by courts in accordance with national law. As a platform, it is therefore important to avoid using legal terms when indicating normative choices of permissible content. Terminology such as 'illegal fascist content' can lead to different implications in different legal systems.[775] Rather, the platform should describe in the terms of the *exact content* or group of content that will be removed. In this way, national variations in the outcome of content restore-claims, as observed in *L'Aquila*, can be avoided.[776]

The pending German case of *HateAid & EUJS v. Twitter* forms an example of a case on the decisive factor determinability plays in relation to a platform's contractual obligations. The details of the case and the interpretational problems are outlined below.

6.4.4.1 The Case of HateAid & EUJS Versus Twitter

At the end of January 2023, HateAid and the European Union of Jewish Students (EUJS) filed a civil action against Twitter for breach of contract. HateAid and EUJS had reported six antisemitic and illegal posts to Twitter, on which the platform has not acted. In relation to one flagged post, Twitter actively refused to remove the content. If

'with or without notice and at any time, for any reason or for no reason at all'. Clause 7. In the event of even potential violations of the Terms of Service, [TikTok] reserves, in its sole discretion, 'the right to permanently or temporarily remove or suspend access to a content at any time and without notice'. Clause 11 (Exclusion of warranties) gives the trader the right to 'modify, suspend, revoke, or limit the availability of all or part of the platform [.] at any time and without prior notice' for general reasons ('commercial and operational reasons').

772. Amended clause 4 (replacing clause 6): The trader may: (i) remove or restrict access to any content, including content uploaded by users, in the event of a breach of contract, injury (potential or actual) to the Company, its affiliates, other users or third parties and (ii) disable the account if the user uses the Platform form again despite the previous disablement. Additionally, it has added procedural safeguards (decision sets out the reasons for suspension/termination and provides possibilities for the user to appeal the decision).
773. *Provvedimento n. 29976 – CV224 – TikTok* (n. 148), §62.
774. *Provvedimento n. 29817 – CV194 – Google Drive* (n. 148), §35.
775. *Corte appello L'Aquila (Correggiari)* (n. 21).
776. *Ibid., see* for a discussion of the case also §2.2.2.

there had been clear and determinable damage on the side of HateAid or EUJS, the case could have been assessed through tort law's rules on direct and indirect liability. Through direct liability, the question as to whether the affected person would be able to claim damages from the speaker for posting a denial of the Shoah would be addressed. Similarly, the field of indirect liability could be applied to find an answer as to whether Twitter would be liable for carrying that content. Since Shoah denials are illegal in over half of the Member States of the European Union,[777] platforms have to abide by the rules in the eCD's Article 14 (soon Article 6 DSA) to be exempted from liability. These rules prescribe that a platform, once it has received a notification pointing to the hosting of illegal content, must act expeditiously to remove or disable access to the illegal content, or it risks intermediary liability. However, in the case at stake, the parties are not personally affected by violations of their rights, rendering a claim for (indirect) liability a tough case. The parties have, therefore, turned to contract law as a legal remedy and complained that Twitter has not upheld its own contractual obligations in the terms of service.[778] Therefore, the claimants argue that Twitter not removing the posts results in a breach of contract.

The case concerns the wording of Twitter's terms of service and the obligations on content moderation included therein. The parties have requested the Berlin Court to determine to what extent Twitter has a contractual obligation to its users, under its terms of service, to remove antisemitic Tweets which contain sedition, including trivialisation and denial of the Shoah.[779] Deciding whether Twitter has the contractual obligation to act on these notifications of illegal content is a question of interpretation of the contractual terms. The terms of service fulfil the formal conditions of a contract. The question, however, relates to the interpretation of the obligation's text and what the scope of the contractual obligations is. First, to determine the parties' obligations, the national court will have to assess on a case-by-case basis the text of the agreement. If there remains unclarity following the textual interpretation, the clause must be interpreted in light of the parties' intent, the meaning commonly given to the terms (if possible), or if neither of those is possible, in the way most favourable to the consumer.[780]

777. These cover Andorra, Austria, Belgium, Cyprus, France, Germany, Hungary, Italy, Latvia, Lichtenstein, Lithuania, Luxemburg, the former Yugoslav Republic of Macedonia, Malta, the Netherlands, Romania, Slovakia, Slovenia, and Switzerland, *see* for an in-depth analysis: Michael Bazyler, 'Holocaust Denial and the Law' in Michael Bazyler (ed.), *Holocaust, Genocide, and the Law: A Quest for Justice in a Post-Holocaust World* (Oxford University Press 2017) https://doi.org/10.1093/acprof:oso/9780195395693.003.0007 (accessed 27 January 2023). Additionally, the ECtHR has consistently excluded holocaust-denials from the protection of the ECHR, pointing to the antisemitic nature of the prohibited statements and qualifying them as abuse of rights.

778. European Union of Jewish Students, 'Lawsuit against Twitter: HateAid and the European Union of Jewish Students Submit Landmark Case' (*EUJS*, 25 January 2023) https://eujs.org/press-releases/lawsuit-against-twitter-hateaid-and-the-european-union-of-jewish-students-submit-landmark-case/ (accessed 27 January 2023): The parties want 'a legal clarification of whether social networks, despite the non-committal wording of their Terms of Service, have the obligation to implement their own rules in order to protect their users.'

779. *Ibid.*

780. Article 5 UCTD.

The contested obligation follows from Twitter's terms of service policy on *'Hateful conduct policy'*[781] and its rules on *'Abusive behaviour'*.[782] The following is stated in these policies in regard to the general binding rule (included in *'The Twitter Rules'*)[783] and the Shoah-denial specific explanation included in the terms of service of the specific policies. Twitter outlines the consequences of a breach of the above policies: 'We will review and take action against reports of accounts targeting an individual or group of people.' Subsequently, Twitter has various ways of enforcing a breach of the terms.[784]

Table 6.2 Twitter's Policies on Hateful Conduct and Abusive Behaviour

Policy	*General Rule*	*Shoah-Denial Content That Is Included in the Contractual Explanation*
Hateful conduct policy	*Hateful conduct*: You may not promote violence against or directly attack or threaten other people on the basis of race, ethnicity, national origin, caste, sexual orientation, gender, gender identity, religious affiliation, age, disability, or serious disease. We also do not allow accounts whose primary purpose is inciting harm towards others on the basis of these categories.	'We prohibit targeting individuals or groups with content that references forms of violence or violent events where a protected category was the primary target or victims, where the intent is to harass. This includes, but is not limited to media or text that refers to or depicts: (...) - genocides, (e.g., *the Holocaust*)'

781. 'Twitter's Policy on Hateful Conduct | Twitter Help' https://help.twitter.com/en/rules-and-policies/hateful-conduct-policy (accessed 27 January 2023).
782. 'How Twitter Handles Abusive Behavior | Twitter Help' https://help.twitter.com/en/rules-and-policies/abusive-behavior (accessed 27 January 2023).
783. 'The Twitter Rules: Safety, Privacy, Authenticity, and More' https://help.twitter.com/en/rules-and-policies/twitter-rules (accessed 27 January 2023).
784. 'When determining the penalty for violating this policy, we consider a number of factors including, but not limited to the severity of the violation and an individual's previous record of rule violations. The following is a list of potential enforcement options for content that violates this policy:

- Downranking Tweets in replies, except when the user follows the Tweet author.
- Making Tweets ineligible for amplification in Top search results and/or on timelines for users who don't follow the Tweet author.
- Excluding Tweets and/or accounts in email or in-product recommendations.
- Requiring Tweet removal.
- Suspending accounts whose primary use we've determined is to engage in hateful conduct as defined in this policy, or who have shared violent threats.'

Further clarification on the order and application of these options follows from Twitter's enforcement policy: 'Our Range of Enforcement Options for Violations | Twitter Help' https://help.twitter.com/en/rules-and-policies/enforcement-options (accessed 27 January 2023).

Policy	*General Rule*	*Shoah-Denial Content That Is Included in the Contractual Explanation*
Abusive behaviour	*Abuse/harassment*: You may not engage in the targeted harassment of someone or incite other people to do so. We consider abusive behaviour an attempt to harass, intimidate, or silence someone else's voice.	We prohibit content that denies that mass murder or other mass casualty events took place, where we can verify that the event occurred, and when the content is shared with abusive intent. This may include references to such an event as a 'hoax' or claims that victims or survivors are fake or 'actors'. It includes, but is not limited to, events like the *Holocaust*, school shootings, terrorist attacks, and natural disasters.

Having the terms in place, an assessment can be made. First, without knowing the exact content of the six posts flagged by the complainants, it is hard to make an exact assessment. Taking as a starting point that the posts indeed denied the Shoah, then those posts would undoubtedly breach Twitter's explanatory rules on abusive behaviour. The general rule is perhaps less crystal clear, but in light of Twitter's *enforcement philosophy*,[785] 'someone' must also be understood as a group of persons. Since the claimants argue that the denial of the Shoah is used in a way to silence their voice, Twitter would be urged to at least review the matter – in line with their own promise ('*we will review*'). That would mean that on a general note, without knowing the facts of the exact cases, it seems as if the only post living up to that obligation is the one post that Twitter denied to act upon because, as a bare minimum, Twitter has reviewed that post. Whether or not Twitter *should* have enforced, and if so, with which measure, cannot be concluded at this point. For the other five posts, Twitter has seemingly breached its own obligation to review the flagged content. Moreover, Twitter stipulates in its *Hateful conduct policy* that the company is 'committed to combating abuse motivated by hatred, prejudice or intolerance, particularly abuse that seeks to silence the voices of those who have been historically marginalized'. Does being committed to combat abuse mean that Twitter should act in case content in breach of this policy is flagged to them? The claimants can rely on the principle of interpretation *contra proferentum* in Article 5 UCTD, meaning that unclear obligations under the contract must be interpreted most favourable to the consumer. In that light, the fact that Twitter states it is 'committed to act' should be interpreted to at least review the content. Obstruction thereof constitutes a breach of contract.

785. 'Twitter's Enforcement Philosophy & Approach to Policy Development' https://help.twitter.com/en/rules-and-policies/enforcement-philosophy (accessed 27 January 2023).

6.5 INTERIM CONCLUSION

As the answer to sub-question (v) depends on the combination of the study on the content layer included in this chapter and the study of the enforcement layer included in Chapter 7 below, the answer to that sub-question is included at the end of Chapter 7. That means that at this point, only an interim conclusion on the content layer is drawn on the scope of social media platforms' freedom of contract.

Social media platforms' moderation decisions can be divided into categories. The division is created by the platform's incentive to make the decision, which can either be mandatory or normative. The former is the result of direct or indirect governmental influence, whereas the latter is the result of the platform's own choice – whether based on economic incentives or represents the platform's political or normative views. A third moderation outcome is caused by the wrongful application/interpretation of the law or the platform's own terms. These wrongful moderation decisions, therefore, constitute a breach of contract. Justifiable mandatory and normative moderation decisions and wrongful moderation decisions can be observed on both open access-platforms as well as on conditional access-platforms.

In physical open access-properties, persons have a general right of use, meaning that a person can, in principle, not be denied from accessing the property or making use of it. In Germany, and arguably in Italy, such a general right of use would/could equally apply to online access-platforms. The general right of use is far-reaching but not absolute. Restrictions on accessing and using open access-platforms cannot be based solely on the subjective intention of the platform operator but must be based on an objective reason. The requirement of an objective reason limits the scope for moderation decisions on open access-platforms to those situations where a user of the service has breached the law or the platform's rules or the platform operator has an objective fear that such breaches could arise in the future. There must be objectively verifiable facts that prove (previous) unlawful conduct or that sustain the existing fear of future disturbances. Moreover, large-scale open access-platforms will most likely have to take the right to non-discrimination into consideration.

The restrictions on conditional access-platforms are subject to (the general principles of) contract law. In principle, the parties are free to decide on the obligations they wish to be bound by, though not everything can form the substance of a contract. If the substance is allowed, the parties must live up to the requirements for the formation of a contract. For contracts between a social media platform and its users, the UCTD and the DSA prescribe mandatory transparency requirements. This follows simultaneously from the principle of mutual consent in contract law, meaning that the contract is only validly formed when both parties know what they say yes to. If a contract has been formed, the individual terms can nonetheless be invalid if they breach mandatory rules of public policy, such as the unfairness test in the Unfair Contract Terms Directive. Contract terms are unfair when a social media platform fully limits the right to freedom of expression. In line with the case law of the ECtHR, a 'full impairment' of the right would destroy the essence of the right's protection. For social media platforms, the criteria to assess whether the platform has a decisive role over the scope of the users' fundamental rights protection in a way that would justify an interference with the private autonomy depends on the degree of market dominance of the operator, the orientation of the platform, the degree of dependence of the users on the platform, and the interests of the platform operators and other third parties affected. In those circumstances where the platform's interests do not outweigh the users, a contractual term that impairs the freedom of expression of the weaker party will not pass the fairness test in the UCTD.

Lastly, the contractual terms must be interpretable to be binding. Terms that are incomprehensible (not written in plain, intelligible language) must be interpreted in the way that is most favourable to the consumer. Where that is not possible, the incomprehensible terms are not binding on consumers.

CHAPTER 7
The Enforcement Layer: The Consequences of Breaching the Terms

7.1 DEALING WITH BREACHES OF THE TERMS OF SERVICE

The aim of this chapter is to gain an overview of the consequences of either a social media platform or a user breaching the terms of service. When the platform's terms of service do not breach mandatory rules, they have been written in a way that meets the transparency and information obligations, and thus, the user has validly consented to the terms, then the terms are binding and form a valid and enforceable contract. If either one of the parties does not live up to the obligations under the contract, a breach of contract occurs. This could be either a social media platform that removes content that it was obliged to host or a user that has uploaded content that is not allowed under the terms of service. A breach of contract of the platform equals a wrongful moderation decision, and users can use both contractual and judicial remedies to (try to) overturn such a decision. If a user posts content that breaches the terms, the platform can make use of the sanctions outlined in the terms. However, with the coming into force of the DSA, social media platforms have to observe increased (procedural) requirements when imposing contractual sanctions.

Figure 7.1 The Enforcement Layer as Applicable to Social Media Platforms

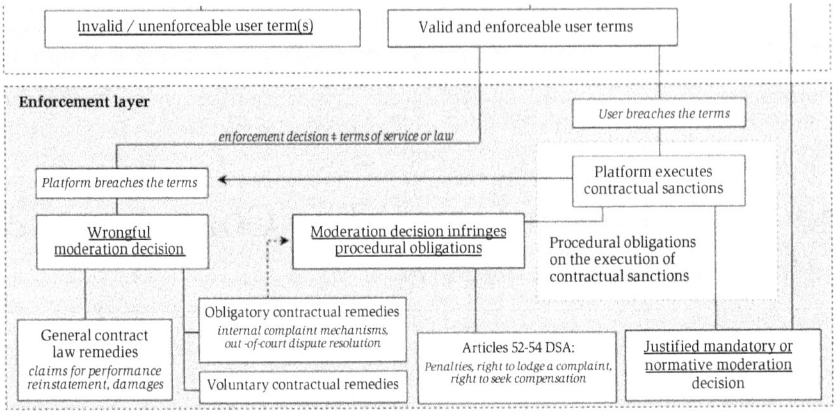

This chapter concerns the sanctions and remedies for breaches of the terms of service. It addresses all the steps between a breach of contract until the final outcome for platform and user (*see* Figure 7.1). First, to define when and which sanctions can be imposed, it must be clear what the obligations of the parties are. Without specifying the obligations of all the individual social media platforms, an abstract overview of the obligations of social media platforms and their users is formed on the basis of the national case law in Italy and Germany. Subsequently, the contractual sanctions that a social media platform can impose for a user's breach of contract are described. Third, with the coming into force of the DSA, a social media platform's ability to execute these contractual sanctions is bound by procedural obligations. These different procedural obligations and the consequences of an infringement of these obligations are discussed. Lastly, the users' contractual and judicial remedies for wrongful moderation decisions (breach of contract by the platform) are outlined and discussed.

7.2 THE MUTUAL OBLIGATIONS OF THE PARTIES

Some of the Member States' national courts have (tried to) determine the platform's obligations according to their terms of service. The national interpretations of these obligations in Italy and Germany are fairly similar. In Italy, the court of L'Aquila found on the basis of the terms of service that Facebook offered a space in which there must be 'balance between the possibility for the user to express himself and share content deemed important and the harm that certain modes of expression or certain content may cause to the safety and well-being of others or to the integrity of the community itself'. This system is subjected to '*rules of civil coexistence*'.[786] The German *Bundesgerichtshof* is more straightforward in its answer and concludes that 'there is a contract

786. *Corte appello L'Aquila (Correggiari)* (n. 21), §9.

of use between the parties, in the context of which the platform makes its products and services available and to enable the user to contact other users and to exchange information with other users, in particular to send messages and share data such as texts, photos and videos.'[787] As such, the platform offers a communication platform for its users, in which they can share opinions and information within the permissible scope as defined by the terms of service and the law.[788] That does not signal an undefined obligation; rather, it signals an obligation on the platform to host the content that falls within the borders of the law and the limits of the terms of service.

Simplified, one could summarise the main mutual obligations of the parties as follows. The platform is obliged to provide access to its communication platform and to host the content as defined in its terms of service. The user has a right to access the service and to have their content hosted. In return, the user is obliged to refrain from sharing illegal content and/or content that is deemed unwanted by the platform. The user is (on most platforms) also obliged to allow the platform to use any contextual and/or personal data that was created by the user during the use of the communication platform.

If the platform operator restricts the access and/or the use of the communication platform in a way that is not outlined in the terms of service, then that would constitute a breach of contract. A wrongful moderation decision is an example of platform behaviour that constitutes a breach of contract. The platform is not hosting the content as it is obliged to. Similarly, when the user shares content on the communication platform that is prohibited in the platform's terms, the user breaches the contract (and/or the law). In case either one of the parties breaches the contract, the other party can make use of the remedies that are either outlined in the terms of service (internal complaint-handling, out-of-court dispute resolution) or national law (reinstatement claim, claim for damages).

7.3 REMEDIES FOR SOCIAL MEDIA PLATFORMS

When a user breaches the terms, the platform can make use of the contractual sanctions outlined in the terms of service. These sanctions can affect the (visibility of the) content or the user's account. For example, content-related sanctions for a breach of the terms could include the removal of content, disabling access to the content, demotion in ranking, or demotion in the recommendation system. User account-related sanctions cover the termination of the user account, suspension of the user account, and a (temporary) restriction to post and share content. The parties are, in principle, free to decide on the contractual sanctions imposed when either one of the parties

787. *Bundesgerichtshof (Inhaltesperrung)* (n. 23), §40.

788. This was also concluded by the EDPB in its Binding Decision 3/2022 discussed further below, *see* point 124: 'The EDPB considers that the main purpose for which users use Facebook and accept the Facebook Terms of Service is to communicate with others, not to receive personalised advertisements.'

breaches the terms.[789] The sanctions must be outlined in the terms of service to be binding on the parties.[790] If the platform imposes a sanction that is not outlined in the terms of service, it would, first, constitute a breach of contract, and second, it would infringe the transparency requirement in Article 14(1) DSA. Moreover, Article 23(1) DSA obliges providers of online platforms to suspend users in case they frequently provide manifestly illegal content.

Sanctions can lead to a restriction of a person's freedoms. In a dispute before the Appeals Court of The Hague in the Netherlands, the question was raised whether a private undertaking, without the mandate and or delegated task from the government, can impose on a natural person a restraint of their liberty (not physically being allowed near and in a stadium). The Court answers in the affirmative, though it clarifies that these are not 'liberty restraints' but merely contractual consequences (suspension of the obligations under the contract and a refusal to enter into an agreement with the supporter to attend the football match). A private undertaking does not need a delegated task from the government 'to agree with an opposing party that certain sanctions may be imposed, or certain powers granted, if that opposing party acts contrary to what has been agreed'. Similarly, the Danish Supreme Court confirmed that parties can agree on the payment of a fine when breaching the terms of service.[791] Moreover, it is settled in German case law that a social media platform is allowed to impose a sanction on those that breach the user terms, whether that sanction contains the removal of content or the blocking of access to the platform.[792]

7.3.1 Obligations for the Execution of Contractual Sanctions

With the enactment of the DSA, social media platforms' execution of the contractual sanctions has been subjected to (procedural) obligations. Before digging into the obligations stipulated by the DSA, it must be noted that the DSA first applies as of the beginning of 2024. The exact scope and application of these (procedural) obligations are therefore far from clear and will depend on future guidelines from the Commission and the Digital Services Coordinators of the Member States, interpretation of the provisions by national courts, or preliminary rulings by the CJEU. Most of the conclusions set out below are either textual interpretations of the provisions or an interpretation of the obligations by analogy to the case law of the Member States.

The obligations applicable to social media platforms when executing the contractual sanctions outlined in their user terms can be found in Article 14(4) and Article 17. The DSA outlines more (procedural) obligations on social media platforms, but these

789. *STEB* (n. 374), §28: 'In that regard, it should be noted that the contracting parties are at liberty – subject to the mandatory rules of public policy – to define the terms of their legal relationship, including the consequences of a cancellation or breach of their obligations.'

790. *See* on the general transparency requirements §6.4.2.1. Sanction on the use of social media platforms must furthermore be outlined according to Art. 14(1) DSA.

791. *Højesteret 16/2013 (Private car parking)* (n. 222).

792. *Landgericht Frankfurt am Main (Access blocks)* (n. 107); *Landgericht Frankfurt am Main (Restore claim)* (n. 102); *Bundesgerichtshof (Kontosperrung)* (n. 23); *Bundesgerichtshof (Inhaltesperrung)* (n. 23).

do not directly affect the execution of contractual sanctions. These cover, respectively, a social media platform's obligation to execute these sanctions in a diligent, objective, and proportionate manner and the obligation to outline the grounds for executing a contractual sanction in a statement of reasons.[793] Infringements of these obligations can have big consequences for social media platforms. The DSA stipulates remedies to deal with and sanctions for the infringements of the obligations in the DSA. However, their effect is restricted to the procedure of applying and enforcing the terms – the terms' binding nature is not affected.[794] The obligations put forward in the DSA are of a procedural nature. They do not affect the *substance* nor the *validity* of the terms. These differences are best demonstrated by examples that demonstrate an unfair term according to the UCTD, as opposed to a term that breaches the proportionality requirement of the DSA.

In situation one, if a social media platform's term of service would, for example, demand that the ownership of a user's cat or dog is automatically transferred to the social media platform when a user's cat or dog video goes viral. That term would not pass the unfairness test of the UCTD.[795] As a result, that term is no longer binding on the user. Also, in future instances, the social media platform cannot invoke that ground in the terms of service. The consequences in the second situation are different. In the second situation, an example could be the termination of a user account by a social media platform for a minor, first-time sharing of copyright-protected content. The terms of service outline that the sharing of copyright-protected content is prohibited, and therefore, the platform operator is, in principle, allowed to impose a sanction (if such a sanction is outlined in the terms in line with the transparency obligations). However, the user has only minorly breached the terms of service. In this case, in line with the Italian case law,[796] the *execution of the sanction* is disproportionate. The application and execution of the contractual sanction, therefore, infringes Article 14(4) DSA. The effect on the term is different from situation one. Whereas the term in situation one is no longer binding and will neither be binding in future situations, the user term in situation two remains valid and enforceable in the future. The binding nature of the term itself is not affected – solely the *application* and *enforcement* of the

793. For example the obligation to provide a notice and action mechanism (Art. 16) including the specific priority rules for trusted flaggers (Art. 22), or the obligation to notify law enforcement of suspicions of criminal offences (Art. 18).

794. *See* more on the consequences of a breach of the DSA's obligations §7.3.6 below.

795. *See* a full outline of the functioning of the unfairness test in §6.4.3.2 above. The UCTD aims to determine whether terms in not-individually negotiated consumer contracts distort the balance between the parties and should therefore be deemed invalid. A contractual term is unfair if it causes a significant imbalance in the parties' rights and obligations arising under the contract – to the detriment of the consumer – and is contrary to the requirement of good faith. Here, that would be the case.

796. *Tribunale di Pordenone (Preliminary reinstatement request)* (n. 153). The user had posted two short video clips including copyright-protected material. The user terms explicitly prohibited this. After making the user aware of the infringing material, the user immediately removed the content and apologised to the copyright holder. The court concluded (preliminary) that suspension of the user account was not proportionate.

term are unjustifiable.[797] Easier said, in situation two, the *execution of the sanction* (termination of the account) was disproportionate, but the reason to delete the content was valid (breach of a contractual term). The disproportionality does not invalidate the reason to remove the content, since that content is still infringing copyright.[798] The same argumentation applies to the mandatory statement of reasons. Failure to send a statement of reasons prior to taking down content that infringes the terms of service affects the interests of the user to appeal that decision, but it does not affect the legitimacy of taking down the content. The situations in which the procedural obligations from the DSA apply and the exact obligations they impose on social media platforms are outlined below.

7.3.2 Article 14(4) DSA: Due Diligence Obligations

The Digital Services Act's Article 14(4) imposes the obligation to act in a diligent, objective, and proportionate way, both when *applying* and when *enforcing* the content moderation restrictions in their terms of service. Both must be carried out 'with due regard to the rights and legitimate interests of all parties involved, including the fundamental rights of the recipients of the service, such as the freedom of expression, freedom and pluralism of the media, and other fundamental rights and freedoms as enshrined in the Charter'. This reference to fundamental rights in the text of Article 14 has been referred to in the literature as a 'revolutionary potential for the indirect horizontal effect of fundamental rights in the relationship between social media platforms and their users'.[799] However, the use of fundamental rights standards in private law is far from revolutionary within the field of contract law, where the indirect horizontal effect of fundamental rights through open norms is an established feature of contract law,[800] especially to balance unequal power relationships. Even without Article 14(4) DSA, principles of fundamental rights law can indirectly be included in the assessment of the unfairness of terms and through other general open norms in national contract law.[801]

797. As also indirectly stated in recital (39) of the DSA, which reserves this option for 'breaches of the terms of service', *see* on this §7.4.2.1.
798. If this case was to be decided on the basis of national contract law, the termination of a user account for a minor breach of contract would likely be contestable, since the termination of a (long-term) contract requires a material breach of the contract.
799. Quintais, Appelman and Fahy (n. 256).
800. The system of open norms of good faith can be traced back to Roman (contract) law (*bonafides*), which 'provided the legal elasticity by giving the judge the possibility to condemn the parties to the requirements of good faith', *see* Talya Şans Uç arıylmaz, 'The Principle of Bona Fides from Roman Law to Contemporary Law' (Thesis, Bilkent University 2018) http://repository.bilkent.edu.tr/handle/11693/47574 (accessed 31 January 2023). The latter equally highlights that 'the most important medium in which bona fides finds its place, has been the law of contracts'. *See* for an extensive study on the inclusion of fundamental rights in open norms in several Member States the 2008-dissertation of: Mak, *Fundamental Rights in European Contract Law* (n. 65).
801. Demonstrated for example by the entire doctrine of *Drittwirkung* in Germany, and the balancing of rights under the 'reasonableness and fairness'-clause in Dutch cases.

7.3.3 The Scope of Application of Article 14(4)

Before digging into the individual obligations in Article 14(4), a remark is to be made on the scope of the article. There seems to be confusion as to the interplay between fundamental rights and the terms of service covered by Article 14. Article 14 forms a limitation to the freedom of contract,[802] and therefore, the obligations in Article 14 should be viewed through that lens. That means that Article 14 is an *exception* to the general freedom of the parties to decide their contractual obligations (private autonomy). Article 14 should, therefore, not be used to *dictate* the content of those obligations.[803] Due to the omission of the word 'design' in the text of Article 14(4), the obligations set forward in the provision should be limited to the application and enforcement of the terms and should not dictate the terms to be included in the contract.[804] That means that a platform is, in principle, free to draw up the rules and restrictions applicable to its service but that the obligations in Article 14(4) must be observed when executing a sanction for a breach of those rules.

Open access-platforms do not have to observe the obligations outlined in Article 14(4). Since these types of platforms generally do not impose any restrictions on the use of their service as outlined in Article 14(1), the obligation in Article 14(4) does not apply. Similarly, the suspension of users that frequently provide manifestly illegal content is excluded from the obligations under Article 14(4) – whether or not applied by conditional or open access-platforms. On the basis of Article 23(1), a platform is obliged to suspend users who frequently disseminate illegal content. This suspension is not affected by Article 14(4) since Article 23 does not refer to the obligations in Article 14(4). That reference has been justly omitted since it is not a free choice of the platform to include that restriction in the terms. It follows from mandatory law, and as such, the platform does not have to take the interests of the party and their fundamental rights into consideration when enforcing – the legislator has already done that when imposing Article 23. It is unclear whether the use of recommender systems falls within the scope of Article 14(4). Such systems would arguably fall in the scope of Article 14(1) since they are used as a tool for the purpose of content moderation. However, recommender systems are regulated as a *lex specialis* in Article 27, which article does

802. *See* recitals (45) and (47) of the DSA, which addresses the restrictions imposed on Art. 14 from the principle to respect the freedom of contract of providers of intermediary services.
803. *See* a similar conclusion reached in: Folkert Wilman, 'The Digital Services Act (DSA) – An Overview' (16 December 2022) 18 https://papers.ssrn.com/abstract=4304586 (accessed 24 January 2023). The conclusion that the DSA lets untouched the content of the terms opposes the idea put forward by other scholars that the DSA will directly regulate the conditions on which platforms can offer their service: Quintais, Appelman and Fahy (n. 256), p. 12, arguing that the DSA will govern the contractual relationship and directly regulate the conditions of the service. Domingos Farinho, 'The Digital Services Act: A European Digital Republic, If We Can Keep It or the Long and Winding Road – The Digital Constitutionalist' (7 December 2022) https://digi-con.org/the-digital-services-act-a-european-digital-republic-if-we-can-keep-it-or-the-long-and-winding-road/ (accessed 1 February 2023). goes even further and refers to a 'duty to align the terms and conditions with the EU Charter of Fundamental rights'.
804. *See* above §6.4.3.1.

not refer to the obligation in Article 14(4). Since the use of recommender systems can have a great influence on the visibility of content, it seems most favourable to subject the use of those systems to the obligations in Article 14(4).

Article 14(4) applies to the *restrictions*, which, according to Article 14(1), must be outlined. The determining factor for the obligation to adhere to the standards in Article 14(4), therefore, depends on the definition of a restriction. What exactly falls within the scope of *restrictions* is unclear from a textual interpretation of Article 14(1). Earlier, I already argued that the obligations under Article 14(4) are solely restricted to *ex post* restrictions that affect the content or the account of the user.[805] A closer examination of Article 14(1) shows that the first sentence and the examples in the second sentence leave room for different interpretations. Whether or not the examples in the second sentence of Article 14(1) are to be interpreted as information subject to the transparency requirement of Article 14(1) or as examples of 'restrictions' is not fully clear. That difference matters, as the obligations of Article 14(4) solely apply to 'the restrictions referred to in paragraph 1'. The second sentence mentions the rules of procedure of an internal complaint-handling system. When the rules of procedure of the internal complaints mechanism fall within the scope of Article 14(4), then a decision on a complaint that was not taken objectively or with due regard to the user's legitimate interests and fundamental rights results in an infringement of the DSA.[806] If the rules of procedure were solely to be included in the terms but would not qualify as a 'restriction', then a breach of these procedural rules solely constitutes a breach of contract. It would not lead to any of the measures available for infringements of the DSA. The discussion on whether internal complaints mechanisms are subjected to the obligations in Article 14(4) is outlined below when discussing the obligation to offer access to such mechanisms.[807]

Article 14(4) differentiates between *ex post* restrictions' application and enforcement. The category 'application' covers those practices of content moderation that do not have a sanctioning effect but merely govern the processes of the platform's content moderation. The category 'enforcement' covers the execution of contractual sanctions on users in relation to their content or their account. The obligations under Article 14(4) do not form a part of the terms of service. It is an obligation that follows directly from the law. The obligations in Article 14(4) are limited to procedural rules only.[808] For infringements of DSA, the Regulation outlines additional remedies available to users.[809]

805. *See* for the conclusion on the exclusion of ex-ante restrictions: §6.4.2.1.
806. The consequences of an infringement are outlined below in §7.3.6.
807. Article 20 DSA, *see also* §7.4.1.1.
808. *See* a similar conclusion pre-DSA on the imposition of procedural safeguards on social media platforms in German case law: Moritz Hennemann and Amélie Heldt, 'Prozedurale Vermessung: Das Kuratieren Kommunikativer Räume Durch Soziale Netzwerke Zugleich Besprechung von BGH, Urteile Vom 29.7.2021 – BGH Aktenzeichen IIIZR17920 III ZR 179/20 (ZUM 2021, ZUM Jahr 2021 Seite 953) Und BGH Aktenzeichen III ZR 192/20 (ZUM-RD 2021, ZUM-RD Jahr 2021 Seite 612)' [2021] ZUM 981. *See* equally *Van Haga v. LinkedIn* (n. 23), §4.14: 'The DSA contains procedural frameworks within which that consideration should take place.'
809. These remedies are outlined below in §7.3.6.

7.3.4 Substance of the Obligations in Article 14(4)

The obligations in Article 14(4) provide a broad-scoped, open norm that users can invoke to rebalance the contractual relationship between them and the social media platform. Article 14(4) forms as such an addition to the national private law systems of those Member States that already offer open norms (e.g., 'reasonableness and fairness' or 'good faith') through which fundamental rights can be included. As such, in those Member States, the obligations set forward in Article 14(4) do not increase the protection of users beyond the scope of national private law. For users in Member States where such balancing is not yet available through open norms in national private law, the article increases their fundamental rights' protection. Article 14(4) is, in that sense, merely a confirmation of this national practice. Arguably, the inclusion of the open norm in Article 14(4) can form a potential gateway for European harmonisation of the indirect horizontal application of fundamental rights, at least on the contractual relationship between the user and social media platform. Article 14(4) opens the door for the CJEU to balance the different interests in light of the unbalanced relationship between platform and user and to create case law that can form a bridge between national contract law, (European) consumer protection law, and fundamental rights protection. Therefore, in addition to the welcoming response of fundamental rights and IHRL scholars on Article 14 as a recognition of the calls and recommendations from international and European human rights bodies,[810] the inclusion is also a welcome addition from a contractual angle.

The interpretation of the exact obligation to observe when executing contractual sanctions is, however, far from clear. According to Article 14(4), the application and enforcement of *ex post* restrictions must be diligent, objective, and proportionate, and with due regard to the rights and legitimate interests of all parties involved. When enforcing the terms of the contract as set by the platform, it will have to adhere to certain safeguards 'in the interests of transparency, the protection of recipients of the service and the avoidance of unfair or arbitrary outcomes'.[811] The DSA's recitals solely prescribe the aimed outcome of the platforms' behaviour: acting diligently, objectively, and proportionately, beholds that the platform acts *non-arbitrary* and *non-discriminatory*.[812] On the aim of the DSA, scholars have argued that the DSA seeks to 'fairly balance the different, often conflicting, fundamental rights of the parties concerned'.[813] However, the DSA does not actually balance the different fundamental rights.[814] Rather, the obligation to balance the fundamental rights and interests has been shifted onto private undertakings without much guidance on what would be expected of them. Whether that has been the right approach could be discussed. Rather than a choice of the (European) legislator to regulate on the basis of a balancing

810. Quintais, Appelman and Fahy (n. 256) 17.
811. Recital (45) DSA.
812. Recital (47) DSA.
813. Wilman (n. 803).
814. Similar: Pietro Ortolani, 'The Resolution of content moderation disputes under the Digital Services Act' 2 544. Ortolani references the new rules in the DSA as a 'procedure before substance'-approach.

assessment of those rights at stake, it has chosen to create (yet another)[815] open norm that can be filled in by 'relevant international standards for the protection of human rights, such as the United Nations Guiding Principles on Business and Human Rights'.[816]

It seems likely that the CJEU will closely build upon the existing tests for diligent, objective, and proportionate behaviour. The principle of proportionality could, for example, be interpreted by reference to the Charter's Article 52 and as applied by the CJEU through the *Gebhard* test.[817] Consequently, a decision by a platform is not proportionate if a less intrusive measure exists which is capable of achieving the same objective or goal.[818] Others have argued that the proportionality test in Article 14(4) is not equal to the proportionality test for States envisaged in the Charter since 'the providers themselves also have fundamental rights'.[819] The platform has a varying margin of appreciation, depending on various factors, such as the platform's size, user dependence, and importance for disseminating ideas and information.[820] Especially since this obligation does not only apply to VLOPs, who presumably would have the resources and manpower to do the necessary research to define their new obligations under Article 14(4), the obligations equally apply to all providers of intermediary services. The right to freely allocate a business's resources falls within the business's own fundamental rights (Article 16)[821] For the latter group, their own fundamental rights protection could potentially be an argument to refrain from applying the obligations under Article 14(4).[822]

All of these arguments obstruct an easy conclusion on the application of the obligations under Article 14(4). The obligation to balance the various fundamental rights at stake in a diligent, objective, and proportionate manner seemingly follows

---

815. For some Member States, including the four examined here, this open norm is just an addition to their own national open norms in private law that would allow the inclusion of fundamental rights to balance contractual relationships. However, for other Member States that do not have such open norms, Art. 14(4) is a new gateway.
816. Recital (47) DSA.
817. *See* on the *Gebhard* test: §4.3.2.
818. *See* similar: Quintais, Appelman and Fahy (n. 256) 18.
819. Amelie Röhling and Johannes Weil, '"Marg bar Khamenei": Art. 14(4) DSA in light of Iranian Online Protest' [2023] Verfassungsblog https://verfassungsblog.de/marg-bar-khamenei/ (accessed 6 February 2023).
820. *Ibid.*, arguing that the tiered approach of the DSA should also apply to the interpretation of the obligations under Art. 14(4). However, the latter seems to be an intepprretation contra legem, since the European legislator has not chosen to apply the tiered system to Art. 14(4), but rather to apply the same standard to all intermediaries. A similar conclusion on the requirements (size, influence) for the margin of appreciation can be drawn from German law and case law, *see*: Heldt, *Intensive Third-Party Effect* (n. 20).
821. *See* the history of the development and an outline of the relevant case law in §4.3.3.3.
822. The text of Art. 14(4) refers to the rights and legitimate interest of *all parties involved*. This also includes the platforms itself, despite the DSA's text focusing mostly on the rights of the users. The assessment thus includes the platforms' freedom to conduct a business and right to property. Arguably, also the platform's freedom of expression must be balanced, *see* on that: Röhling and Weil (n. 819). *See* on the effects of the DSA's obligations on (smaller) businesses: Daphne Keller, 'The EU's New Digital Services Act and the Rest of the World' [2022] Verfassungsblog https://verfassungsblog.de/dsa-rest-of-world/ (accessed 1 February 2023).

from public law. However, even before Article 14(4) came into the picture, proportionality played a role in the execution of such sanctions. Through the open norms in national private law, the balancing of these values in contractual relationships has been addressed in national case law. Therefore, a first interpretation of the application of the obligations under Article 14(4) can be drawn from the Member States' case law of what would expectedly not be 'acting diligently, objectively, and proportionately'. All of the examples of Member States' case law references included below concern the execution of contractual sanctions for *ex post* restrictions. The following can be deducted from these cases. First, insignificant breaches of the terms must not lead to the permanent suspension or termination of the user account. Following Italian case law, minor breaches of the user terms, such as posting in good faith two short clips, including copyright-protected material, should not lead to suspension or termination of a user account, as such an access restriction is disproportionate.[823] Second, the user's data must not be removed before the user has had the opportunity to make use of all contractual and legal remedies.[824] As a result of these remedies, the conclusion may be that a proper balancing of the rights and interests of the parties requires reinstatement. If the user's data has been permanently deleted from the servers, that would cause irreparable harm. Third, following these national cases, a general requirement to send a prior warning to users that infringe the terms of service or the law can be deducted. The omission to send a prior warning to users before suspending a user account was found unfair in Germany and the Netherlands.[825] Lastly, sanctions that are listed in the terms of service may not be used to subjectively harm the user.[826] The case law leading to the conclusion in the second to fourth category will be discussed in more detail below.

7.3.4.1 *Permanent Removal of a User's Data Can Be Disproportionate*

From the case law in the Netherlands and Italy, the conclusion can be drawn that the permanent removal of a user's data that is hosted on a platform's server can be disproportionate. This will generally be the case if the user has not yet exhausted all legal remedies to challenge the platform's decision to impose a contractual sanction for a breach of contract.[827] The argument for disproportionality is simple. If the user has

823. *Tribunale di Pordenone (Preliminary reinstatement request)* (n. 153). The user had posted two short video clips including copyright-protected material. The user terms explicitly prohibited this. After making the user aware of the infringing material, the user immediately removed the content and apologised to the copyright holder. The court concluded (preliminary) that suspension of the user account was not proportionate.
824. *Microsoft OneDrive* (n. 199); *Provvedimento n. 26729 – CV157 – App Pokemon GO* (n. 150); *Provvedimento n. 29818 – CV195 – Dropbox* (n. 150); *Tribunale di Bologna sez. II (De Gaetano)* (n. 21).
825. *Landsgericht München (Reinstatement request)* (n. 110); *Bundesgerichtshof (Inhaltesperrung)* (n. 23); *Stadionverbod* (n. 165).
826. *Tribunale di Bologna sez. II (De Gaetano)* (n. 21).
827. The DSA provides recipients of the service with a right to an internal complaint mechanism (Art. 20) for at least up to six months after the decision took place. Therefore, permanent removal of the recipient's data within that time period would per default be disproportionate.

not exhausted the remedies, the decision of the platform to suspend access to the service might be overturned by the court. For example, if it turns out during the proceedings that the user did not breach the terms, the access to the account must be reinstated with immediate effect.[828] The latter was the case in *Microsoft OneDrive II*, where a user's access to his e-mail accounts was suspended due to an alleged violation of Microsoft's Service Agreement. However, the proceedings showed that the content shared was not illegal, leading to the conclusion that the block of the account was imposed without a ground in the terms. The Court ordered Microsoft to reinstate the user's access to his e-mail accounts with immediate effect.

Opposingly, in *Microsoft OneDrive*,[829] access to a cloud service account was suspended after the user had uploaded a file containing child pornography. In this preliminary ruling, the illegality of the photo was confirmed by the court.[830] The point of dispute is whether the plaintiff, despite breaching the user terms, should be granted access to the remaining non-infringing files on the cloud service. The user wanted to gain access to at least the documents stored in the cloud that do not breach the user terms in order to secure these non-infringing files for further use. Microsoft argued that allowing the user to access the documents stored on the cloud service would not be possible because it could entail risks to the rights and freedoms of third parties. The court dismisses the user's claim. In §4.14, the court concludes that the rule on child pornography and the consequential suspension of access to the files are not unreasonable. Contrarily, these articles serve to guarantee a safe usage of Microsoft's service. The consequence - denying access to *all* of the files on the cloud - is not disproportionate, despite the fact that less far-reaching remedies, such as a temporary ban or removal of the illegal image, existed.[831] Such measures would not have been as effective as the permanent suspension of access. On the proportionality of the chosen measure, the court finds that the user had not argued that the non-infringing files are of (emotional) value and that access to these files is necessary.[832] Potentially, if the plaintiff *had* argued the personal importance of gaining access to the non-infringing files, the outcome of the case would have been different. Therefore, despite the conclusion that Microsoft's user terms are not unreasonably burdensome and the

828. *Camping Olst* (n. 179).
829. *Microsoft OneDrive* (n. 199).
830. *Ibid.*, §§4.6-4.11.
831. Interestingly, the plaintiff had pointed to Facebook's removal strategy and consequences for the same image. Whereas Microsoft blocks the access to the account completely, Facebook had chosen to temporarily ban users. The Court uses this argument against the plaintiff, rather than in its favour. In §4.20 it concludes: 'With respect to [plaintiff's] argument that Facebook had apparently denied a user access to his account for a limited period of time after a similar picture had been found there, the Court observed that this also shows that the finding of this picture is not only a reason for Microsoft to impose sanctions.', thus using it as an argument to strengthen the proportionality of Microsoft's measure as seemingly other platforms would enforce the same content.
832. On the discussion of whether a full and permanent suspension after sharing illegal content was unreasonably burdensome (Art. 6:233(a)), the Court seems to put specific emphasise on the importance to stop the spread of child pornography as opposed to the plaintiff's interest to gain access to the remaining files. As it was not argued that the plaintiff had specific interest in regaining access to the blocked files, the Court weighs the protection of the child higher.

denied access to the cloud service was proportionate, the court imposes a prohibition on the platform to *permanently* delete the plaintiff's files to prevent any irrevocable damage in the timeframe where the plaintiff can start a main legal procedure.

On the assessment of the proportionality of a contractual sanction, the Italian Consumer Authority concluded that when the termination by the platform has the effect that users will lose virtual goods and/or virtual money that has intrinsic economic value, the platform will have to reimburse the costs made by the user. Excluding such refund payments in the user terms was found unfair as it negatively distorts the balance between the platform and the consumer.[833] The *Tribunale di Bologna* goes even further, highlighting the fact that the platform (Facebook) at the time of the proceeding stored and managed the data of 2.7 billion users, 'so that the preservation for some time of the data of the persons removed appears to be part of their normal contractual conduct and the destruction certainly constitutes conduct contrary to good faith'.[834] The court subsequently concludes that the platform has not lived up to its contractual obligations (hosting the user account), leading to a breach of contract for which damages are awardable.[835]

7.3.4.2 The Necessity to Send a Warning Prior to Moderating

For the mandatory suspension of users that frequently provide manifestly illegal content, Article 23(1) outlines the necessity to send a warning prior to enforcing the suspension. That warning must include the reasons for the possible suspension and the means of redress against the decision of the providers of the online platform.[836] Whether or not a similar obligation exists for the execution of sanctions included in Article 14(1) does not follow explicitly from the text of the DSA. One could argue that the omission to send a warning prior to suspending a user account could be a disproportionate execution.

An obligation to send a warning can similarly be observed in Member States' case law. However, in these cases, the omission to send a warning prior to executing sanctions was found *unfair* rather than disproportionate. Only in cases where the platform has a legitimate interest to immediately remove the content (mainly avoiding

833. *Provvedimento n. 26729 – CV157 – App Pokemon GO* (n. 150), §44: 'In particular, what determines a significant imbalance in the rights and obligations of consumers under the contract is the failure to provide any form of reimbursement for those who have purchased Exchange Items, virtual money or virtual goods that have been lost or not used as a result of the unilateral cancellation, suspension or termination of the user's account by the merchant.'

834. *Tribunale di Bologna sez. II (De Gaetano)* (n. 21), §5.2: 'Come si è detto, si tratta peraltro non di documentazione cartacea, ma immateriale, agevolmente conservabile, quantomeno per un certo tempo, senza costi eccessivi, sicchè la loro distruzione è sintomatica di una intenzione soggettiva di provocare un danno ingiusto alla controparte. La resistente vanta di gestire e conservare attualmente dati relativi a 2,7 miliardi di utenti, sicchè la conservazione per qualche tempo dei dati dei soggetti rimossi appare condotta contrattuale assolutamente esigibile e la loro distruzione configura senz'altro un comportamento contrario a buona fede.'

835. *See* more on the possibility to claim damages for wrongful or unjust removals, §7.4.2.2 below.

836. Recital (64) DSA.

liability and providing an attractive platform)[837] or there exists a pressing need to prevent crime,[838] content may be removed, and accounts may be suspended with immediate effect and before the user has been heard. If such an interest or pressing need is not present, the removal of the content is unreasonably disadvantaging for the user. A similar decision was reached by the Appeals Court of The Hague in the Netherlands in relation to a physical access case.[839] The above assessment of fairness applies to the validity of the content of the terms of service. As such, despite the fact that the suspensions under Article 23 do not fall within the scope of Article 14(4),[840] extending the practice in case law to be included in the scope of diligence in Article 14(4) increases the protection of users.

7.3.4.3 Sanctions May Not Be Used to 'Subjectively Do Harm'

The principle of objectivity can be interpreted in line with the conclusion of the Italian *Tribunale di Bologna* in *De Gaetano*. Facebook had permanently deleted *De Gaetano*'s account, without informing the user of the decision nor the underlying reasons. The court is (very) critical of the behaviour of the platform (Facebook) leading up to and during the proceeding and balances on the verge of an abuse of power on the platform's side. The court, on the basis of the behaviour of Facebook,[841] concludes that:

> The destruction of all contractual data reveals, as is evident, a profoundly improper contractual conduct, not allowing the progress of the relationship to be

837. *Bundesgerichtshof (Inhaltesperrung)* (n. 23), §104.
838. *Landsgericht München (Reinstatement request)* (n. 110). The account was suspended with immediate effect because it was used to share Child Exploitative Imagery. After the coming into force of the DSA, this situation will be covered by Art. 23, for which a warning must be sent.
839. *Stadionverbod* (n. 165). In the dispute, the question was raised whether a private undertaking, without the mandate and or delegated task from the government, can impose on a natural person a restraint of their liberty (not physically being allowed near and in a stadium). When a sanction has been agreed upon, it is up to the discretion of the proprietor to decide on the breach of the user terms and the consequential refusal of access. It is of no importance whether the stadium ban had been based on a presumption, rather than a conviction, as 'the criminal law principle of the presumption of innocence does not apply in a contractual relationship (if any) between the parties'. For user terms to be valid, the user terms must have been communicated to the users before invoking them as a basis for the house right. When communicated in due time, these house rules will become a part of the contractual relationship between the parties. Though, a sole reference to the existence of terms and conditions, without including the terms and conditions themselves, can be sufficient to fulfil the requirement of communication.
840. *See* above in §7.3.3.
841. *See* an example the court's critique in §5.1. on the statements made by the platform that it questions whether there is a contractual relationship between the plaintiff and the platform: 'L'eccezione è palesemente infondata e francamente contraddittoria.' (The objection is patently unfounded and frankly contradictory, translation by the author). Subsequently, the court addresses the fact that Facebook had obstructed the proceedings by simply deleting all the relevant data from its servers: 'Tale giustificazione, tuttavia, non persuade, posto che la loro distruzione non appare imposta da alcuna esigenza oggettiva, trattandosi di dati immateriali agevolmente conservabili, quantomeno per un certo periodo.' (This justification, however, is not persuasive, since their destruction does not appear to be imposed by any objective requirement, since we are dealing with intangible data that can be easily preserved, at least for a certain period of time) (§5.2).

> reconstructed, thus a negotiating conduct that is manifestly contrary to the principles of good faith and fairness in the execution of the contract that underpins all the legal systems of countries with a legal civilisation akin to ours.[842]

The decision of the platform to take the decision is attributed to *revenge*. On the basis of the behaviour of the platform (a completely unmotivated removal, followed a few days after the applicant, in his capacity as defence lawyer for another user, had sent a warning letter to Facebook Italia) and the fact that the platform has not given any reasons or explanation for the termination of the account and the destruction of all the data, the court concluded that the sanctions have been applied 'with the desire to retaliate against the lawyer, causing a very serious infringement of clear fundamental rights of the user'.[843] The court concludes that the platform has abused its power to impose sanctions and orders the platform to pay (immaterial) damages.

7.3.5 The Statement of Reasons

In addition to the obligation in Article 14(4), Article 17 obliges providers of hosting services, which includes social media platforms, to send a statement of reasons to the affected users when moderating on the basis of an infringement of the law or the terms of service. As such, Article 17 imposes another procedural obligation on platforms when executing contractual sanctions. The mandatory statement of reasons must be sent when a platform imposes restrictions on: (i) the visibility of content or when it disables access to, removes or demotes content; (ii) when it suspends, terminates, or restricts monetary payments; or (iii) when it suspends, terminates, or restricts the user's account or the entire service.[844] Excluded from the obligation are the application of these restrictions to 'deceptive high-volume commercial content disseminated through intentional manipulation of the service, in particular inauthentic use of the service such as the use of bots or fake accounts or other deceptive uses of the service'.[845] In those circumstances there is no obligation for a statement of reasons, presumably as this would cause an undue burden on the operator.

The obligation to send a statement of reason is not new, though its explicit inclusion in the DSA aids the effective redress of users.[846] The practice has equally been observed in case law of the Member States. In the Netherlands, the District Court of Amsterdam has interpreted the due diligence obligation of the platform under the proposed Article 14 DSA (then Article 12) and concludes that 'such due diligence implies, in any case, an obligation to notify the user of each deletion, where, depending on the content of the message, efforts should be made to justify the deletion in such a

842. §5.2: 'La distruzione di tutti i dati contrattuali rivela, com'è evidente, una condotta contrattuale profondamente scorretta, non consentendo di riscostruire l'andamento del rapporto, dunque un comportamento negoziale palesemente contrario ai canoni di buona fede e di correttezza nell'esecuzione del contratto che informano tutti gli ordinamenti dei paesi a civiltà giuridica a noi affine.'
843. *Tribunale di Bologna sez. II (De Gaetano)* (n. 21), §6.
844. Article 17(1) DSA.
845. Article 17(2) and recital (55) DSA.
846. Wilman (n. 803) 11.

way that the user can learn from the decision'.[847] The Court subsequently orders reinstatement of the claimant's user account, because the platform had not lived up to the due diligence requirements.[848] In Italy, it is settled case law that the omission of a statement of reasons leads to unfairness.[849] Without a provision of the reason(s) for termination or suspension, the users' right to defend themselves would be impaired as they would not have adequate possibilities to complain against the decision.[850] That reasoning also follows from the conclusion that 'the user should be able to learn from its mistake' highlighted in the Dutch case. Those interests are equally reflected in the codification of the statement of reasons in Article 17. Following Article 17(4), the statement of reason's information 'shall, in particular, be such as to reasonably allow the recipient of the service concerned to effectively exercise the possibilities for redress'.

The exact information to be included in the statement of reasons is outlined in Article 17(3). For normative restrictions based solely on the terms of service of the platform, the statement of reason provides the user with the necessary information to challenge the decision. For these restrictions, the platform must include a reference to the contractual ground relied on and explanations as to why the information is considered to be incompatible with that ground.[851]

7.3.6 Consequences of Infringements of the Obligations for Execution

The consequences of an infringement of the procedural obligations for the execution of sanctions in the DSA are outlined in Articles 52-54 DSA. The supervision and enforcement of the obligations in the DSA are designated to the national Member States' Digital Services Coordinators (Article 49-51 DSA).

First, an infringement of the obligations under the DSA can lead to penalty payments.[852] It is up to the Member States to define the rules concerning these

847. *Van Haga v. LinkedIn* (n. 23), §4.21.
848. In *Van Haga v. LinkedIn*, the access to an account was unduly restricted and had to be reinstated. Based on the underlying aim of the (then still only proposed) DSA, the effect that the restriction of access to LinkedIn may have for the plaintiff's freedom of expression, the fact that the user terms give LinkedIn a very broad and undefined scope for terminating the contract, the Court finds that the (permanent) restriction on Van Haga to access his LinkedIn account breached the platform's duty of care, which resulted in a negligent removal from the platform. According to the Court in §4.22: 'LinkedIn should be aware that its obligation to provide reasons in concrete cases increases, the more vaguely defined and/or less known the policy it claims to be applying in its decisions is.' This decision is in line with the previous decision in *Hoge Raad (Goglio/SMQ Group)* (2018) ECLI:NL:HR:2018:141. The Supreme Court concludes in this case that Art. 6:248 can lead to additional requirements for the termination of a 'long-term agreement' (*duurovereenkomst*). The implications of this outcome in a civil case before a national court is discussed in the following paragraph.
849. *Tribunale di Pordenone (Preliminary reinstatement request)* (n. 153); *Tribunale di Bologna sez. II (De Gaetano)* (n. 21); *Provvedimento n. 29976 – CV224 – TikTok* (n. 148); *Provvedimento n. 29817 – CV194 – Google Drive* (n. 141); *Provvedimento n. 26596 – CV154 – Whatsapp* (n. 143).
850. *Provvedimento n. 29817 – CV194 – Google Drive* (n. 141), §34.
851. Article 17(3)(e).
852. Article 52 DSA.

penalties,[853] though they must be effective, proportionate, and dissuasive.[854] Imposable penalties cover the ability of a Digital Services Coordinator to impose fines or to request a judicial authority to impose fines (Article 51 (2)(c)) and/or periodic penalty payment (Article 51 (2)(d)). Article 52 regulates the maximum amount that can be imposed.[855] Second, users have the right to lodge a complaint with the Digital Services Coordinator in the Member State where the user is located.[856] This, in turn, enables the Digital Services Coordinator to use its investigation and enforcement powers under Article 51. Third, users have the right to seek compensation from the platform operator.[857] This right applies irrespective of the exemptions of liability for platform operators under the DSA and covers the damages suffered by users that are caused by an infringement of the obligations.[858]

7.4 REMEDIES FOR USERS

The user has various redress mechanisms available to challenge a content decision taken by a social media platform. The redress mechanisms following from the national legal systems of the Member States are supplemented by voluntary remedies outlined in the terms and service[859] and obligatory contractual remedies prescribed by the DSA. It will be the platform's duty to inform the users about these various redress mechanisms when taking a restriction. Article 17(3)(f) obliges platforms to include in the statement of reasons clear and user-friendly information on the possibilities for redress available to the user, in particular, where applicable through internal complaint-handling mechanisms, out-of-court dispute settlement and judicial redress.[860] Despite arguments that alternative dispute resolution mechanisms would give platforms quasi-judicial power,[861] the DSA does not favour one mechanism over the other and increases the users' free choice of redress by leaving it up to the user to choose which redress mechanism the user would like to use. Users are not obliged to first exhaust the internal complaint-handling system before initiating an out-of-court dispute settlement proceeding or to file a complaint before a national court.[862]

853. Article 52(1) DSA.
854. Article 52(2) DSA.
855. Article 52(3) regarding the fines and Art. 52(4) regarding the penalty payments.
856. Article 53 DSA.
857. Article 54 DSA.
858. Article 54 and recital (121).
859. Based on the general principle of private autonomy, the parties can decide on the remedies available for a breach of contract. These remedies can be freely agreed upon by the parties. It is therefore not possible to give an abstract overview of the possibilities. For a concrete idea of the remedies, the terms of service of social media platforms will have to be consulted. They are therefore not individually addressed in this paragraph. They are included as an element in the roadmap, because of the stricter rules applicable to *obligatory* contractual remedies.
860. Article 17(3)(f).
861. Belli (n. 6), p. 82.
862. Article 21(1) DSA dictates that any user – regardless of whether they have used the internal complaint-handling system – is entitled to select any out-of-court certified dispute settlement body to resolve an issue related to an access or moderation decision. The third paragraph of 21(1) extends that line to national courts: 'The first subparagraph is without prejudice to the

The various possibilities to claim redress are described briefly below to give an idea of the users' increased power to challenge access and moderation decisions. First, the platform's obligation to offer an internal complaint-handling system is addressed (Article 20 DSA), followed by the out-of-court dispute settlement (Article 21 DSA), and lastly, the DSA's obligations on the availability of legal redress in the Member States' national legal systems are outlined. Member States may opt to create an administrative complaint-handling mechanism,[863] but since it is not yet clear which Member States will make use of this option and under which rules, this option is not further addressed in this book.[864]

7.4.1 Obligatory Contractual Remedies

For online platforms that do not fall within the threshold of a small or micro-enterprise, the DSA dictates mandatory contractual remedies. These rules apply to an online platform operator with over fifty employees and an annual turnover of (more than) EUR 10 million.[865]

7.4.1.1 Internal Complaint-Handling Systems

Article 20 DSA obliges providers of online platforms to provide an internal complaint-handling system. Internal complaint-handling systems mainly serve the role of filtering out obviously wrong decisions before these decisions go to court. In case of an evidently wrongful or disproportionate decision, the platform must reverse its decision.[866] This is in line with the aim of the system of internal complaint-handling, which must ensure that the users of platforms are able to 'easily and effectively contest certain decisions of providers of online platforms concerning the illegality of content'.[867] Decisions that can be challenged through the internal complaint-handling system are not limited to access and content moderation decisions. The decision not to act on a notice of allegedly illegal or infringing content can also be challenged. That will significantly aid similar cases as the above-discussed decision of *HateAid & EUJS versus Twitter* (§6.4.4.1), as it would have allowed the claimants to challenge their case internally before filing a civil case against the platform.

---

right of the recipient of the service concerned to initiate, at any stage, proceedings to contest those decisions by the providers of online platforms before a court in accordance with the applicable law.'

863. Recital (39) DSA.
864. Further research would be welcome, *see* more reflections in §9.3.1.
865. Article 19 DSA excludes micro and small enterprises from the rules in section 3. The criteria for micro and small enterprises can be found in the Annex to the Commission Recommendation 2003/361/EC.
866. Article 20(4) DSA.
867. Recital (58) DSA.

The system must be easy to access, user-friendly and enable and facilitate the submission of sufficiently precise and adequately substantiated complaints.[868] In case the internal complaint-handling systems are based on automated means, the final decision on the complaint must be taken under the supervision of a human ('appropriately qualified staff').[869] The procedural rules for the internal complaint-handling system must be outlined in the terms of service. Since the latter obligation follows from Article 14(1) DSA, this leads to a discussion as to what extent the procedural rules are covered by the obligations in Article 14(4).[870] The internal complaints mechanism does not form a part of 'using the service'. It is a remedy to resolve disputes over restrictions that are imposed by a platform. Arguing that the rules of procedure of the internal complaint-handling system itself are a restriction on the use of the platform's service broadens the scope of Article 14(1) to also include the (contractual) remedies available to decisions taken on the basis of Article 14(1). Contrarily, one could argue that the rules of procedure for the internal complaint-handling system are intentionally included by the legislator to safeguard that the decisions on user complaints are taken in compliance with the increased due diligence obligations in Article 14(4).

Not all providers of intermediary services are obliged to offer an internal complaints mechanism. In case they choose to do so, the decisions taken are subject to the obligations in Article 14(4). Providing access to an internal complain-handling system is voluntary for providers of intermediary services that do not qualify as online platform providers. The latter (platform providers) are obliged to offer such a service. Therefore, it would make sense to make the procedural rules of the internal complaints mechanisms subject to the obligations in Article 14(4) since the *voluntary* mechanisms of providers of intermediary services are not subject to the rules in Article 20. However, to make matters more complicated, Article 20 prescribes its own due diligence obligation for the obliged internal complaints mechanism for online platforms, which rules deviate from the obligation in Article 14(4). The obligation in Article 14(4) is stricter than the rules in Article 20(4). Stating that voluntary mechanisms should be subject to stricter rules than mandatory mechanisms is illogical and could discourage intermediary service providers from providing voluntary mechanisms altogether.

The interplay between the obligations in 14(4) and 20(4) is unclear. From the recitals to the DSA, it seems that the legislator intended that these mechanisms would solely be subjected to the obligations in Article 20(4).[871] A reference to the inclusion of the legitimate interests of the users or their fundamental rights is not made.

868. Article 20(3) DSA.
869. Article 20(6) DSA.
870. *See also* above §7.3.3.
871. Recital (58): Recipients of the service should be able to easily and effectively contest certain decisions of providers of online platforms concerning the illegality of content or its incompatibility with the terms and conditions that negatively affect them. Therefore, providers of online platforms should be required to provide for internal complaint-handling systems, which meet certain conditions that aim to ensure that the systems are easily accessible and lead to swift, non-discriminatory, non-arbitrary and fair outcomes, and are subject to human review where automated means are used. (underlining by the author).

Table 7.1 Differences in the Due Diligence Obligation in Articles 14 and 20 DSA

Due Diligence Obligation in Article 14(4)	*Due Diligence Obligation in Article 20(4)*
Providers of intermediary services shall act in a diligent, objective and proportionate manner in applying and enforcing the restrictions referred to in paragraph 1, with due regard to the rights and legitimate interests of all parties involved, including the fundamental rights of the recipients of the service, such as the freedom of expression, freedom and pluralism of the media, and other fundamental rights and freedoms as enshrined in the Charter.	Providers of online platforms shall handle complaints submitted through their internal complaint-handling system in a timely, non-discriminatory, diligent and non-arbitrary manner.

If an internal complaint-handling system does not fulfil the requirements outlined in Article 20, for example, if there is no human supervision, the system is not easily accessible, or the outcome of the decision is arbitrary, then this results in an infringement of the DSA. To these infringements, the same consequences as outlined above in §7.3.6 apply. Since the *rules of procedure* for the internal complaint-handling system must be outlined in the terms of service, not following these rules results in a breach of contract.

7.4.1.2 Out-of-Court Dispute Settlement

The decisions that can be brought before the internal complaint-handling system can equally be brought before an out-of-court dispute settlement body.[872] The users are free to select *any* settlement body that has been certified by a Member State.[873] The decision of the dispute settlement body is not binding.[874] In case the disputed decision has been resolved before in relation to the same information and the same grounds of illegality or incompatibility, platforms are not obliged to take part in resolving the dispute through the settlement body.[875] Exactly which posts fall within that description is unclear. For example, if user A challenges the deletion of a video on the basis of a copyright violation, would the platform then be able to refuse to participate in out-of-court dispute resolution when user B challenges the deletion of a video including the same copyright-infringing material? Must the video be identical to fulfil these requirements? As the answer to this question defines which proceedings the platform can avoid participating in, it is an important point for further research to clarify. It is in the interest of the platform not to participate in proceedings before an out-of-court

872. Article 21(1) DSA.
873. Bodies are approved by the national Digital Services Coordinator for five years at a time. To be approved, bodies need to fulfil the requirements in Art. 21(3) DSA.
874. Article 21 DSA: 'The certified out-of-court dispute settlement body shall not have the power to impose a binding settlement of the dispute on the parties.'
875. Article 21(2) DSA.

dispute settlement body because of the costs involved, which are borne by the platform,[876] and, generally, to prevent burdensome proceedings over the deletion of identical (re-)posted content.

7.4.2 General Contract Law Remedies

Regardless of the applicability of the DSA, a breach of the terms of service can be brought before Member States' national courts in accordance with national private law. Social media platforms are obliged to inform their users of these options.[877] Wrongful moderation decisions constitute a breach of contract because the platform removes content that is not illegal and/or does not breach the terms of service. It, therefore, does not fulfil its contractual obligation to host the content. If outlined in the terms, users can claim performance of the contract (*pacta sunt servanda*). That would concretely mean the reinstatement of unjustly removed content or access to the platform. Moreover, they can claim compensation for damage suffered by the platform's breach of contract in line with the national rules on redress.[878] The right to claim reinstatement and to claim damages for unjust removals or terminations are both discussed below. The results of the comparative study showed that the differences in the outcome of cases between users and social media platforms are minimal between the examined Member States, but there are some.[879] Specifically, with regard to the possibility of claiming damages for unjust removals or suspensions, the case law showed different approaches in the Member States.[880]

7.4.2.1 Put-Back Claims for Wrongful Moderation Decisions

Users' options for put-back claims for wrongful moderation decisions have been explicitly left untouched in the DSA.[881] Put-back claims only apply to breach of contract, not to infringement of the DSA procedural guidelines. Content removed without notifying the user through a statement of reasons should not lead to a

---

876. Article 21(5) DSA. When the user wins, the platform bears all the costs of both parties and the settlement body. If the platform wins, the platform also bears the costs of the proceeding, including its own costs, but not the user's costs. The payment burden solely flips to the user's side in case the user 'manifestly acts in bad faith'.
877. Article 17(3)(f) and recital (39) DSA.
878. These legal systems can differ greatly, especially along the line of continental legal systems and common law systems. *See* for an overview of the rules on performance claims in Europe: Hein Kötz, 'Claims for Performance' in Hein Kötz, Gill Mertens and Tony Weir (eds), *European Contract Law* (Oxford University Press 2017) https://doi.org/10.1093/oso/9780198800040.003.0012 (accessed 13 March 2023).
879. *See* the conclusions of the comparative study above in §2.4.
880. National civil litigation can also lead to jurisdictional problems, *see* for examples of this: Ortolani (n. 814) 567.
881. Recital (39): 'This Regulation shall not prevent the relevant national judicial or administrative authorities from issuing, on the basis of the applicable Union or national law, an order to restore content, where such content was in compliance with the terms and conditions of the provider of the intermediary service but has been erroneously considered as illegal by that provider and has been removed.'

reinstatement claim. In the latter situation, it is the *procedure* that went wrong, not the legal ground for removing it. In case of a wrongful moderation decision, it is the *ground* (whether on the basis of the law or the terms) that is challenged.

Identical to any other contractual dispute, wrongful moderation decisions imply that the platform breaches its own terms. It has not hosted the content that it said it would host, or it has terminated or suspended access to the account outside the scope of the contract, meaning that the platform has failed to supply the service it was obliged to. A discrepancy in access to an effective reinstatement of wrongful content did not follow from the comparative study. The four national systems included in the comparative study all had mechanisms in place to successfully claim the reinstatement of wrongful decisions - both for content and for accounts. Therefore, drastic changes from Member States in the case of a wrongful moderation decision on the basis of terms of service are not to be expected. These cases will be settled by applying national contract law.

7.4.2.2 Claiming Damages for Unjust Removals or Suspensions

Inherently, content restore-claims are time-consuming to challenge before a court. In the months the case is pending before a court, the user potentially loses followers and interaction, and if the user's feed is used professionally, they lose money. Therefore, perhaps for some, the most interesting part of this chapter concerns the possibility of claiming damages in case of a wrongful moderation decision, a decision that is not in line with the principles set out in Article 14(4) DSA or another obligation in the DSA. Damages for a wrongful moderation decision follow the general rules for awarding damages in the Member States' national legal systems. These rules must similarly apply to any damage the user suffers from an infringement of the obligations in the DSA.[882] For the latter, the DSA adds that the platform operator should be liable for any damage that is caused by an infringement of an obligation in the DSA.[883] Since the DSA is included in the *Collective Redress Directive*,[884] it means that infringements of the DSA can be addressed as a collective action.[885]

The DSA's right to claim compensation deviates from the similar right in the GDPR's Article 82. The latter refers explicitly to 'material' and 'non-material' damage, whereas Article 54 DSA speaks of 'any damage or loss'. Whether or not these are to be

882. Article 54: 'Recipients of the service shall have the right to seek, in accordance with Union and national law, compensation from providers of intermediary services, in respect of any damage or loss suffered due to an infringement by those providers of their obligations under this Regulation.'
883. Recital (121): 'Without prejudice to the provisions on the exemption from liability provided for in this Regulation as regards the information transmitted or stored at the request of a recipient of the service, a provider of intermediary services should be liable for the damages suffered by recipients of the service that are caused by an infringement of the obligations set out in this Regulation by that provider.'
884. Directive (EU) 2020/1828 of the European Parliament and of the Council of 25 November 2020 on representative actions for the protection of the collective interests of consumers and repealing Directive 2009/22/EC.
885. Wilman (n. 803) 12.

interpreted equally is not clear. Apart from the differences in the textual wording of damage (material/non-material versus all damage or loss), the respective articles both connect the right to receive compensation to an infringement of the regulation. The text of the DSA beholds a broader scope than the GDPR, which supposes at least a similar, if not broader, right for the user. Since presumably the articles' application is similar, the outcome of the pending questions on the interpretation of 'non-material damages' of Article 82 GDPR before the CJEU will prove useful to interpret the claims for damages for an infringement of the DSA.[886] In his opinion of the case, AG Campos Sánchez-Bordona argues for a strict interpretation of Article 82.[887] First, compensation cannot be awarded for an infringement of the Regulation that has not caused the person to suffer damage. The presumption that an irrebuttable presumption of damage exists once an infringement has occurred is to be dismissed. Even in the case of non-material damage, the infringement must create more harm to the data subject than mere feelings of annoyance or upset.[888] The interpretation of the latter is left to the national courts:

> I am in no doubt that there is a fine line between mere upset (which is not eligible for compensation) and genuine non-material damage (which is eligible for compensation), and I am also aware of how complicated it is to delimit, in the abstract, the two categories and apply them to a particular dispute. That difficult task falls to the courts of the Member States, which will probably be unable to avoid in their rulings the perception prevailing in society at a given time regarding the permissible degree of tolerance where the subjective effects of infringement of a provision in this area do not exceed a de minimis level.[889]

What exactly falls within the scope of 'damage' within the DSA is unclear. The case of the (disproportionate)[890] measures taken by YouTube against the YouTube channel *Tour de Tietema* during the Tour de France of 2021 makes a good example

886. CJEU Case C-300/21 (*Österreichische Post*). The case concerns three questions:

    (1) Does the award of compensation under Art. 82 of Regulation (EU) 2016/679 1 (the GDPR) also require, in addition to infringement of provisions of the GDPR, that an applicant must have suffered harm, or is the infringement of provisions of the GDPR in itself sufficient for the award of compensation?
    (2) Does the assessment of the compensation depend on further EU-law requirements in addition to the principles of effectiveness and equivalence?
    (3) Is it compatible with EU law to take the view that the award of compensation for non-material damage presupposes the existence of a consequence of the infringement of at least some weight that goes beyond the upset caused by that infringement?

887. Opinion of AG Campos Sánchez-Bordona to CJEU Case C-300/21 (*Österreichische Post*) 6 October 2022, ECLI:EU:C:2022:756. *See* criticism on the opinion: Alexia Pato, 'Compensation for non-material damages under the GDPR: An uphill battle' [2022] Verfassungsblog https://verfassungsblog.de/gdpr-non-material/ (accessed 12 March 2023).
888. Opinion of AG Campos Sánchez-Bordona to CJEU Case C-300/21 (*Österreichische Post*), points 112-116.
889. *Ibid.*, point 116.
890. The case shows similarities with the decision of *Tribunale di Pordenone (Preliminary reinstatement request)* (n. 153), where the court concluded that a termination of a user account for minor breaches of the terms of services (short videos with copyright-protected content) was disproportionate.

from practice. *Tour de Tietema* offers a YouTube channel[891] where they report sports events (in a non-traditional way). During the summer of 2021, the channel reported from the Tour de France-route. In two videos, the Tour de France was featured in the background of a video for several seconds. Consequently, the Amaury Sports Organisation (ASO) sent a take-down request to YouTube on the basis of an infringement of broadcasting rights. As a consequence, five videos were taken offline (including three videos that did not show the Tour de France), and the channel was suspended. The three videos not featuring the Tour de France were taken down without the channel breaching the terms. This wrongful moderation decision constitutes, in turn, a breach of contract on the side of YouTube. After complaints, those three videos were reinstated. The other two videos have remained offline. Whether or not the take-down is challengeable depends on whether a fair use-exemption (or similar) would apply to broadcasting rights or not. The suspension of the channel itself will presumably be disproportionate under the new rules in Article 14(4) DSA. Defining their suffered damage is difficult. Bas Tietema, one of the channel's owners, mentioned that during the twenty-three days' period in which the Tour de France takes place, the channel's statistics show that the channel had gained approximately 3,000-4,000 new followers a day during the period the Tour de France took place. When the channel was blocked, this increase stagnated immediately. The channel was blocked for a week during the twenty-three days of the Tour de France. Then, what is their loss? If the trend of followers had continued, they would have gained seven times, on average, 3,500 new followers, which equals a loss of 24,500 potential followers. The transposition of that loss to a monetary amount will be up to the national court.

Leaving the possibility to claim damages and the interpretation of what those damages are up to the Member States' national legal systems puts users in unequal situations across the Union. Following the comparative study, successful claims for damages for unjust removals or suspensions have solely been observed in Italian case law. Following Italian case law, users who had their content wrongfully removed and/or access to their account blocked have successfully claimed non-material damages in several cases. A user was awarded EUR 14,000 for the wrongful removal of two Facebook pages featuring (historical) military items and a suspension of his personal Facebook account.[892] The Court specifically stated that the *economic* value of the pages – estimated at around EUR 100 – was irrelevant to the determination of the damages.[893]

891. https://www.youtube.com/c/TourdeTietema. The channel is operated from the Netherlands and currently has 155,000 subscribers (15 March 2023).

892. *Tribunale di Bologna sez. II (De Gaetano)* (n. 21), point 7: 'Since [Facebook] has not produced any evidence in support of a reduced use of the personal profile and of the two pages, and since the applicant has alleged a very intense use of them, given, moreover, the impossibility alleged by [Facebook] of restoring the account, and consequently, the permanent loss of all the contacts, messages and documents stored therein, it appears therefore fair to estimate the immaterial damage suffered by the applicant at EUR 10,000.00 for the personal profile, which is more directly connected with his personal rights, and Euro 2,000.00 for each of the two pages which, although they are also an expression of his relationship life, appear to be connected with interests of a more purely hobbyist nature.'

893. *Ibid.*, point 7: 'Notwithstanding the well-known estimate of the average value, in commercial terms, of a Facebook account in the order of slightly less than EUR 100, which takes into account the usability by the operator of the personal data provided by the users for advertising

A user cannot monetise the pages in the same way as Facebook monetises them by selling advertisement space. The court based the value of the accounts on the impact the removal has had on the social life of the user included in Article 21 of the Italian Constitution (freedom of expression). Similarly, in the case before the *Corte d'Appello di L'Aquila,* a user was awarded EUR 3,000 for the wrongful removal of three posts.[894] In Germany, the *OLG München* comes to a contrary decision. The German court finds that the request of EUR 1,500 for the (temporary) suspension of a user account must be denied, since the user had not suffered any *material* damages.[895] According to the court, 'a claim for damages, be it from §280 I or §§823 ff. BGB fails – regardless of all other prerequisites – because the plaintiff has not explained in a comprehensible manner that he has suffered material damage in the amount claimed'. The court concludes that 'a temporary restriction of private communication possibilities on Facebook does not in itself have an asset value'. In the other two examined Member States (Denmark, and the Netherlands), the outcome is unclear as damages had not been requested in the assessed cases.[896] These examples point to a problem that is likely to arise, even without comparing all national legal systems in the European Union on users' potential ability to claim (immaterial) damages. The differences at the Member State level are problematic because it means that users in different Member States would or would not be awarded damages for the exact same infringement of an obligation by the exact same social media platform. Unfortunately, the scope of this book does not allow for a full European study on the possibilities to claim damages for breaches by social media platforms, but such a study would be highly necessary to assess the differences in legal redress of users in the various Member States. This is especially important in light of the users' fundamental right to an effective remedy and to a fair trial in Article 47 Charter.

---

and commercial purposes (the estimate suggested by Deutsche Bank Research is approximately EUR 88; an average estimate can be arrived at, for example, by dividing the operator's turnover by the number of users; However, it must be borne in mind that this is an average figure, which is likely to be affected by the existence of a very significant number of registered but unused profiles, against which there are profiles and pages of a very significant value), in the present case it must be borne in mind that it is not the economic value of the user's personal data and account, which is relevant for the operator, that is relevant here, but the damage suffered by the user in the event of its removal, on account of the obvious impairment of his or her relationship life.' (translation by the author).

894. *Corte appello L'Aquila (Correggiari)* (n. 21), point 10: 'taking into account both their duration (approximately three months) and the fact that the period of the plaintiff's suspension from the platform was not continuous, as well as taking into account that the plaintiff complained of not having been able to cultivate his relationships, merely stating their total number (approximately 2.500 persons), without however specifying whether and how many of these temporarily suspended relationships were significant in terms of interpersonal relations nor the frequency of the contacts temporarily lost and not otherwise cultivable. (...) In view of all these elements, it is considered appropriate to estimate, on an equitable basis, the damage suffered by settling at the present time an amount of €3,000.' (translation by the author).

895. *Ibid.*, §1160-164.

896. There is no known case law on request for damages for wrongful moderation on social media platforms in Denmark. *See* for the Netherlands: *BLCKBX/Google* (n. 22); *FvD/Google* (n. 189); *Van Haga v. LinkedIn* (n. 23); *Café Weltschmerz/YouTube* (n. 190).

7.5 CONCLUSION ON THE CONTENT AND ENFORCEMENT OF USER TERMS

This research's final sub-question – *when and how can users oppose a platform's moderation decision?* – can be answered through a combination of factors. The extent to which social media platforms can freely draft their terms of service, along with the procedural rules outlined in the Digital Services Act for executing contractual sanctions, as well as the available national and contractual remedies for breaches of contractual obligations, will all play a role in determining the answer.

A social media platform's terms must be valid before any contractual sanctions can be executed. Terms are valid if their substance is not prohibited (e.g., 'signing-up for the platform means your organs become the platform's property'), the transparency obligations in the UCTD and the DSA must have been fulfilled, and the term may not be unfair. The latter means, *inter alia*, that platforms are not at liberty to fully restrict the fundamental rights of a contracting party through their terms of service. Lastly, the obligations under the terms must be interpretable. If any of the above requirements for validity are not fulfilled, the terms as a whole or the specific term are not binding on the user. A moderation decision taken on the basis of a non-binding term constitutes a breach of contract on the side of the social media platform. A social media platform equally breaches the contract if it wrongfully removes content or suspends/terminates a user account. The user can invoke legal remedies against that breach. The number of options for redress depends on the contract between platform and user. First, users can make use of the remedies that follow generally from contract law. These include a request for an injunction to reinstate the content (performance of the contract) and a claim for compensation for the damages caused by the breach. Second, the DSA obliges the platform to include two types of remedies in the terms of service: an internal complaints mechanism and an out-of-court dispute resolution. Third, the platform can voluntarily include additional contractual remedies in the terms.

A user's breach of a valid term can be enforced. The sanctions that a social media platform can impose on users for a breach of the terms must be outlined in the terms of service. Moreover, these contractual sanctions will be subjected to the procedural requirements after the DSA becomes applicable. Following the DSA, a social media platform must, first, act diligently, objectively, and proportionately when executing contractual sanctions, and second, it must send a statement of reasons to the affected user. The DSA equally lists the consequences in case a platform fails to comply with the procedural obligations for executing contractual sanctions. Based on Articles 52-54 DSA, a social media platform can be subjected to penalties defined by the Member States, which can consist of fines and/or periodic penalty payments. Users have the right to complain about the infringement to a Digital Services Coordinator, and they have the right to claim compensation for any damage that was caused by the infringement. Since the obligatory contractual remedies (internal complaints-mechanism, out-of-court dispute resolution) follow from the DSA, an infringement to offer those remedies constitutes an infringement to which the above consequences apply equally.

Concluding Part

CHAPTER 8

A Roadmap Fit for Platform Purpose

8.1 ANSWER TO THE MAIN RESEARCH QUESTION

The objective of the study underlying this book is to provide a harmonised approach to addressing issues related to access and moderation decisions on social media platforms in the European Union. The book comprises six substantive chapters that outline four independent layers for the roadmap, designed to reflect the current legal landscape applicable to social media platforms' terms of service. This results in a final roadmap that answers the main research question: *How can the positive law applicable to access and moderation decisions by social media platforms be consolidated into a guide for decision-makers in the European Union?*

If you are a predominantly visual thinker (like me), you can turn to the end of this section to see the visual representation of *the European roadmap to navigate online access rights* as the answer to the research question. For others, a translation of the visual representation into text is included here. The roadmap is made up of four layers: the foundational, access, content, and enforcement layers. These layers correspond to the various legal discussions concerning access and moderation decisions on social media platforms. The first, the foundational layer, outlines the legal basis for social media platforms to impose access restrictions. The elements of the foundational layer are the result of the observations in the Member States' national legal systems in the comparative study in Chapter 2. Following the case law of the Member States, national courts have almost exclusively relied on the right to property to resolve access and moderation decisions, both concerning physical and online property. This finding in the case law has subsequently been contextualised within the legal literature in Chapter 3 and the doctrinal study in Chapter 4 to conclude that the right to property forms the best foundational starting point to address access and content restrictions on social media platforms. The foundation layer's elements consist of the platform's right to property and the two choices a platform has in relation to its property: the right to exclude the use and access to the property and the freedom to use the property. The latter, in turn, is further supported by the platform's freedom to exercise an economic activity – a sub-freedom of the freedom to conduct a business in Article 16 of the Charter of Fundamental Rights.

The second layer, the access layer, covers the three ways a platform operator can shape the access possibilities to its platform by exercising its right to property: open, conditional, and denied access. Issues addressed in this layer cover access restrictions and denials to the platform's service. This layer also outlines the limitations to the platform's right to exclude, which form a legal basis for users to force the platform to contract. These limitations that can lead to an obligation to contract include secondary legislation (equality and non-discrimination), the horizontal direct effect of fundamental and constitutional rights, and the public' and the users' social interest. Currently, competition law does not form a basis for access claims, but regulatory intervention could change that in the future. Competition law has, therefore, been included optionally in the roadmap by means of a dotted line. A successful access claim on either of these grounds obliges the platform operator to provide access to the platform. To what extent the platform operator can freely dictate the terms when executing an obligation to contract is unclear. This legal uncertainty has been indicated in the roadmap as the *infinity loop of forced access.*

After accessing the platform through either open, conditional, or forced access, the legal issues shift from accessing the platform to decisions that the platform takes in relation to the users' content. The third layer, therefore called the content layer, covers two paths: the doctrine of the general right of use on open access-platforms and the validity and enforceability of user terms on conditional access-platforms.

The relationship between an open access-platform and its users is neither contractual nor is there specific legislation covering these platforms, which makes addressing and resolving access and moderation issues difficult. Following the German doctrine on general rights of use, a platform operator that has chosen to provide access to the general public without access restrictions must, in principle, allow anyone to freely use the service within the scope of the law. This general right of use can only be restricted on the basis of an objective reason. The open norm of an 'objective reason' can be interpreted by balancing the fundamental rights of the parties involved. If the use of an open access-platform has been restricted without an objective reason, the user can invoke its general right of use to oppose the operator's decision. If there is an objective reason, the decision is justified and cannot be opposed by the user.

On conditional access-platforms, the platform operator makes use of user terms to limit the use of the service. These terms must follow the basic principles of contract law, which define the permissible substance and the rules for the formation of a contract. Furthermore, the validity of the terms is assessed in light of the obligations that follow from mandatory rules of public policy. In Member States where national private law includes open norms such as good faith, reasonableness, and/or (un)fairness, fundamental rights can be included in the interpretation of those norms in a similar way as the open norm of 'objective reason' is interpreted for open access-platforms. Terms that are not in compliance with the basic principles of contract law or the mandatory rules of public policy are invalid and not binding on the users of the platform. As such, they cannot form a valid basis for a moderation decision. Terms that fulfil the basic principles of contract law and stay within the borders of the mandatory rules of public policy form a valid and binding contractual agreement between the platform operator and the user.

In case either user or platform breaches the valid, binding obligations of the terms of service, the other party can execute the contractual sanctions and/or the remedies provided by law or by the contract. The fourth and final layer, the enforcement layer, is formed by users' legal redress against a content moderation decision, the laws on procedural obligations that platform operators have to uphold when enforcing contractual sanctions for a user's breach of contract, and the consequences outlined in the Digital Services Act for infringements of platform's procedural obligations. In case a user breaches the terms, the platform operator can execute the sanctions that are outlined in the terms of service. If (i) the sanctions are in line with the terms, (ii) the execution of the sanction does not breach the obligatory due diligence obligations in the DSA, and (iii) the operator has sent a statement of reasons to the user, then the moderation decision is justified. In case the platform operator does not uphold the procedural obligations in the DSA, the moderation decision infringes the DSA. In the latter situation, the affected user has a right to claim compensation and can file a complaint, and the platform operator can be subjected to the penalties defined by the Member States. The platform operator can also breach the terms. This would be the case when the operator (including any algorithmic system it applies) removes content or suspends a user account without a basis in the law or the terms. Against such a wrongful moderation decision, the user can, first, invoke the general contract law remedies available in the national legal systems, such as, *inter alia*, claims for performance (reinstatement claims) and a claim to compensate the damage the user suffered as a consequence of the wrongful moderation decision. Second, the user can make use of any contractual remedies that have been voluntarily included by the platform operator in the terms of service. Third, the DSA stipulates that the terms must include two obligatory contractual remedies: an internal complaint mechanism, and a possibility for out-of-court dispute settlement. Since the latter two are included in the DSA, non-compliance with the obligations outlined in the DSA constitutes an infringement. The user can, therefore, also, in that situation, lodge a complaint or seek compensation for damages, and the platform operator can be subjected to penalties.

Lastly, the roadmap has five final outcomes ('exit-points') for access/moderation decisions. In the roadmap, these elements are indicated by a white colour and underlined text. These exit-points are *access denied* in the access layer, *invalid/unenforceable user term(s)* in the content layer, and three exit-points in the enforcement layer: *a justified mandatory or normative moderation decision, a moderation decision that infringes procedural obligations*, and *a wrongful moderation decision* (*see* Figure 8.1).

Figure 8.1 Full Roadmap to Navigate Access Rights and Moderation Issues on Social Media Platformsm

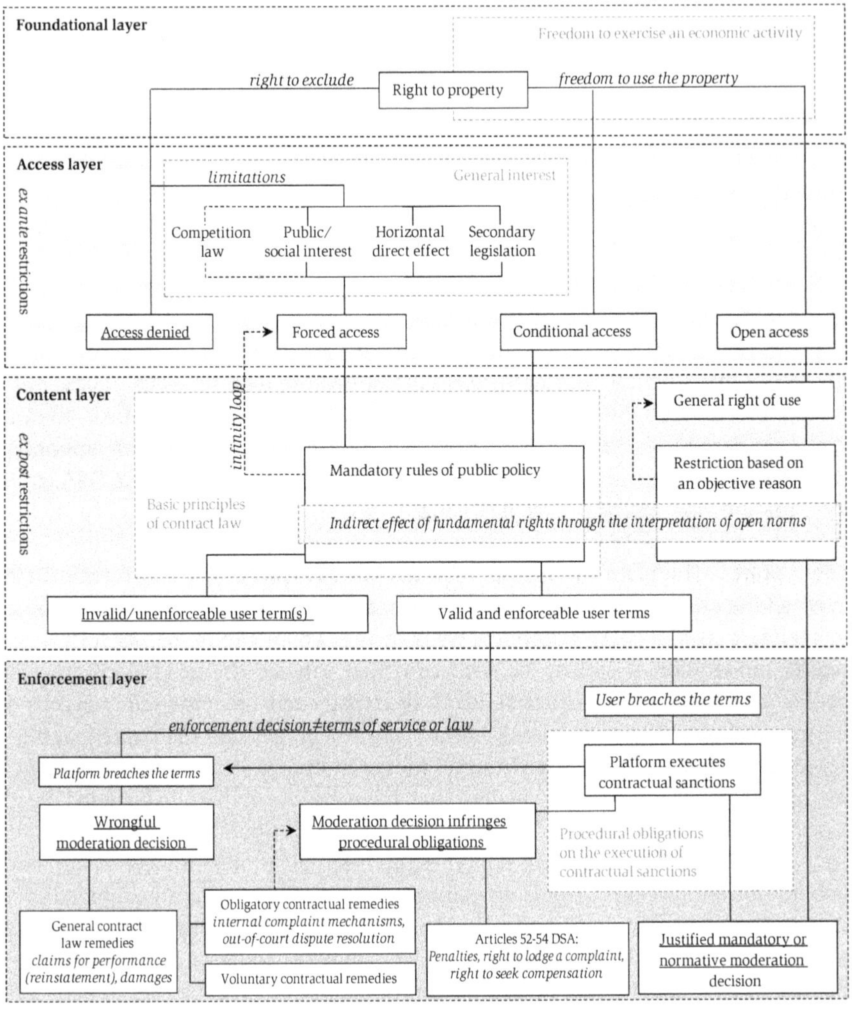

8.2 CASE STUDIES TO DEMONSTRATE THE ROADMAP'S FUNCTIONING

Here are five fictitious examples that illustrate how the roadmap works. These case studies showcase the various elements that decision-makers should consider when deciding on similar cases. Additionally, they can serve as a deterrent for social media platforms to avoid activities or behaviours that may breach procedural or contractual obligations.

8.2.1 Denial of Access to a Social Media Platform

The first examples concern the access to social media platforms. Before addressing an issue of a denial of access, it must be clarified whether the access refusal concerns a conditional or an open access-platform. The qualification depends on the characteristics of either platform. Recalling §5.4, for open access-platforms, these are the temporary nature of the service offered, the limited individual consequences of a breach of any rules, and the lack of general access restrictions. For conditional platforms, these concern the continuous nature of the service, the necessity to create a user account before interacting on the service, and the platform operator's power to exercise normative power.

8.2.1.1 Denial of Access to a Conditional Access-Platform

A new social media platform markets itself as an LGBTQ+ platform.
The platform operator refuses to contract heterosexual cisgender users.

In line with the literature on property rights in virtual spaces, it is defendable that the virtual space offered by a platform operator falls within its right to property. That means that, in principle, the operator is free to deny access to their virtual space by using their right to exclude (*ius excludendi*). The platform operator's right to exclude is not absolute. The limitations to this right can form an opportunity for refused persons to claim forced access, meaning the platform operator is obliged to contract. In the example case, the platform distinguishes on the basis of a person's sexual orientation, denying the access to the entire group of heterosexual cisgender users. If the group can successfully invoke any of the limitations to the platform operator's right to exclude, then the operator must allow them to access the platform.

The situation of discrimination on the basis of sexual orientation or gender identity is not covered by any secondary European legislation. The DSA does not apply to *ex ante* restrictions, and (in)direct discrimination on the basis of sexual orientation is not covered by Directive 2004/113/EC (Gender Goods and Services Directive). However, since the latter Directive solely prescribes the minimum requirements for national transpositions, differences exist from Member State to Member State. The outcome of this example case differs, therefore, from Member State to Member State due to their national implementation of the Gender Goods directive.

Under Danish, Dutch, and German law, the refused person will be able to complain over this refusal, as direct discrimination on the basis of sexual orientation is prohibited. That option is not open for Italian users. Perhaps Italian users could invoke the horizontal direct effect of their Charter right to non-discrimination, but the outcome of such a claim is unclear. The balancing of the user's right to non-discrimination against the interest of the platform's freedom to conduct a business is unsettled. Lastly, Italian users might be able to invoke an individual legitimate interest to access the platform's service. That assessment would depend on the individual circumstances of the person concerned, the scale and dominance of the platform, and any existing or potential networking effect (*see* Figure 8.2).

Figure 8.2 Pathway of a Denial of Access to a Conditional Access-Platform

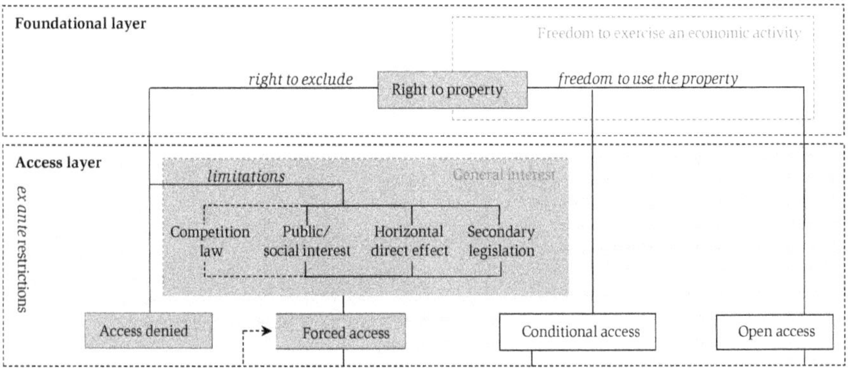

8.2.1.2 *Denial of Access to an Open Access-Platform*

> An online chat box operator limits access to its service to users who are located in Denmark. A user from the Netherlands attempts to access the service, but their access is automatically blocked on the basis of their IP address.

The platform's open nature obstructs differentiation between persons wishing to access it. In general, persons that wish to access an open access-platform must be free to do so, and once they have entered the platform, they have a general right to use that platform. However, platform operators can restrict access to their service on the basis of formal restrictions following from national law, and the operator can confine the service to the boundaries of one or several jurisdictions. If a platform is solely offered to users in a certain part of the world, they do de facto impose an access restriction for potential users from outside this jurisdiction. As is the case in this case-example, the platform applies territorial restrictions. The platform's nature remains open access for the territory the platform operates in (Denmark). It qualifies as an unavailable service outside that jurisdiction (the Netherlands). The jurisdiction restriction does not change the platform into a conditional platform since users in the blocked jurisdiction have no means to comply with the restriction. Solely a move from the Netherlands to Denmark will allow the user to access the service on equal terms with other users in Denmark.

According to the German doctrine on general access to publicly available property, in case a platform is 'open' to any type of content, the restriction of a certain type of content requires an objective reason. A moderation decision on open access-platforms can only be imposed if a user of the service has breached the law or the platform operator has an objective fear that such breaches could arise in the future. There must be objectively verifiable facts that prove (previous) unlawful conduct or that sustain the existing fear of future disturbances. Moreover, large-scale open access-platforms will most likely have to take the right to non-discrimination into consideration. The latter conclusion is, however, unsettled and will have to be addressed based on national law (*see* Figure 8.3).

Figure 8.3 Pathway of a Denial of Access to an Open Access-Platform

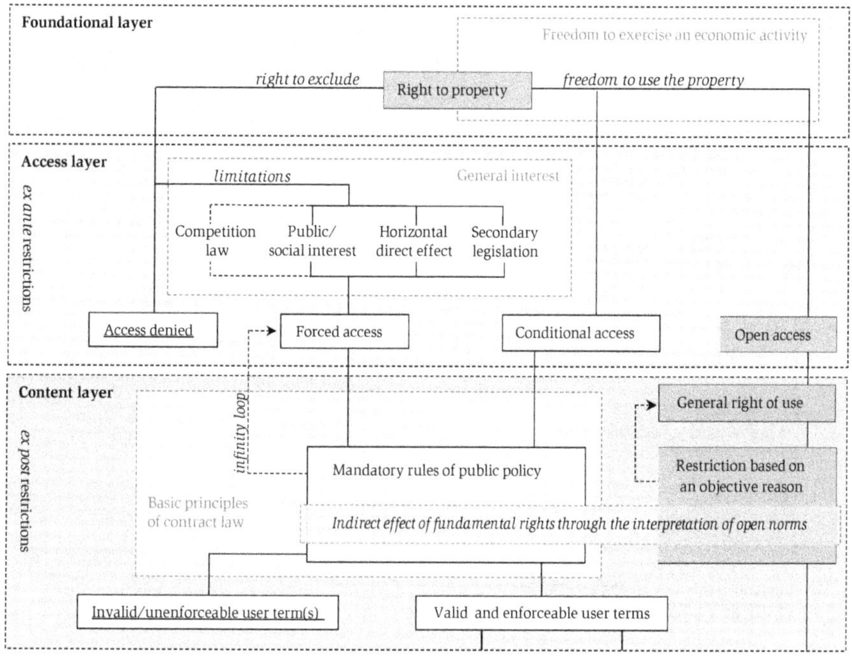

8.2.2 User Terms That Are More Restrictive Than National Law

> A social media platform prohibits the dissemination of euthanasia content in its terms of service.
>
> A user shares content discussing euthanasia from a medical perspective. The content gets deleted.

Within the borders of the law, a conditional access-platform is free to dictate the terms of service applicable on their platform. Hosting euthanasia content is not prohibited by law, nor is there an explicit must-carry obligation for such content. The decision to prohibit the dissemination of euthanasia content in the terms of service is, therefore, a normative restriction of the use of the service. The validity of the term is assessed by the general requirements for contracts (substance, formation, mandatory rules of public policy). There seem to be no indications that there are problems with the formation or the substance of the contract. Following the DSA's Article 14(1), the restriction must be outlined clearly, in plain, intelligible, user-friendly, and unambiguous language in the terms of service. Moreover, the restriction on this social media platform does not render it impossible for the user to express their opinion elsewhere. Users can turn to other means of communication (websites, media), and the restrictions, therefore, do not form a full restriction of the right to freedom of expression. In case the latter would be true, or the term would cause a significant imbalance in the parties' rights and obligations, it will not pass the unfairness test in the UCTD. This does not seem to be the case in this example (*see* Figure 8.4).

Figure 8.4 Pathway of User Terms That Are More Restrictive Than National Law

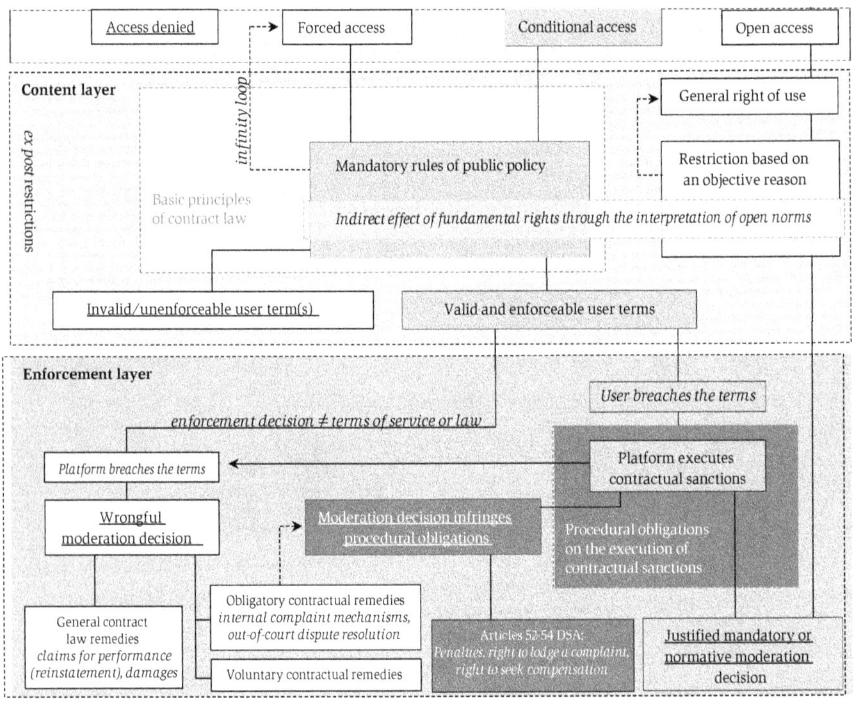

If all the above requirements are fulfilled, then the prohibition of disseminating euthanasia content is a valid contractual term that is binding on the platform and the user. When the user shares euthanasia content, (s)he breaches the term. Against that breach, the platform can execute the sanctions that are outlined in the terms of service (ex. Article 14(1) DSA). When executing those sanctions, the platform must live up to the due diligence obligations in Article 14(4). The decision to remove the euthanasia content must, therefore, be taken diligently, objectively, and proportionately, with due regard to the rights and legitimate interests of all parties involved. The decision would seemingly fulfil the requirements of objectivity (content breaches terms) and proportionality (there is no lesser measure available to enforce the prohibition than to delete the content), but one could contemplate whether the requirement to act in a diligent manner means that the decision should reflect the user's or society's interest in gaining access to objective medical information on euthanasia. There is room for various conclusions here, based on the balancing of the parties' interests by the national courts. The platform must also send the user a statement of reasons outlining the decision (Article 17 DSA). If a statement of reasons is missing or does not contain the mandatory information, or when the decision breaches the due diligence obligations, the platform's execution of the contractual sanction (removing the post) infringes the procedural obligations in the DSA. Articles 52-54 DSA subsequently outline the consequences of such an infringement (penalty, right to lodge a complaint, right to seek compensation).

8.2.3 Removal of a Post Outside the Scope of the User Terms

> A social media platform's terms of service do not specify any restrictions on the content that is allowed to be shared on the platform. The platform removes a user's video that promotes abortion.

Figure 8.5 Pathway of a Content Moderation Decision That Is Outside the Terms' Scope

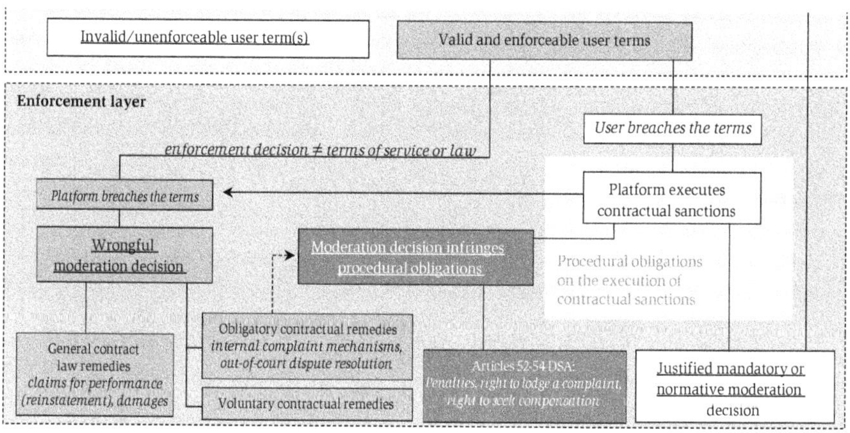

In case a conditional access-platforms does not outline the limitations of the use of their service in their terms, then in principle, the platform operator is held to host all legal content. In the example case (*see* Figure 8.5), the platform, first, infringes on the DSA. Any restriction imposed on the use of the service must be outlined according to Article 14(1) DSA. Second, any moderation of legal content will form a breach of contract. In jurisdictions where the promotion of abortion is not illegal, the platform is contractually obliged to host the content shared by the user. Against this wrongful moderation decision, the user can invoke the general contract law remedies and the contractual remedies. In case the platform operator does not offer obligatory contractual remedies (internal complaints-mechanism or out-of-court dispute resolution), the operator infringes Articles 20 and 21 DSA. Equally, not including the restrictions on the use of the service is a violation of the transparency requirements in Article 14(1) DSA. Against these infringements, the consequences listed in Articles 52-54 DSA are applicable (penalty, right to lodge a complaint, right to seek compensation).

8.2.4 Removal of Content Breaches Procedural Obligations in the DSA

> The terms of service of a social media platform prohibit the dissemination of cat videos. A user shares a video of their daughter taking her first steps. A cat is walking in the background of the video. The platform decides to terminate the user's account and deletes the account's data with immediate effect.

In line with the example case on euthanasia above, the platform operator is, in principle, free to define normative restrictions on the use of the service. If the requirements for validity are met, then the prohibition to disseminate cat videos forms a valid and binding contractual term. When the user shares a cat video, (s)he breaches the term. Against that breach, the platform can execute the sanctions that are outlined in the terms of service (ex. Article 14(1) DSA). When executing those sanctions, the platform must live up to the due diligence obligation in Article 14(4).

Figure 8.6 The Removal of Content Breaches the DSA's Procedural Obligations

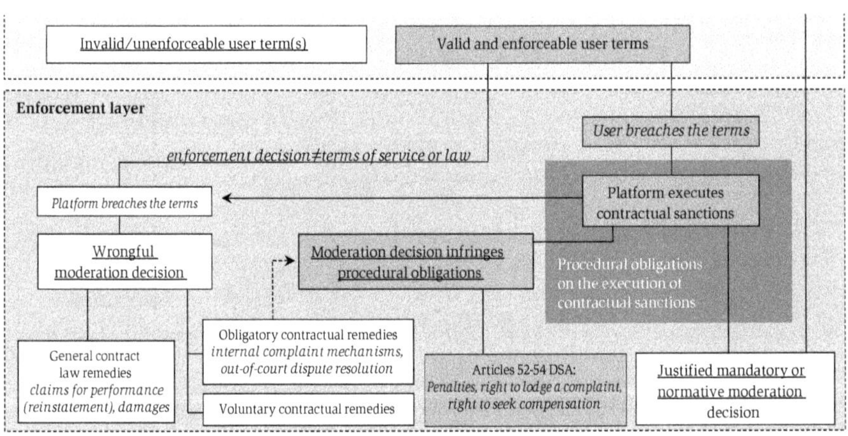

In this example (*see* Figure 8.6), it is, first, arguable whether the user breaches the terms. Is the simple crossing of a cat in the back of the video enough to qualify the entire video as a 'cat video'? If so, the execution of the contractual sanction by the platform operator is in line with the terms. The platform operator does not breach the terms. However, the execution of the contractual sanction is by any means disproportionate to the breach of the terms as there is a less proportionate measure available (removal of the post). Moreover, the user account's data should be retained until the user has been able to appeal the decision. Therefore, the decision infringes on the procedural obligation in Article 14(4) DSA. The consequences for an infringement in Articles 52-54 apply.

Chapter 9

Thoughts and Findings Along the Road

9.1 ADDITIONAL CONTRIBUTIONS TO THE FIELD

This study has been designed as a 'surfer'-study. Therefore, this project does not offer one specific contribution to the legal field. The projects' biggest contribution to the legal field lies in the unifying power of the roadmap. Streamlining the application of the various fields of law allows decision-makers to reach (more) uniform outcomes, which will ultimately benefit European platform users. In addition to developing the roadmap, the research has yielded several other noteworthy findings that are worth highlighting.

Viewing this study through the lens of technological neutrality, specifically comparing physical property restrictions to those on social media platforms, has offered a fresh perspective on platform law. Based on the examined case law, the courts in the Member States rely predominantly on property law to adjudicate access and moderation restrictions on both physical and social media platforms, whether directly or indirectly. This study's focus on property law has revealed a new distinction not previously highlighted in the literature: the differentiation between *ex ante* and *ex post* access restrictions. *Ex ante* restrictions have not been highlighted as a separate problem in the academic literature before. They have been included in the general scope of content moderation and freedom of expression issues, which is understandable but does not do justice to the severity of the problem, nor will such a combined approach allow for any adequate solutions. *Ex ante* access problems result from the fact that the platform operator *refuses* to contract. The discussion on content moderation falls within the scope of contract law. *Ex ante* access problems can thus not be resolved by applying the same rationale, arguments, and laws as applicable to content moderation issues. Singling out *ex ante* access restrictions as a separate problem opens up a discussion on how to tackle them.

Furthermore, this study demonstrates that the primary way to safeguard fundamental rights is through national contract law. Directly imposing fundamental rights obligations on social media platforms is not feasible, but overarching European norms such as the European Declaration on Digital Rights and Principles can be used indirectly through open norms in private law to streamline approaches taken by Member States' courts.

9.2 REFLECTIONS AND RECOMMENDATIONS

9.2.1 General Reflections

This book mapped the road between the origin of a social media platform operator's decision to restrict access to content on its platform and the legal redress available to users to oppose those decisions. By size and number of elements, the enforcement layer has turned out to be the largest and most complex layer of the roadmap. To rebalance the power imbalance between user and platform, both the regulatory, judicial, and academic focus have seen a shift to (procedural) fairness, which is effectuated predominantly when enforcing sanctions on the use of social media platforms' services. The conclusion that effective mechanisms for redress are essential to rebalancing the power between users and social media platforms is a crucial one. Given that platforms are unlikely to voluntarily relinquish their profitable, data-driven business models, users must have legal remedies available to hold platforms accountable for their actions.

The significant normative power that social media platforms can assert through their terms of service has led scholars to call for better protection of users' rights and interests. National legislators have sought to curb the power of platforms by increasing their obligations to remove illegal and harmful content. Some national courts have tried to increase fairness in the contractual relationship between platform and user by including fundamental rights protection through the open norms in their national private law systems. The adoption of the Digital Services Act (DSA) by the European legislator reflects the growing trend towards increased regulation of social media platforms and their freedom to restrict their services. The DSA will also have important implications for the use of fundamental rights protection as a tool to ensure fairness in contractual relationships between private parties. With the coming into force of the DSA, even Member States that do not have open norms as an inherent part of their national private law system will be able to rely on Article 14(4) to achieve outcomes similar to those observed in the four Member States analysed in this book. For those Member States that already have open norms, the DSA will simply codify existing practices in their national courts. Overall, the DSA represents an important step towards ensuring greater fairness and protection of users' rights and interests in their relationships with social media platforms.

The DSA seems to be a wish come true for procedural fairness, but to what extent can *procedural fairness* actually balance the relationship between platform and user? In fact, an infringement of similar transparency requirements as outlined in the DSA, particularly in Article 14(1), has already been deemed unreasonable or unfair for users in national case law prior to their inclusion in the DSA. Moreover, the imposition of a contractual sanction that is not explicitly outlined in the terms of service can be considered a breach of contract. Such a breach can be perfectly dealt with by national contract law. This raises questions about whether the DSA truly represents a meaningful step forward in protecting users' rights and interests.

While this book has focused on analysing the legal framework for access and content moderation decisions by social media platforms, it is worth taking a step back to consider the broader intentions behind the inclusion of specific obligations in the DSA. Were these obligations included in an attempt to harmonise the national practices? Unfortunately, based on the findings of this study, it seems unlikely that we can expect truly harmonised outcomes as a result of the DSA. While the Act represents an important effort to create a more comprehensive legal framework for addressing the challenges posed by social media platforms, it is ultimately up to individual Member States to interpret and implement the Act's provisions within their own national legal frameworks. The DSA leaves the substantial assessment and, more importantly, the consequences for infringements and the legal redress for breaches of contracts up to the Member States.

One significant concern with the DSA is the way it leaves the rules on penalties to the discretion of individual Member States (Article 52). While this approach may have been intended to allow for greater flexibility in implementation, it also creates the risk of significant variations in how penalties are enforced across the EU. This could result in a lack of consistency and transparency, which could, in turn, undermine the effectiveness of the DSA. In short, the decision to leave penalties entirely to the Member States represents a missed opportunity to create a more coherent and unified approach to addressing infringements of the DSA. However, it remains to be seen how individual Member States will choose to implement the Act's provisions and whether they will be successful in promoting greater accountability and transparency across the social media landscape. On a more positive note, the European legislator has succeeded in harmonising some options for contractual redress for all users in the Union through the DSA. Specifically, the Act establishes a right to claim compensation for damages, which is a significant step towards providing users with greater protection and legal recourse in the event of contractual disputes with social media platforms. Despite this progress, however, there remains a risk of differentiated outcomes in Member States, as individual countries may interpret and apply the provisions of the DSA differently. Differences will likely emerge as a consequence of the choice to leave the right to reinstatement in the case of a wrongful moderation decision to the national legal systems of the Member States (Recital 39), as well as the lack of guidance in the DSA on what should be considered 'damage' (material/non-material and their thresholds). These omissions have the effect of creating uneven protection for users across the Union, with some Member States offering greater protections than others. This creates a situation in which social media platforms will need to undertake a risk assessment on a Member State-by-Member State basis, taking into account differences in penalties and compensation claims for material and non-material damages. Given the fact that claims for compensation under the DSA are covered by the Collective Redress Directive, platforms potentially face class-action cases in those jurisdictions where users can effectively claim compensation for (non-)material damages suffered due to wrongful moderation decisions.

Moreover, the failure to address access restrictions in the DSA is a missed opportunity. Future legislation addressing *ex ante* access restrictions would be highly welcomed. Ideally, the legal uncertainty concerning access rights on the basis of non-discrimination legislation can be addressed by updating the Directives on consumer's access to goods and services. Additionally, the ongoing debate on the direct horizontal effect of fundamental rights suggests that an access claim to a social media platform based on the right to non-discrimination could potentially succeed, leading hopefully to insightful case law in the coming years. It only takes one person who wishes to re-enter a social media platform after having had his/her account terminated permanently to challenge a platform operator's decision to deny re-entry to the platform. In that same instance, the applicability of the doctrine of social/public interest can be put to the test.

In conclusion, the research underlying this book aimed to clarify the positive law applicable to the adjudication of access and content moderation issues on social media platforms in the European Union. The ultimate goal is to establish a legal system that ensures uniform outcomes for users throughout the Union, providing users with the same tools to challenge restrictive decisions regardless of the Member State in which they signed up for a social media platform. Achieving this goal requires continued efforts to harmonise legal frameworks and establish clear guidelines and obligations for platform operators. It is crucial to ensure that users' fundamental rights are protected and that access and content moderation decisions are fair, transparent, and subject to effective redress mechanisms. As mentioned in the introduction, that goal does not necessarily entail *equal* outcomes. The Union is not one country, nor should we strive to make it one. However, overarching digital norms can be taken into consideration when addressing online issues in an attempt to bring the national approaches closer together. The European Union has recently united those overarching digital norms in a European Declaration on Digital Rights and Principles for the Digital Decade.[897] Over the next years, we will hopefully see more guidance on the legal value and legal effect of the Declaration.[898] Apart from these abstract digital norms, the concrete interpretation of morality and desirability of information in the Member States will differ as a result of their cultural differences. Those differences must be cherished, at least to a certain extent, but they may under no circumstances lead to unfair outcomes for users in the Union.

Lastly, this framework has been inspired by the legal systems of four Member States and does, therefore, not reflect all details in all European Member States' legal systems. My aim has not been to precisely map all existing national laws that could possibly affect the outcome of access or moderation decisions. Rather, elements that

897. 'European Declaration on Digital Rights and Principles | Shaping Europe's Digital Future' (7 February 2023) https://digital-strategy.ec.europa.eu/en/library/european-declaration-digital-rights-and-principles (accessed 19 March 2023).

898. *See* reflections on the current uncertainty regarding its legal value: Elizabeth Quinn, 'Much Ado About Nothing: The European Declaration on Digital Rights and Principles' [2022] Verfassungsblog https://verfassungsblog.de/much-ado-about-nothing-2/ (accessed 19 March 2023).

represent the same type of rule were grouped together and included if they were observed in all or the majority of the examined Member States. For example, the inclusion of a public/social interest-right is based on the existence of such a rule in three out of four of the examined Member States. Even though the exact laws in those three Member States differ, the *overarching rule* of allowing access to private property on the basis of public or social interest was present in all three. As such, the roadmap must not be interpreted nor applied as something static. Rather, the judiciary, national lawyers, social media platforms, and scholars are encouraged to use the roadmap as a starting point to resolve these problems and as a source to streamline their decisions.

9.2.2 Regulating Social Media Platforms as Public Utilities

One aspect that deserves further consideration and exploration is the potential for regulating social media platforms as public utilities. Social media platforms have not been regulated as public utilities, neither as SGEI nor as universal services. In §5.5.5, I already hinted in the direction that such regulation would be undesirable but that the discussion on that desirability would fall outside the scope of defining *lex lata*. For discussions in the future, I will here elaborate on my recommendation not to regulate social media platforms as public utilities.

First, it is debatable whether social media platforms fulfil the criteria for SGEIs that 'the objective cannot be ensured by private actors alone'. One the one hand, one could argue that social media platforms are up and running and the objective (providing a communication platform) is fulfilled sufficiently since users have access to and can make effective use of the service. On the other hand, in favour of regulating social media platforms as SGEI, if the objective aimed at is the provision of a safe communication environment that is free from illegal and harmful content, then one could argue that the current practice of private companies is not able to reach that objective without interference from the state. Platforms' for-profit, advertisement-heavy business models that run on users' personal data do not allow to put the consumer's benefit first. However, despite perhaps fulfilling this first criterion, the other arguments for SGEI regulation rule out the inclusion of social media platforms. There are most certainly adequate investors, an adequate infrastructure, and numerous competing services. Moreover, it is counterproductive to leave the regulation up to individual Member States, as social media platforms do not solely offer their services on a Member State level; they operate worldwide. A patched European legislative framework would, therefore, be more harmful than that it would actually solve access and/or content moderation issues. A good step to a more uniform regulation and treatment of these platforms would be to at least create a uniform European approach, which would be more suitable through the system of universal services.

However, for the conclusion on the answer to whether the regulation of social media platforms as universal services can aid a solution to access problems on platforms, the same argumentation applies as for SGEI. Recalling the aim of universal services' regulation – *providing a safety net to ensure that a set of at least the minimum services is available to all end-users and at an affordable price to consumers, where a risk of social exclusion arising from the lack of such access prevents citizens from full social and economic participation in society* – seemingly no obstacles exist as related to the price and the continuity of the platform itself. Users can access and use the service, and the service is financed by its underlying advertisement business. However, any normative restrictions that impede access to a social media platform could potentially pose a risk for social exclusion since these platforms are used as a main source of communication in society. As such, access restrictions could prevent citizens from participating in society, which could be an incentive for universal service regulation. Similar to the discussion on SGEI, any main issues thus revolve around access and quality problems on social media platforms.

In the case of access problems, do these problems relate to citizens not being able to *technically access* the platform or is it rather a problem that the characteristics or behaviour of the user do not allow access to the platform? If the latter is the case, the exact access problem could potentially be equally effectively addressed through less severe measures, for example, by increasing the rules on unfair contractual terms in consumer contracts.[899] Compare, for example, accessing a social media platform to a person who is living in a European rural area and who does not have access to an internet connection. In the latter situation, the person is technically not able to connect to the internet and participate in the digital society. In the first, on the contrary, access is not obstructed as such (anyone with an internet connection can enter), but *the way* the access to the platform is set up creates access problems. Rules on universal services are a tool to guarantee access to a service that is of importance to all European citizens. The rules are intended to prevent citizens from social exclusion and to provide a service that would not adequately be covered by the market itself. In that sense, social media platforms do not fit within this line of reasoning. In principle, all Europeans have access to these platforms if they are willing to accept the terms and abide by the rules. Comparing social media platforms to services like telecommunications and broadband internet connection is therefore unjust. The differences between the characteristics and the nature of these different services are simply too big. Social media platforms are not infrastructures, which is demonstrated by the fact that numerous social media platforms exist, which all offer a similar, slightly different product, whereas all companies offering broadband internet offer, in fact, the very same product: a broadband internet connection. Recalling the ECtHR's conclusion on the *internet* as the principal means of communication, social media platforms only form one realisation of the potential means of online communication.[900]

899. The user terms governing the relationship between the user and the social media platform fall within the scope of the Council Directive 93/13/EEC of 5 April 1993 on unfair terms in consumer contracts. However, the current black and grey list do not reflect the infrastructure of the internet in the 2020s. Inclusion of certain practices carried out by social media platforms in the scope of the unfair contract terms directive could safeguard the interests of consumers without excluding the service from the free market.

900. ECtHR, *Cengiz and Others v. Turkey* (1 December 2015) CE:ECHR:2015:1201JUD004822610, §52, and ECtHR, *Vladimir Kharitonov v. Russia* (23 June 2020) CE:ECHR:2020:0623JUD0010 79514, §33.

Comparing and equating social media platforms to broadcasting and telecommunication services as an argument for public utility regulation is a misapplication of public utility rules. When the telecommunication services were regulated, one of the aims of doing so was 'to provide users on request with a connection to the public telephone network at a fixed location, at an affordable price'.[901] European citizens could not simply set up their own communication networks. The lacking infrastructure was the main problem. Similarly, when looking at broadcasting services, the barriers for users to set up their own broadcasting service were high. Users were not able to easily set up their own broadcasting service, or if they would (e.g., a pirate radio channel), the costs were high enough to refrain the general public from setting up individual broadcasting channels. Rather, the equivalent to the communication network services offered by the telecommunication and broadcast companies in the online environment is access to *the internet*. Consequently, access to broadband internet has been regulated as a universal service. In the Directive (EU) 2018/1972 on the European Electronic Communications Code, it is stated that one of the reasons to include broadband internet access in the sphere of universal services is because, without access, citizens face an obstacle to full social and economic participation in society. Access and quality problems on social media platforms are caused by the extensive power of these platforms to dictate the requirements on which users can enter their services. As such, access problems do not form an infrastructural problem. In principle, all European users can enter the service. It is the terms of services that lead to access problems. As such, these access problems are better addressed by increasing the rules on (consumer) contracts, rather than regulating the access to social media platforms under universal services.

However, the recommendation on whether social media platforms should be regulated as universal services differs (slightly) from the conclusion on the regulation of platforms such as SGEI. Contrary to the conclusion that the regulation of social media platforms within the framework of SGEI is unfit because of the national scope of this regulatory tool, social media platforms *could* be regulated as universal services. The regulation of platforms as universal services is not ruled out per se. However, the choice to do so is a normative one and should be substantiated as such, taking into consideration the aimed goals of the service. Social media platforms are not, per default, universal services and cannot be included within the scope without extensive argumentation as to why they should be because, seemingly, the market produces sufficient competition, and the individual operators provide an accessible and efficient service to European consumers. This is evidenced by the constant rise of new dominant platforms (e.g., TikTok and BeReal in the most recent years) and their success in attracting and retaining new users. The conclusion that social media platforms *could* be regulated as universal services is, therefore, a sceptic one. One could fear that assigning a universal service status to (a selective number of) social media platforms could create new problems, namely, deciding which ones are so essential that they should be

901. Directive 2002/22/EC of the European Parliament and of the Council of 7 March 2002 on universal service and users' rights relating to electronic communications networks and services (Universal Service Directive), preamble (8).

included in the regulation. To what extend should their business models be regulated, and how is the freedom to conduct a business (Article 16 of the Charter) of these social media platforms then subsequently guaranteed? Therefore, *if* social media platforms are deemed so essential that all European citizens must be guaranteed access to them and the current platforms are deemed not to sufficiently provide this, then Van Dijck's argument for a public equivalent of a social media platform which reflects public values, rather than commercial values, forms the best way forward.[902] Alternatively, regulation should steer far away from the sphere of competition law and preferably focus on the permissible restrictions in the terms of services applied by these platforms, as such (less far-reaching) interventions possess sufficient potential to effectively curb access problems or on the interoperability of social media platforms.

9.2.3 Interoperability as the Holy Grail?

Social media platform users do not have the same luxury to switch to another service as users of other services. Customers of a hardware store, an online video streaming service, or an (online) newspaper have the option to choose another provider with similar services or products if they find the subscription or entry ticket too high. Switching social media platforms would mean losing all connections and data associated with their account, making users dependent on the platform to stay connected with their online social circle. This lock-in effect on social media platforms gives platform operators significant power to control the information shared between users and the freedom of expression of individual users. Therefore, users must comply with the platforms' terms to avoid losing access to their data and online social relations. As such, the house rules of a restaurant or hardware store in the physical world are not nearly as impactful as the terms of service set by social media platforms. When persons do not agree with the house rules in these types of spaces, they will simply go somewhere else. The case law in the Netherlands, however, demonstrated clearly that some physical properties face similar 'lock-in' problems, namely those private properties where the *aim of visiting* is the predominant factor. Examples are nursing homes, football stadiums, and houses of worship. For these properties, there are no solutions other than to find a way to unite the interests of the proprietor and the visitor. Alternatives do not exist, as one cannot simply ask their football team to play in another stadium simply because one of their fans has a stadium ban for the stadium in which they usually play. For social media platforms, however, an alternative does exist in the form of *interoperability*.

Interoperability for social media platforms means that a user who has a user account on platform A can view content and/or communicate with users of platform B without necessarily having a user account on both platforms. As that would be a promising solution for the lock-in effects of users, interoperability has become a

902. Dijck, Poell and Waal (n. 31); van Dijck (n. 35). Van Dijck urges (local) governments, independent public institutions, and non-profit organisations to be proactive in negotiating public values on behalf of citizens and consumers, in order to secure European values in a foreign-dominated social media landscape.

popular topic in debates on platform power.[903] A reference to interoperability popped up in the European Electronic Communications Code (Directive (EU) 2018/1972) and has been explicitly included as an obligation for European gatekeeper platforms in the Digital Markets Act. According to the latter, a gatekeeper must ensure effective interoperability to their communications services, which would mean that, for example, a person with a *WhatsApp* account will be able to send a message to a person who only uses *iMessage* or *Facebook Messenger*. Some (or most) of the biggest social media platforms will presumably be included in the list of gatekeepers.[904] Combining the obligation of interoperability with the right to data portability in Article 20 of the GDPR, users might finally gain an effective sword to cut themselves loose from the lock-in effect of dominant social media platforms.

With the rise of alternative social media platforms – and especially platforms that offer a *fediverse*-type service[905] – the potential efficacy of interoperability on the accessibility and freedom of expression of individual users becomes more apparent. Scholars have argued that decentralised communication (such as offered through Mastodon's protocol) provides users with increased autonomy,[906] and their open-source software, non-profit and non-commercial nature, allows users to participate in the service's communication culture in ways not possible on mainstream social media platforms.[907] As opposed to centralised social media platforms, as addressed in this book, these decentralised services are managed locally, meaning that different parts of the service function independently and can draw up their own access and moderation rules. If a user disagrees, they can simply switch to another server without losing the possibility to interact with people on other servers.

903. Graef (n. 9); Wolfgang Kerber and Heike Schweitzer, 'Interoperability in the Digital Economy Special Issue on Contracts on Digital Goods and Services' (2017) 8 Journal of Intellectual Property, Information Technology and Electronic Commerce Law 39; Chris Riley, 'Unpacking Interoperability in Competition' (2020) 5 Journal of Cyber Policy 94; Rishab Bailey and Prakhar Misra, 'Interoperability of Social Media: An Appraisal of the Regulatory and Technical Ecosystem' (12 February 2022) https://papers.ssrn.com/abstract=4095312 (accessed 19 March 2023), including an entire dissertation on the topic: Ana Belen Ruival, 'The Promises of Interoperability in Social Media Platforms, Too Good to Be True?' (Cornell University 2022) https://ecommons.cornell.edu/handle/1813/112043 (accessed 19 March 2023).

904. The dissertation on which this book is based was submitted in March 2023. At that time, the process of qualification as gatekeepers was ongoing. Since then, several companies have been designated as gatekeepers, including Alphabet, Amazon, Apple, Booking, ByteDance, Meta and Microsoft.

905. *See* for a thorough explanation: 'What on Earth Is the Fediverse? – Lawfare' https://www.lawfareblog.com/what-earth-fediverse (accessed 19 March 2023). 'The Fediverse is a network of interconnected servers, which communicate with each other based on decentralized networking protocols. These servers can be used for any number of different services, such as social media or file hosting. The most popular services are Mastodon, PeerTube (video hosting, like YouTube), and Pleroma (social networking and microblogging similar to Mastodon).'

906. Diana Zulli, Miao Liu and Robert Gehl, 'Rethinking the "Social" in "Social Media": Insights into Topology, Abstraction, and Scale on the Mastodon Social Network' (2020) 22 New Media & Society 1188.

907. Kate Mannell and Eden T Smith, 'Alternative Social Media and the Complexities of a More Participatory Culture: A View From Scuttlebutt' (2022) 8 Social Media + Society 20563051221122450.

The question is to what extent these interoperable decentralised servers can offer a viable alternative and solution to the problems created by restrictive normative terms on social media platforms. Opposed to the promising nature outlined above, there are, unfortunately, downsides to these decentralised platforms. The use of these systems requires a higher level of technical literacy then mainstream social media platforms like Facebook or Twitter,[908] meaning that it does not prove an alternative for everyone. Furthermore, challenging these new systems against the obligations under the DSA reveals more friction. First, most of the individual decentralised servers will not qualify as a medium enterprise (50 employees and 10 million annual turnover).[909] Therefore, the obligatory contractual remedies in the DSA do not apply.[910] That means that users will lose their access to internal complaints mechanisms and out-of-court dispute resolutions. However, since the users have the possibility to directly interact with the moderator of a server and to move to another server in case there is no consensus reached, the risks for users seem negligible.[911] Second, every instance on Mastodon or another decentralised platform service will have to outline its content moderation policies in line with Article 14(1) DSA and send a statement of reasons for executing any of the restrictions in line with Article 17. This burden falls fully on the individual moderators of the server, creating a heavy labour and financial burden.[912] As such, these obligations could become problematic for some Mastodon instances. Scholars have pointed out that some instances do not outline the rules applicable to their instances but that content restrictions are nonetheless imposed on users.[913]

As these platforms continue to expand, they will likely encounter similar challenges related to illegal content and criticism of their moderation practices, just like mainstream social media sites. Additionally, the implementation of interoperability could give rise to novel content moderation issues. While it remains unclear whether interoperability will ultimately solve the problem of (overly restrictive) normative content moderation policies, it is worth monitoring the issue closely.

908. Zulli, Liu and Gehl (n. 906).
909. Konstantinos Komaitis, 'Can Mastodon Survive Europe's Digital Services Act?' (*Tech Policy Press*, 16 November 2022) https://techpolicy.press/can-mastodon-survive-europes-digital-services-act/ (accessed 19 March 2023).
910. *See* §7.4.1.
911. Zulli, Liu and Gehl (n. 906): 'Moreover, open organizational abstraction (e.g., having moderator contact information, negotiating rules) and horizontal scaling lead to monitorial sociality on ASM. Because moderation policies result from processes of negotiation, users remain vigilant regarding the types of behaviours they deem (in)appropriate for an instance. Users in violation of an instance's expectations are managed at the communal level and, in some cases, through platform adaption (e.g., adopting new rules or features to prevent inappropriate posts). As an extension of technosocial negotiation, users are inadvertently conditioned and technologically enabled to monitor their own engagement and that of fellow users in line with the values of the community.'
912. *Ibid.*
913. Alan Z Rozenshtein, 'Moderating the Fediverse: Content Moderation on Distributed Social Media' (23 November 2022) https://papers.ssrn.com/abstract=4213674 (accessed 19 March 2023).

9.2.4 Dealing with Infringing Activity on Open Access-Platforms

Lastly, it is important to address a pressing societal issue – the prevalence of illegal conduct on open access-platforms. In Denmark (and presumably equally in other Member States), open access-platforms are used as vehicles for criminal activity.[914] Because of their open access design, which enables users to use the platform without having to create a user profile, and their liberal content policies, these platforms make it easier to engage in such activities compared to conventional social media platforms. Recent convictions and increased incidents of *grooming*[915] on open access-platforms have led to a call for increased monitoring of open access-platforms and the content shared on their services.[916] However, obliging open access-platforms to generally monitor their service for illegal activity is prohibited.[917] Calls to increase monitoring follow further from a belief that the platform's service in itself forms an inherent factor contributing to and exacerbating the existence of criminal activity. Rather than increasing monitoring based on platform exceptionalism, the criminal activity – grooming – must be viewed in the bigger context of online illegal activity. If a minor sends child exploitative material, then that is in itself not any different from other online illegal activity, such as the dissemination of terrorist content or intellectual property infringements. The material is equally illegal outside the scope of open access-platforms.

The problem with grooming is that currently, under Danish law, it is not qualified as a criminal offence. Any material, including minors, can qualify as illegal child pornography, but the act of grooming itself is not illegal. The discussion, therefore, mainly concerns the *illegality* of the behaviour, and this discussion is not limited to online access-platforms. Grooming also occurs in the physical world. After a school teacher was acquitted of rape and instead convicted of sexual intercourse with a minor, calls to criminalise grooming appeared in Denmark.[918] As a consequence, in February 2023, the Danish Ministry of Justice put forward a bill to criminalise grooming,[919] but

914. '"Digitale børnelokkere" udnytter chatrouletter: Mand tiltalt for overgreb på mere end 160 børn' (*DR*, 22 February 2023) https://www.dr.dk/nyheder/indland/digitale-boernelokkere-udnytter-chatrouletter-mand-tiltalt-overgreb paa mere-end-160 (accessed 24 February 2023). *See also* Retten i Roskilde (14 November 2022), 9-2787/2022, where a person was convicted for grooming on online chat boxes (amongst other criminal activities).

915. Grooming refers to the process of befriending and establishing an emotional connection with a minor to lower the child's inhibitions with the objective of sexual abuse. 'Child Grooming', *Wikipedia* (2023) https://en.wikipedia.org/w/index.php?title=Child_grooming&oldid=1145153208 (accessed 19 March 2023).

916. *Ibid.* (*DR*, 22 February 2023), referring to the call of *Børns Vilkår* to increase the monitoring of these platforms.

917. Article 15 eCommerce Directive and equally Art. 8 DSA.

918. Rasmus Hylleberg, 'Børn skal per lov sikres mod seksuel manipulation' https://www.k-news.dk/nyheder/børn-skal-per-lovgivning-sikres-mod-seksuel-manipulation (accessed 19 March 2023).

919. Pressevagt, 'Nyt lovforslag skal kriminalisere grooming' (*Justitsministeriet*, 22 February 2023) https://www.justitsministeriet.dk/pressemeddelelse/nyt-lovforslag-skal-kriminalisere-grooming/ (accessed 19 March 2023). The proposal can be found at https://www.ft.dk/ripdf/samling/20222/lovforslag/l50/20222_l50_som_fremsat.pdf (accessed 19 March 2023).

the provision does not include any reference to the digital world.[920] A similar discussion can be observed in relation to *doxing* in the Netherlands.[921]

The internet, including (open access) social media platforms, can exacerbate behaviour that can have significant effects on other persons. These practices might not be as harmful in the physical world as is, for example the case with doxing. It can also be that the same criminal behaviour is more harmful online, which would justify more severe punishments. In the future, criminals will most likely find new types of online criminal behaviour, and national laws might be behind in criminalising such harmful online behaviour. That, in turn, does not mean that open access-platforms must – unlawfully – be obliged to monitor their services for illegal activity. It means that the legislator must step in adequately where the law clearly omits behaviour that is harmful to society, and simultaneously, that law enforcement must turn to online surveillance and adapt their techniques to also enforce criminal behaviour effectively on online access-platforms.

9.3 OPPORTUNITIES FOR FURTHER RESEARCH

Throughout this book, opportunities for further research have been highlighted. These included aspects that were directly related to the topic of access and/or content moderation decisions by social media platforms or more indirectly related to the general topics addressed in this book. I have included an overview of the opportunities for further research that were mentioned throughout this book in a list below.

9.3.1 Digital Services Act

I have four recommendations for further research related to the Digital Services Act. First, following the results and research carried out to form this book, the most pressing unanswered question concerns the compensation for damages that users can claim for unjust removals, suspensions, and terminations. The comparative study in four Member States showed the discrepancy in the outcome of claims for damages – a bigger discrepancy is to be expected when comparing these four Member States to the remaining twenty-three. With the coming into force of the DSA within the next year, a long-term study into the damages awarded and injunctions imposed by courts in the Member States for infringements of the DSA could prove very useful to further map

920. '§231. Grooming is punishable by a fine or up to 2 years' imprisonment if a person systematically or by manipulation and by taking advantage of a superior position based on age and experience establishes a relationship with a person under 18 years of age with the intention of subjecting that person to a sexual offence.' From the explanatory memorandum it follows that: 'Grooming covers the situation where a person builds a relationship of trust with a child or young person with the intention of a sexual offence against that person or to lure the child or young person to send nude photos or images of a sexual nature.'
921. Equally in February 2023, the discussion on doxing (sharing a person's personal data to intimidate them) has led the Dutch Ministry of Justice to put forward a bill to criminalise doxing. Dutch parliament voted in favour of the law (150/150 votes) on 7 February 2023, *see* https://www.tweedekamer.nl/kamerstukken/wetsvoorstellen/detail?cfg=wetsvoorsteldetails&qry=wetsvoorstel%3A36171 (accessed 19 March 2023).

these differences and, hopefully, to effectively resolve them in the future. It would, after all, go directly against the idea of a European Digital Single Market if users in one Member State were better off in these situations than their fellow European users.

Second, the interaction between the due diligence obligations in Articles 14(4) and 20(4) should be clarified. Currently, as shown above, in Chapter 7, a textual interpretation of these provisions does not resolve the overlap in the application of these two due diligence obligations to internal complaints mechanisms. It remains, therefore, unclear whether the decisions brought before these internal complaints mechanisms are to be assessed in light of the fundamental rights of the users or not. The inclusion of the principle of proportionality, the legal interest and the fundamental rights of the users calls for a more thorough (and therefore costly) process than a simple assessment of whether the moderation decision was taken timely, non-discriminatory, diligently, and non-arbitrary. This creates legal uncertainty for the providers of platform services that are obliged to offer such a mechanism.

Third, Member States will have the opportunity to create an administrative complaint-handling mechanism to settle disputes over access and content moderation issues (on social media platforms). Over time, a comparative study into the availability of administrative complaint-handling mechanisms, their rules, and an analysis of the outcome of the cases brought before these administrative complaints bodies will be desirable.

Fourth, different types of governmental influence on mandatory moderation decisions were discussed in Chapter 6. This revealed a problem concerning cross-border jurisdiction. Social media platforms must find a way to balance the (un)intentional influence from states on the content that can be hosted in other jurisdictions. This would be the case if national legislation demands that certain illegal content must be removed from the platform on a worldwide scale. Since social media platforms are, in principle, free to define the service they would like to offer, they can, in principle, take the strictest regime as a base line for their terms of service. Defining to what extent this extraterritorial effect of national law through private contracting can be tackled by the due diligence obligation in Article 14(4) DSA would be highly relevant to prevent a regulatory race to the bottom from happening. The research should preferably focus on balancing the interest of the national state to effectively block their nationals from accessing illegal content against the interests of the users to have certain legal content hosted in another jurisdiction.

9.3.2 National and Comparative Private Law

Two concrete problems can be identified within the scope of national and comparative private law. First, more research is desirable on the scope of the freedom of contract in situations where a more powerful party is obliged to contract a consumer. The unclarity concerning the scope of the freedom of contract in this situation gives rise to legal uncertainty, as highlighted when discussing the *infinity loop* in Chapter 5. It is unclear whether and to what extent the more powerful party can deviate from terms it would offer to other parties, nor is it clear what standard to use if that party has not previously contracted with other third parties.

Second, from the research done in Chapter 6, it was concluded that weaker parties could not be forced to accept a full waiver of their fundamental rights protection. However, a full waiver of fundamental rights (e.g., the right to privacy or the freedom of expression) seems unlikely to be included in the terms of service of social media platforms. Therefore, there is a need to explore the grey area between a full waiver of fundamental rights protection and a contractual term that significantly restricts the protection. The scope of immoral contracts poses an interesting and promising basis for a project to look further into the possibility of weaker parties to waive fundamental rights protection in contracts (and especially in terms of services). Combined with the theory on the principle of abuse of rights – which principle also indirectly seems to be protected by the balancing of rights in Article 14(4) – an academic contribution addressing this unclarity would be highly welcome.

9.3.3 Equality and Non-discrimination Law

More research into access rights to social media platforms would be highly welcome too. Academic research has had a main focus on the *ex post* access and moderation restrictions imposed by social media platforms, but *ex ante* access restrictions have equally substantive effects on the right to freedom of expression of users. This is especially the case when focusing on the re-entry of previously permanently terminated user accounts. The field of equality and non-discrimination law proves promising to tackle (some) of the problems that follow from *ex ante* access restrictions. Studies in this field could focus on the recent developments on the direct effect of the right to non-discrimination under the Charter. Especially since this research has highlighted that there are (significant) differences in the implementation of Council Directive 2004/113/EC.

9.3.4 Social and Public Interest Rights

Finally, it follows from national case law that under certain circumstances, a person's interest in accessing private property outweighs the owner's interest in freely regulating access to the property. That is, *inter alia,* the case if a person's *aim* of visiting that exact private property cannot be fulfilled by visiting another similar property. Currently, the requirements to successfully invoke social and public interests as a limitation to the proprietor's right to exclude are not clearly defined. As this stream of case law can form a promising basis for access rights to social media platforms, further exploration into this legal opportunity is encouraged. As a starting point, a quote from Vinding Kruse in the 1951 version of *Ejendomsretten* can serve as inspiration for further research within the field of property law: 'Where values are created by the individual as the result of his activity, they belong primarily to him; where, on the other hand, values arise – in nature or in the course of the development of social life – which cannot reasonably be attributed to the *activity of one or more individuals, they belong to society as a whole.*'[922] It is debatable who creates the value for social media platforms. Would that be the platform offering the service, the individual users creating the content, or the community of users all together interacting with that content? And would that be enough to consider the value a product of the development of social life? Moreover, a query into the existence and discussion of similar rights in the remaining twenty-three Member States of the European Union could serve as an opening to kindle the debate on the regulation of access to social media platforms on the basis of social and public interest. Given the obligation for social media platforms to take the interests of the users into consideration when making an *ex post* decision (Article 14(4) DSA), the relevance of social and public interest rights will only increase over the next years.

922. Vinding Kruse (n. 203), p. 94): 'hvor værdier skabes af den enkelte, som resultater af hans virksomhed, hører de i første række ham til; opstår der derimod værdier – i naturen eller under samfundslivets udvikling – der ikke med nogen rimelighed kan henføres til nogen enkelts eller flere bestemtes virksomhed, hører værdierne samfundet til'.

Bibliography

Á Costello R, 'Faux Ami? Interrogating the Normative Coherence of "Digital Constitutionalism"' 2023 Global Constitutionalism

Almada M and others, 'Opportunities and Limits of European Social Network Regulation' (2022) 62 Demokratie und Öffentlichkeit im 21. Jahrhundert – zur Macht des Digitalen 327

Ananny M, 'From Noxious to Public? Tracing Ethical Dynamics of Social Media Platform Conversions' (2015) 1 Social Media + Society 2056305115578140

'Avoid Fraudulent Message Attacks on TikTok | TikTok Help Center' https://support.tiktok.com/en/safety-hc/account-and-user-safety/avoid-fraudulent-message-attacks-on-tiktok accessed 27 January 2023

Bagnoli V, 'Digital Platforms as Public Utilities' (2020) 51 IIC – International Review of Intellectual Property and Competition Law 903

Bailey R and Misra P, 'Interoperability of Social Media: An Appraisal of the Regulatory and Technical Ecosystem' (12 February 2022) https://papers.ssrn.com/ abstract =4095312 accessed 19 March 2023

Balkin JM, 'Free Speech Is a Triangle', *Columbia Law Review* https://columbialawreview.org/content/free-speech-is-a-triangle/ accessed 1 June 2022

Bar C von, *Gemeineuropäisches Sachenrecht* (CH Beck 2015)

Bassini M, 'Fundamental Rights and Private Enforcement in the Digital Age' (2019) 25 European Law Journal 182

Bassini M, 'Libertà di espressione e social network, tra nuovi 'spazi pubblici' e 'poteri privati'. Spunti di comparazione' 33

Bazyler M, 'Holocaust Denial and the Law' in Michael Bazyler (ed.), *Holocaust, Genocide, and the Law: A Quest for Justice in a Post-Holocaust World* (Oxford University Press 2017) https://doi.org/10.1093/acprof:oso/9780195395693.003.0007 accessed 27 January 2023

Belli L, 'Structural Power as a Critical Element of Social Media Platforms' Private Sovereignty' in Edoardo Celeste, Amélie Heldt and Clara Iglesias Keller (eds),

Constitutionalising Social Media (Bloomsbury Publishing Plc 2022) http://ebook central.proquest.com/lib/kbdk/detail.action?docID = 7027117 accessed 28 January 2023

Belli L and Venturini J, 'Private Ordering and the Rise of Terms of Service as Cyber-Regulation' [2016] Internet Policy Review https://policyreview.info/articles/analysis/private-ordering-and-rise-terms-service-cyber-regulation accessed 22 March 2021

Benda-Beckmann K von and Turner B, 'Legal Pluralism, Social Theory, and the State' (2018) 50 The Journal of Legal Pluralism and Unofficial Law 255

Benoliel U and Becher SI, 'The Duty to Read the Unreadable' (2019) 60 Boston College Law Review

Bermejo N, 'Fundamental Rights and Horizontal Direct Effect Under the Charter' in Cristina Izquierdo-Sans, Carmen Martínez-Capdevila and Magdalena Nogueira-Guastavino (eds), *Fundamental Rights Challenges: Horizontal Effectiveness, Rule of Law and Margin of National Appreciation* (Springer International Publishing 2021) https://doi.org/10.1007/978-3-030-72798-7_5 accessed 13 December 2022

Binder M, 'Mastodon Has Gained Millions of New Users since Elon Musk Bought Twitter' (*Mashable*, 20 December 2022) https://mashable.com/article/mastodon-millions-users accessed 29 January 2023

Birnhack M and Elkin-Koren N, 'The Invisible Handshake: The Reemergence of the State in the Digital Environment' (10 April 2003) https://papers.ssrn.com/abstract = 381020 accessed 9 February 2023

Bradford A, *The Brussels Effect: How the European Union Rules the World* (Oxford University Press 2020)

Brkan M, 'Freedom of Expression and Artificial Intelligence: On Personalisation, Disinformation and (Lack Of) Horizontal Effect of the Charter' (17 March 2019) https://papers.ssrn.com/abstract = 3354180 accessed 13 December 2022

Bruns A and Highfield T, 'Is Habermas on Twitter?: Social Media and the Public Sphere', *The Routledge Companion to Social Media and Politics* (Routledge 2015)

Buratti A, 'Framing the Facebook Oversight Board: Rough Justice in the Wild Web?' 19

Burkell J and others, 'Facebook: Public Space, or Private Space?' (2014) 17 Information, Communication & Society 974

Busch C, 'Reguliering Digitaler Plattformen als Infrastrukturen der Daseinsvorsorge' 36

Caro RA, *The Power Broker: Robert Moses and the Fall of New York* (Vintage Books Edition September 1975, Vintage 1975)

Castells M, 'The New Public Sphere: Global Civil Society, Communication Networks, and Global Governance' (2008) 616 Annals of The American Academy of Political and Social Science - ANN AMER ACAD POLIT SOC SCI 78

Celeste E, 'Terms of Service and Bills of Rights: New Mechanisms of Constitutionalisation in the Social Media Environment?' (2019) 33 International Review of Law, Computers & Technology 122

Celeste E, Heldt A and Keller CI, *Constitutionalising Social Media* (Bloomsbury Publishing Plc 2022) http://ebook central.proquest.com/lib/kbdk/detail.action?docID = 7027117 accessed 28 January 2023

CESI Europe Academy, 'Providing High-Quality Public Services in Europe Based on the Values of Protocol 26 TFEU' (2012) https://www.cesi.org/wp-content/uploads/2012/10/121129_Brochure-Protocole26-2-EN_DEF.pdf

'Child Grooming', *Wikipedia* (2023) https://en.wikipedia.org/w/index.php?title=Child_grooming&oldid=1145153208 accessed 19 March 2023

Ciacchi AC, '28 Jurisdictions and 12 Types of Morally Dubious Contracts. To What Extent Is There a Common Core?' in Aurelia Colombi Ciacchi, Chantal Mak and Zeeshan Mansoor (eds), *Immoral Contracts in Europe* (Intersentia 2020) https://www.cambridge.org/core/books/immoral-contracts-in-europe/BA5381E 5A2BE 0A231DF703547888C1C9 accessed 16 January 2023

Ciacchi AC, 'Immoral Contracts in Europe: The First Common Core' in Chantal Mak, Zeeshan Mansoor and Aurelia Colombi Ciacchi (eds), *Immoral Contracts in Europe* (Intersentia 2020) https://www.cambridge.org/core/books/immoral-contracts-in-europe/BA5381E5A2BE0A231DF703547888C1C9 accessed 16 January 2023

Ciacchi AC, Mak C and Mansoor Z (eds), *Immoral Contracts in Europe* (Intersentia 2020) https://www.cambridge. org/core/books/immoral-contracts-in-europe/BA5381E5A2BE0A231DF703547888C1C9 accessed 26 January 2023

Cockfield A and Pridmore J, 'A Synthetic Theory of Law and Technology' (2007) 8 40

Cosio R, 'Facebook e Social. Natura del contratto tra utente e social' [2020] Ricerche giuridiche JournalArticle_3077

Costello RÁ, 'Faux Ami? Interrogating the Normative Coherence of 'Digital Constitutionalism'' [2023] Global Constitutionalism 1

De Gregorio G, 'The Rise of Digital Constitutionalism in the European Union' (2021) 19 International Journal of Constitutional Law 41

De Gregorio G, *Digital Constitutionalism in Europe: Reframing Rights and Powers in the Algorithmic Society* (Cambridge University Press 2022) https://www.cambridge.org/core/books/digital-constitutionalism-in-europe/A3F 61C6368D17D95345 7234B8A59C502 accessed 6 July 2022

''Digitale børnelokkere' udnytter chatrouletter: Mand tiltalt for overgreb på mere end 160 børn' (*DR*, 22 February 2023) https://www.dr.dk/nyheder/indland/digitale-boernelokkere-udnytter-chatrouletter-mand-tiltalt-overgreb-paa-mere-end-160 accessed 24 February 2023

Dijck J van, Poell T and Waal M de, *The Platform Society: Public Values in a Connective World* (Oxford University Press 2018)

Dinar C, 'The State of Content Moderation for the LGBTIQA + Community and the Role of the EU Digital Services Act'

Dizon MAC, 'From Regulating Technologies to Governing Society: Towards a Plural, Social and Interactive Conception of Law' (Social Science Research Network 2012) SSRN Scholarly Paper ID 2123105 https://papers.ssrn. com/abstract=2123105 accessed 6 April 2021

Douek E, 'The Limits of International Law in Content Moderation' (Social Science Research Network 2020) SSRN Scholarly Paper ID 3709566 https://papers.ssrn.com/abstract=3709566 accessed 24 February 2021

Dupret B, 'Legal Pluralism, Plurality of Laws, and Legal Practices':

Easterbrook FH, 'Cyberspace and the Law of the Horse' The University of Chicago Legal Forum 11

ECHR, 'Guide on Article 1 of Protocol No. 1 – Protection of Property' 89

Elkin-Koren N, 'Government-Platform Synergy and Its Perils' in Edoardo Celeste, Amélie Heldt and Clara Iglesias Keller (eds), *Constitutionalising Social Media* (Bloomsbury Publishing Plc 2022) http://ebookcentral.proquest.com/lib/kbdk/detail.action?docID=7027117 accessed 7 February 2023

Elkin-Koren N, Perel (Filmar) M and De Gregorio G, 'Social Media as Contractual Networks: A Bottom up Check on Content Moderation' (Social Science Research Network 2021) SSRN Scholarly Paper ID 3797554 https://papers.ssrn.com/abstract=3797554 accessed 29 March 2021

Elsaß L, Labusga J-H and Tichy R, 'Internet und E-Commerce. Löschungen und Sperrungen von Beiträgen und Nutzerprofilen durch die Betreiber sozialer Netzwerke' (2017) 33 Computer und Recht 234

Erp SV, 'European Property Law as New Private Law?' (*Property*, 12 July 2016) https://property.jotwell.com/european-property-law-as-new-private-law/ accessed 27 February 2023

'EUR-Lex – Public_service – EN – EUR-Lex' https://eur-lex.europa.eu/EN/ legal-content/glossary/public-service.html accessed 5 March 2023

'EUR-Lex – Services_general_economic_interest – EN – EUR-Lex' https://eur-lex.europa.eu/ EN/legal-content/glossary/services-of-general-economic-interest.html accessed 5 March 2023

'EUR-Lex – Universal_service – EN – EUR-Lex' https://eur-lex.europa.eu/ EN/legal-content/glossary/universal-service.html accessed 5 March 2023

European Commission, 'Explanations Relating to the Charter of Fundamental Rights' (2007)

'European Declaration on Digital Rights and Principles | Shaping Europe's Digital Future' (7 February 2023) https://digital-strategy.ec.europa.eu/en/library/european-declaration-digital-rights-and-principles accessed 19 March 2023

Fairfield J, 'Virtual Property' 85 Boston University Law Review 56

Farinho D, 'The Digital Services Act: A European Digital Republic, If We Can Keep It or the Long and Winding Road – The Digital Constitutionalist' (7 December 2022) https://digi-con.org/the-digital-services-act-a-european-digital-republic-if-we-can-keep-it-or-the-long-and-winding-road/ accessed 1 February 2023

Fauvarque-Cosson B and Mazeaud D, *European Contract Law: Materials for a Common Frame of Reference: Terminology, Guiding Principles, Model Rules* (Walter de Gruyter 2009)

Feldmann T and Heidrich J, 'Rechtsfragen Des Ausschlusses von Usern Aus Internetforen' (2006) 22 Computer und Recht https://www.degruyter.com/ document/doi/10.9785/ovs-cr-2006-406/html accessed 2 February 2022

FRA – European Union Agency for Fundamental Rights, 'Freedom to Conduct a Business: Exploring the Dimensions of a Fundamental Right'

Frantziou E, 'The Horizontal Effect of the Charter of Fundamental Rights of the EU: Rediscovering the Reasons for Horizontality' (2015) 21 European Law Journal 657

Frantziou E, 'The Horizontal Effect of the Charter: Towards an Understanding of Horizontality as a Structural Constitutional Principle' (2020) 22 Cambridge Yearbook of European Legal Studies 208

Friso Bostoen, 'Are Online Platforms the New Utilities – And Should They Be Regulated as Such? Inspiration from over 100 Years of Telecommunications Regulation' https://fsr.eui.eu/bostoen-f-are-online-platforms-the-new-utilities-and-should-they-be-regulated-as-such-inspiration-from-over-100-years-of-telecommunicat ions-regulation/ accessed 14 September 2021

Galgano F, *Trattato Di Diritto Civile. Volume II* (III, Wolters Kluwer 2020)

Gillespie T and Mike Ananny, 'Exceptional Platforms' (*The Internet, Policy & Politics Conferences*, 2016) http://blogs.oii.ox.ac. uk/ipp-conference/2016/programme-2016/track-b-governance/platform-studies/tarleton-gillespie-mike-ananny.html

Golunova V, 'In Tech We Trust? Fixing the Evolutionary Interpretation by the Court of Justice of the Prohibition of General Monitoring in the Era of Automated Content Moderation' in Evangelia Psychogiopoulou and Susana de la Sierra, *Digital Media Governance and Supranational Courts* (Edward Elgar Publishing 2022) https://www.elgaronline.com/display/book/9781802203004/book-part-97818022 0300 4-8.xml accessed 6 March 2023

Gorwa R, Binns R and Katzenbach C, 'Algorithmic Content Moderation: Technical and Political Challenges in the Automation of Platform Governance' (2020) 7 Big Data & Society 2053951719897945

Graef I, 'Mandating Portability and Interoperability in Online Social Networks: Regulatory and Competition Law Issues in the European Union' (2015) 39 Telecommunications Policy 502

Graef I, 'Rethinking the Essential Facilities Doctrine for the EU Digital Economy' https://papers.ssrn.com/sol3/papers.cfm?abstract_id = 3371457

Grantham R, 'The Legitimacy of the Company as a Source of (Private) Power' in Kit Barker, Simone Degeling and Karen Fairweather (eds), *Private law and power* (Hart Publishing 2017)

Griffin R, 'A Progressive View of Digital Constitutionalism – The Digital Constitutionalist' (14 June 2022) https://digi-con.org/a-progressive-view-of-digital-constituti onalism/ accessed 28 January 2023

Grimm D, 'The Achievement of Constitutionalism and Its Prospects in a Changed World' in Petra Dobner and Martin Loughlin (eds), *The Twilight of Constitutionalism?* (Oxford University Press 2010) https://doi.org/10.1093/ acprof:oso/9780 199585007.003.0001 accessed 28 January 2023

Grimmelmann J, 'Virtual Worlds as Comparative Law' (2004) New York Law School Law Review

Groussot X, Petursson GT and Pierce J, 'Weak Right, Strong Court – The Freedom to Conduct Business and the EU Charter of Fundamental Rights' (Social Science Research Network 2014) SSRN Scholarly Paper ID 2428181 https://papers.ssrn.com/abstract = 2428181 accessed 10 November 2020

Hansen O and Ritchie HG, 'Unilateral Variation Clauses in Professional Platform-User Agreements' (2022) 6 European Review of Private Law

Hansen O, Ulfbeck V and Petersen CS, 'Private Governance and the Potential of Private Law' (2020) 28 European Review of Private Law https://kluwerlawonline. com/api/Product/CitationPDFURL?file=Journals\ERPL\ERPL2020017.pdf accessed 23 January 2023

Hartley TC (ed.), 'Contracts: The Principle of Party Autonomy', *International Commercial Litigation: Text, Cases and Materials on Private International Law* (Cambridge University Press 2009) https://www.cambridge. org/core/books/international-commercial -litigation/contracts-the-principle-of-party autonomy/899C42C4D91C0736A2C823C97AC308B1 accessed 25 January 2023

Helberger N, Pierson J and Poell T, 'Governing Online Platforms: From Contested to Cooperative Responsibility' (2018) 34 The Information Society 1

Heldt A, 'Intensivere Drittwirkung: Die Mittelbare Drittwirkung Der Meinungsfreiheit in Öffentlichkeiten Der Digitalen Gesellschaft – Eine Verfassungsrechtliche, Rechtsvergleichende Und Interdisziplinäre Analyse' (2022)

Heldt A, *Intensive Third-Party Effect* (1st edn, Mohr Siebeck 2023)

Heldt A, 'Content Moderation and Freedom of Expression – Digital Society Blog' (*HIIG*, 18 January 2023) https://www.hiig.de/en/content-moderation-on-digital-platforms/ accessed 19 January 2023

Heldt AP, 'Merging the 'Social' and the 'Public': How Social Media Platforms Could Be a New Public Forum' (Social Science Research Network 2019) SSRN Scholarly Paper 3460067 https://papers. ssrn.com/abstract=3460067 accessed 22 April 2022

Helvacı İ, 'Obligation to Contract' in İlhan Helvacı (ed.), *Turkish Contract Law* (Springer International Publishing 2017) doi.org/10.1007/978-3-319-60061-1_7 accessed 21 January 2023

Hennemann M and Heldt A, 'Prozedurale Vermessung: Das Kuratieren Kommunikativer Räume Durch Soziale Netzwerke Zugleich Besprechung von BGH, Urteile Vom 29.7.2021 – BGH Aktenzeichen IIIZR17920 III ZR 179/20 (ZUM 2021, ZUM Jahr 2021 Seite 953) Und BGH Aktenzeichen III ZR 192/20 (ZUM-RD 2021, ZUM-RD Jahr 2021 Seite 612)' [2021] ZUM 981

'How Twitter Handles Abusive Behavior | Twitter Help' https://help.twitter.com/en/rules-and-policies/abusive-behavior accessed 27 January 2023

Human Rights Council (Advisory Committee), 'New and Emerging Digital Technologies and Human Rights. Study of the Human Rights Council Advisory Committee' (2021) A/HRC/AC/25/CRP.2

Hylleberg R, 'Børn skal per lov sikres mod seksuel manipulation' https://www.k-news.dk/nyheder/børn-skal-per-lovgivning-sikres-mod-seksuel-manipulation accessed 19 March 2023

Justitia, 'The Digital Berlin Wall: How Germany (Accidentally) Created a Prototype for Global Online Censorship – Act Two' (2020) https://justitia-int.org/wp-content/uploads/2020/09/ Analyse_Cross-fertilizing-Online-Censorship-The-Global-Impact-of-Germanys-Network-Enforcement-Act-Part-two_Final-1.pdf accessed 17 February 2023

Karanicolas M, 'Too Long; Didn't Read: Finding Meaning in Platforms' Terms of Service Agreements' (2021) 52 University of Toledo Law Review 1

Kaye D, *Speech Police: The Global Struggle to Govern the Internet* (Columbia Global Reports 2019) https://www.jstor.org/ stable/j.ctv1fx4h8v accessed 15 January 2023

Keller D, 'Lawful but Awful? Control over Legal Speech by Platforms, Governments, and Internet Users' (*The University of Chicago Law Review Online*, 28 June 2022) https://lawreviewblog.uchicago.edu/2022/06/28/keller-control-over-speech/ accessed 3 August 2022

Keller D, 'The EU's New Digital Services Act and the Rest of the World' [2022] Verfassungsblog https://verfassungs blog.de/dsa-rest-of-world/ accessed 1 February 2023

Keller D, 'Who Do You Sue? State and Platform Hybrid Power Over Online Speech' Stanford University www.hoover .org/sites/default/files/research/docs/who-do-you-sue-state-and-platform-hybrid-power-over-online-speech_0.pdf

Keller D, 'Why D.C. Pundits' Must-Carry Claims Are Relevant to Global Censorship' http://cyberlaw.stanford.edu/blog/2018/09/why-dc-pundits-must-carry-clai ms-are-relevant-global-censorship accessed 3 August 2022

Kerber W and Schweitzer H, 'Interoperability in the Digital Economy Special Issue on Contracts on Digital Goods and Services' (2017) 8 Journal of Intellectual Property, Information Technology and Electronic Commerce Law 39

Kettemann MC, *The Normative Order of the Internet: A Theory of Rule and Regulation Online* (Oxford University Press 2020)

Kettemann MC and Klausa T, 'Regulating Online Speech: Ze German Way' (*Lawfare*, 20 September 2021) www.lawfareblog.com/regulating-online-speech-ze-german-way accessed 27 September 2021

Kettemann MC and Tiedeke AS, 'Back up: Can Users Sue Platforms to Reinstate Deleted Content?' (2020) 9 Internet Policy Review https://policyreview.info/ articles/anal ysis/back-can-users-sue-platforms-reinstate-deleted-content accessed 3 August 2022

Kim NS, *Wrap Contracts: Foundations and Ramifications* (Oxford University Press 2013)

Kischel U, 'Variety of the Civil Law Context' in Uwe Kischel and Andrew Hammel (eds), *Comparative Law* (Oxford University Press 2019) https://doi.org/10.1093/ oso/9780198791355.003.0007 accessed 9 February 2023

Klappstein V, 'The Obligation to Contract in British Law' (2014) 3 Journal of Governance and Regulation 15

Klos M, 'Wrongful Moderation Regulation of Internet Intermediary Service Provider Liability and Freedom of Expression' (2022)

Komaitis K, 'Can Mastodon Survive Europe's Digital Services Act?' (*Tech Policy Press*, 16 November 2022) https://techpolicy.press/can-mastodon-survive-europes-di gital-services-act/ accessed 19 March 2023

Koninkrijksrelaties M van BZ en, 'Algemene Wet Gelijke Behandeling – Discriminatie op de woningmarkt – Home | Volkshuisvesting Nederland' (15 March 2022) https://www.volkshuisvesting nederland.nl/onderwerpen/discriminatie-op-de-woningmarkt/algemene-wet-gelijke-behandeling accessed 15 March 2023

Lagioia F and others, 'AI in Search of Unfairness in Consumer Contracts: The Terms of Service Landscape' (2022) 45 Journal of consumer policy 481

Lastowka G and Hunter D, 'The Laws of the Virtual Worlds' (29 May 2003) https://papers.ssrn.com/abstract=402860 accessed 15 November 2022

Leerssen P, 'An End to Shadow Banning? Transparency Rights in the Digital Services Act Between Content Moderation and Curation' (2023) 48 Computer Law & Security Review 105790

Lenaerts, Koen, 'The Court of Justice and the Comparative Law Method' (2016) https://www.europeanlawinstitute.eu/fileadmin/user_upload/p_eli/General_Assembly/2016/K._Lenaerts_ELI_AC_2016.pdf accessed 27 September 2021

Lessig L and Lessig L, *Code* (Version 20, Basic Books 2006)

Llansó EJ, 'No Amount of "AI" in Content Moderation Will Solve Filtering's Prior-Restraint Problem' (2020) 7 Big Data & Society 2053951720920686

Loos M and Luzak J, 'Update the Unfair Contract Terms Directive for Digital Services' https://www.europarl.europa. eu/RegData/etudes/STUD/2021/676006/IPOL_STU(2021)676006_EN.pdf accessed 26 February 2021

Loos MBM, 'Transparency of Standard Terms under the Unfair Contract Terms Directive and the Proposal for a Common European Sales Law' (2015) 23 European Review of Private Law https://kluwerlawonline.com/api/Product/CitationPDFURL?file=Journals\ERPL\ERPL2015015.pdf accessed 24 January 2023

Loughlin M, 'What Is Constitutionalisation?' in Petra Dobner and Martin Loughlin (eds), *The Twilight of Constitutionalism?* (Oxford University Press 2010) https://doi.org/10.1093/acprof:oso/9780199585007.003.0003 accessed 28 January 2023

Lynge Andersen L, *Aftalelovens §36-Fra Kontraktfrihed Til Urimelighedskontrol* (Foerste udgave, foerste oplag, Ex Tuto Publishing 2018)

MacDonald M, 'The Case for Virtual Property' (2016)

Mak C, *Fundamental Rights in European Contract Law: A Comparison of the Impact of Fundamental Rights on Contractual Relationships in Germany, the Netherlands, Italy, and England* (Kluwer Law International; Sold and distributed in North, Central, and South America by Aspen 2008)

Mak C, 'Immorality of Contracts in Europe: Four Approaches' in Aurelia Colombi Ciacchi, Chantal Mak and Zeeshan Mansoor (eds), *Immoral Contracts in Europe* (Intersentia 2020) https://www .cambridge.org/core/books/immoral-contracts-in-europe/BA5381E5A2BE0A2 31DF703547888C1C9 accessed 26 January 2023

Mak V, *Legal Pluralism in European Contract Law* (First edition, Oxford University Press 2020)

'Managing Spam on Facebook | Facebook Help Centre' https://www.facebook. com/help/217854714899185 accessed 27 January 2023

Mannell K and Smith ET, 'Alternative Social Media and the Complexities of a More Participatory Culture: A View From Scuttlebutt' (2022) 8 Social Media + Society 20563051221122450

Maronick TJ, 'Do Consumers Read Terms of Service Agreements When Installing Software? – A Two-Study Empirical Analysis' (2014) 4 International Journal of Business and Social Research 137

Mattei U and Quarta A, *The Turning Point in Private Law: Ecology, Technology and the Commons* (Edward Elgar Publishing 2019)

Maume P, 'Bestehen Und Grenzen Des Virtuellen Hausrechts' [2007] Multimedia und Recht Zeitschrift für Informations-, Telekommunikations- und Medienrecht 620

McCartney M, 'Online Is Not a Private Space' (2011) 343 BMJ d7109

McMullan J, 'A New Understanding of 'New Media': Online Platforms as Digital Mediums' (2020) 26 Convergence 287

Michele Everson and Rui Correia Gonçalves, 'Article 16', *The EU Charter of Fundamental Rights: A Commentary* (Hart Publishing 2014)

Micklitz H-W, *The Politics of Justice in European Private Law* (Cambridge University Press 2020)

'Misleading and Deceptive Identities Policy' https://help.twitter.com/ en/rules-and-policies/twitter-impersonation-and-deceptive-identities-policy accessed 27 January 2023

Mollers TM, 'Working with Legal Principles – Demonstrated Using Private Autonomy and Freedom of Contract as Examples' (2018) 14 European Review of Contract Law (ERCL) 101

Monti M, 'Privatizzazione della censura e Internet platforms: la libertà d'espressione e i nuovi censori dell'agorà digitale' (2019) 1 Rivista italiana di informatica e diritto 35

Morelli A and Pollicino O, 'Metaphors, Judicial Frames and Fundamental Rights in Cyberspace' (2019) https://papers.ssrn .com/abstract=3422946 accessed 29 September 2022

Morris PL and Sarapin SH, 'You Can't Block Me: When Social Media Spaces Are Public Forums' (2020) 54 First Amendment Studies 52

Moses LB, 'How to Think about Law, Regulation and Technology: Problems with "Technology" as a Regulatory Target' (2013) 5 Law, Innovation and Technology 1

Muckel S, 'Mittelbare Drittwirkung Des Allgemeinen Gleichheitssatzes' [2018] Juristische Arbeitsblätter 553

'Names Allowed on Facebook | Facebook Help Centre' https://www.facebook. com/help/112146705538576 accessed 6 March 2023

Obar JA and Oeldorf-Hirsch A, 'The Biggest Lie on the Internet: Ignoring the Privacy Policies and Terms of Service Policies of Social Networking Services' (Social Science Research Network 2018) SSRN Scholarly Paper ID 2757465 https://papers.ssrn.com/abstract=2757465 accessed 21 September 2021

Oderkerk M, 'The Need for a Methodological Framework for Comparative Legal Research: Sense and Nonsense of 'Methodological Pluralism' in Comparative Law' (2015) 79 Rabels Zeitschrift für ausländisches und internationales Privatrecht / The Rabel Journal of Comparative and International Private Law 589

Oliver P, 'What Purpose Does Article 16 of the Charter Serve?', *General Principles of EU Law and European Private Law* (Kluwer Law International 2013)

Ortolani P, 'The Resolution of Content Moderation Disputes under the Digital Services Act' 2

'Our Range of Enforcement Options for Violations | Twitter Help' https://help.twitter.com/en/rules-and-policies/enforcement-options accessed 27 January 2023

Palka P, 'Virtual Property: Towards a General Theory' (Thesis, 2017) https://cadmus.eui.eu/handle/1814/49664 accessed 15 November 2022

Palka P, 'Czy Istnieje Prawo Do Własności Danych? Plusy, Minusy, Alternatywy' https://klubjagiellonski.pl/2022/02/02/czy-istnieje-prawo-do-wlasnosci-danych-plusy-minusy-alternatywy/ accessed 28 February 2023

Palka PJ, 'Terms of Service Are Not Contracts – Beyond Contract Law in the Regulation of Online Platforms' in Stefan Grundmann (ed.), *European Contract Law in the Digital Age*, vol. 3 (Intersentia 2018)

Pandya T, 'In Academia, We Need Two Types of Researchers: Divers and Surfers' (*University Affairs*) https://www.university affairs.ca/career-advice/career-advice-article/in-academia-we-need-two-types-of-researchers-divers-and-surfers/ accessed 6 February 2023

Pato A, 'Compensation for non-material damages under the GDPR: An uphill battle' [2022] Verfassungsblog https://verfassungsblog.de/gdpr-non-material/ accessed 12 March 2023

Patti S, 'Contractual Autonomy and European Private Law' in Jacobien Rutgers and Pietro Sirena (eds), *Rules and Principles in European Contract Law* (Intersentia 2015) https://www.cambridge.org/core/books/rules-and-principles-in-european-contract-law/contractual-autonomy-and-european-private-law/3B9B01AFFDEA67 5CCF0840311EC0F19F accessed 25 January 2023

Pecora A, 'L'art. 187 del Regolamento T.U.L.P.S. (R.D. 6.5.1940. N. 635): Problemi Interpretativi' 4

Piras G, *Virtuelles Hausrecht?*, vol. 7 (1st edn, Mohr Siebeck 2016)

Plantin J-C and others, 'Infrastructure Studies Meet Platform Studies in the Age of Google and Facebook' (2018) 20 New Media & Society 293

Pollicino O, 'Internet Regulation: Not a Matter of Freedom of Speech, but Freedom to Conduct Business' (*Help Net Security*, 26 January 2021) https://www.helpnet security.com/2021/01/26/internet-regula tion-freedom/ accessed 8 February 2021

Praduroux S, 'Property and Expropriation: Two Concepts Revisited in the Light of the Case Law of the European Court of Human Rights and the European Court of Justice' (2019) 8 European Property Law Journal 172

Pressevagt, 'Nyt lovforslag skal kriminalisere grooming' (*Justitsministeriet*, 22 February 2023) https://www.justits ministeriet.dk/pressemeddelelse/nyt-lovforslag-skal-kriminalisere-grooming/ accessed 19 March 2023

'Public Undertakings/Services in the EU: Summary – Part 2 (DG4 Study ECON W21) – Public Undertakings and Public Services in the European Union: Summary – Part 2' https://www.europarl.europa.eu/workingpapers/econ/w21/sum-2_en.htm accessed 5 March 2023

Quarta A, 'Ripensare la proprietà a partire dall'accesso' (2014) https://fair.unifg.it/retrieve/de2a638f-3e47-8577-e053-3705fe0aa5f3/Ripensare%20la%20propriet%c3%a0_AQ.pdf

Quarta A, 'La Dicotomia Bene-Servizio Alla Prova Del Supporto Digitale'

Quarta A, 'Contenuti digitali e beni con elementi digitali: c'è ancora posto per la proprietà privata?' in Teresa Pasquino, Alberto Rizzo and Mauro Tescaro (eds), *Questioni attuali in tema di commercio elettronico* (Edizioni scientifiche italiane 2020)

Quarta A, 'Beyond Assimilation: Are Terms of Use Really Contracts?'

Quinn E, 'Much Ado about Nothing: The European Declaration on Digital Rights and Principles' [2022] Verfassungsblog https://verfassungsblog.de/much-ado-about-nothing-2/ accessed 19 March 2023

Quintais JP, Appelman N and Fahy R, 'Using Terms and Conditions to Apply Fundamental Rights to Content Moderation' (25 November 2022) https://papers.ssrn.com/abstract=4286147 accessed 31 January 2023

Quintais JP, De Gregorio G and Magalhães JC, 'How Platforms Govern Users' Copyright-Protected Content: Exploring the Power of Private Ordering and Its Implications' (2023) 48 Computer Law & Security Review 105792

Raffaele C, 'Cyberspazio, Social Network e Teoria Generale Del Contratto' (2011) 20 AIDA. Annali italiani del diritto d'autore, della cultura e dello spettacolo 93

Rahman KS, 'The New Utilities: Private Power, Social Infrastructure, and the Revival of the Public Utility Concept' (2017) 39 Cardozo Law Review 1621

Ramaekers E, *European Union Property Law: From Fragments to a System* (Intersentia; Metro 2013)

Ratner JR, 'Should There Be an Essential Facility Doctrine' (1987) 21 U.C. Davis Law Review 327

Reich N, *General Principles of EU Civil Law* (Intersentia 2014)

Ribeiro MH, Cheng J and West R, 'Automated Content Moderation Increases Adherence to Community Guidelines' (arXiv, 19 October 2022) http://arxiv.org/abs/2210.10454 accessed 8 January 2023

Riley C, 'Unpacking Interoperability in Competition' (2020) 5 Journal of Cyber Policy 94

Rinaldi L, 'Le Piattaforme Tra Diritto Pubblico e Diritto Privato: Libertà d'espressione, Discorso Politico e Social Network in Alcuni Casi Recenti Tra Italia e Stati Uniti' 211

'Ristoranti vietati ai bambini, l'ingresso "childfree" è legale?' (*LCA Studio Legale*, 25 October 2022) https://www.lcalex.it/ ristoranti-vietati-ai-bambini-lingresso-childfree-e-legale/ accessed 20 February 2023

Röhling A and Weil J, 'Marg bar Khamenei': Art. 14(4) DSA in light of Iranian Online Protest' [2023] Verfassungsblog https://verfassungsblog.de/marg-bar-khamenei/ accessed 6 February 2023

Rott P, 'Powerful Private Players in the Digital Economy: Between Private Law Freedoms and the Constitutional Principle of Equality' (2020) 18 Baltic Yearbook of International Law Online 32

Rozenshtein AZ, 'Moderating the Fediverse: Content Moderation on Distributed Social Media' (23 November 2022) https://papers.ssrn.com/ abstract=4213674 accessed 19 March 2023

Ruival AB, 'The Promises of Interoperability in Social Media Platforms, Too Good to Be True?' (Cornell University 2022) https://ecommons.cornell.edu/ handle/1813/112043 accessed 19 March 2023

Sakariassen H, 'A Digital Public Sphere: Just in Theory or a Perceived Reality for Users of Social Network Sites?' (2020) 36 MedieKultur: Journal of media and communication research 126

Şans Uçaryılmaz T, 'The Principle of Bona Fides from Roman Law to Contemporary Law' (Thesis, Bilkent University 2018) http://repository.bilkent.edu.tr/handle/11693/47574 accessed 31 January 2023

Schäfer MS, 'Digital Public Sphere', *The International Encyclopedia of Political Communication* (American Cancer Society 2016) https://onlinelibrary.wiley.com/doi/abs/10.1002/9781118541555.wbiepc087 accessed 14 September 2021

Schulze G, 'Das private Hausrecht. Schutzrecht für die Gebrauchsnutzung von Räumen' (2015) 70 JuristenZeitung 414

Schwartze A, 'Comparative Law' in Karl Riesenhuber and Fritz Thyssen-Stiftung (eds), *European legal methodology* (Intersentia 2017)

Settis S, 'The Cultural Heritage of the Church in Contemporary Culture' in Francesco Buranelli, Jean-François Rauzier and Katholische Kirche (eds), *Ventennale della Pontificia Commissione per i Beni culturali della Chiesa: Twenty Years of the Pontificial Commission for the Cultural Patrimony of the Church* (Libreria editrice Vaticana 2011)

Slaughter J, 'Virtual Worlds: Between Contract and Property' [2008] Student Scholarship Papers https://openyls.law. yale.edu/handle/20.500.13051/5676 accessed 27 February 2023

Smed Larsen M, 'A Right to Post? Structural Human Rights Law and Social Media' (2022) 6 Retskraft

Smits JM, 'What Is Legal Doctrine? On the Aims and Methods of Legal-Dogmatic Research' (1 September 2015) https://papers.ssrn.com/abstract=2644088 accessed 9 February 2023

Spindler G, 'Löschung und Sperrung von Inhalten aufgrund von Teilnahmebedingungen sozialer Netzwerke – Eine Untersuchung der zivil- und verfassungsrechtlichen Grundlagen' (2019) 35 Computer und Recht 238

Stella R, 'È legale vietare l'accesso alle famiglie con bambini nei ristoranti?' (*Studio Cataldi*, 27 July 2017) https://www.studio cataldi.it/articoli/26965-e-legale-vietare-l-accesso-alle-famiglie-con-bambini-nei-ristoranti.asp accessed 31 May 2022

Stephens M, 'Sales of In-Game Assets: An Illustration of the Continuing Failure of Intellectual Property Law to Protect Digital-Content Creators' (2002) 80

Students EU of J, 'Lawsuit Against Twitter: HateAid and the European Union of Jewish Students Submit Landmark Case' (*EUJS*, 25 January 2023) https://eujs.org/press-releases/lawsuit-against-twitter-hateaid-and-the-european-union-of-jewish-students-submit-landmark-case/ accessed 27 January 2023

'Suicide and Self-Injury | Transparency Centre' https://transparency.fb.com/en-gb/policies/community-standards/suicide -self-injury/ accessed 6 March 2023

Susan B, 'But Facebook's Not a Country: How to Interpret Human Rights Law for Social Media Companies' (*Yale Journal on Regulation*) https://www. yalejreg.com/bulletin/but-facebooks-not-a-country-how-to-interpret-human-rights-law-for-social-media-companies/ accessed 13 September 2021

Suzor N, 'Digital Constitutionalism: Using the Rule of Law to Evaluate the Legitimacy of Governance by Platforms' (2018) 4 Social Media + Society https://doi.org/10.1177/2056305118787812 accessed 5 March 2021

Telegen M, 'You Can't Say That!: Public Forum Doctrine and Viewpoint Discrimination in the Social Media Era' (2018) 52 University of Michigan Journal of Law Reform 235

'The Twitter Rules: Safety, Privacy, Authenticity, and More' https://help. twitter.com/en/rules-and-policies/twitter-rules accessed 27 January 2023

Thierer A, 'The Perils of Classifying Social Media Platforms as Public Utilities' [2012] SSRN Electronic Journal

Thierer A, 'The Perils of Classifying Social Media Platforms as Public Utilities' (2013) 21 CommLaw Conspectus: Journal of Communications Law and Technology Policy (1993-2015) 249

'Twitter's Enforcement Philosophy & Approach to Policy Development' https://help. twitter.com/en/rules-and-policies/enforcement-philosophy accessed 27 January 2023

'Twitter's Platform Manipulation and Spam Policy | Twitter Help' https://help. twitter. com/en/rules-and-policies/platform-manipulation accessed 27 January 2023

'Twitter's Policy on Hateful Conduct | Twitter Help' https://help.twitter.com/ en/rules-and-policies/hateful-conduct-policy accessed 27 January 2023

Tworek H and Leerssen P, 'An Analysis of Germany's NetzDG Law' https://www. ivir.nl/publicaties/download/NetzDG_Tworek_Leerssen_April_2019.pdf

Udsen H, 'Personoplysninger som en modydelse', *Festskrift til Palle Bo Madsen* (Djøf 2021)

Usynin M, 'Sailing in All Winds: Extraterritorial Regulation as a Trigger for Self-Regulatory Practices in the Shipping Industry' (2020) 26 JIML

van der Donk B.B.E., 'Should Critique on Governmental Policy Regarding Covid-19 Be Tolerated on Online Platforms? An Analysis of Recent Case-Law in the Netherlands' (2021) 13 Journal of Human Rights Practice 426

van der Donk B.B.E., 'Circumventing Ambiguous Qualifications and National Discrepancies: A European Roadmap to Define Social Media Platforms', *Re:constitution workshop* (2022)

van der Donk B.B.E., 'European Views on the Privatization of the "Online Public Space"' (*Media Research Blog*, 29 June 2022) https://leibniz-hbi.de/de/blog/european-views-on-the-privatization-of-the-online-public-space

van der Donk B.B.E., 'Ex-Ante and Ex-Post Access Restrictions in Online Marketplace's Terms of Service' (2022) 6 European Review of Private Law

van der Donk B.B.E., 'Regulating Behaviour on Data Platforms: The Online Restraining Order as an Administrative Sanction'

van der Donk B.B.E., 'The Freedom to Conduct a Business as a Counterargument to Limit Platform Users' Freedom of Expression' (Springer International Publishing) https://doi. org/10.1007/16495_2021_33 accessed 20 April 2022

van Dijck J, 'Governing Digital Societies: Private Platforms, Public Values' (2020) 36 Computer Law & Security Review 105377

Van Hoecke M, *Methodologies of Legal Research: Which Kind of Method for What Kind of Discipline?* (Bloomsbury Publishing Plc 2013) http://ebookcentral. proquest. com/lib/kbdk/detail.action?docID = 1772966 accessed 8 February 2023

Vander Maelen C, 'Hardly Law or Hard Law? Investigating the Dimensions of Functionality and Legalisation of Codes of Conduct in Recent EU Legislation and the Normative Repercussions Thereof' (2022) 47 European Law Review 752

Vasarienė D and Jakulevičienė L, 'Freedom to Conduct Business During the Covid-19 Pandemic' (2021) 26 Tilburg Law Review 16

Veltri GA and others, 'The Impact of Online Platform Transparency of Information on Consumers' Choices' (2023) 7 Behavioural Public Policy 55

Venturini J and others, *Terms of Service and Human Rights: An Analysis of Online Platform Contracts* (Editora Revan 2016) http://bibliotecadigital.fgv.br/dspace/handle/10438/18231 accessed 3 March 2021

Venturini J and others, 'Terms of Service and Human Rights: An Analysis of Online Platform Contracts'

Vinding Kruse F, *Ejendomsretten* https://jura.ku.dk/jurabog/pdf/juridiske-monografier/kruse_ejendomsretten_foerste_bind_3-udgave_1951.pdf accessed 14 September 2022

Wachter S, 'The Theory of Artificial Immutability: Protecting Algorithmic Groups under Anti-Discrimination Law' (15 February 2022) https://papers.ssrn.com/abstract = 4099100 accessed 14 December 2022

Waller S, 'Antitrust and Social Networking' (2011) 90 North Carolina Law Review

Werden GJ, 'The Law and Economics of the Essential Facility Doctrine' (1987) 32 Saint Louis University Law Journal 433

'What on Earth Is the Fediverse? – Lawfare' https://www.lawfareblog.com/what-earth-fediverse accessed 19 March 2023

Wiemann J, 'Obligation to Contract and the German General Act on Equal Treatment (Allgemeines Gleichbehandlungsgesetz)' (2019) 11 German Law Journal 1131

Wilman F, 'The Digital Services Act (DSA) – An Overview' (16 December 2022) https://papers.ssrn.com/abstract = 4304586 accessed 24 January 2023

Zulli D, Liu M and Gehl R, 'Rethinking the 'Social' in 'Social Media': Insights into Topology, Abstraction, and Scale on the Mastodon Social Network' (2020) 22 New Media & Society 1188

Table of Cases

Court of Justice of the European Union

European Court of Human Rights

Denmark

Germany

Italy

The Netherlands

EUROPEAN MONOGRAPH SERIES

1. Lammy Betten (ed.), *The Future of European Social Policy,* 1991 (ISBN 90-654-4585-4).
2. Annemarie Loman, Kamiel Mortelmans, Harry H.G. Post & Stewart Watson, *Culture and Common Law: Before and After Maastricht,* 1992 (ISBN 90-654-4638-9).
3. John A.E. Vervaele, *Fraud against the Community: The Need for European Fraud Legislation,* 1994 (ISBN 90-654-4634-6).
4. Philip Raworth, *The Legislative Process in the European Community,* 1993 (ISBN 90-654-4690-7).
5. Jules Stuyck, *Financial and Monetary Integration in the European Economic Community,* 1993 (ISBN 90-654-4718-0).
6. Jules Stuyck & A.J. Vossestein (eds), *State Entrepreneurship, National Monopolies and European Community Law,* 1993 (ISBN 90-654-4773-3).
7. Jules Stuyck & A. Looijestijn-Clearie (eds), *The European Economic Area EC-EFTA,* 1994 (ISBN 90-654-4815-2).
8. Rosita B. Bouterse, *Competition and Integration: What Goals Count?,* 1995 (ISBN 90-654-4816-0).
9. René Barents, *The Agricultural Law of the EU, 2nd Edition,* 2022 (ISBN 978-94-035-4411-3).
10. Nicholas Emiliou, *Principles of Proportionality in European Law: A Comparative Study,* 1996 (ISBN 90-411-0866-1).
11. Eivind Smith, *National Parliaments as Cornerstones of European Integration,* 1996 (ISBN 90-411-0898-X).
12. Jan H. Jans, *European Environmental Law,* 1996 (ISBN 90-411-0877-7).
13. Síofra O'Leary, *The Evolving Concept of Community Citizenship: From the Free Movement of Persons to Union Citizenship,* 1997 (ISBN 90-411-0878-5).
14. Laurence W. Gormley (ed.), *Current and Future Perspectives on EC Competition Law,* 1983 (ISBN 90-411-0691-X).
15. Simone White, *Protection of the Financial Interests of the European Communities: The Fight against Fraud and Corruption,* 1998 (ISBN 90-411-9647-1).
16. Morten P. Broberg, *Broberg on the European Commission's Jurisdiction to Scrutinise Mergers*, 4th Edition, 2013 (ISBN 978-90-411-3339-7).
17. Doris Hildebrand, *The Role of Economic Analysis in the EC Competition Rules: The European School,* 2nd Edition, 2002 (ISBN 90-411-1706-7).
18. Christof R.A. Swaak, *European Community Law and the Automobile Industry,* 1999 (ISBN 90-411-1140-9).

19. Dorthe Dahlgaard Dingel, *Public Procurement: A Harmonization of the National Judicial Review of the Application of European Community Law,* 1999 (ISBN 90-411-1161-1).
20. John A.E. Vervaele (ed.), *Compliance and Enforcement of European Community Law,* 1999 (ISBN 90-411-1151-4).
21. Martin Trybus, *European Defence Procurement Law: International and National Procurement Systems as Models for a Liberalized Defence Procurement Market in Europe,* 1999 (ISBN 90-411-1167-0).
22. Helen Staples, *The Legal Status of Third Country Nationals Resident in the European Union,* 1999 (ISBN 90-411-1277-4).
23. Damien Geradin (ed.), *The Liberalization of State Monopolies in the European Union and Beyond,* 1999 (ISBN 90-411-1264-2).
24. Katja Heede, *European Ombudsman: Redress and Control at Union Level,* 2000 (ISBN 90-411-1413-0).
25. Ulf Bernitz & Joakim Nergelius (eds), *General Principles of European Community Law,* 2000 (ISBN 90-411-1402-5).
26. Michaela Drahos, *Convergence of Competition Laws and Policies in the European Community,* 2002 (ISBN 90-411-1562-5).
27. Damien Geradin (ed.), *The Liberalization of Electricity and Natural Gas in the European Union,* 2001 (ISBN 90-411-1560-9).
28. Gisella Gori, *Towards an EU Right to Education,* 2001 (ISBN 90-411-1670-2).
29. Brendan P.G. Smith, *Constitution Building in the European Union,* 2001 (ISBN 90-411-1695-8).
30. Friedl Weiss & Frank Wooldridge, *Free Movement of Persons within the European Community,* 2nd Edition, 2007 (ISBN 978-90-411-2545-3).
31. Ingrid Boccardi, *Europe and Refugees: Towards an EU Asylum Policy,* 2002 (ISBN 90-411-1709-1).
32. John A.E. Vervaele & André Klip (eds), *European Cooperation Between Tax, Customs and Judicial Authorities,* 2001 (ISBN 90-411-1747-4).
33. Wouter P.J. Wils, *The Optimal Enforcement of EC Antitrust Law: Essays in Law and Economics,* 2002 (ISBN 90-411-1757-1).
34. Damien Geradin (ed.), *The Liberalization of Postal Services in the European Union,* 2002 (ISBN 90-411-1780-6).
35. Nick Bernard, *Multilevel Governance in the European Union,* 2002 (ISBN 90-411-1812-8).
36. Jill Wakefield, *Judicial Protection through the Use of Article 288(2) EC,* 2002 (ISBN 90-411-1823-3).
37. Sebastiaan Princen, *EU Regulation and Transatlantic Trade,* 2002 (ISBN 90-411-1871-3).
38. Amaryllis Verhoeven, *The European Union in Search of a Democratic and Constitutional Theory,* 2002 (ISBN 90-411-1872-1).
39. Paul L.C. Torremans, *Cross Border Insolvencies in EU, English and Belgian Law,* 2002 (ISBN 90-411-1888-8).

40. Malcolm Anderson & Joanna Apap (eds), *Police and Justice Cooperation and the New European Borders*, 2002 (ISBN 90-411-1893-4).
41. Christin M. Forstinger, *Takeover Law in EU and USA: A Comparative Analysis*, 2002 (ISBN 90-411-1919-1).
42. Antonio Bavasso, *Communications in EU Antitrust Law: Market Power and Public Interest*, 2003 (ISBN 90-411-1974-4).
43. Fiona G. Wishlade, *Regional State Aid and Competition Policy in the European Union*, 2003 (ISBN 90-411-1975-2).
44. Gareth Davies, *Nationality Discrimination in the European Internal Market*, 2003 (ISBN 90-411-1998-1).
45. René Barents, *The Autonomy of Community Law*, 2003 (ISBN 90-411-2251-6).
46. Gerhard Dannecker & Oswald Jansen (eds), *Competition Law Sanctioning in the European Union*, 2004 (ISBN 90-411-2100-5).
47. Nauta Dutilh (ed.), *Dealing with Dominance: The Experience of National Competition Authorities*, 2004 (ISBN 90-411-2211-7).
48. Stefaan van den Bogaert, *Practical Regulation of the Mobility of Sportsmen in the EU Post Bosman*, 2005 (ISBN 90-411-2327-X).
49. Katalin Judit Cseres, *Competition Law and Consumer Protection*, 2005 (ISBN 90-411-2380-6).
50. Philipp Kiiver, *The National Parliaments in the European Union: A Critical View on EU Constitution Building*, 2006 (ISBN 978-90-411-2452-4).
51. Alexander Turk, *The Concept of Legislation in European Community Law*, 2006 (ISBN 978-90-411-2472-2).
52. Dimitrios Sinaniotis, *The Interim Protection of Individuals before the European and National Courts*, 2006 (ISBN 978-90-411-2498-2).
53. M. Holoubek & D. Damjanovic, M. Traimer (eds), *Regulating Content: The European Regulatory Framework for the Media and Related Creative Sectors*, 2006 (ISBN 978-90-411-2597-2).
54. Anneli Albi & Jacques Ziller (eds), *The European Constitution and National Constitutions: Ratification and Beyond*, 2006 (ISBN 978-90-411-2524-8).
55. Gustavo E. Luengo, *Regulation of Subsidies and State Aids in WTO and EC Law: Conflicts in International Trade Law*, 2007 (ISBN 978-90-411-2547-7).
56. Eniko Horvath, *Mandating Identity: Citizenship, Kinship Laws and Plural Nationality in the European Union*, 2007 (ISBN 978-90-411-2662-7).
57. Rass Holdgaard, *External Relations Law of the European Community: Legal Reasoning and Legal Discourses*, 2007 (ISBN 978-90-411-2604-7).
58. Jill Wakefield, *The Right to Good Administration*, 2007 (ISBN 978-90-411-2697-9).
59. Dimitry Kochenov, *EU Enlargement and the Failure of Conditionality: Pre- accession Conditionality in the Fields of Democracy and the Rule of Law*, 2008 (ISBN 978-90-411-2696-2).
60. Despina Mavromati, *The Law of Payment Services in the EU: The EC Directive on Payment Services in the Internal Market*, 2008 (ISBN 978-90-411-2700-6).

61. Anne Meuwese, *Impact Assessment in EU Lawmaking*, 2008 (ISBN 978-90-411-2720-4).
62. Ulf Bernitz, Joakim Nergelius & Cecilia Cardner (eds), *General Principles of EC Law in a Process of Development*, 2008 (ISBN 978-90-411-2705-1).
63. Johan van de Gronden (ed.), *The EU and WTO Law on Services: Limits to the Realisation of General Interest Policies within the Services Markets?*, 2008 (ISBN 978-90-411-2809-6).
64. Alina Tryfonidou, *Reverse Discrimination in EC Law*, 2009 (ISBN 978-90-411-2751-8).
65. Mikael Berglund, *Cross-Border Enforcement of Claims in the EU: History Present Time and Future*, 2014 (ISBN 978-90-411-4564-2).
66. Theodore Konstadinides, *Division of Powers in European Union Law: The Delimitation of Internal Competence between the EU and the Member States*, 2009 (ISBN 978-90-411-2615-3).
67. Mattias Derlén, *Multilingual Interpretation of European Union Law*, 2009 (ISBN 978-90-411-2853-9).
68. René Barents, *Directory of EU Case Law on the Preliminary Ruling Procedure*, 2009 (ISBN 978-90-411-3150-8).
69. Yan Luo, *Anti-dumping in the WTO, the EU and China: The Rise of Legalization in the Trade Regime and Its Consequences*, 2010 (ISBN 978-90-411-3207-9).
70. Patrick Birkinshaw & Mike Varney (eds), *The European Union Legal Order after Lisbon*, 2010 (ISBN 978-90-411-3152-2).
71. Thomas Gr. Papadopoulos, *EU Law and Harmonization of Takeovers in the Internal Market*, 2010 (ISBN 978-90-411-3340-3).
72. Bas van Bockel, *The* Ne Bis In Idem *Principle in EU Law*, 2010 (ISBN 978-90-411-3156-0).
73. Veljko Milutinović, *The 'Right to Damages' under EU Competition Law: From* Courage v. Crehan *to the White Paper and Beyond*, 2010 (ISBN 978-90-411-3235-2).
74. Amandine Garde, *EU Law and Obesity Prevention*, 2010 (ISBN 978-90-411-2706-8).
75. Leonard Besselink, Frans Pennings & Sacha Prechal (eds), *The Eclipse of the Legality Principle in the European Union*, 2011 (ISBN 978-90-411-3262-8).
76. Sacha Garben, *EU Higher Education Law: The Bologna Process and Harmonization by Stealth*, 2011 (ISBN 978-90-411-3365-6).
77. Dimitry Kochenov (ed.), *EU Law of the Overseas: Outermost Regions, Associated Overseas Countries and Territories, Territories Sui Generis*, 2011 (ISBN 978-90-411-3445-5).
78. Pablo Ibáñez Colomo, *European Communications Law and Technological Convergence: Deregulation, Re-regulation and Regulatory Convergence in Television and Telecommunications*, 2012 (ISBN 978-90-411-3829-3).
79. Elise Muir, *EU Regulation of Access to Labour Markets: A Case Study of EU Constraints on Member State Competences*, 2012 (ISBN 978-90-411-3823-1).
80. Tim Corthaut, *EU Ordre Public*, 2012 (ISBN 978-90-411-3232-1).

81. Oana Ştefan, *Soft Law in Court: Competition Law, State Aid and the Court of Justice of the European Union*, 2013 (ISBN 978-90-411-3997-9).
82. Francesco Rossi dal Pozzo, *Citizenship Rights and Freedom of Movement in the European Union*, 2013 (ISBN 978-90-411-4660-1).
83. Jens Hartig Danielsen, *EU Agricultural Law*, 2013 (ISBN 978-90-411-3280-2).
84. Ulf Bernitz, Xavier Groussot & Felix Schulyok (eds), *General Principles of EU Law and European Private Law*, 2013 (ISBN 978-90-411-4683-0).
85. Michelle Everson, Cosimo Monda & Ellen Vos (eds), *European Agencies in between Institutions and Member States*, 2014 (ISBN 978-90-411-2843-0).
86. Stefan Leible & Matthias Lehmann (eds), *European Contract Law and German Law*, 2014 (ISBN 978-90-411-2588-0).
87. Piero Leanza & Ondrej Pridal, *The Right to a Fair Trial: Article 6 of the European Convention on Human Rights*, 2014 (ISBN 978-90-411-4855-1).
88. Patrick J. Birkinshaw, *European Public Law: The Achievement and the Brexit Challenge*, 3rd Edition, 2020 (ISBN 978-90-411-9751-1).
89. George Cumming, *Expert Evidence Deficiencies in the Judgments of the Courts of the European Union and the European Court of Human Rights*, 2014 (ISBN 978-90-411-4123-1).
90. Vesna Rijavec, Tomaž Keresteš & Tjaša Ivanc (eds), *Simplification of Debt Collection in the EU*, 2014 (ISBN 978-90-411-4854-4).
91. Nina Półtorak, *European Union Rights in National Courts*, 2015 (ISBN 978-90-411-5863-5).
92. Kyriaki-Korina Raptopoulou, *EU Law and Healthcare Services: Normative Approaches to Public Health Systems*, 2015 (ISBN 978-90-411-5013-4).
93. Torsten Frank Koschinka & Piero Leanza, *Preliminary Injunctions: Germany, England/Wales, Italy and France*, 2015 (ISBN 978-90-411-5833-8).
94. Vesna Rijavec, Tomaž Keresteš & Tjaša Ivanc (eds), *Dimensions of Evidence in European Civil Procedure*, 2016 (ISBN 978-90-411-6662-3).
95. Stefan Leible (ed.), *General Principles of European Private International Law*, 2016 (ISBN 978-90-411-5955-7).
96. Patrick J. Birkinshaw & Andrea Biondi (eds), *Britain Alone!: The Implications and Consequences of United Kingdom Exit from the EU*, 2016 (ISBN 978-90-411-5832-1).
97. René Barents, *Remedies and Procedures before the EU Courts*, 2nd Edition, 2020 (ISBN 978-94-035-1140-5).
98. Luca Prete, *Infringement Proceedings in EU Law*, 2017 (ISBN 978-90-411-6900-6).
99. Robert van den Hoven van Genderen, *Privacy Limitation Clauses: Trojan Horses under the Disguise of Democracy*, 2017 (ISBN 978-90-411-8599-0).
100. Mariusz Krzysztofek, *Post-Reform Personal Data Protection in the European Union: General Data Protection Regulation (EU) 2016/679*, 2017 (ISBN 978-90-411-6237-3).
101. Gianni Lo Schiavo, *The Role of Financial Stability in EU Law and Policy*, 2017 (ISBN 978-90-411-8230-2).

102. Emmanuel Guinchard & Marie-Pierre Granger (eds), *The New EU Judiciary: An Analysis of Current Judicial Reforms*, 2017 (ISBN 978-90-411-6834-4).
103. Kirsten Henckel, *Cross-Border Transfers of Undertakings: A European Perspective*, 2017 (ISBN 978-90-411-9227-1).
104. Vesna Rijavec, Wendy Kennett, Tomaž Keresteš & Tjaša Ivanc, *Remedies Concerning Enforcement of Foreign Judgements: Brussels I Recast*, 2018 (ISBN 978-90-411-9416-9).
105. Albert Sanchez-Graells & Constant De Koninck, *Shaping EU Public Procurement Law: A Critical Analysis of the CJEU Case Law 2015–2017*, 2018 (ISBN 978-94-035-0160-4).
106. Andrea Biondi, Patrick J. Birkinshaw & Maria Kendrick, *Brexit: The Legal Implications*, 2019 (ISBN 978-90-411-9540-1).
107. Mariusz Krzysztofek, *GDPR: General Data Protection Regulation (EU) 2016/679: Post-Reform Personal Data Protection in the European Union*, 2019 (ISBN 978-94-035-0594-7).
108. Giovanni Bassani, *The Legal Framework Applicable to the Single Supervisory Mechanism: Tapestry or Patchwork?*, 2019 (ISBN 978-94-035-0872-6).
109. Piotr Staszczyk, *A Legal Analysis of NGOs and European Civil Society*, 2019 (ISBN 978-94-035-1251-8).
110. Patrizio Messina, *Finance for SMEs: European Regulation and Capital Markets Union – Focus on Securitization and Alternative Finance Tools*, 2019 (ISBN 978-94-035-0161-1).
111. Jacques H.J. Bourgeois (ed.), *EU Framework for Foreign Direct Investment Control*, 2020 (ISBN 978-94-035-1883-1).
112. Ulf Bernitz, Xavier Groussot, Jaan Paju & Sybe de Vries (eds), *General Principles of EU Law and the EU Digital Order*, 2020 (ISBN 978-94-035-1165-8).
113. Aleksandra Drożdż, *Protection of Natural Persons with Regard to Automated Individual Decision-Making in the GDPR*, 2020 (ISBN 978-94-035-2045-2).
114. Mariusz Krzysztofek, *GDPR: Personal Data Protection in the European Union*, 2021 (ISBN 978-94-035-3270-7).
115. Katarzyna Gromek-Broc (ed.), *Public Law in a Troubled Era: A Tribute to Professor Patrick Birkinshaw*, 2023 (ISBN 978-94-035-3576-0).
116. Guido Alpa, *Solidarity: A Normative Principle*, 2023 (ISBN 978-94-035-3596-8).
117. Frederik Behre, *Fixing the Euro Within the National Constitutional Guardrails: A Comparative Assessment of the National Constitutional Space for EU (Fiscal) Integration*, 2023 (ISBN 978-94-035-3586-9).
118. Berdien B.E. van der Donk, *Digital Bouncers: A European Roadmap to Navigate Access Rights and Moderation Issues on Social Media Platforms*, 2024 (ISBN 978-94-035-2858-8).